Snake Ring

The serpent is a metaphor for the apparently spiraling, entwined path of the sun around the viewer. The number of coils in this illustration is reduced from 365 in a year to 5, in order to focus attention on the coil containing the sun during the day when the springtime season is to begin. Virtually the entire cluster of images represented as icons along this coil appeared in the first art in the world, during the terminal Ice Age, and in most cultures of the world therafter.

- Dragon 🐦- Bird ⍱- Bull 🔥- Fire ✝▮ - Cross West, Vertical 〰- Crustacean, Water ▲- Mountain, Pyramid ⌂- Cave, House, Marriage ❀- Flora, Young Sun 🐋- Whale ▬ - Levels Underworld ▽- Trinity 👁- Feline ✺- War ✋⊙- Raised Hand, Leaping Animal ☁- Levels, Celestial ⊙- Raptor 🧎- Society as at the Axis Mundi ⊙- Ring Motif 🐎- Horse

Typical

ABBREVIATIONS, SIGNS, ETC.

• Altars with bulls horns at the top were found in the oldest city known to man *See* ALTAR & BULL & SOCIETY AS AT THE AXIS MUNDI -70a TURKEY, CATAL HUYUK \BRAs

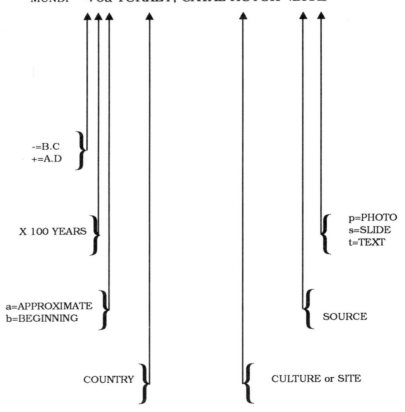

-=B.C
+=A.D
}

X 100 YEARS }

p=PHOTO
s=SLIDE
t=TEXT
{

a=APPROXIMATE
b=BEGINNING
}

SOURCE {

COUNTRY }

{ CULTURE or SITE

IMAGES

ENCYCLOPEDIA

Allan Wesler

JOURNEY INTO THE LANGUAGE OF LIFE

Enterprises • Publishers

Box 546665
Surfside, FL. 33154-6665, U.S.A.

Contents

Dedicated to
Phyllis

in Memory of
Jill

ENTERPRISES

PUBLISHERS

Library of Congress Catalog Number 92-071622

ISBN # 0-9627472-0-3

BOOK COVER DESIGN	Richard Carter
SNAKE RING ART	Linda Nye
MATHEMATICAL GRAPHICS	Carl Gerle
PHOTOGRAPHIC ART	Carlos Stoliar Robert Wesler
DATABASE MANAGEMENT	Leslie Blanchard
TYPESETTING/EDITING	Enid Drummond-Smith Erin Svolos
PRODUCTION MANAGEMENT	Jeffrey Peterson

IMAGES ENCYCLOPEDIA

INTRODUCTION

The Images Encyclopedia contains descriptions of over 3,200 images, drawn from an unprecedented computer database of over 200,000 images (Images DataBank) that was developed by Allan Wesler over the past 20 years. The material in the DataBank, and the book, is like nothing ever assembled, being academically cross-disciplinary and geographically universal. It opens an astounding new door to understanding the persistent urges of mankind, from primitive societies to modern times.

Large serpents, some with wings, were painted on the surfaces of Ice Age caves. A winged serpent stood as a statue in Solomon's Temple. The winged serpent was in golden relief on the throne in King Tutankhamen's tomb, and was carved in stone in classical Greek art. As a feathered serpent, it appeared on the surfaces of pyramids in preColumbian America. Yet, as you know, winged or feathered serpents never existed in nature.

In these same areas, weapons or armies of clay soldiers were placed in ancient burials. Tribal people of northern Asia, today, bury their dead with sticks to defend themselves in the underworld, their shaman moving in imitation of the movement of snakes and wearing figures of serpents on his clothes, even though the weather in northern Asia has always been too cold for snakes. You and I might ask why there is this fear of attack in the underworld (even in contemporary religions) and what has this to do with a mythic serpent?

myths and microchips
Joseph Campbell and other comparativists have made the public aware of the mythic themes which one culture shares with another. Mr. Wesler went beyond this to the next stage. He analyzed these themes image by image, and proposed an understanding of what the myths mean, and where and why they began.

By extensive computer analyses of his Images DataBank, Mr. Wesler found that the images and symbols from these shared mythic themes were found in virtually all cultures, back to the decorated Ice Age caves. Further analyses discovered specific "roles" for each of the images, which are defined by the image's orientation and/or its association with other images.

a fable from the mists
Focusing on those societies that are the most ancient, primitive, and/or isolated, Mr. Wesler determined that the recurring images and their relationships formed a single story. He named the story the Snake Ring when he discovered that it was the snake that provided continuity between the scenes in the story.

The Snake Ring story begins with a regenerating sun joining with a mother goddess to produce a new sun that causes the change in the seasons. The snake represented the path of the sun. To the primitive viewer, the sun spiralled serpent-like around the earth, through the sky and the underworld, from solstice to solstice. Later in the story, the sun is attacked by demons in the underworld, which is the bottom portion of this serpentine path. This was the attack that was feared in worldwide burials.

Revealed in the Images Encyclopedia, for the first time, is how the scenes of this single story were seminal to all of mankind's mythic themes, images, and ritual activities.

hard hats as shamans

In Mr. Wesler's time-factored Images DataBank, the images of the Snake Ring story made their first appearance in the cave art of the terminal Ice Age. This was the time when huge glaciers advanced and retreated, in successive waves, covering much of Europe and North America. The chaos in nature devastated flora and fauna alike. Human dental remains from the terminal Ice Age show that mankind suffered widespread diseases from starvation.

Our branch of mankind -- advanced tool-makers who created superior tools -- may have created a new "tool" in this most desperate time in human history. This "tool" would be the language of images and symbols in the Ice Age caves, which until now have never been explained. As a result of Mr. Wesler's analyses of the Images DataBank, it becomes clear that the images and symbols were instructions to the sun on how to right the seasons: the Snake Ring story.

> *Examples of the "hard hat" approach: Early evidences of the wheel were on small clay figures excavated in Mesoamerica (which never made practical use of the wheel) and the Indus Valley. The placement of wheels on these figures of bulls, felines, etc., of the Snake Ring story, suggest they were used to simulate movement along the Snake Ring path. Similarly, the earliest use of the block and tackle was in ancient Greek theater, where it was used to lower an actor to the stage to begin scenes of the Snake Ring story. Massive blocks of stone or marble (suggesting "mountain") were engineered into place to cover ancient pyramids and sacred houses, serving as models of the mother goddess' mountain house in the western horizon where the new sun was born.*

hieroglyphs on cave walls

The Images Encyclopedia uses the Snake Ring story to interpret the painted sprigs of plants and galloping herds of animals in the Ice Age caves as being inspirations to the sun to restore the bountiful fauna and flora devastated by the chaotic climate of the time. The other painted symbols, images and scenes in these caves -- including rows of dots, figures of men whose heads are those of birds, bison, or felines, and figures of faceless women -- are defined as specific reminders of what the sun must do to restore fertility.

The images and symbols of these instructions were the beginning of hieroglyphic writing. When these elements were no longer painted in the Ice Age caves, they were molded and impressed on tens of thousands of clay tokens, which were found assembled into various clusters at many ancient sites. Later, these images were impressed on clay tablets to form messages and, still later, schematized in the Middle Eastern precursors to the letters of our own alphabets.

> *Examples of letters: In the ancient Greek and Hebrew alphabets the letters corresponding to the English letters A, B, D, K, and N were originally representations of a bull's head, house, fish, raised-hand, snake, respectively. The bull in the Snake Ring story is a metaphor for the desired virility of the old sun when he enters the house of the mother goddess in the western horizon water. Their joining produces the new sun of the next season, who rises from the eastern horizon water, and assumes the snake path in the sky. Before now no explanation has been offered as to why all alphabets begin with A, which was originally the pictograph of a bull's head, and which is followed by B, originally the pictograph of a house.*

Much of what we today regard as culture, the Images Encyclopedia shows, began as supplements to Ice Age "writing". Music, dance, and theater, in their earliest forms, were urgent communications to the sun to maintain its path to the death, marriage, rebirth, and battle of the Snake Ring story.

do as I do

Although most images in the terminal Ice Age caves were painted, there is also the evidence of people ritually circle-dancing on their heels (those impressions, now hardened in the glacial clay floor, resemble bull/bison hoofs) and hundreds of stencils of human raised hands. From the proximity of these evidences to the images painted and sculpted on the cave surfaces, the Images Encyclopedia determines that the people were using themselves, as well, as part of the symbol language. Their activities appear to be models of what the sun must do: circle the earth to its virile descent in the western horizon (bull-metaphor), and rise to the sky in the eastern horizon (raised-hand-metaphor).

> *Examples in contemporary life: The groom giving a ring to the bride is a historical rite of marriage. Evidence indicates that it was practiced as long ago as the ancient Egyptian and Greek civilizations. The rite echoes the Snake Ring story of the old sun joining with the mother goddess: the old sun transfers its solar characteristics to the goddess (the ring was used worldwide as a symbol for the sun) for rebirth in the new sun of the next season. The new sun resulting from this union is born in the western horizon waters, suggesting the present day baptism of the newborn. In the Snake Ring story this child is the newborn sun of the season of fertility upon which our very existence depends (therefore abortions may be a negative aspect of the symbol language, greatly feared by many in their subconscious).*

what makes man man?

The Images Encyclopedia suggests that this art and ritual in the Ice Age caves may have been the beginnings of religion. At this time one finds the earliest evidence of mankind applying his societal endeavors to a higher purpose: to communicate with a supernatural power. Many present-day religions still see man as made in the image of God. This does not seem far different from the Ice Age idea of presenting man as a symbol of the sun. It is also not unusual in the present day for us to communicate with God for our survival (as Ice Age man did); i.e. for Him to bring rain or to end a hurricane, earthquake or famine.

Scholars say that culture "exploded" in these Ice Age caves. In the Images Encyclopedia, for example, are evidences that warfare and sports began as reenactments of the underworld conflict in the Snake Ring story.

> *Examples of warfare: The legions of Rome and the armies of medieval Europe marched off to war under banners shaped as dragons that were inflated by the wind. The Images Encyclopedia suggests that when these armies marched from their motherland (envisioned as the western horizon place where the new sun was born) they were within the dragon path ("dragon" is from the Greek word "drakon", meaning simply "snake") of the Snake Ring story. Metaphorically the soldiers were venturing into the underworld, where all of the dead father suns descended to after they birthed new suns in the western horizon house. But the old suns' husks did not willingly yield their souls and their serpent path (the trinitarian aspect of the sun in the western horizon house was: the old sun, the "father"; the new sun, his "son" who received his soul; and the old sun after he lost his soul, the "ghost" of the old sun remaining in the underworld). The old suns' attacks on the new sun in the underworld (sun gods devouring or attacking their progeny are common themes in worldwide mythologies) accounted for the next season not always appearing on time, and sometimes not at all. The fear of these attacking demons in the underworld is the reason weapons and model armies of soldiers are often found in worldwide graves.*

There is no sign of warfare, no evidence of weapons killing humans, before the terminal Ice Age and its Snake Ring story. Thereafter, warfare was present in virtually every tribal culture and civilization.

The roots of warfare then seem to have been laid when ancient societies began to envision themselves as occupying the Western horizon place within the Snake Ring story. When they ventured away from their homeland in the only direction possible according to the configuration of the Snake Ring -- toward the underworld -- their neighboring societies had to be the forces of the demonic enemy, to be defeated in battle for the new sun of the next season to arise.

Examples of sports contests: The ancient Egyptians, Greeks and Romans played ritual ball-games to seasonally renew their crops, and whenever else there was a great scarcity of food. A ritual contest representing the struggle between the forces of winter and spring took place in the most ancient ceremonies dedicated to the young sun god Osiris. The first Greek Olympics were held in memory of the fight between the sun gods Zeus and his father Kronos (winners were presented with palm branches and were showered with flowers as symbols of the resulting seasonal fertility). When traditional religion faded in the fifth century B.C. (see the Ionian discoveries below) the Olympic games lost their religious significance. Romans had furious ritual games of combat at the start of spring, in which many were killed. Their gladiator games, copied after the Etuscans', were originally religious and represented a struggle in the underworld. Medieval ball-games were played in England at the start of springtime for the benefit of the crops. In an early version of these games a sack containing the head of a sacrificed bull (the Snake Ring story's dead old sun in the underworld) was used instead of a ball.

Continuing in this vein: murals from the pre-Greek Minoans depict youths leaping over the heads of bulls. There were bull fights in the Artemis Ephesius cult rituals. Even today, amateurs are killed each year fighting bulls at the start of springtime in Portugal. The toreadors of the Latin world wear a "suit of light" and feline-type ears on their hats as they fight the bull who, although color blind, is taunted by a red cloak (Red is the Snake Ring story's metaphor for death and regeneration in the sunset. The feline is the Snake Ring story's hero of the young sun in its underworld combat with the old suns. Carved stone murals from an ancient Olmec period ball-court in present day Mexico depict players with feline ears on their headdress). Finally, European tennis courts until the eighteenth century were painted with lamp black and the blood of bulls.

one step at a time

Tally marks, the first evidence in the world of counting, were found in the Ice Age caves associated with the images of the story. The Images Encyclopedia relates how prominent tallies in the cave art corresponded to the sun's imagined passage through numbered levels above and below the earth (7 levels in the sky and 5 levels in the underworld) and how these levels were derived from the seven moving bodies visible in the sky to the unaided eye.

Examples of numbers: The seven moving bodies that were assigned their own levels in the sky were the sun, moon, Mercury, Venus, Mars, Jupiter and Saturn. The sun's steps from dawn to sunset through these levels each day, were numbered. "One" was where the sun broke through the eastern horizon, "two" through "six" were where it ascended through the steps between the paths of the other six stars, and "seven" was where it reached its own zenith in the sky. After appearing to pause at this seventh level (note that Sun-day, the seventh day, is regarded as the day of rest) the sun descended through the opposite paths of the six stars ("eight" through "twelve"), finally reaching level "thirteen" at the western horizon place where the sun of each season dies and joins with the mother goddess. Thirteen was the key number in the Mayan calendar.

The sun-worshiping Egyptians and Greeks divided the complete day into twenty-four parts, our "hours", apparently from the sun going up and down 7 levels in the sky plus 5 levels in the underworld in its daily path around the world. There is a 7:5 ratio at springtime of the duration of daylight (when the sun is supposed to be in the seven levels in the sky) to the duration of nighttime darkness (when the sun is supposed to be in the underworld). The Mayan universe had seven levels in the sky and five levels in the underworld.

xiv

In the stone relief of a pregnant Ice Age mother goddess discovered in Laussel, France, she holds aloft a truncated bull's horn inscribed with thirteen tally marks. The truncated horn is the Snake Ring story's composite metaphor for the death and virility of the old sun when it joins with the mother goddess at the number thirteen.

The fear of thirteen, called triskaidekaphobia, is so acute in our subconscious that the count of floors of many buildings and the rows on many airlines skip past it. The royal family of England alters the official records to show the next day if the birthday of a royal progeny falls on the thirteenth of a month. Particularly unlucky is Friday the thirteenth. Friday is named after the Anglo Saxon mother goddess "Frig", and as the Snake Ring story indicates, there are ominous implications of death and loss of soul at the western horizon conjunction (13th level) of the old sun with the mother goddess.

Members of the great cultures of Mesoamerica, such as Olmec, Maya, and Aztec -- together with the other Indians in the Americas -- were descendants of terminal Ice Age men and women who had crossed over Beringia from the Old to the New World, to be isolated in the New World by rising oceans thousands of years ago. When explorers from Spain invaded the New World, in the 16th century, they were stunned to see great civilizations, more sophisticated in many respects than in Europe at the time. However, they also encountered strange images and significance attributed to certain numbers. In the Images Encyclopedia one sees that these images and numbers, inexplicable to the explorers, were virtually the same as those that were used in the Ice Age caves, and that they were used in the same manner.

Einstein and his fiddle

The earliest musical instruments were also unearthed in the Ice Age caves. The Images Encyclopedia notes that the first evidence of written music, found in Mesopotamian burials, used a 7-note diatonic musical scale, the scale that is still used today in most parts of the world. Reconstructed Mesopotamian instruments on which this music was played were decorated with themes of the Snake Ring story.

Examples of music: Modern pianos have clusters of 7 white and 5 black keys. In the Snake Ring story, where the sun makes its daily journey through 7 levels in the sky and 5 levels in the underworld, black is a metaphor for the underworld. The Images Encyclopedia suggests that the complex relationship of music to mathematics has its roots in the eternal path of the sun crossing the numbered levels around the earth, from solstice to solstice and back again.

From Greek sources, the 7-note scale was played in descending order. This sequence suggests the sun's path down the seven levels of the sky to the western horizon. In the Snake Ring story the sun dies in the flaming sky of the horizon sunset at the end of its season, and is reborn Phoenix-like in the horizon underworld as the sun of the next season. Its eternal "solar" characteristics are transferred from the old sun, after its death, to the new sun. This theme may have begun our concept of the "soul" continuing after death. It may also explain why musical instruments, bearing images of the Snake ring story and with its message of life after death, were placed in the underworld burials of some Mesopotamian rulers.

to the four winds

Ice Age art and rituals ended abruptly in the caves, thousands of years after they began, when the seasons finally stabilized near the present level. This seems to support the Images Encyclopedia premise as to the original purpose of art and ritual in the caves: to control nature.

In the meantime, groups of Ice Age people had left their homelands during the Ice Age period of starvation, migrating to such distant places as the Americas and the Azores searching for sustenance. The Images Encyclopedia suggests that the exodus spread the story and its symbol language to all other parts of the world. The Images Data

Bank reveals that the story and its language are found in the foundation of every one of the ancient cultures and religions. The images and scenes continue even in present-day cultures and religions. Wendell Willkie said "one world", and he was right!

Examples of the spread of the story and its symbol language (as related to Springtime ceremonies): Springtime is the time of fertility, "When April showers bring May flowers". In the Snake Ring story, the change in seasons is effected when the old sun comes bird-like from the sky down the serpent path, dies in the western horizon mountain house, joins bull-like with the mother goddess and makes the new sun of springtime. The new sun then leaps up deer-like into the sky at the east and brings the springtime rain, causing the crops to grow so all the life will be be able to go on.

The Images Encyclopedia points to evidence that peoples of the world draw parts or all of their springtime scenes from this basic story. The Sarmat people of Indonesia have a festival in which they erect a ladder with seven rungs (the seven levels of the sky) on a fig tree. They pray, "Grandfather sun come down and make our empty rice basket full". During the ceremony the Sarmats make animal sacrifices and have a collective orgy. The Chinese emperor made sacrifices on a mound before the city gate at the start of spring. The Dai people of China have dragon-boat races and splash one another with water. In Japan, there is a Shinto procession at the start of spring where a giant phallus is carried into the temple. Springtime processions of dragons are still common in Italy at the start of springtime. People of the Ukraine decorate eggs at this time (the practice is said to have its origins in pagan rites and not related to the Christian Easter eggs) which they give as gifts all year.

In Mexico at springtime, street vendors sell figures of large skeletons with crosses painted on their foreheads (the old sun's death in the horizon). Each village hangs large stuffed "Judas" figures by nooses tied around their necks (red devils with long beards; defeated old suns in the underworld), and deer dances are held, where dancers dressed as deer (the leap up of the new sun) are serenaded "Comes the light of day, the sun is high and rains come". **American Indians' Sun Dance:** *The Mandans' Okipa ceremony at the start of springtime began with a lone figure descended from a bluff at the west to announce that he alone survived the catastrophe of a great flood (memory of the Ice Age great flood, accompanied by chaos in nature and starvation), and that the sun dance lodge, which had been closed all year, should be opened. During the ensuing ceremony, screams of alarm went up as a dancer dressed as a bull arrived with a colossal artificial penis. Women outside the lodge threw him down, removed his penis and threw yellow dirt in his face (the virile old sun replaced by the new sun). In the Arapaho Sun Dance, a couple representing the sun and the moon (a common metaphor for the mother goddess) had intercourse on the bull's hide which the male wore to their meeting place at the lodge. After their intercourse, he (as the old sun) placed the root of a plant in her mouth which she brought back to her husband and the dancers, all of whom thanked her and prayed for her success, "Man above give more light for our vegetation, our stock and ourselves".*

Jewish Passover: *The ceremony was celebrated by herdsmen before the Hebrews entered the region, and was performed to insure fertility of the cultivated regions. It was originally a ceremony where the herdsmen spread the blood of a sacrificed animal on the doorposts and the lintels of their houses. Later, it was made into a domestic ceremony of the Hebrews celebrating the feast of the Exodus. The present day ceremony has offerings on a plate including a roasted shank of a lamb (representing sacrifice), parsley which is dipped in salt water (representing the sea) and an egg, the traditional symbol of birth.* **Christian Easter:** *On the Saturday before Easter at Christ's tomb in the Holy Land, the church is in darkness. Men dance and women wail until Easter, when torches are lit and the worshipers celebrate the resurrection of the Light of the World waving branches of trees. In the Greek orthodox ceremonies, the Easter celebration is said to insure good crops.*

a serpent in the noodle

Incredibly, the story and its language appear to have also deeply affected our psyche, without apparent effort. As indicated in the Images Encyclopedia, they appear in dreams, and in the complexes and archetypes of modern psychology. The Oedipal myth and complex is a sequence of images and scenes that are precisely dictated by the Snake Ring path of the sun: the young sun defeating his father in the underworld and returning to his mother goddess to create the new sun of the next season.

Mr. Wesler turned to present-day science for an explanation of the reverberations of this story and of its language in our psyche. He noted agreement among sociobiologists that life-forms inherit memories of activities which have proven essential for the survival of their gene pool. Other researchers, operating on laboratory cats, severed the portion of cats' brains which suppresses the acting out of their dreams. The felines went through the motions of catching mice while dreaming. From this, the scientists surmised that mammals generally dream of the activities they need to perform for their survival. Mr. Wesler's astounding proposition, documented in the Images Encyclopedia, is that we in our gene pool have inherited the Snake Ring story from the terminal Ice Age. This language of symbols seemed to inspire the natural progression of the seasons in the Ice Age, enabling mankind to survive even when whole branches of animal species died off. Perhaps that is why there are scenes in our dreams which psychologists find so difficult to explain, such as those of flying, falling, and being chased by wild animals. These are scenes from the Snake Ring story in our subconcious. According to the story, we are within the snake ring path of the sun in the sky, falling to the mountain home of the mother goddess in the western horizon waters (see Story enclosed).

The founder of psychoanalysis, Sigmund Freud, decried that his ideas had become the preserve of medical science and thus emptied of the mystery of the prehistoric past that he had discovered in everyone. In a recently discovered manuscript he said the chaos of the Ice Age, with its severe food shortages, is still seen in the infant mentality.

in the land of make-believe

The Images Encyclopedia reveals that tribal societies in different parts of the world say that their ceremonial house, sacred mountain or body of water is modeled on the home, mountain or water of the gods. Many great civilizations of the past have said the same.

It appears that people around the world were subconsciously placing themselves within the snake ring path, envisioning their homelands as models of the western horizon place where the sun descends and is reborn. Each homeland was a stage on which the people presented the arts and rituals handed down from their ancestors in the Ice Age caves. These arts and rituals had saved nature from chaos. We are the heirs to that legacy. In the Images Encyclopedia one finds that this "modelling" provides the skeleton for mankind's present-day cultural esthetics and, even, the concept of urban life.

The decorated Ice Age caves were mainly on the west coast of Europe. When they were abandoned, sacred houses were built containing virtually the same images as in the caves. Entrances to these structures were usually in the roof or the east wall. Their builders may have been consciously suggesting the path of the old sun into the western horizon house. This consistent aspect of sacred houses is noted in the Images Encyclopedia.

Examples of sacred houses: Kivas, the buried sacred houses of the Pueblo Indians, are, to this day, entered by an opening in the roof. The first true city in the world, excavated at Catal Huyuk, Turkey, has many shrine rooms entered by ladders from openings in the roofs (there is no evidence of warfare necessitating such an entrance for defense). Remarkable art is in these rooms, unexplained, alluding to the Snake Ring story: Reliefs of bull's heads are associated with goddesses giving birth; pilasters painted with snake markings are at each side of a feline in relief; and murals are facing west with reliefs of bull's heads, and the symbols of crosses, ring signs, raised hands, etc.

All Egyptian mastabas -- the mortuary temples abutting the eastern walls of the great pyramids -- were entered from the east. Ancient Middle Eastern temples, including the great temple of the Hebrews, had their entrances at the east, and frets at their roofs suggesting staircases for the god's descent. Until the practice was ended by the Reformation, major Christian cathedrals, wherever they were, were built with this same east-west orientation.

Tribal societies in different parts of the world say that their ceremonial house, sacred mountain or body of water is modeled on the god's mountain, house, or water. Many great civilizations of the past have said the same.

Examples of sacred locations: The Mesopotamian pyramid-temples, or ziggurats, on the sacred Euphrates River represented hills with staircases for the god's descent. Aboriginal malocas -- sacred houses of the South American Amazon area -- are entered by an opening in the east walls. The malocas are said by the aboriginals to represent their god's house at the west where the waters of the world fall into the underworld. Virtually all major Egyptian cities were said to be the place where the Mountain of the Gods rose from the water of the primeval flood.

Throughout history, when humanity enters ceremonial huts, tents, churches, synagogues, mosques, and temples it is exposed to images and rituals with a very ancient and rich lineage.

go back to the farm
Authorities cannot agree on the reason why urban life emerged after the end of the terminal Ice Age. The radical proposal in the Images Encyclopedia is that urban centers are sophisticated stage sets. They are known to have developed around shrines and temples which, historical societies have said, represented the world mountain at the axis mundi. This is very much the way our earliest ancestors, before leaving their nomadic hunter-gatherer existence, gathered in their Ice Age caves for ritual purposes.

The Images Encyclopedia explains that the axis mundi, widely regarded as at the center, or "navel" of our world, stems from our subconscious visualization of the vertical segment of the Snake Ring coil descending from the sky, to the mountain home at the abyss of the western horizon.

thirty thousand years, and wrong?
In spite of the powerful Snake Ring story in the human subconscious, a new thinking emerged in the western world about 700 B.C.. An Ionian group of philosophers, already famed for forecasting the exact time of a solar eclipse, forcefully argued that the sun was simply a solid object in the sky, not a god. The sun, they said, did not move around the earth.

Following this, and related to these discoveries, there was a severe decline in Greek art. Its mythic themes vanished for a time, including the pervasive snake image. The sun no longer had an underworld path around the earth in which to be reborn and bring on each new season. Instead the sun became one, everlasting, and the underworld became the taboo world of the unknown and of terrifying danger.

Of course, in the areas of the world isolated from the Ionian discoveries, this demytholization of the Snake Ring story did not occur. When the Spanish landed in Mesoamerica, which had been isolated by rising ocean levels from other continents for some 10,000 years, they came upon a great civilization, with larger and better organized cities than were in Europe at the time. Unknowing, they had come upon the pre-Ionian roots of their own religion and civilization.

God is great!

What are now the major religions in the world skillfully rewove the Snake Ring images into new dogmas. Of the many examples in the Images Encyclopedia: Lord Buddha rode the dragon path to the western horizon when he died. In Judeo-Christian-Islamic lore, Adam and Eve's primal sin was touching the snake-entwined Tree of Knowledge in the Garden of Eden. Was the act a sin because the tree was a powerful symbol in the Snake Ring story, and like the axis mundi, a metaphor for the vertical portion of the Snake Ring path between the sky and the underworld? From the preponderance of Snake Ring images in the Garden of Eden, the Images Encyclopedia suggests that it became the new model for the western horizon place of solar rebirth.

the echo lingers

Only Hinduism, among the present-day major religions, retains the original Snake Ring story, its early Indus Valley roots surviving the Ionian period of revisionism. Sacred stones, temples, and ritual baths of the Hindu are still decorated with serpents. The Hindu gods are sun gods. Without the dragon who twirls around, according to the Rg Veda, there would be no sun god Indra. Perhaps our distance in time from that ancient Indus horizon explains why present scholars have no clear idea of Hinduism, lamenting that the Hindu "Bible" is unknown.

There are also many tribal people in the Images Encyclopedia who, like the Hindu, retain the original Snake Ring themes and images. For example, African Bushmen, the world's most ancient tribal people, exaggerate snakes beyond all subjects in their art, and associate the snake with their supreme god Ruwa, whose name means "sun". All later African art developed on Bushmen themes.

Darwinian to the core

Several proposals derived from the vast Images DataBank, and merely touched on in the Images Encyclopedia, may modestly contribute to forthcoming studies in the social sciences:

1. In spite of the differences which exist between the various cultures and religions, there is a definable spirituality in common.

2. This spirituality inspires all people to engage in ritualistic practices (religions, sports, music, etc.) that subconsciously promote the natural progression of the seasons.

3. Places of worship and societal residence are essential backdrops to these practices.

4. The Snake Ring story that was crafted in the Ice Age is by now a schema of spiritual scenes and images in the human mind, passed through the genes from generation to generation.

5. Mental or social ills may result if the totality of these scenes and images, which gives a uniquely human ("tool-making") purpose to life, is greatly diminished or distorted.

Will mankind listen to the story behind these collective inner memories and voices? Will the uncovered story be used to better understand, and possibly improve society? Hopefully, this book will prompt masses of people to enter the ancient lineage of images in the Images Encyclopedia, and become conscious of the meanings of the visuals and activities that are all about us.

The Snake Ring story which Mr. Wesler identified from his research is briefly set forth on the following page. It is explained more fully, of course, in the Images Encyclopedia, with its worldwide illustrations and references. As with any unfamiliar language, the language of the Snake Ring story does require diligent study.

IMAGES ENCYCLOPEDIA

-The Snake Ring Story-

The sun traveled around the earth in a spiral path. Each evening the sun died at its descent into the western horizon, went through the nighttime Land of the Dead in the underworld, and rose again in the eastern horizon. When a season ended, the sun of the ending season copulated with the mother goddess in her home under the western horizon waters, and made a baby sun who would begin the next season. The suns are like the flowers blooming in the field: the sun of this season has all the tendencies and appearance of the sun last season, only they are different suns.

When droughts and floods brought widespread starvation as the glaciers advanced and retreated during the last Ice Age, it fell to us tool-makers to inspire the errant sun to give birth to a new sun that would restore our food. To that end, we presented scenes and images, using art and even ourselves, in decorated caves which served as models for the western horizon house into which the sun descended at the end of each season. We showed the old sun how to generate a new sun, the baby sun how to defeat his jealous father in the hazardous passage through the underworld and, then, leap into the sky. A new sun finally restored harmony to the seasons. The animals' stomachs became full, and berries grew again for us to eat.

IMAGES ENCYCLOPEDIA

- Template: The Snake Ring Story Language -

A - Spiral symbols and serpents were metaphors for the sun's spiralling path around the earth.

B - Birds were metaphors for the sun's flight through this path in the sky.

C - Bulls and other virile animals were metaphors for the old sun's superhuman virility in the western horizon. Their death, human death, and the virile animals' truncated horns were metaphors for the old sun's death in the sunset sky.

D - Flames, blood and the color red were metaphors for the fiery appearance of the sunset, where the old sun dies and the new sun is born.

E - Vertical stones, altars, trees, vertical signs, flagpoles and crosses were metaphors for the old sun's descent into the western horizon.

F - Water, shells and fish were metaphors for the waters of the western horizon.

G - Mountains, mounds, caves and sacred structures were metaphors for the earth mother's western horizon mountain house. The concept that the mountain house was under the waters of the horizon was likely inspired by European mountains and huge caves appearing under the flood-waters as the Ice Age glaciers began to melt.

H - Vagina signs and goddess figures were metaphors for the copulation of the old sun with the earth mother in her horizon mountain house. The descending old sun goes into her house to make her pregnant with the new sun.

I - Flora and fauna were metaphors for the newborn sun of the season of fertility.

J - Whales (including dolphins) were metaphors for the passage of the new sun from the waters of the western horizon to the east.

IMAGES ENCYCLOPEDIA

- Template: The Snake Ring Story Language -

 **K -** The color black, clefts in the earth and cascades of falling water were metaphors for the underworld. There were five levels to the underworld.

 **P -** There were seven levels to the sky.

 **L -** Horned demons, like our own devil, were metaphors for the husk of the virile old sun who remains in the underworld after the father sun has passed his solar soul to his son, the new sun.

 **9 -** Vultures, hawks, eagles, etc., were metaphors for the sun's ascent to the highest level of the sky.

 **M -** Felines were metaphors for the heros who save the new suns from the demonic old suns in the underworld.

 R - Orientation to the west was a ritual metaphor for the sunset location where the axis mundi penetrates the horizon.

 **N -** Sports and battles were metaphors for the under-world struggle between the old suns and the new suns, in which the new suns must triumph.

 **S -** Circles, round signs, balls, mirrors and the color yellow/gold were metaphors for the sun.

 **0 -** Leaping animals and raised hands were the metaphors for the leap-up of the new sun above the eastern horizon at the beginning of the day.

 **T -** Horses, chariots, and time were metaphors for the speed of the sun's movement up, down and around the sky and the underworld.

Dragon

dragon *The letter A of the Snake Ring Template.* A metaphor for the apparently serpentine path of the sun around the earth. Within this apparent path the sun undergoes seasonal changes which bring about changes in nature, such as fertility. When there was extreme chaos and famine in nature, our tool-making forbearers created and used terminal Ice Age art, consisting of a language of images to inspire changes, in effect rebirths, of the sun along this serpentine path. Since birth occurs after male penetration, and the sun appears to penetrate the earth's western horizon at dusk, the new sun must be born afterwards in the nighttime underworld. From this starting point a language of metaphors began -- and we shall see that in many ways it continues -- to the thought of the sun within its serpentine path. This path includes the sun's rebirth as a new sun in the nighttime underworld bringing springtime fertility (Letter *I*), to this new sun's water passage from the western horizon (Letter *J*), through the levels of the underworld (Letter *K*), to its confrontation with the husks of the previous seasons' suns that remain in the underworld (Letter *L*). Fearing that the new sun might fail to take its place in the sky because of this conflict, a carrier feline, a feline because it is the lord of the jungle and because it can also see in the underworld darkness (Letter *M*),was provided for inspiration to the new sun. This new sun triumphs in the underworld (Letter *N*), and rises through the eastern horizon to leap-up like raised hand or a deer (Letter *O*) into the levels of the sky (Letter *P*). This sun (Letter *S*), like its father before it, flies bird-like (Letter *B*) into the sky to heights where only raptors, such as eagles or vultures, can reach (Letter *Q*), covering the reaches of the daytime sky and the nighttime underworld with the speed of a racing horse (Letter *T*). At the ebbing of its own season, this sun, again like its father before it, must be virile as a bull (Letter *C*) when it dies into the flaming sky of sunset (Letter *D*) along the vertical element of the serpentine path (Letter *E*), to penetrate into the horizon waters (Letter *F*). Instructions to the sun (Letter *R*) do not end there. Likely drawing on their own terminal Ice Age experience when they saw mountains and caves emerging from the waters of the huge melting glaciers, our Homo sapien ancestors postulated that the aged sun within this fantastic serpent path descended into a mountain (Letter *G*) in the western horizon waters (Letter *F*) to join with a female element in a cave there (Letter *H*) and give birth to the next successor sun along this eternally spiralling serpentine path. *Ref* ART, CAVE, CHAOS IN NATURE, FERTILITY, FIRE, FLOOD, HOUSE, PATH, SEASON, SERPENT ENTWINED, SNAKE FEATHERED/ WINGED, SNAKE, SUN OLD/ YOUNG.

• Flying serpentine figures painted on the ceiling of an Ice Age cave in Spain appear to be the front and side views of serpents with wings *See* DRAGON & SNAKE FEATHERED/ WINGED -350b SPAIN, ALTAMIRA *Figure* 1

Figure 1

• Most dragons of the ancient world were benevolent *See* FERTILITY & SEASON +19a ANTHONY AVENI \AVDt

• Dragons dwell in the clouds, have sacred power of the abyss, and are hidden in the depths of the ocean *See* UROBORUS +19a MIRCEA ELIADE \ELIt

• Dragons are common dream images *See* DREAM & PSYCHOLOGY CHILD/ GENERAL +19a \JUNt

• A bronze pendant depicts a plumed snake with the small figure of a man in its mouth *See* PATH & REGENERATION -34b IRAN, ELLAMITE *Figure 2*

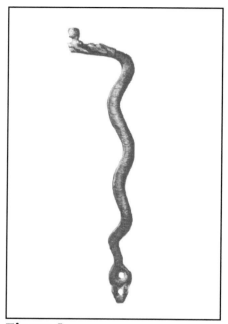

Figure 2

• A golden throne from the Tutankhamun tomb depicts winged snakes on the sides and the heads of felines at the front of the seat *See* CARRIER & FELINE & GOLD & PATH & REGENERATION & RULER -30b EGYPT *Figure 3*

• The general meaning of the dragons' names in the Rig Veda is "to cover"; specifically the name of the dragon Asat means "non-existence" and "Vrtra" means "to twirl" or "turn around" *See* CALABASH & PATH & SERPENT ENTWINED & UROBORUS -19b INDIA, HINDU \MCCt

• Mankind originated in the "land of the bird-snake" *See* SNAKE FEATHERED/ WINGED & SOCIETAL ASPECT -6b MEXICO, MAYAN \MUTt

• The dragon was both the yang and the yin, the male and female spiritual force, respectively *See* CELESTIAL & MARRIAGE & PATH & UNDERWORLD -1b CHINA, TAOIST \RAWt

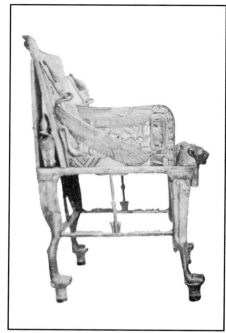

Figure 3

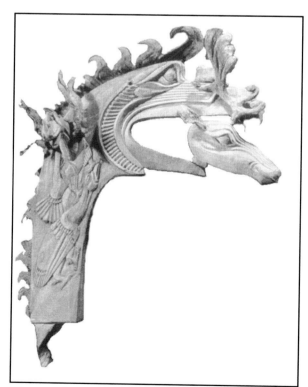

Figure 4

• A wood and leather dragon's head from a frozen Scythian burial has a small deer's head in its mouth and ascending birds on its neck *See* CELESTIAL & DEER & FUNERAL & LEAP-UP & PATH & REGENERATION -5a RUSSIA, PAZYRYK *Figure 4*

• Buddha rode a dragon to the western paradise *See* FUNERAL & PATH & WEST ORIENTATION -5b CHINA, BUDDHA *Figure 5*

• In Revelations the Red Dragon's tail drew stars behind him which he plunged to the earth, the apparent celestial path of the stars to the western horizon. There he stood before "the whore" ready to consume her baby who was to rule the world when he was born. Instead God defeated the dragon. "That old serpent" was thrown into the bottomless pit and God took the newborn boy to sit beside Him thus ending the path and the solar regenerations *See* ABYSS & BABY BOY & DEMYTHOLIZATION & DRAGON & GODDESSES & MARRIAGE & PATH & RED +9a ITALY, CHRISTIAN \MERt

Figure 5

• Sisiutl, the fabulous serpent of the Northwest Coast Indians, also possesses aspects of the thunderbird and the whale, symbolizing the upper and lower worlds respectively *See* RAPTOR & REGENERATION & WHALE +6b CANADA \MUNt

• Stelae frequently depict rulers and deities with bodies of celestial dragons *See* PATH & RULER & STELLA & STONE +7a GUATEMALA, MAYAN \EXPp

• Large fantastic representations of snakes in the French Ice Age caves of Rouffingac and Baume-Latrone and La Pileta in Spain are surprisingly similar, considering the distance between them. Serpent images made of bone were burned with organic matter and completely hidden by a six-foot stone slab. Nearby were pits filled with seashells and red ochre *See* CAVE & CRUSTACEAN & FIRE & RED & SNAKE & UNDERWORLD -350b SPAIN, EL JUYO \NAUt \MUNt

• A mythical fire-serpent, represented as a feathered snake with crossbands in its eyes, was the path of the sun through the sky *See* CELESTIAL & FIRE & PATH & SUN OLD & X-CROSSING -15b MEXICO, OLMEC \COEt

• An illustration in the Dresden Codex depicts a deluge of rain falling from the mouth of a "rain-serpent" with crossed bands on its body *See* CELESTIAL & RAIN & X-CROSSING +12a MEXICO, MAYAN *Figure 6*

• Feathered serpents are depicted wrapped around the poles of the palace in the Forbidden City. The Emperor walked down the front staircase of the palace along a balustrade which depicted a sky-dragon [as on the balustrade of many Mesoamerican pyramid-temples] descending to mountains surrounded by water *See* COLUMN & HOUSE & PATH & RULER & SOCIETY AS AT THE AXIS MUNDI +16a CHINA \SMJp

• Regicide was common until 1810; every four years they strangled their king with the foot sinew of a bull; his body was sealed in a cave until his soul emerged in the form of a dragon *See* BULL & CAVE & PATH & REGENERATION & RULER & SACRIFICE HUMAN +18a RHODESIA, MATABELAND \CAAt

• The word "dragon" comes from the Greek word "drakon" which means "snake" +19a GREEK \WEBt

• The Latin word "draco" means both "snake" and "dragon" +19a ITALY, ROMAN \HAKt

Figure 6

• The Flag of the Empire until the 19th century was a dragon with the sun in its maw; dragons and snakes are interchangeable in Chinese myths *See* FLAG & RULER & SUN OLD/ YOUNG +18a CHINA \CAIt \ELIt

• A sky-snake is in the creation story +18a USA, YUMA \HEEt

• Dragons were synonymous with serpents in the myths of the native people; they lived in the water and caused the death of the gods *See* DEATH & PATH & WATER +19a JAPAN, AINU \MUNt

snake *The letter A of the Snake Ring Template.* A metaphor for the entwined serpent path of the sun, specifically for the vertical segment of the path penetrating the horizon. *Ref* HORIZONTAL MOTIF, SERPENT ENTWINED, VERTICAL LINE/ SHAPE.

• The sacred text "Chilam Balam" of Tizimin laments the destruction of their religion by the Spanish conquest: Once there was truth, which we derived from the serpent in ancient days, from the clear unclouded heavens to the evil knotted earth beneath *See* DEMYTHOLIZATION & UROBORUS +15b MEXICO, MAYAN \AVDt

• A divine snake is coiled around the earth and carries the gods, establishing order. The snake was created first to carry the creator gods *See* PATH & SEASON & REGENERATION +18a NIGERIA \PAQt

• During the annual festival at Epirus a naked virgin presented cakes to snakes kept in a grove sacred to the sun god **Apollo**; "snakes, the sun, and nakedness are related in some way which can no longer be defined" *See* BABY BOY & DEMYTHOLIZATION & FERTILITY & MARRIAGE & SUN OLD/ YOUNG & TREE +19a HANS LEISEGANG \LEIt

• In the Egyptian Book of the Dead the serpent Sata, of infinite years, dwelled at the ends of the earth, renewing his youth every day *See* HORIZON & PATH & REGENERATION -30b EGYPT \SANt

• **Okeanos Achelous** was not an ocean and was separate from the other gods. He was the primal water in the form of a serpent which encircled the universe generating all. *See* BIRTH & UROBORUS & WATER & WATERFALL -20b GREEK \SANt

• The meaning of the serpent and Tree of Knowledge in the Garden of Eden, said to be at the source of the great world rivers, is widely debated *See* DEMYTHOLIZATION & TREE & WATER -10b ISRAEL, JEWISH \ENDt

• St. Patrick is famed for having chased the snakes out of Ireland, a country which has never had snakes *See* DEMYTHOLIZATION & WATER & WEST ORIENTATION +4a IRELAND, CHRISTIAN \HEOt

• The Indians of Bolivia worshipped Yaurinkha a huge lake-dwelling serpent *See* PATH & WATER & WEST ORIENTATION +14a BOLIVIA \MUNt

• During ceremonial rites the shaman chants about a mythic serpent as he moves in a path to represent the course of the sun [in an area which is too cold to have ever had snakes]. *See* PATH & PRIEST & SUN +19a RUSSIA, EVENKI \MUNt

• The king never has contact with the sacred python although he derives his power from the creature. It is both a powerful benefactor and destroyer *See* DEATH & PATH & RULER & REGENERATION & SEASON +19a ANGOLA \MUNt

• The great python deity known as the Rainbow Serpent is associated with the weather. It is the focus of the fertility cult, and is believed to live in a sacred waterhole *See* ABYSS & FERTILITY & PATH & RAINBOW & SEASON & WATER +19a AUSTRALIA, MURNGIN \COTt

• Although snakes are not known to the islands, the islanders believe that Radaulo, the "miles long king of snakes" emerged from a crack in a mountain and chased away a flood which covered the whole earth *See* FLOOD & INFANT MENTALITY & MOUNTAIN & PATH & SEASON +19a NEW GUINEA \ELHt

• Although they are rarely encountered, snakes are of extraordinary mythic importance to the Cheremis, Ostyak, Ainu, Goldi, Tungus, the Mansi and other Russian tribal people. During rituals among these widely separated groups, the shaman suspends a drum with effigies of serpents attached to it at the center of the "Yurt", a practice common to the Tuva as well who were originally Turkish *See* DESCENDING & HOUSE & MUSIC & PATH & SOCIETY AS AT THE AXIS MUNDI +19a RUSSIA \MUNt

• Ritual carvings include forked drumsticks and staffs which depict attributes of a mythic serpent, although snakes have never existed north of the Arctic Circle +19a RUSSIA, SIBERIA \MUNp

• Ritual charms used by the shaman were carved in the form of a double-headed serpent. At times the heads of the serpent are those of a bear *See* BEAR & NORTH/ SOUTH ORIENTATION & PATH +5a ESKIMO *Figure 7*

Figure 7

**See The Following Entries in Section Three
For Some Related Metaphors and Concepts**

- *alligator*
- *arch*
- *basilisk*
- *calabash*
- *circle motif*
- *clock*
- *cobweb*
- *collapse mysterious*
- *cosmology*
- *crest*
- *crocodile*
- *dance*
- *devouring*
- *fan*
- *flag*
- *guilloche*
- *heaven*
- *Hermes*
- *hour*
- *information destroyed/ secret*
- *integer*
- *journey*
- *mandala*
- *meander motif*
- *Mercury*
- *millstone*
- *mouth*
- *net*
- *north orientation*
- *path*
- *pilgrimage*
- *procession*
- *quarters of the world*
- *quipu*
- *rainbow*
- *reptile carrier*
- *return*
- *ribbon*
- *rope*
- *salamander*
- *season*
- *serpent entwined*
- *shoe or stocking*
- *snake feathered/ winged*
- *snake wheel*
- *south orientation*
- *spider*
- *spiral motif*
- *streamer*
- *string or cord*
- *string knotted*
- *structur- alism*
- *thread*
- *time*
- *tortoise*
- *turtle*
- *twenty*
- *umbrella*
- *uroborus*
- *weaving*
- *wheel*
- *wheel of fortune*
- *worm*
- *woven fabric*
- *X-crossing*
- *year*

Bird

bird **1.** *The letter **B** of the Snake Ring Template.* A metaphor designating "celestial", for the descent of the old sun from the sky into the western horizon. **2.** *The letter **O** of the Snake Ring Template.* A metaphor designating "celestial", for the ascent of the young sun into the sky at the eastern horizon. *Ref* FEATHERED.

• An Ice Age cave painting depicts a bird-headed figure carried by a flying figure with an elongated neck. **[Note:** A frontal view of the winged serpent in other Ice Age art**]** *See* CELESTIAL & PATH -350b FRANCE, PECH MERLE *Figure 8*
Refer also to *Figure 1*

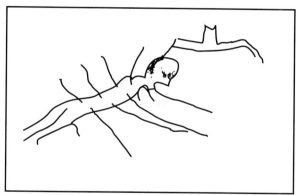

Figure 8

• The hand-wear along the edges of an engraved Ice Age antler suggests it had ritual importance. The engraving depicts a series of a bird's head with enlarged round eyes alongside the body of a large snake; round motifs are in sequence on the snake's body. At the end of the series of bird heads are engraved sprigs of plants *See* EYE & FERTILITY & FLORA & HEAD & PATH & ROUND MOTIF IN SEQUENCE & SNAKE -350b FRANCE, LORTHET *Figure 9*

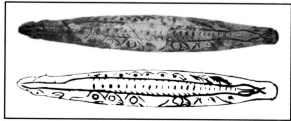

Figure 9

• A roll-out of a seal depicts the sun god with flames at his shoulder as he descends, accompanied by a bird, into the cleft of a mountain *See* ABYSS & DESCENDING MOTIF & FIRE & MOUNTAIN & SUN OLD -23a IRAQ, ACCADIAN \PRIp

• The sun sings as a bird at dawn *See* MUSIC & REGENERATION & SUN YOUNG -19b INDIA, HINDU \MCCt

• A brick fragment from the palace at Nimrud depicts the sun deity with the wings and body of a bird, within a radiant ring motif *See* ASCENDING & HOUSE & RULER & SUN YOUNG -8a IRAQ, ASSYRIAN *Figure 10*

Figure 10

• A figurine from a burial at Jaina, the cemetery island off the west coast of Yucatan, depicts the moon goddess **Ixchel** in her usual role as a weaver, with her mate the sun god **Itzamna** as the solar bird at her knee. Another figurine of the goddess shows her with the aged deity Itzamna lifting her dress *See* FUNERAL & MARRIAGE & REGENERATION & SUN OLD & WATER & WEST ORIENTATION +3b MEXICO, MAYAN *Figure 11* *Figure 12*

• A ruler's sarcophagus from deep within the west, facing the main pyramid at Palenque depicts the solar bird perched at the top of a foliated cross; the dead ruler is below the cross, descending into the open maw of **Kukulkan** the feathered serpent *See* CROSS & FLORA & PATH & REGENERATION & RULER & WEST ORIENTATION +3b MEXICO, MAYAN

Figure 11

Figure 12

• The caduceus, the symbol of healing, is often depicted with a bird or wings at the top of its vertical staff *See* CADUCEUS & BIRD & HEALING & PATH & REGENERATION & SOCIETAL ASPECT & WINGED +15a SWITZERLAND *Figure* 13

Figure 13

• The annual springtime arrival of the Sooty Tern from the east represented the coming of the sun; a festival was held at the appearance of its first egg *See* EGG & REGENERATION & SOCIETY AS AT THE AXIS MUNDI & SPRINGTIME (EASTER) & SUN OLD & WATER & WEST ORIENTATION +15b EASTER ISLAND \HEUp

• One of the figurines most often placed in ritual caves depicts an aged and phallic man with or without the head of a bird *See* CAVE & MARRIAGE & REGENERATION +17a EASTER ISLAND *Figure* 14

• Until recently, dildos with bird bodies and phallic shaped heads were openly sold in European market places *See* BIRD & MARRIAGE & PSYCHOLOGY CHILD & SOCIETAL ASPECT +17a FRANCE \RAUt

• The sun is a bird that flies from east to west +18a USA, SIOUX \NABt

Figure 14

• Kwakiutl Indians wait in reverence in their Potlach lodge for a dancer wearing a raven mask who is identified with the sun, to descend from the rafters at the smoke hole in the roof. **[Note:** Western theatrical performances, from the time of ancient Greeks to Shakespeare's plays, began with an actor descending on a block-and-tackle arrangement referred to as the "deux mechanica"**].** The mural on the wall of the lodge depicts a young beaver with his paws raised between two eagles rising along the circle of the encircling **Sisiutl** feathered serpent *See* BEAVER & FIRE & HAND RAISED & HOUSE & PATH & RAPTOR & REGENERATION & RITUAL & SUN OLD & SNAKE FEATHERED & THEATER & UROBORUS & WATER +19a CANADA, KWAKIUTL \MUNt \WESt
Figure   15

Figure 15

• A panel uncovered from Pompeii depicts ducks in attendance to a phallic cockerel. Some scholars believe that similar sexual art would be found in many places of the ancient world if a fraction of it survived as it did in West-oriented Pompeii *See* BIRD & DUCK & PHALLUS & WATER & WEST ORIENTATION +1a ITALY, POMPEII \GRBt *Figure   16*

Figure 16

**See The Following Entries in Section Three
For Some Related Metaphors and Concepts**

- *cock*
- *cockatrice*
- *crane*
- *crow*
- *dove*
- *duck*
- *heron*
- *ibis*
- *peacock*
- *pelican*
- *phoenix bird*
- *swallow*
- *turkey*

Bull

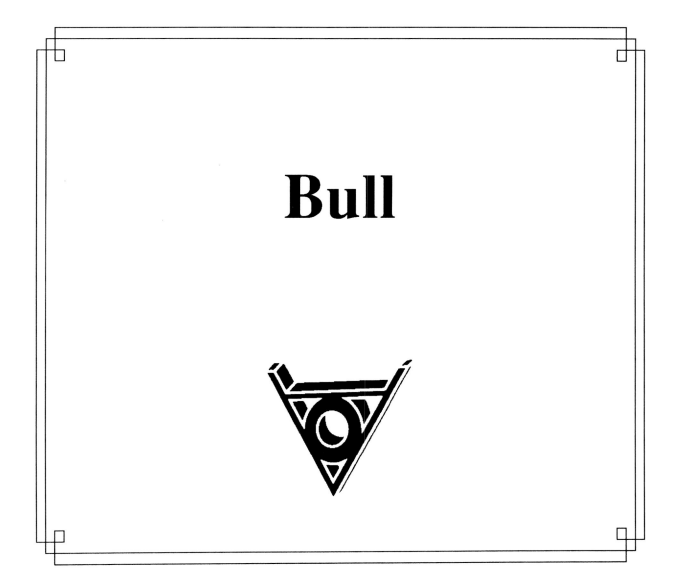

bull *The letter C of the Snake Ring Template.* A metaphor for the virile old sun who dies in the western horizon mountain-house, joins with the mother goddess to produce the new sun of the next season, then remains in the underworld with the numerous father-suns of the past seasons as fearsome husks who jealously oppose their own sons taking the solar path in the sky. *Ref* TRINITY, WAR.

• Leaping bulls are painted on the ceilings of the French cave of Lascaux, France, some with spears through their rump; the paintings are high from the ground where it was difficult for the artists to reach. Dying and charging bulls are on the ceiling of the Spanish cave of Altamira. An impression of a bull made in the wet clays, made after the flood waters of the melting glacier's course through the cave of Calbiere in France, has a painted arrow through its chest and round motifs on its body *See* BULL & CELESTIAL & CHAOS IN NATURE & DEATH & ROUND MOTIFS IN SEQUENCE -350b \ EUROPE, ICE AGE \BRFp \CAAt \NATp CONt

• A ceramic model of a sanctuary that was buried in a necropolis contains figurines of females and bull-headed males holding snakes. Around the base of the walls are bulls in pens [the husks of the suns of the previous past seasons] *See* DEATH & HOUSE & REGENERATION & SEASON & SOCIETAL ASPECT & TRINITY -22a CYPRUS, VOUNOUS *Figure* 17

Figure 17

• The central figure of a Celtic bas relief depicts the god **Cernunnos** with a bull's head and with legs formed of entwined snakes ending in fish-tails (as do the tails of many of the dragons in Chinese art). At their festivals, Celts sacrificed a bull under sacred trees (as do present-day practitioners of Voodoo) *See* PATH & SACRIFICE ANIMAL & TRANSCULTURAL SIMILARITY & TREE & TRINITY & WATER -5b SCOTLAND, CELTIC \SCKt \DATt \WESp *Figure* 18

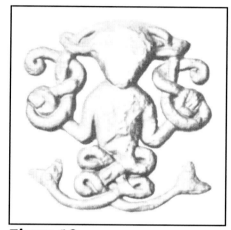

Figure 18

• In front of Solomon's temple there were twelve bronze bulls supporting a thirty-three ton bronze vessel filled with water called "The Sea" *See* HOUSE & TRINITY & UNDERWORLD & WATER -10b ISRAEL, JEWISH \ENDt

• The deity **Vrthrhehna** appeared to **Zoroaster** as a bull, ram, he-goat, and boar [all symbols of male virility] *See* BOAR & BULL & GOAT -6b IRAN, ZOROASTER \ELIt

• A shaped and painted burial vessel depicts a figure with bulls horns copulating with a woman *See* DEATH & EARRING & MARRIAGE & REGENERATION -5b PERU, NAZCA *Figure* 19

• The city of the young sun god, Baalbek (Heliopolis), was the center for worship of the bull god **Baal** *See* REGENERATION & SOCIETY AS AT THE AXIS MUNDI & SUN OLD/ YOUNG +1a LEBANON, ROMAN \HAWt

• The most important object of the Arapaho sun dance is a buffalo skull decorated with vertical rows of red and black dots. It is placed on the altar as a temporary home for the "above one" *See* ALTAR & BLACK & DANCE & PATH & RED & REGENERATION & ROUND MOTIF IN SEQUENCE & SKULL +18a USA, ARAPAHO \DOCp

Figure 19

• In a segment of the Okipa sun dance ceremony of Plains Indians performed until this century, a "dark shaped evil one" imitated a bull and wore a bull's tail; his body was painted black with white rings, and strapped to him was a three foot long wooden penis with a red ball on its end [which shocked George Catlin to the point of him excluding it from his illustrations]. The bull-dancer fell to the ground as spectators broke his wooden penis

and threw yellow paint on his face, saying that his black paint "became the yellow of daylight". Married women of the village then danced lasciviously and had sex with the old men of the tribe, calling them bulls. After having sex, the women said they had strengthened their marriage vows. Present day Indian informants disagree on the meaning of the sun dance except that it was for the benefit of their crops, cattle, and all mankind, and that it was to celebrate man's escape from the flood and chaos *See* CHAOS IN NATURE & CIRCUMCISION (CASTRATION) & DEMYTHOLIZATION & FLOOD & HUSK & MARRIAGE & RED & REGENERATION & RING MOTIF & ROUND MOTIF & SOCIETAL ASPECT +18a USA, MANDAN *Figure 20*

Figure 20

**See The Following Entries in Section Three
For Some Related Metaphors and Concepts**

- *Aries*
- *bear*
- *boar*
- *bucentaur*
- *bucranium*
- *Capricorn*
- *father*
- *goat*
- *he-goat*
- *llama*
- *ox*
- *pig*
- *ram*
- *Santa Claus*
- *sheep (male)*
- *stranger*
- *Taurus*

Fire

fire *The letter D of the Snake Ring Template.* A metaphor for the sunset death of the old sun into the underworld house of the mother goddess.

• A special lamp, decorated and of finer construction than other lamps found in the painted chambers was placed together with a red painted seashell, above the painted scene on the floor in the Well, a natural depression in the floor of the Ice Age cave of Lascaux *See* ABYSS & CAVE & CRUSTACEAN & LAMP & RED & UNDERWORLD & WATER   -350b FRANCE, LASCAUX *Figure 21* **Refer also to** *Figures 33, 34*

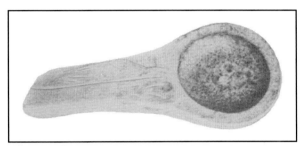

Figure 21

• The earliest known examples of writing in the Far East are pictographs depicting the sun and fire, sometimes shown above the symbol for a mountain *See* LETTERS & MOUNTAIN & PATH & SUN OLD -30a CHINA, NEOLITHIC *Figure 22*

• According to the Rig Veda, one of the most sacred of Hindu books, there is fire at the confluence of rivers, and fire-sticks belong to the millstone *See* CONFLUENCE OF RIVERS & VERTICAL STICK & WHEEL -19b INDIA, HINDU \SANt

• Remnants of purposefully broken figurines and pottery were found at the sacred precints of Eleusis in association with the remains of sacrificial fires lit in honor of the goddess **Demeter** *See* DEATH & MOTHER GODDESS & OBJECTS RITUALLY BROKEN & RITUAL & SACRIFICE ANIMAL & SOCIETY AS AT THE AXIS MUNDI -7b GREEK \MYLt

• Women exposed their genitals over ritual bonfires at the solstice festivals *See* MARRIAGE & PATH & SEASON -5b ENGLAND, CELTIC \RAUt

• In the legend of Atlantis, deemed by scholars to represent the western horizon, a sacrificed bull was burned on the altar of the temple around which were seven concentric planetary rings where **Prometheus** married **Kleito** *See* ALTAR & BULL & DEATH & HORIZON & MARRIAGE & PATH & SUN OLD & WEST ORIENTATION -4a GREEK \BREt

Figure 22

• Ancient Mexican legend tells of a diety who descended into the fiery entrance to the underworld but emerged as the sun, bringing equilibrium to the dry and the rainy seasons *See* ABYSS & CHAOS IN NATURE & RAIN & REGENERATION & SUN YOUNG -1b MEXICO, TEOTIHUACAN \CUPt

• The fallen angel **Lucifer** brought the light of Heaven as fire down to Hell *See* DESCENDING MOTIF & RAYED MOTIF & SUN OLD & UNDERWORLD 0b ITALY, CHRISTIAN \ELHp

• During the Easter ceremony in Jerusalem a holy fire is lit at Christ's tomb *See* DEATH & DEMYTHOLIZATION & REGENERATION & SPRINGTIME 0b ISRAEL, CHRISTIAN \ARCt

• Many church altars bear the image of a flaming heart which is cut and bleeding *See* ALTAR & DEATH & HOUSE   0b FRANCE, CHRISTIAN \WESp

• A brazier from Cerro de las Mesas with early Olmec influence depicts an aged figure seated below a cross-form with a ring motif at its center *See* CROSS WEST & FIRE & RING MOTIF & SUN OLD & TRINITY & UNDERWORLD +2a MEXICO, MAYAN \BEQp **See** *Figure 27*
Refer also to *Figure 31*

• Many "incensarios" were discovered at the bottom of the lake at Flores, a ceremonial center with pyramids *See* DESCENDING MOTIF & INCENSE & PYRAMID & SOCIETY AS AT THE AXIS MUNDI & WATER +2b GUATEMALA, MAYAN \FOUt

• A detail of the roll-out of a cylindrical burial vase (one of several called "Popol Vuh", because of their images' resemblance to legends in a book by that name) depicts a deity falling in flames from the maw of a celestial serpent *See* DESCENDING MOTIF & PATH & SNAKE FEATHERED/ WINGED +3b MEXICO, MAYAN *Figure 23*

Figure 23

• Cremations had been performed in front of several of the colossal stone statues **[Note:** The boat engraved on the figure's submerged stomach] *See* ART & BOAT (WATER) & DEATH & FIRE & HEAD & STONE & VERTICAL LINE/ SHAPE +6b EASTER ISLAND \HEUt *Figure 24*

• In the boiling red inferno of the river Styx there is a waterfall plunging into an abyss where great figures end their mortal life *See* ABYSS & DESCENDING MOTIF & DEATH & RED & TRINITY & WATERFALL +12a ALIGHIERI DANTE \SANt

Figure 24

• **Tezcatlipoca**, "Smoking Mirror", was a fallen sun god who was said to be associated with burning water *See* DESCENDING MOTIF & MIRROR & SUN OLD & WATER +13b MEXICO, AZTEC \LARt **Refer to** *Figure 29*

• At the annual New Fire ceremony, a fire was lit in the open breast of a sacrificed victim captured during ritual warfare between neighboring kingdoms *See* DEATH & SACRIFICE HUMAN & SEASON & WAR +16a MEXICO, AZTEC \LEYp

• The First Ancestor broke his sinuous arms and legs when he took fire down the rainbow *See* ANCESTOR & FOOT & PATH & RAINBOW +19a MALI, DOGON \PAQp

• Grave site posters often depict a winged devil falling into a flaming pot *See* DEATH & DESCENDING MOTIF & HUSK & REGENERATION & TRINITY & VESSEL & WATER   +19a HAITI, VOODOO \WESp

• Woman's vulva is regarded as the place of fire and sacrifice *See* DEATH & MARRIAGE & VAGINA +19a INDIA \MCCt

• Detail from a drawing made while under the influence of hallucinogens depicts a figure descending in flames through a cross-form *See* CROSS WEST & DESCENDING MOTIF & HALLUCINOGEN   +19a COLOMBIA, TUKANO \REJp

• At an annual ritual in honor of **Huitzlipotli**, the young sun god, paper serpents were burned in front of the main temple *See* HOUSE & PATH & REGENERATION & RITUAL & SUN YOUNG +13b MEXICO, AZTEC \NAUt

**See The Following Entries in Section Three
For Some Related Metaphors and Concepts**

- *anvil*
- *blacksmith*
- *bullroarer*
- *burial*
- *candle*
- *castration*
- *chevron pointing
  down*
- *chicken*
- *circumcision
  male*
- *cremation*
- *Crucifixion*
- *Death*
- *decapitation*
- *descending motif*
- *flame*
- *fowl*
- *Golden
  Fleece*
- *hammer*
- *hand down*
- *hanged man*
- *hearth*
- *lamp*

- *lantern*
- *objects ritually broken*
- *oven or furnace*
- *red*
- *sacrifice animal*
- *sacrifice human*
- *Sagittarius*
- *scorpion*
- *scythe*
- *skeletal*
- *skull*
- *smoke*
- *southwest orientation*
- *springtime sunset
  orientation*
- *sulphur*
- *swordfish*
- *thirteen*
- *tobbacco*
- *torch*
- *triangle motif inverted*
- *T-inverted*
- *west orientation*

Cross West,
Vertical Shape

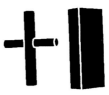

cross *The letter E of the Snake Ring Template.* Christ. *Widely used as a symbol of Christianity.* A metaphor for: **a**. The intersection of the downward path of the sun with the western horizon. *Ref* CRESCENT MOTIF, CRUCIFIXION, DEATH, MARRIAGE, REGENERATION, SOCIETY AS AT THE AXIS MUNDI, STAR, STAR SIX POINTED **b**. Less often, the sun's upward path through the eastern horizon from below. *Ref* CROSS EAST/ WEST, LEAP-UP.

• **Tata Dios** put up a cross in the west where the sun sets at the end of the world, another cross in the east where the sun rises. We are prevented from going to the crosses by large bodies of water, so we set up crosses in front of our houses where we worship. We go to the cross in the west when we die. *See* DEATH & HOUSE & SOCIETY AS AT THE AXIS MUNDI & WATER & WORSHIP +19a MEXICO \FONt

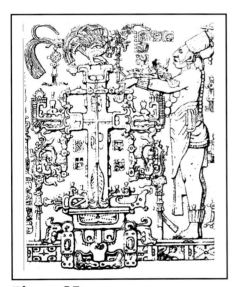

Figure 25

cross west *The letter E of the Snake Ring Template. Ref* CROSS.

• Mesoamericans believed that the entrance to the underworld was in the form of a cross -6b MEXICO \AVDt

• A foliated cross with a fantastic "sun bird" at its top is the central motif of a Palenque pyramid-temple called "the place where the sun died." This most western of the lowland Mayan ceremonial centers is located on the side of a mountain with a small waterfall descending from above. A rubbing of the cover of a royal burial discovered deep within its west-facing major pyramid-temple depicts the bird and foliated cross above the deceased ruler's head as he descends into the mouth of the feathered serpent *See* BIRD & BURIAL & FERTILITY & HOUSE & MOUNTAIN & PATH & PYRAMID & RULER & SNAKE FEATHERED & SOCIETY AS AT THE AXIS MUNDI & SUN OLD & WATERFALL & WEST ORIENTATION +4a MEXICO, PALENQUE \GREt \NASt *Figure 25 Figure 26*

Figure 26

• A Mayan brazier with much older Olmec characteristics, depicts a seated aged man below a border of cross symbols with a ring motif at their center; these decorate the rim of the container in which the fire was built *See* FIRE & RING MOTIF & TRINITY +2a MEXICO, CERRO DE LAS MESAS *Figure 27*

• Present day Maya place sun-crosses on mountains, in caves and at waterfalls. This cross is unrelated to the Christian cross *See* SOCIETY AS AT THE AXIS MUNDI +19a MEXICO, ZINACANTECO \VOGt

• The present-day Maya decorate their braziers with a vertical line to signify a male deity and a horizontal one for a female deity *See* FIRE & HORIZONTAL MOTIF & MARRIAGE & VERTICAL LINE/ SHAPE +19a MEXICO, LACANDONES \FONp

Figure 27

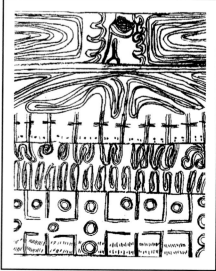

Figure 28

• The great slit-drum is played vertically at ceremonial gatherings of the patrilineal clans and horizontally for matrilineal clans *See* HORIZONTAL MOTIF & MARRIAGE & MUSIC & VERTICAL LINE/ SHAPE +19a NEW HEBRIDES, AMBRYM \METp

• Suns and crosses at the bottom of a Tukano drawing are suns and the suns' male virility respectively. The red symbol at the top of the drawing depicts the sun as a phallus. The central winged figure depicts their maloca, or sacred house, which they copied after the first maloca "the vagina house of the waters" *See* HALLUCINOGEN & HOUSE & MARRIAGE & PHALLUS & SUN OLD & RING MOTIF IN SEQUENCE & VAGINA +19a COLOMBIA, TUKANO \REJt *Figure 28*

• Another drawing made under the influence of hallucinogenic drugs represents creation. It depicts a figure falling headfirst in flames through a line drawing of a cross *See* FIRE & HALLUCINOGEN & REGENERATION +19a COLOMBIA, TUKANO *Figure 29*

Figure 29

• The royal tomb of Mendez is carved in the form of a cross into the side of a mountain; bull figures are carved in relief on columns at the entrance, and a victorious battle scene is carved below the cross-entrance *See* BULL & COLUMNS & FUNERAL & REGENERATION & RULER & WAR -5b IRAQ \GIRp

• Until recent times, rural peoples of Europe bound a dummy on a cross and threw it into the water at the start of springtime for the good of their crops. Scholars conjecture that this was prefigured by similar human sacrifice in olden times, but are puzzled as to why it was done *See* FERTILITY & SACRIFICE HUMAN & SEASON & WATER +18a BOHEMIA \FRBt

• A cross representing the God of Death is placed in every cemetery *See* SOCIETY AS AT THE AXIS MUNDI +19a HAITI, VOODOO \COTt

• Until the seventeenth century, the Christian cross had equilateral arms +16a \JUNt

• Roman Catholics make the sign of the cross with Holy Water as they enter the church *See* HOUSE & PATH & SOCIETAL ASPECT & WATER +19a \TULt

• Scenes of the Crucifixion are often associated with crops, such as grapes *See* DEATH & FERTILITY & REGENERATION & SPRINGTIME +12a SWITZERLAND, CHRISTIAN \CAMp

vertical line/ shape 1. *The letter E of the Snake Ring Template.* A metaphor for the vertical segment of the entwined serpent path penetrating the mother goddess' mountain-house in the waters of the western horizon. *Ref* ALTAR, CROSS, HOUSE, MOTHER GODDESS, SERPENT ENTWINED, SOCIETY AS AT THE AXIS MUNDI, STELA, VERTICAL STICK, WEST ORIENTATION. **2**. *The letter O of the Snake Ring Template.* A secondary use of the metaphor is for the vertical segment of the entwined serpent path at the eastern horizon. *Ref* CROSS EAST.

• Ice Age cave drawings show meanders crossing an image of a pregnant female.

Another image of a headless female in a different cave has lines entering into her vagina *See* GODDESSES & MEANDER MOTIF & VAGINA -250b FRANCE, LA ROCHE \GIEp

vertical stick *The letter E of the Snake Ring Template* : VERTICAL LINE/ SHAPE.

• In an Ice Age cave, the tine of a deer's antler was stuck into a ritual mound which was layered with red ochre *See* CAVE & MOUND & PATH & RED -120b SPAIN \NAUt

• Two pilasters of a shrine room in the first true city in the world were painted with the same pattern as on the scales of a local snake. Between the pillars were two figurines of the same fertility goddess, one pregnant and one lean *See* BABY BOY/ GIRL & BIRTH & COLUMN & FERTILITY & HOUSE & MOTHER GODDESS & PATH & SOCIETY AS AT THE AXIS MUNDI -70b TURKEY, CATAL HUYUK \TILp **Refer to** *Figure 175* SECTION THREE.

• The central axis of the universe is at Mythical mount Meru around which are seven concentric planetary rings [refer to Atlantis above] *See* LEVELS CELESTIAL & MOUNTAIN -5b INDIA, HINDU \BOPt

• The remaining arm of a carved stone cross depicts the god **Heimdall** who holds, in addition to his symbolic bull's horn, a vertical staff which connects between the open mouths of an upper and lower entwined serpent. The lower one is inverted *See* BULLROARER & CROSS WEST & HORIZON & PATH & SERPENT ENTWINED & UNDERWORLD +1b SWEDEN, TEUTONIC
Figure 30

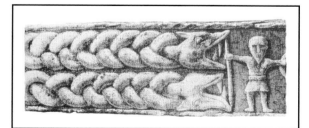

Figure 30

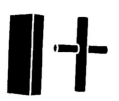

• Maypoles were condemned by the church as "stinking idols" because couples went to them to copulate around them at nighttime *See* MARRIAGE & SPIRAL & SPRINGTIME +15a ENGLAND \FRBt

• The handle of a cleric's crozier is in the form of a coiled snake, whose mouth in the innermost coil disgorges a falling bearded man *See* CROZIER & DESCENDING & PRIEST & STAFF +17a IRELAND, CHRISTIAN *Figure 31*

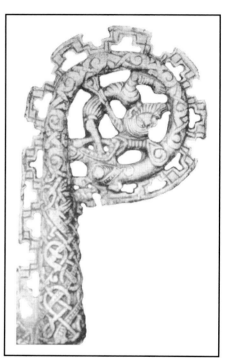

Figure 31

• The Indians believe the creator of the earth marked the center of the earth for them with an ash tree *See* CELESTIAL & PATH & UNDERWORLD & SOCIETY AS AT THE AXIS MUNDI +18a USA \NABt

• A double-bladed "axe" is the vertical path of the people's ancestral deity. His western descent is symbolized by the fish on the blades at its top. A female figure, penetrated below by the shaft, has a circle of beads at her waist *See* ANCESTOR WORSHIP & BEAD & CROSS & FISH & MOTHER GODDESS & UNDERWORLD +18a NIGERIA, YORUBA *Figure 32*

Figure 32

**See The Following Entries in Section Three
For Some Related Metaphors and Concepts**

- *acorn*
- *altar*
- *apple*
- *arrow*
- *baton*
- *blade*
- *bow*
- *branch*
- *bundle of rods*
- *caduceus*
- *center of the world*
- *Christmas tree*
- *column*
- *comb*
- *coral*
- *cromlech*
- *crook*
- *cross circled*
- *cross west*
- *crozier*
- *cypress*
- *distaff*
- *dolmen*
- *drum*
- *elephant*
- *forest*
- *herm*
- *Hermit*
- *hour-glass motif*
- *incense*
- *knife*
- *labrys*
- *lance or spear*
- *libation (oil)*
- *lightning or thunderbolt*
- *lingam*
- *menhir*
- *minaret*
- *mistletoe*
- *monolith*
- *oak*
- *obelisk*
- *paddle*
- *palm*
- *papyrus*
- *phallus*
- *pillar*
- *pine*
- *pine-cone*
- *plow*
- *pole*
- *poplar*
- *rudder or steering paddle*
- *scepter*
- *spindle*
- *spinning*
- *spire*
- *staff*
- *stele or stella*
- *swastika*
- *tombstone*
- *totemism*
- *totem pole*
- *tower*
- *tree*
- *tree worship*
- *twisted shapes*
- *verticality*
- *wand*
- *wood*
- *world axis*

Crustacean, Water

crustacean *The letter F of the Snake Ring Template.* A metaphor for the western horizon waters, the place of solar regeneration. *Ref* REGENERATION, WATER.

• Among present-day tribal cultures the shell is regarded as a symbol of the maternal waters +19a \RAUt

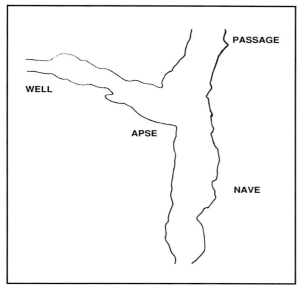

Figure 33

• In addition to the special lamp which had been placed on top of the floor-painting in the Well, a depression in the cave located in a chamber northwest of the main passage, was a seashell stained with red ochre *See* ABYSS & CAVE & FIRE & RED & SPRINGTIME ORIENTATION & TRINITY -350b FRANCE, LASCAUX *Figure 33*
Figure 34

• The goddess of love and fertility, **Aphrodite**, is often depicted within a scallop shell *See* FERTILITY & GODDESS & MARRIAGE & WATER -20b GREEK \RAUt

Figure 34

• From infancy, girls wore a shell pendant over their vulva until after their marriage *See* MARRIAGE & SOCIETAL ASPECT +3b MEXICO, MAYAN \RAUt

• A shell containing red ochre was placed in a royal Mayan burial deep within the main pyramid-temple *See* FUNERAL & PYRAMID & RED & WATER +3b MEXICO, PALENQUE \NASp

• Medicine bags made of the skin of an otter, an aquatic mammal, containing sacred shells are buried with the deceased *See* FUNERAL & REGENERATION & SOCIETAL ASPECT +18a USA, ALGONKIAN \TUQp

• An oyster shell containing dried blood was buried beneath the altar at the foot of a Mayan pyramid-temple *See* ALTAR & BLOOD (RED) & PATH & PYRAMID & SOCIETY AS AT THE AXIS MUNDI +7a HONDURAS, COPAN \ARCt

**See The Following Entries in Section Three
For Some Related Metaphors and Concepts**

- *anchor*
- *Aquarius*
- *ark*
- *boat*
- *confluence
  of rivers*
- *crustacean:
  cowrie*
- *deluge*
- *duck*
- *fish*
- *flood*
- *fountain*
- *horizon*
- *jade*
- *lake*
- *marine bird*
- *night-sea
  crossing*
- *oar*
- *octopus*
- *Red (Reed)
  Sea*
- *reed*
- *river*
- *rushes*
- *sail*
- *sea*
- *shell*
- *ship*
- *stork*
- *swan*
- *water*
- *wave*

Mountain, Pyramid

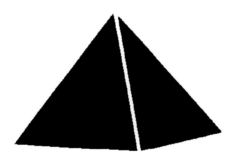

mountain *The letter G of the Snake Ring Template.* A metaphor for the western horizon mountain-house within the serpent path at the watery abyss. *Ref* CAVE, (CHAOS IN NATURE, DEATH, FLOOD, MOTHER GODDESS, RETURN), SOCIETY AS AT THE AXIS MUNDI.

• Every culture has its sacred mountain where the sky and earth meet, where the "axis mundi" goes through *See* AXIS MUNDI/ SOCIETY AS AT THE AXIS MUNDI +19a MIRCEA ELIADE \ELIt

• When the Aztecs were instructed to prepare maps of their territory for the Spanish conquerors, they used their convention of depicting each town as a mountain glyph, with it's base curved as if on water *See* FLOOD & SOCIETY AS AT THE AXIS MUNDI +15a MEXICO, AZTEC *Figure 35*

Figure 35

• Maeve's Cairn is believed to be a replica of the mythic mountain at the navel of the world *See* ABYSS & SOCIETY AS THE AXIS MUNDI & STONE -45b IRELAND \ELHt

• A papyrus illustration shows the sun-disk received into the arms of a goddess in the western mountain on its way to the realm of the dead *See* DEATH & GODDESS & MARRIAGE & WEST ORIENTATION -15a EGYPT \PIDp \ELHt
Figure 36

• Gorgotha was the mountain at the center of the world, where Adam [the Hebrew letters of a bull, fish and water, respectively, forming the name "Adam" are from the proto-Sanaitic {old Hebrew} pictogram] was born and where he is buried *See* ANCESTOR WORSHIP & BULL & DEMYTHOLIZATION & FISH & LETTERS & REGENERATION & WATER 0b ITALY, CHRISTIAN \ELIt

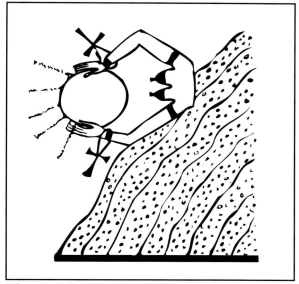

Figure 36

• Mount Himingbjorg, the "celestial mountain" of the Edda myths, was where the rainbow touched the earth *See* HORIZON & RAINBOW +7b GERMAN, TEUTONIC \ELIt

• Legendary king **Mu** reached the setting sun by crossing a river formed of melted snow at Mount Kunlun *See* FLOOD & RULER -15b CHINA \ELHt

• Ancient myths tell of the Queen of the West, who reigned at the abode of the dead in a jade palace on top of a mountain surrounded by water *See* DEATH & GODDESSES & JADE & PALACE & WATER & WEST ORIENTATION -15b CHINA \LARp

• Mount Everest is the "goddess mother of the world". Like Mount Kailas, which is mystically connected with heaven, it is said to be the home of the sun god Siva and at the center of the world *See* MOTHER GODDESS &

SOCIETY AS AT THE AXIS MUNDI & SUN OLD/ YOUNG +19a TIBET, TANTRIC \TIMp \EXQp

• Figures of bulls were depicted in shrine rooms which were entered through openings in their roofs of the world's first true city, but only on walls facing a range of mountains and a river to the west of the city See BULL & HOUSE & SOCIETY AS AT THE AXIS MUNDI & UNDERWORLD & WATER & WEST ORIENTATION -70b TURKEY, CATAL HUYUK \REAt

• In **Gilgamesh's** voyage to the mountains at the mouth of the world's rivers, he went along the sun-road to where he met **Siduri** (a barmaid) in the deep waters of death at the edge of the sea See ABYSS & CONFLUENCE OF RIVERS & DEATH & PATH & SUN OLD & WATER -35b IRAQ, SUMERIAN \SANt

• **Shamash** the sun god travels in a chariot at evening to the west; there he enters a mountain, crosses the underworld and rises in the east See HORSE (CHARIOT) & PATH & UNDERWORLD -20b IRAQ, ACCADIAN \LARt

• The top of the altar in Solomon's temple, with the stone horn of a bull at each of its corners, was called the "mountain of God"; the bottom of the altar was referred to as the "bosom of the earth", or the underworld See ALTAR & BULL & HOUSE & STONE & VERTICAL LINE/ SHAPE & SOCIETY AS AT THE AXIS MUNDI -10b ISRAEL, JEWISH \ENDt

• The vast crater of the Haleakala volcano is called "the house of the sun" and is regarded as holy ground by the islanders See ABYSS & HOUSE & SOCIETY AS AT THE AXIS MUNDI & SUN OLD/ YOUNG +19a HAWAII \NYTp

• Indians of Tierra del Fuego, whose ancestors migrated from northern Asia during the terminal Ice Age, recall a long-ago time when it snowed so hard at springtime that the whole earth was covered; the snow melted and the earth was flooded; only a very lucky few survived on the mountain peaks above the waters See CHAOS IN NATURE & FLOOD & SEASON & SPRINGTIME +19a CHILE, YAMANA \CAIt

• Approximately one-hundred peaks were worshiped as the abode of the earth mother.

According to legend, the Anahuarque mountain at Cuzco rose from the waters of the mythic flood See CHAOS IN NATURE & FLOOD & SOCIETY AS AT THE AXIS MUNDI +9b PERU, INCA \AVDt \OMNp

• The walls of the maloca, their communal house, represented the mountains at the edge of the world See CAVE & HOUSE & SOCIETY AS AT THE AXIS MUNDI & WEST ORIENTATION +19a COLOMBIA, TUKANO \HUGp **Refer to** *Figure 90*

pyramid *The letter G of the Snake Ring Template. Ref* MOUNTAIN.

• The Nippur ziggurat on the sacred Euphrates river [actually a pyramid-temple), was built to imitate the world mountain. It was dedicated to the young sun god **Enlil,** and its stairway was for his divine descent See HOUSE & INFERNAL & MOUNTAIN & STAIRS & SUN YOUNG & WATER -20a IRAQ, SUMERIAN *Figure 37*

Figure 37

• The pyramids, located for the most part on the west bank of the Nile, were symbols of the "world mountain", the home of the "mountain mother" where all life was born and returned to at death See MOTHER GODDESS & MOUNTAIN & SOCIETAL ASPECT & SOCIETY AS AT THE AXIS MUNDI & WATER -30b EGYPT \CAMt *Figure 38*

• Coatepec, "serpent mountain" was the name of the mythic mountain of the west where the young sun god was born. It was also the

name given to the main pyramid of the Aztec nation in present-day Mexico City *See* BIRTH & MOUNTAIN & PATH & SNAKE & SOCIETY AS AT THE AXIS MUNDI & SUN YOUNG & WEST ORIENTATION +13b MEXICO, AZTEC \AVDt

Figure 38

Figure 39

• The lofty pyramid at Tikal has a stone temple with a soaring roof comb at its top *See* HOUSE & PATH & STONE & VERTICAL LINE/ SHAPE +3b GUATEMALA, MAYAN *Figure 39*

• The remains of the pyramid of Quetzlcoatl bear striking reliefs of the mythic feathered serpent, from which the pyramid got its name,

with seashells and fish depicted alongside its body *See* CRUSTACEAN & DRAGON & FISH & PATH & FEATHERED SERPENT & WATER -1b MEXICO, TEOTIHUACAN *Figure 40*

Figure 40

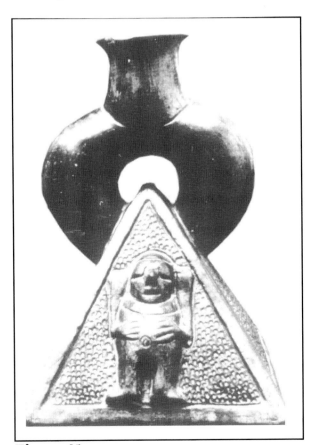

Figure 41

• A stirrup vessel from the mother culture of the Andean civilizations is in the shape of a pyramid with a pregnant woman standing inside *See* BABY BOY/ GIRL & MOTHER GODDESS & VESSEL -8b PERU, CHAVIN *Figure* 41

• El Castillo pyramid, as seen from the statue in the Jaguar Temple at the main ball-court of Chichen Itza, is now more commonly known as Kukulkan, the Maya name for the mythic feathered serpent. At the time of the equinox, the shadow of serpents carved on the balustrade of the staircase appear to descend the staircase and then disappear into the nearby cenote *See* ABYSS & DRAGON & FELINE & GAME SPORT & WELL +8a MEXICO, MAYAN *Figure* 42

Figure 42

**See The Following Entries in Section Three
For Some Related Metaphors and Concepts**

- *abyss*
- *ashlar*
- *cenote*
- *center of the world*
- *cone*
- *crater*
- *garden*
- *Garden of
  Eden*
- *gargoyle*
- *gopher*
- *helmet*
- *hill*
- *hole*
- *hollow*
- *hood*
- *horizontal
  motif*
- *marble*
- *mound*

- *mouse*
- *navel of
  the world*
- *omphalos*
- *palace*
- *pediment*
- *pit*
- *pyramid*
- *rat*
- *reef*
- *rock*
- *stone*
- *triangle
  motif upright*
- *valley*
- *void*
- *volcano*
- *waterfall*
- *well*
- *whirlpool*

Cave, House, Marriage

cave *The letter ℋ of the Snake Ring Template.* A metaphor for the mountain-house within the vertical segment of the entwined serpent path where the old sun joins with the mother goddess in the waters of the western horizon. *Ref* HOUSE.

• . The Mayan word najtunich means both "stone house" and "cave" +8a GUATEMALA, MAYAN \NATp

• The lowland Mayan word "huitz" for a pyramid-temple means "divine mountain" *See* MOUNTAIN & PYRAMID +8a BELIZE, MAYAN \WESt

• The sun abides at night in caves of the City of the Sun at the west, where the sky, land, and water come together *See* HORIZON & WEST ORIENTATION +10b MEXICO, TOLTEC \CAAt

• A bone fragment from a French Ice Age cave depicts the hind legs and phallus of a bull standing above a recumbent, pregnant female wearing bracelets and a necklace, who holds her hands up to the animal *See* BABY BOY/ GIRL & BULL & CIRCLE MOTIF & JEWELRY & MARRIAGE & MOTHER GODDESS & SOCIETAL ASPECT -350b FRANCE, LAUGERIE BASSE *Figure* 43

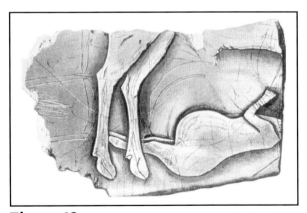

Figure 43

• A pregnant female with traces of red pigment on her body and an emphasized pubic, was carved into the wall of an Ice Age shelter above a river in France. Her blank face is turned to a bull's horn bearing thirteen tally marks which she holds aloft in her right hand, while her left hand rests on her enlarged stomach. There are Venus figures at several other Ice

Age sites also holding bull's horns *See* BABY BOY/GIRL & BULL & LEVELS & MOTHER GODDESS & PATH & RED & RIVER & UNICORN & VAGINA & WATER -350b FRANCE, LAUSSEL *Figure* 44

Figure 44

• The entrance to a ceremonial cave high up on a mountain, is carved out of solid rock into the form of an open dragon's mouth. Huge stone jaguar remains are at either side of the stone staircase to the entrance *See* FELINE & MOUNTAIN & PATH & RITUAL & STAIRS INFERNAL +15a MEXICO, AZTEC \HEKp

house *The letter ℋ of the Snake Ring Template.* A metaphor for the mountain-house of the western horizon where the solar soul is regenerated. *Ref* CAVE.

• Cathedrals and temples derive from caves +19a JOSEPH CAMPBELL \CAAt

• The temple is a metaphor in our minds; we may never know why *See* CHAOS IN NATURE & INFANT MENTALITY +19a \OMNt

• Buildings worldwide are decorated with motifs of serpents, felines, sea-shells, and goddesses *See* CRUSTACEAN & FELINE & GODDESSES & PATH & SNAKE +19a \WESt

• Cities developed around their temples *See* SOCIETY AS AT THE AXIS MUNDI +19a ROBERT ADAMS \FAGt

• The house socializes humans into becoming members of their culture *See* SOCIETAL ASPECT +19a PIERRE BORDIEU \NABt

• The distinguishing characteristic between primitive cultures and civilizations is that the latter builds their sacred houses for posterity *See* MOUNTAIN & STONE +19a KENNETH CLARK \WESt

• Every dwelling, town, pyramid, and temple is projected to the "center of the world" *See* SOCIETY AS AT THE AXIS MUNDI +19a MIRCEA ELIADE \ELIt \ELHt

• Sacred architecture renders visible the passage from the unmanifest to the "here-below" *See* SOCIETY AS AT THE AXIS MUNDI +19a ROBERT LAWLOR \OMNt

• All ritual houses are different stages of development of the same conception: mountains were the models for the "first house" which many people believe was bestowed on them at a distant time or mythic age as a container for their culture *See* CAVE +19a \NABt

• Tomb houses are symbols of the prefigured sacred marriage *See* DEATH & MARRIAGE & MOTHER GODDESS & SOCIETAL ASPECT & SUN OLD +19a ERICH NEUMANN \NEUt

• The earliest known man-made structure consisted of a circular stone Ice Age wall surrounding a floor that is partly sunken into a hill; clay images of bears, lions and women were recovered from a hearth at its center *See* BEAR & CAVE & FELINE & FIRE & MOTHER GODDESS & MOUNTAIN & SOCIETY AS AT THE AXIS MUNDI & STONE -270a CZECHOSLOVAKIA, VESTONICE \MAQp

• The roll-out of a lapis cylinder seal, attributed to the Sumerians or the Assyrians, depicts entwined serpents with a series of round motifs between their bodies descending to the roof of a shrine house, where one of the serpents deposits a round-motif from its mouth. At the front of the house is a rampant feline and a seated figure with bull's horns *See*

BULL & CELESTIAL & FELINE & PATH & ROUND-MOTIF IN SEQUENCE & SERPENT ENTWINED & TRINITY -25a IRAQ, SUMERIAN \PRIs *Figure 45*

Figure 45

• Clay figurines of the entwined serpent Ninshibur, were placed in boxes beneath the doorways of domiciles *See* PATH & SOCIETAL ASPECT -35b IRAQ, SUMERIAN \CAAt

• A house-snake was sealed in the wood doorsteps of Nordic and Baltic houses and fed through a special hole made in the doorsteps. This practice continued until the late Nineteenth Century *See* PATH & SOCIETAL ASPECT +18a SWEDEN; LITHUANIA \MUNt

• In Crete and Cyprus, and later throughout the Greek world, there were feeding stations for snakes in the houses and temples *See* SNAKE & SOCIETY AS AT THE AXIS MUNDI -20b GREEK \MUNt

• Temples were referred to as the Sun Temple of the Primeval Mound; bronze water wheels squirted water on the clothes of the worshippers as they entered *See* FLOOD & MOUND & REGENERATION & SOCIETY AS AT THE AXIS MUNDI & SUN OLD & WATER & WHEEL -30b EGYPT \DEDt

• The name of the mother goddess **Hathor** means literally "Hat-Hor" or "House-of-Horus" *See* BABY BOY & MOTHER GODDESS & SUN YOUNG -30b EGYPT \SANt

• The inscription on the Temple of Luxor is, "from where the sun-god goes forth" *See* BABY BOY & SUN YOUNG AND SOCIETY AS AT THE AXIS MUNDI -30b EGYPT \WESt

• Before the earliest pyramid was constructed, there was a pyramid-shaped mound in the pre-dynastic Temple of Nekhen (Narmar) *See* MOUND & PYRAMID -30b EGYPT \BAJt

• Sanctuaries were called literally, "God's Booth" *See* SUN OLD & TRINITY -24a EGYPT, SAHURE \EDWp

• The Demeter temple was for the goddess to live in; its roots were "below the earth, the beginning and end of life" *See* FERTILITY & GODDESSES & REGENERATION & SOCIETY AS AT THE AXIS MUNDI & UNDERWORLD -7b GREEK, ELEUSIS \MYLt

Figure 46

• The main structure at Knossos served the combined functions of a palace and a

mortuary temple. According to legend, a half-bull and half-man minotaur lived in a labyrinth under the building. Labyrinth comes from the same root "labys" as does the labrys or double-axe; images of the double-axe were found carved into the upper part of the labyrinth at Knossos *See* BULL & DEATH & HOLE & LABRYS & MAZE & PATH & RULER & SOCIETY AS AT THE AXIS MUNDI & STAFF & TRINITY & WATER -20b CRETE, MINOAN \WOOt

• A statue of the goddess **Athene** was the central figure in the Parthenon temple at the Acropolis on the top of an Athens hill. A copy of the statue shows her holding a winged youth in her hand, with a small Sphinx on her helmet and a large snake standing erect behind the shield at her side. Every year a goat was sacrificed in front of the temple, where there was an enormous marble water basin supported by figures of goddesses standing on the backs of lions *See* BABY BOY & DEATH & FELINE & GOAT & MOTHER GODDESS & MOUNTAIN & PATH & SNAKE & SOCIETY AS AT THE AXIS MUNDI & SPHINX & STONE & SUN OLD & TEMPLE & UNDERWORLD & WAR & WATER -20b GREEK \FRBt \BOAp *Figure 46 Figure 47*

Figure 47

• The ziggurat, a stepped pyramid often covered with bricks in the form of snake scales and called "the great binding post", which the Babylonians associated with the waters of the underworld *See* PATH & PYRAMID & ROPE & SNAKE & SOCIETY AS AT THE AXIS MUNDI & UNDERWORLD & VERTICAL LINE/ SHAPE & WATER -35b IRAQ, KISH \FAGt \SANt \ELIt

• Each major city had at least one ziggurat. The ziggurat was considered the crest of a mountain linking heaven to earth. The temple at its top was called "mountain-house"; its temples as well as Babylon itself were often referred to as "the bond between heaven and earth" or the "gate of the waters of chaos" *See* CHAOS IN NATURE & FLOOD & HOLE & HORIZON & MOUNTAIN & PYRAMID & SOCIETY AS AT THE AXIS MUNDI & WATER -20b IRAQ, ACCADIAN \BOPt \ELIt

• Images of serpents were placed over the doorknobs and the portals of Babylonian cities *See* PATH & SNAKE & SOCIETY AS AT THE AXIS MUNDI -20b IRAQ, ASHUR \MUNt

• "Horns of consecration" (bulls' horns) were placed on the facades of all of the religious buildings *See* BULL & DEATH & SOCIETY AS AT THE AXIS MUNDI -17a CRETE, MINOAN \NATp

• An ancient belief of the Chinese is that their temples are counterparts of the sacred temple in the underworld *See* SOCIETY AS AT THE AXIS MUNDI -15b CHINA \ELHt

• Palaces and domiciles were identified with the mythic central mountain of the universe which was penetrated by the axis mundi, the pivot on which all turns; the balustrade of the main palace staircase at the Forbidden City, where the emperor descended on ritual occasions, depicts a dragon descending to mountain peaks surrounded by water; the temple precincts were entered through the All Truth Serpent Gate *See* DRAGON & MOUNTAIN & PATH & RITUAL & RULER & SOCIETY AS AT THE AXIS MUNDI & WATER -15b CHINA \CUPp \DOQp \NYTp

Figure 48

• Before entering Solomon's Temple, the priests ritually immersed themselves in a giant bronze basin which was supported by bronze bulls and called the Sea of Solomon. The Temple was modeled on the Tabernacle built by Moses during the Exodus. It was covered with red-colored dolphin skins and likened to "a cave by the sea" *See* BRONZE & BULL & CAVE & PRIEST & RED & SOCIETY AS AT THE AXIS MUNDI & TRINITY & UNDERWORLD & WATER & WHALE -10b ISRAEL, JEWISH \ENDt

• Aborigines of Tierra del Fuego, at the southern tip of South America, say that their original house was in the form of a mountain, and whoever thinks of it will find many sea lions and whales there *See* CAVE & MOUNTAIN & SOCIETAL ASPECT & WATER & WHALE +19a ARGENTINA, ONA \CAIt

• The Maya regarded their world as a house within an encircling serpent or iguana (the Mayan word has both meanings) which formed its roof, walls, and floor *See* PATH & SERPENT ENTWINED & SOCIETY AS AT THE AXIS MUNDI -6b MEXICO, MAYAN \MUTt \THPt

Figure 49

• Scholars are puzzled by the bas relief on the pediment of a Roman temple, depicting water nymphs at each side of the head of the sun-god *See* GODDESSES & SOCIETY AS AT THE AXIS MUNDI & SUN OLD & TEMPLE & WATER +1a ENGLAND, BATH *Figure* 48

• A Pompeiian wall painting depicts the goddess **Isis** with a snake in her hand greeting the cow-horned priestess **Io**, who, as a virgin, copulated with the old sun god **Zeus** *See* BULL

& COW & MARRIAGE & PATH & SOCIETAL ASPECT & SOCIETY AS AT THE AXIS MUNDI & SUN OLD & WATER & WEST ORIENTATION +1a ITALY, ROMAN \GRBp *Figure 49*

• Every temple represents the cosmic mountain at the center of the world *See* SOCIETY AS AT THE AXIS MUNDI -5b TIBET, TANTRIC \ELIt

• A decorated vase from a burial depicts an old god within a dragon's mouth caressing a half-naked woman; the ornate background of the scene suggests that it is taking place in a temple or a palace *See* DEATH & DRAGON & MARRIAGE & PALACE & PATH & REGENERATION & SUN OLD & TEMPLE +3b MEXICO, MAYAN *Figure 50*

Figure 50

• The earliest settlement of Great Zimbabwe, the ceremonial center, was built on a hill and venerated as "stone house". Pedestals, bearing soapstone statues of birds with columnar necks, were ubiquitous within the precincts; often decorated with ring and zig-zag motifs and figures of crocodiles *See* BIRD & CROCODILE & MOUNTAIN & RING MOTIFS IN SEQUENCE & SOCIETY AS AT THE AXIS MUNDI & STONE & VERTICAL LINE/ SHAPE & ZIG-ZAG MOTIF (HORIZONTAL). +3b ZIMBABWE *Figure 51* *Figure 52*

• Muhammad taught that a black serpent dwells in a pit under the Ka'ba, the Muslim "holy of holies" in Saudi Arabia *See* BLACK & HOLE & PATH & SOCIETY AS AT THE AXIS MUNDI & SNAKE & STONE +5b IRAN, ISLAM \MUNt

• Each igloo is modeled after the house of **Sedna**, the old woman of the sea. Natiq, a recess in the floor, is associated with the sea *See* GODDESS & HOLE & PATH & SOCIETAL ASPECT & SOCIETY AS AT THE AXIS MUNDI & WATER +5b ESKIMO \CAIt \NABp

• Stylized dragons decorate the eaves of the native stave churches *See* PATH & SOCIETY AS AT THE AXIS MUNDI & VERTICAL LINE/ SHAPE +7b NORWAY, VIKING *Figure 53*

Figure 51

• A mural from the west wall of the Temple of the Tigers depicts a great battle between two forces. The two leaders are surrounded by rays and attended by large feathered serpents. At the top of a temple depicted in the scene there is a large "calendar stone" [similar to the disk with an encircling serpent border from the top of the main pyramid-temple of the Aztecs] mounted vertically on a pillar *See* BATON & FELINE & PATH & RAYED MOTIF & RING MOTIF & STAFF & SOCIETY AS AT THE AXIS MUNDI & TRINITY & UROBORUS & WAR & WEST ORIENTATION & WHEEL +7a MEXICO, CHICHEN ITZA \WIKp

• Hindu sanctuaries, called "sun temples", have surrounding moats called "the cosmic ocean". Hindu stupas are considered to be replicas of the legendary mount Meru. The mast at the center of their domes is the world axis extending to the watery depths below. Lingams within the sacred structures [a stone phallus, often surrounded by serpents] are said to be in the "womb's house"; the ritual baths in front of these temples have their sides decorated with snakes *See* CASTRATION (CIRCUMCISION) & MOUNTAIN & PATH & REGENERATION & SNAKE & SOCIETY AS AT THE AXIS MUNDI & STAFF & SUN OLD & WATER +7a INDIA, HINDU \ARCt \BOPt \COTt \EXQt

Figure 52

• Borobudur, one of the largest religious centers on the island, has its temple constructed in the form of a mountain *See*

MOUNTAIN & SOCIETY AS AT THE AXIS MUNDI & WATER +8a JAVA, BUDDHIST \ELIt

• Present-day Maya hang a rope from the center of their domicile to mark the entry of the "earth lord" *See* DESCENDING MOTIF & PATH & ROPE & SOCIETAL ASPECT +9a MEXICO, ZINACANTECO \AVDt

Figure 53

Figure 54

• Tula, the capital of the Toltecs, was called the "city of rushes". Sculpted on its encircling wall is the repeated figure of a skeletal deity, with a scroll emanating from his mouth, carried in the mouth of a fantastic serpent *See* DEATH & DRAGON & HEAD & MOUTH & PATH & REGENERATION & RUSHES & SOCIETY AS AT THE AXIS MUNDI & SOUL +10b MEXICO, TOLTEC

Figure 54

• Notre Dame Cathedral has images of dragons peering downwards as its rain-spouts [called "gargoyles" from the word "gurgle" sound of water], and figures of Devils along its gallery pointing skyward. The edifice and its decorations were made under strict control of the Clergy to "complete the picture of the world" *See* DRAGON & HUSK & PATH & SOCIETY AS AT THE AXIS MUNDI & TRINITY & UNDERWORLD & WATERFALL +12a FRANCE, CHRISTIAN \WESp \HAJp

• The enclosure wall of Templo Mayor was studded with stone heads of the feathered serpent Quetzlcoatl. Aztecs considered the temple "the navel of the world" and named it after the mythic mountain Coatepec, "serpent mountain", located where the sky and earth meet at the entranceway to Mictlan, the underworld of the dead. It was the home of the goddess **Coatlicue**, "serpent skirt", who gave birth to the young sun god **Huitzlipochtli** *See* BABY BOY & DRAGON & MOTHER GODDESS & MOUNTAIN & PRECINCT & NAVEL OF THE WORLD & PATH & PYRAMID & SOCIETY AS AT THE AXIS MUNDI & SUN YOUNG +13b MEXICO, AZTEC \AVDt \MAXt
Figure 55   Figure 56

Figure 55

• Within the Templo Mayor enclosure was the smaller Red Temple, whose painted walls are capped with a series of stone rings *See* PATH & RED & RING MOTIFS IN SEQUENCE +13b MEXICO, AZTEC \BANp

• Giant stone sea-shells ornamented the roofs of the pyramid-temples in Templo Mayor representing the place "in the water among reeds where **Huitzlipotli** was born" *See* BABY BOY & CRUSTACEAN & RUSHES & SOCIETY AS AT THE AXIS MUNDI & SUN YOUNG & UNDERWORLD & WATER +13b MEXICO, AZTEC \NYMp

• A great gold disk of a radiant sun was in the main temple at Cuzco, called the Temple of the Sun *See* GOLD & SUN YOUNG & REGENERATION +14b PERU, INCA \MASt

• Southeast Indians built their ritual houses with a tree protruding at the top *See* SOCIETY AS AT THE AXIS MUNDI & TREE +17a USA, CREEK \NABp

Figure 56

• Northwest Coast Indians decorate their lodge houses with figures of beavers with their hands raised. The beavers are sometimes surrounded by sun-rays. Beavers bear their young in houses which appear as mounds protruding from the water *See* BEAVER & BIRTH & HAND RAISED & MOUND & RAYED MOTIF & WATER +18a ALASKA, TLINGIT *Figure 57*
Refer also to *Figure 15*

Figure 57

• Posts and beams of the Kwakiutl ceremonial houses were carved and painted to represent winged serpents, with ring motifs along their bodies. Entranceways to these structures were shaped and painted to represent the outstretched legs and open vagina of the moon-mother, the "symbol of death and rebirth" *See* DEATH & DRAGON & MOON & MOTHER GODDESS & PATH & REGENERATION & RING MOTIFS IN SEQUENCE & SOCIETY AS AT THE AXIS MUNDI & VAGINA +18a CANADA, KWAKIUTL *Figure* 58 *Figure* 59

• The California Indian's primary loyalty was to his house-group, often taking the house name for his own. He used the house pit for healing ceremonies and for a world-renewing Jump Dance *See* DANCE & FERTILITY & HEALING & HOLE & LEAP-UP & PATH & REGENERATION & SEASON & SOCIETAL ASPECT & SUN YOUNG +18a USA, YUROK \NABt

• Plains Indians planted seven trees in the earth next to their Sun Dance altar. The digging stick used for this purpose was then placed at the top of the center pole of the lodge. The Indians called the pole the "link between heaven and earth". Arapaho Indians

pray in their Sun Dance lodge: "Grandfather sun, we desire that this lodge be the *painting [sic]* that brings prosperity"; a similar prayer is made by the Sioux, to which they add "so that our people may live" *See* ALTAR & ANCESTOR WORSHIP & ART & AXIS MUNDI & CHAOS IN NATURE & FERTILITY & HAND RAISED & HOLE & LEVELS CELESTIAL & PATH & REGENERATION & SOCIETAL ASPECT & SOCIETY AS AT THE AXIS MUNDI & SUN OLD +18a USA, ARAPAHO, SIOUX \DOPt \NABt \CAIt

Figure 58

• When building a modern skyscraper it is customary to place a tree and a flag at the top of the new structure *See* FLAG/ RIBBON & PATH & SOCIETY AS AT THE AXIS MUNDI & TREE +19a \TULp

• The central pole of Siberian tribal dwellings is regarded as the cosmic axis +19a RUSSIA, SAMOVED \ELIt

• A Plains Indian's myth tells of people who were facing starvation when they ventured into "hollow mountain" during a storm, from where they learned how to build the Sun Dance lodge and perform its rituals *See* CAVE & CHAOS IN NATURE & FERTILITY & RITUAL +18a USA, CHEYENNE \NABt

Figure 59

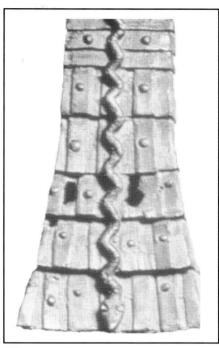

Figure 60

• Sun Dancers of the Walpi village in Arizona place cornmeal in the crevices of "snake rock", a sacred sandstone pillar, as offerings to snakes. Next to the stone is the hatchway to an underground "sun hill" kiva, whose ladder symbolizes descent into the underworld. The secret "soyal" ceremonies performed in the kiva are intended to inspire the sun to perform similar activities at the winter solstice in his own "southern house". These rituals are the most important obligations in the life of the Greater Southwest Indians, involving sacrifices which they make "for the whole world" *See* CHRISTMASTIDE & FERTILITY & INFORMATION DESTROYED OR SECRET & LADDER INFERNAL & MEANING OF LIFE & MONOLITH & PATH & REGENERATION & RITUAL & SACRIFICE ANIMAL/ HUMAN & SNAKE & SOUTHWEST ORIENTATION & SUN OLD +18a USA, HOPI \NABp \NATt \SINt

• Until the sixteenth century, the king's meeting house had an immense brass snake down its metal roof, over the doorway. The image remains on a bronze plaque, which was polished to resemble gold, that sheathed one of the columns in the meeting house *See* BRASS/ BRONZE & COLUMN & DESCENDING MOTIF & PATH & RULER & SNAKE & UNDERWORLD +18a NIGERIA, BENIN *Figure 60*

• The men's house in each public square was built on rows of pillars in the plan of a coiled serpent, and had a millstone on its roof *See* BATON & PATH & RING MOTIF & SOCIETY AS AT THE AXIS MUNDI & SPIRAL & STAFF & WHEEL +19a MALI, DOGON \GRKt

Figure 61

• Rooms of their houses are said to represent caves *See* CAVE & SOCIETAL ASPECT +19a MALI, DOGON \GRKt

• **Mammy Wata** lives in the "house of the dead" in sacred lakes. She is depicted wrapped in the coils of a snake with the sun painted on its body *See* DEATH & MOTHER GODDESS & PATH & SNAKE & SOCIETY AS AT THE AXIS MUNDI & SUN OLD/ YOUNG & WATER +19a NIGERIA, IBIBIO \NATt *Figure 61*

• The incursion of a serpent into the dwelling is considered beneficial, and milk and butter are always offered to it. On the other hand, they kill and burn serpents, mixing the ashes with ox blood as a ritual offering *See* BLOOD & BULL & DEATH & FERTILITY & FIRE & PATH & REGENERATION & SACRIFICE ANIMAL & SOCIETAL ASPECT & +19a ETHIOPIA, GALLA \MUNt

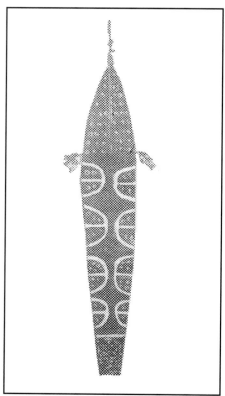

Figure 62

• Granaries are a realization of the anthill after which their men's houses were modeled; what is eaten from the granary "is sunlight" *See* FERTILITY & MOUND & SEASON & SUN YOUNG +19a MALI, DOGON \GRKt

• Sanctuaries dedicated to the **Binu** ancestor serve as models for the Dogon private dwellings. Binu's name is a contraction of two phrases meaning "gone" and "come back". On the sanctuary's roof is a metal hook whose curved branches represent the "celestial ram." This hook is between mounds on the roof representing the "world altar". A hollow stone inside the sanctuary contains holy water. The ground below the sanctuary is regarded as the tomb of the serpent-god **Lebe** *See* ALTAR & ANCESTOR WORSHIP & DEATH & MOUND & PATH & RAM & REGENERATION & SNAKE & SOCIETAL ASPECT & SUN OLD/ YOUNG & UNDERWORLD & WATER +19a MALI, DOGON \GRKt

• There is a palace under the water where the spirits live *See* HUSK & MOTHER GODDESS & PALACE & RULER & UNDERWORLD & WATER +19a NIGERIA, IBIBIO \AFAt

• Indians of Chamula believe that beneath their house floors are water-filled caves *See* CAVE & PATH & SOCIETAL ASPECT & SOCIETY AS AT THE AXIS MUNDI & WATER +19a MEXICO, TZOTZIL \AVDt

• To present-day Aztecs the ruins of their temples are still considered doorways into the underworld *See* PATH & SOCIETY AS AT THE AXIS MUNDI & TEMPLE +19a MEXICO, AZTEC \NAUt

• The vast crater of the extinct Haleakala volcano is holy ground, referred to as the "house of the sun" *See* HOLE & MOUNTAIN & SOCIETY AS AT THE AXIS MUNDI & SUN OLD/ YOUNG +19a HAWAII \NYTp

• All temples are modeled after the house of the creator deity, referred to as "his bed" *See* FERTILITY & MARRIAGE & REGENERATION & TRINITY +19a TAHITI \COTt

• They whirl their bullroarers as they chant and sing at night in the dance area of the men's house *See* BULLROARER & DANCE & MUSIC & NIGHT & PATH +19a BOLIVIA, BORRORO \LETt *Figure 62*

• At death their souls go to a stone house which they have carved into the natural rock *See* CAVE & PATH & REGENERATION & SOUL & STONE & TRINITY +19a BRAZIL, GE \LEVt

• Tukano people believe that their maloca, or ritual house, is the center of the world. The vertical post at its roof is the "seat of the sun" *See* NAVEL OF THE WORLD & PATH & SOCIETY AS AT THE AXIS MUNDI & STAFF & SUN OLD +19a COLOMBIA, BARASANA \AVDt \REJt
Refer to *Figure 108*

• The first maloca was "the house of the waters", depicted in their sand paintings as a red upright triangle. Below the triangle a vagina symbol represents "life in the maloca" *See* ART & MOUNTAIN & RED & REGENERATION & TRIANGLE MOTIF UPRIGHT & VAGINA & WATER +19a COLOMBIA, TUKANO \REJt
Refer to *Figure 33*

marriage *The letter H of the Snake Ring Template.* A metaphor for the joining of the old sun with the mother goddess in the mountain-house of the western horizon waters, where the solar soul is transferred to the mother goddess, who births it in the new sun of the next season. This sun, in turn, returns to the mother goddess at the completion of its season to produce the successive sun of the next season. *Ref* COPULATION, INCEST, PSYCHOLOGY CONTEMPORARY, GODDESSES, SOCIETAL ASPECT.

• Marriage between the gods of heaven and earth was the first sacredness, and man in turn imitated them, placing sacred value on copulation *See* DEMYTHOLIZATION & MARRIAGE & SOCIETAL ASPECT +19a MIRCEA ELIADE \ELIt

• Marriage is one of the highest achievements of mankind +19a SIR JAMES FRASER \NYTt

• Sexuality was once experienced as a chthonic (infernal) divinity +19a ERICH NEUMANN \NEUt

• Carl Jung had recurrent "house dreams" in which his mother entertained male guests while his father was in the basement dissecting fish. When he eventually associated the dreams with a vision that he had of an elderly sun god joined with a nude moon goddess, he was cured *See* DEATH & FISH & HOUSE & MOTHER GODDESS & PSYCHOLOGY CHILD/ DREAM & SUN OLD & TRINITY & WATER +19a \JUNp

• A pre-historic African rock painting depicts a phallic human figure with the legs of a bull standing over a recumbent female with her legs raised up to him; a curving serpentine line connects the two figures *See* ART & BULL & PATH & PHALLUS & STONE -200b SOUTH AFRICA, BUSHMAN \AFAp

• The groom in ancient Egypt placed a ring on the finger of his bride. The Greeks began our present-day custom of placing the ring on the third finger of her hand *See* HAND RAISED & JEWELRY & PATH & RING MOTIF & SOCIETAL ASPECT -3a GREEK -30b EGYPT \MIAt \HEHt

• The sun god **Nergal** was lured back to bed by the goddess **Ereshkagal**. If he did not return, it would mean the end of all life *See* FERTILITY & MOTHER GODDESS & REGENERATION & SEASON & SUN OLD/ YOUNG -20b IRAQ, ACCADIAN \COTt

• Figurines of men with enormous penises and naked women with their genitals exposed were often found at dwelling sites *See* SOCIETAL ASPECT -7a EGYPT \BAJp *Figure 63*

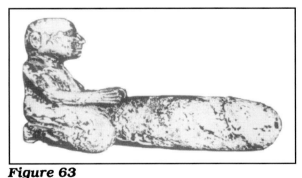
Figure 63

• The marriage bed was located in the darkest place in the house, directly above the spot where the dead were buried. Seeds for planting were kept beneath the bed. At springtime, boys and girls mated on the ground to regenerate nature *See* FERTILITY & HOUSE & PATH & SOCIETAL ASPECT & TRINITY -15b CHINA \ELIt

• Women raised their dresses to expose their genitals to the Apis bull *See* BULL & COPULATION & RITUAL -4a EGYPT \NYLt

• The bride-to-be waited inside the house with a jar of water where the guests and the celebrants washed their feet. "Snake-hand" cowries were placed at the sides of the groom's path which he would follow to join her *See* CRUSTACEAN(COWRIE) & HOUSE & PATH & SNAKE & WATER +13a MALDIVE \HEVt

• In the fairy tale Beauty and the Beast as originally written by Madame de Beaumont, a father loses all of his money and a beast bribes him for his beautiful daughter. When the beast lies with her in the form of a snake he turns into a young prince *See* BULL & FAIRY TALE & MONEY & PATH & PRINCE & REGENERATION & SNAKE +17a FRANCE \BEUt

• An old man who returned to his youth through the love of a woman, was a theme for centuries before the Faustian version *See* REGENERATION +18a GERMAN, TEUTONIC \WESt

• The sleeping rug is identified with the earth. Its traditional motifs of a celestial dragon and a phoenix bird are said to be good for domestic and marital harmony *See* BIRD & PATH & REGENERATION & SOCIETAL ASPECT +18a TIBET, TANTRIC \WESp

• Sexual lust often fades after less than two years of marriage [thereafter the pair is bonded by mythic elements]. (Recent studies reveal that there is no attempt at monogamy in the animal kingdom except among humans). Weddings are a social act on which society places a special meaning; June is the favorite month for the ceremony [a baby conceived at that time is born at the start of spring, as is the young sun god who brings on the season of fertility] *See* SOCIETAL ASPECT +19a \WESt

• It is good luck in Italian superstition if rain falls on the wedding day *See* FERTILITY & RAIN & SOCIETAL ASPECT & SUPERSTITION +19a ITALY \TIMt

• A contemporary sculpture titled "Family" by Max Ernst in the Maeght Museum depicts a bull-headed man holding a staff in the form of a snake, his spouse is a mermaid with a fish on her head, and their child is accompanied by a feline *See* ART & BABY BOY & BULL & FELINE & MERMAID & MOTHER GODDESS & PATH & UNDERWORLD & WATER +19a FRANCE \DORp

• Scholars are puzzled by the meanings of paintings by Pablo Picasso depicting carnal scenes between nude females and lusting bulls or old men *See* BULL & MOTHER GODDESS & SUN OLD +19a FRANCE \JUNp \TIMp

• "Dreamtime" paintings by Marc Chagall juxtapose images of winged fish, a violin and clock, with an amorous couple at the water's edge *See* FEATHERED & FISH & MUSIC & PSYCHOLOGY CHILD & TIME & WATER +19a RUSSIA \JUNp

• The sun married the moon *See* MOON & SUN OLD +19a TOGO, KRACHI \PAQt

• Sunset, particularly over the water, is associated with romance *See* DEATH & PATH & PSYCHOLOGY CHILD & SUN OLD & TRINITY & WEST ORIENTATION +19a \REDt \WESt

• Women slide bare-bottomed down the Brise menhir at springtime to have children *See* BABY BOY/ GIRL & MENHIR & PATH & SOCIETAL ASPECT & SPRINGTIME & STONE +18a FRANCE, LOCMAR \SMJt

• Some European women rub on megaliths to marry and to have children; it is still traditional for French brides to rub on a stone after their wedding *See* BABY BOY/ GIRL & MENHIR & MOUNTAIN & SOCIETAL ASPECT & STONE +18a FRANCE \RAUt \ELIt

• **Great Nyami** in Ashanti mythology is the sun and king. His wife, **Nyami**, is the moon and queen *See* MOON & RULER & SUN OLD +19a GHANA, ASHANTI \PAQt

• In the courting rites the girls wear veils. The boys' faces are painted with vertical red stripes and rams' beards, and cowrie shells and feathers are entwined in their hair *See* CRUSTACEAN & FEATHERED & PATH & RAM & RED & SOCIETAL ASPECT & VEIL & VERTICAL LINE/ SHAPE +18a AFRICA, FULANI \BRBp

• A python appearing in the river is said to cause couples to join and conceive *See* PATH & SOCIETY AS AT THE AXIS MUNDI & SUPERSTITION & WATER +19a GHANA, ASHANTI \COTt

• The sun as the serpent-god copulates with the moon to order the universe *See* MOON & PATH & SEASON & SUN OLD/ YOUNG +18a BENIN, FON \COTt

• Girls copulate with the temple priests as symbolic brides of the serpent-god, then serve as sacred prostitutes in the temple to insure the world's fertility *See* FERTILITY & HOUSE & PATH & PRIEST & RITUAL +18a WEST AFRICA, EWE \ELIt

• The god of death is also the god of erotic love. Fusion with his rainbow wife animates the blood which passes through all male testes to create semen. The serpent Dambala, an entwined cosmic snake represents the sexual unity of the world. As a great spiral enveloping the universe, he is the father of falling water *See* BLOOD & CALABASH & COPULATION & PATH & RAINBOW & SOCIETAL ASPECT & SPIRAL & TRINITY & WATERFALL +19a HAITI, VOODOO \DATt

• Sexually explicit decorations were on the walls of the chief's palaces and on his throne *See* PALACE & RULER +18a CAMEROON, BAMUM \RAUt

• The secret Poro and Sandogo societies regulate the worship of the great mother; they also regulate all phases of society including female and male relationships *See* INFORMATION DESTROYED/ SECRET & MOTHER GODDESS & SOCIETAL ASPECT +19a IVORY COAST, SENUFO \METt

• Human copulation reproduces the incest of the sun god **Amma** and of his oldest son with mother earth. There are many legends of rams luring girls into the water for sex *See* GOAT & GODDESSES & INCEST & PATH & SOCIETAL ASPECT & SUN OLD/ YOUNG & WATER +19a MALI, DOGON \GRKt

• Dancers wear cut-outs of snakes and airplanes pinned together on their clothes during an erotic dance to bring on the rainy season *See* DANCE & DRAGON & PATH & RAIN & SEASON & SNAKE FEATHERED/ WINGED +19a NIGER, WODAABE \NATp

• A dance mask worn during the initiation ceremonies of the Sande secret society is carved at its top to represent a bird entering into a vulva *See* BIRD & DANCE & INFORMATION DESTROYED/ SECRET & VAGINA +19a SIERRA LEONE, MENDE \RAUp

• When the crops or the herds failed, the king was strangled and his body interred with a virgin buried alive *See* BIRTH & FAUNA & FLORA & REGENERATION & RULER & SACRIFICE HUMAN & SOCIETAL ASPECT & VIRGIN +18a SUDAN \CAAt

• An illustration from the Dresden Codex depicts the old sun-god **Itzamna** mating with **Ixchel** the moon and water goddess; she is often depicted with a serpent on her head or in other scenes as spinning or mating with the solar bird; a figurine depicts the aged god reaching under the dress of the goddess *See* BIRD & PATH & SNAKE & SUN OLD +3b MEXICO, MAYAN \FURt \COTt *Figure 64*
Refer also to *Figure 12*

Figure 64

• Spanish explorers named an island off the coast of Mexico, La Isla de Mujeres, in honor of a temple they saw on the island with sculpted columns of half-naked women raising their skirts up to their navel. Early voyagers to the area reported seeing sex symbols on the temples *See* COLUMN & HOUSE & TRANSCULTURAL SIMILARITY & WATER   +3b MEXICO, MAYAN \RAUt

• A vase painting depicts an old god within a dragon's mouth caressing a goddess seated in a palace setting; the body of the serpent surrounds both figures *See* HOUSE & PATH +3b MEXICO, MAYAN **Refer to** *Figure 57*

• During a Christmas dance held on December 24, present-day Maya women lift their skirts to a dancer dressed as a bull. In their marriage ceremonies, the groom wearing a red turban stands on a bull's hide next to his bride who is called "earth". **[Note:** There were no cattle in Mesoamerica until brought in by the Spanish] *See* BULL & CHRISTMASTIDE & DEMYTHOLIZATION & EARTH GODDESS & HAT(CAP) & PSYCHOLOGY CHILD & RED & SOCIETAL ASPECT   +19a MEXICO, ZINACANTECO \VOGt

• The cosmic layers in a codex illustration depicts the old deity couple (who created the other gods) in the "navel of the world", the thirteenth, or last, position of the seven celestial layers.   Another codex illustration depicts the creator couple in a cave in the water, with a deer's head emerging from the cave *See* BABY BOY/ GIRL & CAVE & DEER & LEVELS CELESTIAL & WATER & WEST ORIENTATION +15a MEXICO, AZTEC \NATp *Figure 65*

• **Tezcatlipoca**, "smoking mirror", was the old sun god who joined with the moon goddess in the western horizon; he was a god of music and dancing *See* DANCE & FIRE & MIRROR & MOON & MUSIC & SUN OLD   +13b MEXICO, AZTEC \LARt

• The Little Old Man Dance was performed at the main pyramid in pre-conquest times and continues to this day in the form of a folk dance.   Performers costumed as old men dance in a circle, titillating the spectators by poking their canes under the dresses of ladies in the audience *See* CIRCLE MOTIF & DANCE & DEMYTHOLIZATION & HOUSE & PATH & STAFF +19a MEXICO, AZTEC *Figure 66*

• The Aztec goddess **Coatlicue**, who gave birth to the young sun god **Huitzilopochtli**, was the same name as the Maya goddess of the moon and water, who was a wife of the sun god *See* BABY BOY & GODDESSES & MOON & REGENERATION & SUN OLD/ YOUNG & WATER   +13b MEXICO,AZTEC \NYTt \RAUt

• Leaping bulls, or bisons, on ceilings of the Ice Age caves, such as those at Lascaux, are interpreted as energetic sex symbols [of the old sun] *See* BULL & CAVE & CELESTIAL & PATH & SUN OLD -350b FRANCE \CAAt \RAUt

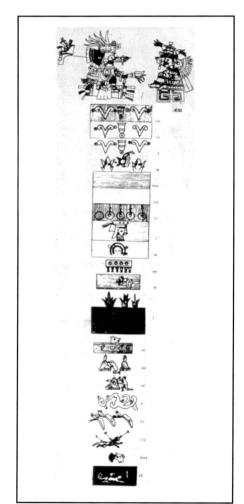

Figure 65

Figure 66

• Deep within an Ice Age cave, footprints remain in the clay floor from ritual dancing before the images of a male bison mounting a female bison *See* BULL & CAVE & DANCE & RITUAL -350b FRANCE, TUC D'ADOUBERT *Figure 67*

Figure 67

• An inscribed bone fragment from Laugerie Basse depicts the lower portion of a phallic animal, identified as a bull, standing over a pregnant woman wearing bracelets and necklace, and raising her hands to the animal *See* BABY BOY/ GIRL & BULL & JEWELRY -350b FRANCE, LAUGERIE BASSE
Refer to *Figure 50*

• The Venus figure from the decorated Ice Age shelter of Lauselle has one hand on her pregnant stomach, while the other holds aloft an excised bull's horn bearing thirteen inscribed tally marks *See* BABY BOY/ GIRL &

BULL & DEATH & LEVELS CELESTIAL & MATHEMATICS -350b FRANCE, LAUSELLE
Refer to *Figure 51*

• Female figures at the entrance to some of the decorated Ice Age caves are shown with their legs parted and with emphasized pubics [images which may have been intended to inspire the old sun to join with the mother goddess] *See* CAVE & SUN OLD & VAGINA -350b FRANCE \RAUt

• Over many Christian church doors in England and Ireland are reliefs of females with their legs parted, holding their vulvas open with their hands -14b ENGLAND, CELTIC *Figure 68*

Figure 68

• Indian illustrations depict goddesses showing their genitals *See* GODDESSES & VAGINA -19b INDIA, HINDU \NEUt

• In the sun temple at Konara, noted for its many erotic carvings, a stone depicts the amorous **Naga** with his consort **Nagini**, their lower bodies in the form of entwined serpents +12a INDIA, HINDU *Figure 69*

• A terra cotta house model depicts **Astarte** of the mountain and sea seated at an upper window with her thighs spread apart. In front of the house is a large upright serpent and her spouse, the deity **Baal**, watching her. A feline's head is in relief on the house wall, and remnants of goat hooves are at its base *See* FELINE & GOAT & HOUSE MODEL & MOTHER GODDESS & MOUNTAIN & SNAKE & SUN OLD & VERTICAL LINE/ SHAPE & VAGINA & WATER -15b ISRAEL, PHOENECIAN \MUNt

Figure 69

• Snakes or ring motifs in sequence are inscribed on the legs leading to the pubic area, of nude female figurines found in burials *See* REGENERATION & RING MOTIF IN SEQUENCE & SNAKE & SOCIETAL ASPECT & UNDERWORLD -20a RUSSIA, TURKMEN REPUBLIC \MUNp

• Seductive bare-breasted female figurines from the Knossos palace believed by some to have been a mortuary temple, hold snakes in their hands and have a small feline or bird perched on their heads *See* BIRD & FELINE & HOUSE & MOTHER GODDESS & PATH & REGENERATION -16a CRETE, MINOAN *Figure 70*

Figure 70

• **Helios** copulated in the form of a bull with his earth mother *See* BULL & INCEST & REGENERATION & SUN OLD/ YOUNG -20b GREEK, MINOAN \ELIt

• Bullroarers were sounded during the Greek orgies *See* BULL & BULLROARER & RITUAL -20b GREEK \CAAt

• The Greeks originated our biological signs for genders: the male sign is a ring motif with an arrow pointing upwards to the right; the female sign is a cross with a ring motif at it's top *See* ARCH & CROSS WEST & EAST ORIENTATION & PATH & RING MOTIF & SOCIETAL ASPECT -20b GREEK *Figure 71*

• Brides were called "nymphs" and were veiled like the departed *See* NYMPH & SOCIETAL ASPECT & UNDERWORLD & VEIL -20b GREEK \KERt \PINt

• There were many illustrations of phallic images and of goddesses exposing their genitals during the classical period *See* PHALLUS & VAGINA -20b GREEK \RAUt \NEUt

• The sun god **Poseidon** mated with **Klito** on the island mountain of Atlantis "beyond the pillars of Hercules", suggesting to scholars the western limits of the known world, where the sky appeared to fuse with the earth at the horizon waters. During their joining Poseidon surrounded the bridal bower with the "numerate equivalent of marriage" *See* ARCH & BOWER & LEVELS CELESTIAL & MATHEMATICS &

MOUNTAIN & SUN OLD & WATER -4a GREEK, ATLANTIS \BREt

Figure 71

• In the legend of **Attis**, the hero was slain and mourned by his mother who was also his lover, and he was reborn through her *See* DEATH & GODDESSES & INCEST & PATH & REGENERATION SUN OLD/ YOUNG -20b GREEK \NEUt

• The sun god **Zeus** appeared in the forms of a serpent, bull, cuckoo, swan, and a shower of gold to approach his beloveds *See* AVATAR & BIRD & BULL & GOLD & MARINE BIRD & PATH & SNAKE & SUN OLD -20b GREEK \FRBt \JUNp \MUNp \ELHt

• The creator couple consisting of **Ouranos**, the sky god and **Gaia** the earth, produced the sun god **Kronos** and other gods. Kronos and his mate **Rhea** who were Titans living under the volcano known as Mount Etna, joined to produce the family of Olympians. These were successive sun gods who overthrew their fathers and ruled in their place *See* GODS & HOLE & MOTHER GODDESS & MOUNTAIN & SEASON & TRINITY & UNDERWORLD & WAR -20b GREEK \WEBt

• The sun god **Amon** joined with the goddess **Mut** to birth a divine child in the primordial watery abyss [(the Egyptian glyph for marriage "mni" depicts the mooring of a boat)]. The sun

god **Osiris**, in turn, after his death joined with the goddess **Isis** below the western horizon in the sea to conceive the young sun god **Horus** who succeeded to his father's throne. She entreated him "beloved bull, pillar, come to thy house" *See* BABY BOY & BOAT & BULL & DEATH & HORIZON & HOUSE & PATH & PILLAR & SOCIETAL ASPECT & SUN OLD/ YOUNG & UNDERWORLD & WATER -30b EGYPT \COTt \ARCt \NEUt \PATt \EDWt

• A phallus-shape stone monument at the extreme west coast of England depicts in relief a plumed serpent with a fish in its mouth. On the opposite side a round face is screaming, apparently in agony *See* CASTRATION (CIRCUMCISION) & DEATH & DRAGON & FISH & HEAD & PATH & PHALLUS & ROUND MOTIF & STONE & WATER & WEST ORIENTATION -14a ENGLAND, CELTIC *Figure 72*

• All of the earth's waters feed into a whirlpool which leads to the abode of the dead, where a goddess called "whore" sits with a mill in her hall in the sea *See* ABYSS & CONFLUENCE OF RIVERS & DEATH & GODS & HOUSE & PATH & WATER & WHEEL & WHIRLPOOL +9b FINNO-UGARITIC \SANt

Figure 72

• The Siberian shaman presses a drumstick, representing a serpent, to his brow, at which time he is transformed into a bull who couples with his spirit wife *See* BULL & HEAD & MUSIC &

PATH & PRIEST & SNAKE +19a RUSSIA, YAKUT \RAUt \CAIt

• The arch over the path of newly married Swedish couples is the same arch which is placed over their graves to receive the corpse; the Christmas tree is used at both weddings and at funerals. Swedish women are sometimes buried in their wedding gowns with a piece of their wedding cake See ARCH & DEATH & FERTILITY & REGENERATION & SOCIETAL ASPECTS & TREE +18a SWEDEN \ELIt

• Powdered rhinoceros horns and deer antlers are used as aphrodisiacs See DEATH & DEER & REGENERATION & RHINOCEROS +19a CHINA \RAUt

• Tao, the ever-turning wheel, represents the joining of the male yang principle, the sun, and the female yin principle, the moon, to preserve the orderly changes in the seasons; their copulation is the "penetration by the yang dragon of the yin vase" See DRAGON & MOON & PATH & SEASON & SUN OLD & VESSEL & WHEEL -5a CHINA, I CHING \CAAt \RAWp

• The creator couple copulated on an island in the sacred sea; traditional Japanese couples immerse themselves in water and bow before house shrines preceding their copulation. See HOUSE MODEL & SOCIETAL ASPECT & WATER +19a JAPAN, SHINTO \WESt

• In order to have a bountiful crop, festivals are held throughout Japan in which women caress a giant phallus carried in processions See FERTILITY & PHALLUS & REGENERATION & RITUAL & SEASON & SOCIETAL ASPECT +19a JAPAN, SHINTO \WESp

• In the Andaman islands off the west coast of Burma, the creator couple was the sun and the moon. At wedding ceremonies the attendants weep over the bride and groom who are decorated with snake patterns drawn in white clay See BODY PAINTING & DEATH & MOON & PATH & REGENERATION & SOCIETAL ASPECT & SUN OLD & TRANSCULTURAL SIMILARITY +19a ANDAMAN ISLANDS \CAIp

• Court dancers, with their arms undulating in curves, are regarded as descendants of the snake woman who copulated with the original king. He had renewed the fertility of the land by inseminating the snake woman See FERTILITY & GODDESSES & MYTH & PATH & RULER & SNAKE +19a CAMBODIA \NAUp \NAUt

• In Vedic writings the great self of the **Upanishad** divided into male and female halves; the male became a bull [(he also appears at times as a stallion, goat, and ram)] and the female a cow before they joined as the creator couple See BULL & COW & GOAT & HORSE & RAM -8a INDIA, HINDU \CAAt

• A prayer from the Rig Veda entreats, "earth mother open thyself, let him in lightly, arch thy broad back on the next lap of his journey" See EARTH MOTHER & PATH & SERPENT ENTWINED -19b INDIA, HINDU \NEUt

• A carved stone in the Konara Sun Temple depicts the embracing deities **Naga** and **Nagini** with their lower bodies formed of entwined serpents See ART & HOUSE & PATH & STONE & SUN OLD -19b INDIA, HINDU
Refer to *Figure 84*

• Orgies are conducted prior to the rainy season under a "sun pennant" depicting a man with a large stuffed penis See FLAG & PHALLUS & RAIN & REGENERATION & RITUAL & SEASON & SUN OLD +19a INDONESIA, BABAR ISLANDS \RAUt \ELIt

• Indonesians smear oil on stones in order to have children; the central object of their worship is the sun's masculine principle and the earth's female principle See BABY BOY/ GIRL & EARTH MOTHER & LIBATION & SOCIETAL ASPECT & STONE & SUN OLD & VERTICAL LINE/ SHAPE +18a INDONESIA, KAI \ELIt

• **Ishtar's** husband **Damuzzi** died annually and remarried her; therefore her lovers were legion and sacred prostitution was part of her cult; Ishtar's love lured **Damuzzi** to his death at the gates of the underworld where, "water is between the lovers' thighs". Their marriage, at the start of springtime, marked the new year and was the most important event of the Sumerian calendar *See* NEW YEAR & PROSTITUTION & REGENERATION & SPRINGTIME & UNDERWORLD & WATER -35b IRAQ, SUMERIAN \COTt \LARt \NYTt

• In the legends of the sun god **Shamash**, the deity **Nergal** must die and return to the bed of his consort **Ereshkagal**, "death", or all life on earth would end *See* CHAOS IN NATURE & DEATH & FERTILITY & MOTHER GODDESS & REGENERATION & SEASON & SUN OLD -20b IRAQ, ACCADIAN \COTt \WESt

Figure 73

• A pottery incense stand from Megiddo depicts female figures with one hand on their breasts and the other on their privates *See* INCENSE & GODDESSES & PATH & REGENERATION -11a ISRAEL *Figure 73*

• A Roman illustration of the snake in the Garden of Eden, which was at the confluence of rivers, also described by prophet Ezekiel as the location of the Holy Mountain and the Stones of Fire, depicts ring motifs along the serpent's body as it wraps around the Tree of Knowledge where Adam and Eve joined in sin. The Hosts of Heaven said that by their act "man has become like one of us" [which suggests that their sin was to emulate the regenerating sun god's copulating at the vertical serpent path in the western horizon] *See* ANCESTOR WORSHIP & CONFLUENCE OF RIVERS

& DEMYTHOLIZATION & FIRE & MOUNTAIN & RING MOTIF IN SEQUENCE & TREE & SNAKE & STONE -10b ISRAEL, JEWISH \ENDt *Figure 74*

• **Sampson**, whose name means "sun" and who was born in the place called "house of the sun", suffered his downfall when he joined with **Delilah** whose name means "night" *See* DEMYTHOLIZATION & HOUSE & NIGHT & SUN OLD -10b ISRAEL, JEWISH \ENDt

• In Orthodox marriages, held after nightfall, the groom wears a burial gown and breaks a glass; a double ring ceremony invalidates the marriage, as the ring must pass only from the groom to the bride. A ritual bath, the Mikvah, must be performed in "living water" before the couple has sex, as the potential exists for them to have a baby *See* BABY BOY/ GIRL & DEATH & NIGHT & OBJECTS RITUALLY BROKEN & PATH & RING MOTIF & SOCIETAL ASPECT & WATER -10b ISRAEL, JEWISH \ENDt \MOMp \MIAp

• Koran: "Your wives are your field, you go in as you will" *See* EARTH MOTHER +5b IRAN, ISLAM \NYTt

• A popular belief is that a girl will dream of a snake biting her before she is going to marry *See* DREAM & PATH & SNAKE +5b JAVA, BUDDHIST \GEFt

Figure 74

• The creator couple was the sky-father and the great mother **Sedna**, who lived under the sea *See* MOTHER GODDESS & WATER +18a ESKIMO \WESt

Figure 75

• A wooden uroborus hung with eagle feathers was on a staff above the altar for the Sun Dance. A buffalo skull painted with vertical rows of red and black discs was on the altar when the lodgemaker of the previous season, representing the sun as a buffalo, took present lodgemaker's wife, who represented the moon, aside to copulate with her. She returned with a sprig of plant held in her mouth when her husband and all in the lodge thanked her. *See* ALTAR & BLACK & BULL & DEATH & FERTILITY & MOON & PATH & RED & REGENERATION & RITUAL & ROUND MOTIF IN SEQUENCE & SNAKE FEATHERED/ WINGED & SUN OLD & STAFF & TRANSCULTURAL SIMILARITY & UROBORUS +18a USA, ARAPAHO Figure 75

• In the Okipa Sun Dance, married women danced lasciviously before old men dressed as bulls and later joined with them for sex; they said that the adultery strengthened their marriage bonds *See* BULL & DANCE & RITUAL & SOCIETAL ASPECT +18a USA, MANDAN \CATt

• Our father and our mother are the sky-man facing down and the earth mother facing up; they made the little sun and moon in the underworld *See* ANCESTOR WORSHIP & BABY BOY/ GIRL & EARTH MOTHER & GODDESSES & INCEST & MOON & SOCIETAL ASPECT & SUN OLD/ YOUNG & UNDERWORLD +18a USA, APACHE \CAIt

• The hogan (house) was copied after a New Mexico mountain called "lungs of the earth"

which was the home of "changing woman, the wife of the sun" *See* GODDESSES & HOUSE & MOUNTAIN & SOCIETY AS AT THE AXIS MUNDI & SUN OLD & UNDERWORLD +18a USA, NAVAJO \NABp

• Villages were divided into two moieties in which members of the sky moiety married the members of the earth moiety *See* SOCIETAL ASPECT +18a USA, WINNEBAGO \NABt

• Aborigine women visit sacred stones at night to become pregnant; if women pass near the stone and do not want a child they say "do not come to me, I am old" *See* BABY BOY/ GIRL & SOCIETAL ASPECT & STONE +18a AUSTRALIA \ELIt \RAUt

• In the Engwura ceremony, initiates carrying bullroarers ford a river to reach the girls who are gesturing invitingly from the far side. When they reach the river bank, they fall with the bullroarer in front of the women. Then they return to the Engwura ground for the conclusion of the ceremony below a bullroarer hanging at the top of a tall pole when the boys are delivered to their assigned women *See* BULLROARER & PATH & POLE & SOCIETAL ASPECT & SOCIETY AS AT THE AXIS MUNDI & UNDERWORLD +19a AUSTRALIA, ARANDA \CAAt Figure 76

Figure 76

• At Woman Island on the Yule river there are archaic petroglyphs of vulvas below an engraved figure of the "rainbow snake" *See* RAINBOW & SNAKE & SOCIETY AS AT THE AXIS MUNDI & STONE & VAGINA & WATER +18a AUSTRALIA \CAAt

• Large wooden figures of females, their hands holding their legs open, are mounted on the gables of the men's houses on Palau Islands *See* HOUSE & TRANSCULTURAL SIMILARITY +19a CAROLINE ISLANDS \NESp [Figure 77]

Figure 77

• The souls of married men only, cross the sea to a serpent deity who is at the precipice of a mountain overlooking a bottomless lake *See* ABYSS & DEATH & MOUNTAIN & SOCIETAL ASPECT & SOUL & WATER +19a FIJI \ELHt

• The creator couple was a boar who came down a vine to mate with a sow from the sea *See* BOAR & PATH & VINE & WATER +19a NEW HEBRIDES \RAUt

• According to the Ona, one of the tribal peoples living in isolation at the tip of South America, the forest became green only when **Kran**, the sun, joined with **Kra**, the moon. Men of the Yamana people duplicate in a secret festival the "sun man's" activities with the moon woman **Kina** *See* FERTILITY & INFORMATION DESTROYED/ SECRET & MOON & REGENERATION & RITUAL & SUN OLD & TRANSCULTURAL SIMILARITY +19a ARGENTINA, TIERRA DEL FUEGO \CAAt \CAIt

• An erotic pot from a Moche burial depicts a male skeleton, with a round cap on his head, embracing a woman. A pot from a Nazca burial depicts a bull-horned man, wearing large earplugs, copulating with a woman *See* BULL & DEATH & FUNERAL & HAT(CAP) & JEWELRY & QUESTIONS BY SCHOLARS & REGENERATION & RING MOTIF & SKELETAL & VESSEL +2b PERU,

MOCHICAN & NAZCAN [Figure 78]
Refer also to [Figure 19]

Figure 78

• The Pope kisses the earth when he arrives at a new destination; parishioners hail him as "light" *See* DEMYTHOLIZATION & EARTH MOTHER & LIGHT & PRIEST +19a ITALY, CHRISTIAN \NYTp

• Dances are held to inspire **Sun-Father** to join with his daughter, **Yaje Woman,** in the Water House **[Note:** "Yaje" is the name given to the vine *Banisteriopsis Caapi,* the source of the hallucinogen that they use in their rituals. It is also the name given to their mythic snake**]** *See* DANCE & HOUSE & INCEST & MOTHER GODDESS & PATH & SNAKE & SUN OLD & VINE & WATER +19a COLOMBIA, TUKANO \REJt

• The creator couple was the sun and his wife the moon *See* MOON & TRANSCULTURAL SIMILARITY & SUN OLD +9b PERU, INCA \MASt

• The Macumba festival features lascivious dancing in honor of **Iemanja,** the goddess of the sea *See* DANCE & MOTHER GODDESS & WATER +19a BRAZIL \ATLt

• The Desana believe that Solar energy is a regenerative sexual force. The present sun is the child of the creator couple, consisting of **Primal Sun** as the male half and **Woman Shaman** as the female half *See* GODDESSES & REGENERATION & SUN OLD/ YOUNG +19a COLOMBIA, TUKANO \AVDt \REJt

• The rulers of Rome kissed the earth as if it were their mother *See* BABY BOY & EARTH MOTHER & INCEST & RULER & SUN YOUNG -5b ITALY, ROMAN \SANt

Figure 79

• Like Niagara Falls in Canada and many other waterfalls around the world, Iguacu Falls in Argentina and Brazil, has a special appeal to honeymooners *See* ABYSS & HORIZON & SOCIETAL ASPECT & WATER & WATERFALL +19a BRAZIL
Figure 79

• Scholars are puzzled by the purpose of the many erotic scenes in private Pompeiian houses. If a fraction of the ancient world's sexual art survived, as it did in Pompeii due to the eruption of Vesuvius, it would be found all over *See* ART & HOUSE & SOCIETAL ASPECT & SOCIETY AS AT THE AXIS MUNDI & WATER & WEST ORIENTATION +1a ITALY, POMPEII \GRBt

**See The Following Entries in Section Three
For Some Related Metaphors and Concepts**

- *ancestor worship*
- *architecture*
- *arch triumphal*
- *baby girl*
- *baptism*
- *bat*
- *bath*
- *bower*
- *Cancer*
- *canopy*
- *castle*
- *church*
- *circumcision female*
- *city*
- *clover*
- *coffin*
- *copulation*
- *cow*
- *crescent motif*
- *crocket*
- *crossroads*
- *demytholization*
- *door*
- *duality*
- *eye*
- *frog*
- *goddesses numerous*
- *Great Mother*
- *hare*
- *hermaphrodite*
- *hippopotamus*
- *honeymoon*
- *house haunted*
- *house model*
- *incest*
- *intersection*
- *island*
- *Janus*
- *Justice*
- *key*
- *knot*
- *ladder infernal*
- *lodge*
- *marriage*
- *mermaid*
- *metamorphosis*
- *moon*
- *mother goddess*
- *mother goddess worship*
- *nymph*
- *orgy*
- *paradise*
- *prime matter*
- *psychology child*
- *queen*
- *rabbit*
- *regeneration*
- *ritual house*
- *romantic love*
- *room*
- *sarcophagus*
- *Seal of Solomon*
- *siren*
- *societal aspects*
- *society as at the axis mundi*
- *society contemporary*
- *stairs infernal*
- *star and crescent motif*
- *star motif*
- *temple*
- *tipi or tent*
- *threshold*
- *tomb*
- *trefoil motif*
- *vagina*
- *virgin*
- *Virgo*
- *walled enclosure*
- *window*
- *woman*
- *yang-yin*

Flora,
Young Sun

flora *The letter I of the Snake Ring Template.* A metaphor for the fertility brought on by regeneration of the solar soul from the dead old sun of winter to the vibrant new sun of springtime to provide food for the hunter-gatherers as well as for their quarry during the terminal Ice Age famine and chaos in the seasons. *Ref* FAUNA, FERTILITY.

• Dental remains from the terminal Ice Age indicate widespread starvation and diseases from malnutrition *See* ART & CHAOS IN NATURE -350b \SMJt

• A carved wooden mummy was kept in a coffin at banquets *See* DEATH & REGENERATION & SOCIETAL ASPECT & SUN OLD -30b EGYPT \CASt

• The original divinities plunged headlong into the sea with hunger and thirst, and out of them "the form that arose was food" *See* CHAOS IN NATURE & RAIN & REGENERATION & SUN OLD & WATER -19b INDIA, HINDU \NEUt

• **Xochitl** is the Nahuatl word for both "flower" and the name of the young sun god +15a MEXICO, AZTEC \RECt

• The food we eat is sunlight *See* SUN YOUNG +19a MALI, DOGON \GRKt

• Rural Mexicans place stylized serpents in the earth before planting *See* PATH & REGENERATION & SOCIETY AS AT THE AXIS MUNDI +19a MEXICO, HUICHOL \FONt

• At the conclusion of the Sun Dance ceremony, participants raise their hands to the rising sun, move the snake ring in the sun's apparent east to west direction, then break their fast with a feast *See* HAND RAISED & PATH & RITUAL & SPRINGTIME & SUN YOUNG & UROBORUS +19a USA, ARAPAHO \DOPt
Refer to *Figure 91*

• If their festivals and daily rituals to the sun are not accurate, the crops will fail *See* MEANING OF LIFE & RITUAL SUN OLD/ YOUNG +19a USA, HOPI \COSt

• The sun and a flute are emblazoned on the clothing of a celebrant who joins in the Lake Titicaca festival at the beginning of the planting season, when present-day Inca look to their sacred lake for the son of the sun god to rise and "end the evil" *See* BABY BOY & CHAOS IN NATURE & LEAP UP & MUSIC & RITUAL & SOCIETY AS AT THE AXIS MUNDI & SUN OLD/ YOUNG & WATER +19a PERU, INCA *Figure 80*

Figure 80

• At Indonesian birth rituals, the wife presents symbolic sweets to the guests *See* BABY BOY & SOCIETAL ASPECT +19a JAVA, MODJUK \GEFt

• Hansel and Gretel houses presented at Christmas and New Year are covered with sweets *See* CHRISTMASTIDE & FAIRY TALE & HOUSE MODEL & REGENERATION +19a ITALY, CHRISTIAN \WESt

sun young *The letter S of the Snake Ring Template.* A metaphor for the regenerated sun, who negotiates a hazardous underworld then leaps into the eastern sky at the beginning of a season, possessing the solar soul passed from his father when the father joined with the mother goddess in the mountain-house of the western horizon *Ref* BABY BOY, EAST ORIENTATION, HAND RAISED, LEAP-UP, SEASON, TRINITY, WAR.

• The young sun god **Apollo [Note:** whose name means "from the mouth of the lion"], first appeared after a great flood covered the earth. Thereafter, he arrives each spring bringing the harvest; he also heals the sick and is the patron of music and poetry *See* CHAOS IN NATURE & FELINE & FLOOD & HEALING & MUSIC & POETRY -20b GREEK \GAWt

• The sun died into the mouth of the goddess **Nut** at sunset and was born of her body at daybreak [(on the day the season changed)]. The image of the goddess **Nut** was often painted on the bottom of sarcophagi as the protector of the dead *See* DEATH & REGENERATION & SOCIETAL ASPECT -6b EGYPT \BRAt

• A plaque placed in temples of the Mithraic cult depicts the young sun god **Mithras** killing a bull along the path of a plumed serpent; a dog is his helper in the battle *See* BULL & HERO & PATH & SNAKE FEATHERED/ WINGED +1a ITALY, ROMAN *Figure 81*

Figure 81

• **Xochipilli** was the young sun god of flowers and food born in the west to the great water goddess. Many stone effigies of him were erected in the ball-courts *See* BABY BOY & FAUNA & FLORA & GAME SPORT & HERO & MOTHER GODDESS & WATER & WEST ORIENTATION +11a MEXICO \CAMt

• A mask displayed to musical accompaniment in ceremonies depicts the rayed face of the king of the sea who lives in the underworld. At the conclusion of the music a string is pulled to fling open the mask and reveal a radiant sun inside *See* DANCE & MASK & MUSIC & REGENERATION & SUN OLD/ YOUNG & TRINITY & WATER +18a CANADA, KWAKIUTL *Figure 82*

Figure 82

• At the conclusion of the Sun Dance lodge ceremony when the participants raise their wooden snake ring up into the sky to hasten the appearance of the new sun, they hang discarded children's clothes on the center pole of the lodge before returning to their homes +19a USA, ARAPAHO *Figure 83*
Refer also to *Figure 91*

• During the spring festival at Lake Titicaca when participants look to the water for the son of the sun god to rise; "warriors" carry an actor portraying the young sun god to the soccer

stadium where the people sing the legend of the "first Inca" in the Inca language *See* ANCESTOR WORSHIP & BIRTH & GAME SPORT & HERO & SOCIETY AS AT THE AXIS MUNDI & WAR & WATER +19a PERU, INCA \REVt

Figure 83

**See The Following Entries in Section Three
For Some Related Metaphors and Concepts**

- *agriculture*
- *angel*
- *apple*
- *baby boy*
- *badger*
- *banking*
- *beaver*
- *bee*
- *brass*
- *bronze*
- *catastrophe*
- *chaos in nature*
- *children*
- *Christmastide*
- *climate*
- *commerce*
- *copper*
- *cornucopia*

- *crook*
- *cupid*
- *duck*
- *ear of corn*
- *earthquake*
- *Easter*
- *eclipse*
- *egg*
- *fertility*
- *flora*
- *flower*
- *fruit*
- *gift giving*
- *gold*
- *hand down and up*
- *healing*
- *herb*
- *honey*

- *ivy*
- *lamb*
- *laurel*
- *leaf*
- *llama*
- *materialism*
- *mistletoe*
- *money*
- *new year*
- *olive branch/ tree*
- *palm*
- *pearl*
- *perfume*
- *pomegranate*
- *prince*
- *pumpkin*
- *rain*

- *resurrection*
- *rose*
- *seasons*
- *sheaf*
- *shepherd*
- *soul*
- *springtime*
- *storm*
- *toad*
- *trade*
- *treasure*
- *trepanning*
- *triform*
- *vegetation*
- *wheel of fortune*
- *wine*
- *wreath*

Whale

whale *The letter J of the Snake Ring Template.* A metaphor for the carrier of the new sun through the water, from the waters of the western horizon towards the east. *Ref* BABY BOY, EAST ORIENTATION, MARINE CARRIER.

• A decorated Ice Age cave painting depicts a large black fish with a ring motif at its mouth and the outline of a small bird on its body *See* BIRD & CARRIER & RING MOTIF -350b SPAIN, LA PILETA *Figure 84*

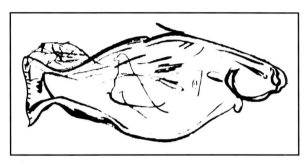

Figure 84

• Special religious importance is given to the story of Jonah carried within a whale from the west to east **[Note:** as depicted here in a 14th century illustration]. It is read in the afternoon on the Day of Atonement. **[Note:** The whale is traditionally associated with Leviathan, a huge aquatic animal variously interpreted as a dragon or a whale. Leviathan's root "lwy" means "to coil"] *See* CARRIER & DRAGON & PATH & WATER & EAST ORIENTATION -10b ISRAEL, JEWISH \ENDt *Figure 85*

Figure 85

• A large salmon with a series of engraved round motifs on its body is carved into the ceiling of a decorated Ice Age Cave, located below the small Gorge D'Efner waterfall, just before it tumbles down into the Vezere river *See* CAVE & PATH & ROUND MOTIF IN SEQUENCE & WATERFALL & UNDERWORLD -350b FRANCE, ABRI \BRFp

• An early American Indian painting on the ceiling of a west coast cave depicts a whale whose front half is colored red and its rear half is colored black *See* BLACK & CARRIER & CAVE & PATH & RED & UNDERWORLD -60b USA, CALIFORNIA \NATp

• **Osiris'** body was cut into thirteen parts which were regenerated within a giant fish *See* CARRIER & DEATH & LEVELS CELESTIAL & REGENERATION & SUN OLD/ YOUNG -30b EGYPT \MCCt

• The name Delphi, chosen land of the young sun god **Apollo**, comes from the word dolphin. Apollo went in the form of a dolphin to Southwest Asia Minor each year and returned bringing the season of good weather *See* CARRIER & SEASON & SOCIETY AS AT THE AXIS MUNDI & SUN YOUNG -20b GREEK \LARt

• Many fountain figures in the Roman world depict **Cupid** riding on a dolphin *See* BABY BOY & CARRIER & SOCIETY AS AT THE AXIS MUNDI & WATER +1a ITALY, POMPEII *Figure 86*

Figure 86

• **Vishnu** was incarnated from within a giant fish -19b INDIA, HINDU \KAPt

• A carving on a mountainside at an Olmec site shows a man being carried within the mouth of a composite serpent-fish *See* CARRIER & MOUNTAIN & PATH & SOCIETY AS AT THE AXIS MUNDI -9b MEXICO, CHALCACINGO *Figure 87*

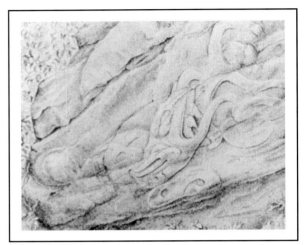

Figure 87

• The image of a youth holding a torch and a snake while riding on the back of a fish is embossed on the gold panel of the Gundenstrup bowl *See* BABY BOY & CARRIER & LIGHT & PATH & SNAKE -1b DENMARK, CELTIC \LARp

• One of the earliest Christian creeds as well as born-again Christians use the symbol of a fish, with the acronym in Greek letters for "Jesus Christ, Son of God" on its body. Jonah in the whale signifies Christ's resurrection *See* BABY BOY & CARRIER & RESURRECTION 0b ITALY, CHRISTIAN \KENp \ARCp

• A ground drawing on the Nazca plain depicts a whale facing east and carrying a human. A

Nazca effigy pot with precisely this same configuration has, in addition, a large ringsymbol around the eye of the whale *See* CARRIER & EAST ORIENTATION & EYE & RING MOTIF +1b PERU, NAZCA \ISBp

• The detail of a relief on the side of a ball-court depicts a deity figure perforating his penis; the penile blood is directed to the face of a young man within the mouth of a large fish *See* CARRIER & CASTRATION (CIRCUMCISION) & PATH & REGENERATION +14b MEXICO, EL TAJIN *Figure 88*

Figure 88

• The painting on an American Indian bowl depicts a man within the body of a fish +5b USA, MIMBRES \ARCp

• The ceremonial house was formed of whalebones, with the whale's head forming the entrance. Participants in the rituals sat inside the space encompassed by the whale's ribs *See* HOUSE & INFORMATION DESTROYED & SECRET & SOCIETAL ASPECT & WATER +14a ALASKA, ESKIMO \ARCt

• Frequent drawings in the native art are of a man within a whale's body +18a EASTER ISLAND \HEUp

**See The Following Entries in Section Three
For Some Related Metaphors and Concepts**

- *dolphin*
- *marine carrier*
- *porpoise*

Levels,
Underworld

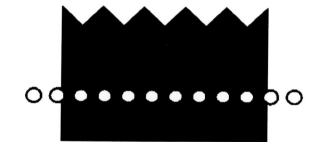

levels *The letters 𝒦 & 𝒫 of the Snake Ring Template.* The supposed daily movement of the sun through seven levels in the sky and five levels in the underworld. The earth itself was the first level counting in both directions *Ref* TIME, UROBORUS \MUTt

levels underworld *The letter 𝒦 of the Snake Ring Template.* Five equidistant levels through which the serpent path of the sun must pass down and up each night. The sun's steps through these levels are numbered; "one" where the new sun begins its underworld path at the western horizon then down four steps to "five" where it reaches its nadir in the underworld, and then up four steps again to "nine" at the eastern horizon. *Ref* LEVELS, NIGHT.

• The Merkabah, or Throne Mystery, was an early Judaic mystery similar to the Greek Mysteries; it focused on the safe passage of the soul through the levels of the underworld, where there was peril from demons, followed by its ascension through the levels of heaven *See* HUSK & OCCULT & SOCIETAL ASPECT & SOUL & WAR +2a ISRAEL, JEWISH \OCTt

• The maloca, ceremonial house, is located between two branches of a river symbolizing the center of the world. Its walls and posts represent mountains and hills at the western edge of the world. The sun descends to the river of the dead, travels the underworld path in a "snake-canoe" then rises again in the east *See* CONFLUENCE OF RIVERS & HOUSE & MOUNTAIN & PATH & PILLAR & SOCIETY AS AT THE AXIS MUNDI & WATER +19a COLOMBIA, TUKANO *Figure* 89

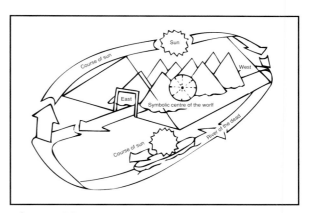

Figure 89

underworld *The letter 𝒦 of the Snake Ring Template.* The portion of the sun's path beneath the horizons. *Ref* CALABASH, VESSEL.

**See The Following Entries in Section Three
For Some Related Metaphors and Concepts**

- *black*
- *cauldron*
- *checkerboard design*
- *darkness*
- *five*
- *goblet*
- *Grail*
- *hemisphere motif*
- *invisibility*
- *labyrinth*
- *levels*
- *levels underworld*
- *loving cup*
- *mathematics*
- *maze*
- *night*
- *nine*
- *number*
- *owl*
- *questions by scholars*
- *science*
- *snail*
- *south orientation*
- *twelve*
- *urn*
- *vase*
- *veil*
- *vessel*
- *yoke motif*

Trinity

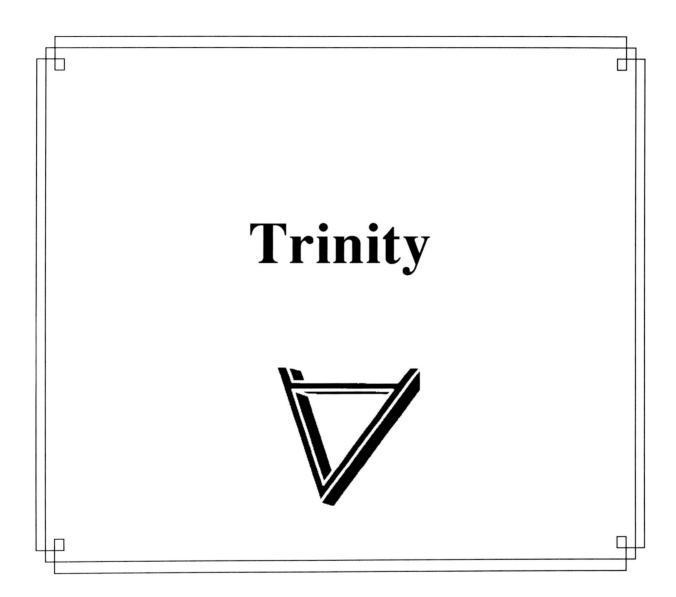

trinity *The letter L of the Snake Ring Template.* A metaphor for the climatic moment of godhead regeneration at the western horizon which brings about a change in nature, such as a season of fertility (springtime): the celestial father transfers his soul to a newborn son, at which time he immediately becomes a ghost of his former virile self, no longer able to travel the serpent path.

• An Ice Age painting on the floor of the Well, a natural depression in the north-of-west chamber of a cave depicts three figures. The celestial figure is a fallen, phallic bird-man [the "father"]. One of his outstretched hands points to a small bird rising on a stick [the "son"]. The other hand points to a bull which is castrated by a spear through its privates [the once "virile" ghost]. At the bottom of the scene there is a leafed branch *See* ASCENSION & BIRD & CASTRATION & FERTILITY & FLORA & HUSK & PHALLUS & RED & REGENERATION & SPRINGTIME SUNSET ORIENTATION & SUN OLD/ YOUNG & VERTICAL LINE / SHAPE & WELL -350b FRANCE, LASCAUX *Figure* 90

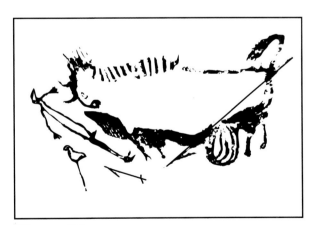

Figure 90

• On the pediment of a temple of the Athenian Acropolis, is a figure of three winged deities with an entwined serpent's body. They are holding the water symbol, sparks of fire and a bird *See* PATH & SERPENT ENTWINED & WATER & HOUSE & BIRD & FIRE -20b GREECE \LARt *Figure* 91

Figure 91

• A triform figure which decorated a temple pediment of the Acropolis consists of reddish skinned figures with wings and the scaly tail of a snake. The figure on the right with blue hair and beard holds a bird. The similar figure on the left holds an ear of corn. The central figure with white hair holds a water symbol -20b GREEK \BOAp

• The three leafed clover is representative of the Father, the Son, and the Holy Ghost; the Holy Ghost descends into one's Christian soul at the baptism +4b FRANCE, CHRISTIAN \WESt

**See The Following Entries in Section Three
For Some Related Metaphors and Concepts**

- *clown*
- *demons*
- *devil*
- *Fool*
- *ghost*
- *giant*
- *husk*
- *jester*
- *Minotaur*
- *negro*
- *ogre*
- *rhinoceros*
- *scale*
- *shadow*
- *ternary*
- *three*
- *trident*
- *unicorn*
- *wild man*
- *wolf*

Feline

feline *The letter* ***M*** *of the Snake Ring Template.* A metaphor for the successful passage of the newborn sun through the perilous underworld to its ascent in the east, with the characteristics of fiercely protecting its young, carrying the young in its mouth and of its eyes shining in the dark. *Ref* CARRIER, EYE, HERO, WAR.

• One of the earliest anthropomorphic statuettes is an Ice Age ivory figurine of a lion-headed man *See* CARRIER -300a GERMANY, HOHLENSTEIN \NATp

• A boulder on a small mound facing outward from an Ice Age cave is carved in the form of a composite head with the features of a man and a feline on each half of the face *See* CARRIER & CAVE & FELINE & PATH -120a SPAIN, EL JUYO *Figure* 92

Figure 93

• During the Tiger Dance held in local churchyards, participants wear a tiger mask with mirrors for eyes and a deer's head painted on their upper body *See* CARRIER & DEER & EYE & HOUSE & MIRROR & PATH +19a MEXICO *Figure* 94

Figure 92

• An aggressive figure painted on a wall facing out from another Ice Age cave entrance has a feline's face on a human body, with antlers at its head and large round eyes. This is the only figure in the cave painted black *See* BLACK & CARRIER & CAVE & DEER & EYE & FELINE -350b FRANCE, TROIS FRERES *Figure* 93

Figure 94

• A small stone carving from Catal Huyuk, the first true city, is described by its discoverers as the figure of a young deity riding on the back of a leopard *See* BABY BOY & CARRIER & SOCIETY AS AT THE AXIS MUNDI -70b TURKEY, CATAL HUYUK *Figure 95*

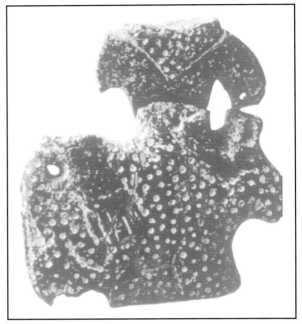

Figure 95

Figure 96

• A roll-out drawing of a cup from the king's burial at Uruk (Warka) depicts winged felines, wearing the hair fold which is common in Egyptian art for designating a royal boy-child, holding what appear to be swords, standing as guardians at either side of vertically entwined serpents *See* BABY BOY & CADUCEUS & CARRIER & REGENERATION & RULER & PATH & SERPENT ENTWINED -35b IRAQ, SUMERIAN *Figure 96*

• A box from a royal burial was decorated with ivory plaques depicting a lion defeating a bull *See* BULL & REGENERATION & WAR -35b IRAQ, SUMERIAN *Figure 97*

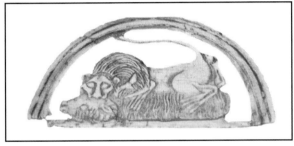

Figure 97

• During decipherment of the Egyptian heiroglyphs, Jean Francois Champollion discovered that the symbol for a lion was used in the same context as the Greek word for "war" *See* WRITING -30b EGYPT \CASt

• Bronze cats wearing gold earrings were not unusual. One was uncovered at a cemetery containing thousands of mummified cats *See* CARRIER & GOLD & REGENERATION & RING MOTIF & SOCIETAL ASPECT -30b EGYPT \HAWp

• A detail from an Egyptian plaque depicts lion-headed **Bes** with eye-signs covering his body; Bes is winged and phallic and holds a "snake-holder", as he treads on the uroborus, which is said to symbolize the underworld *See* CARRIER & EYE & PATH & SOUL & SUN YOUNG & UROBORUS -30b EGYPT *Figure 98*

• The face of lion goddess **Tefnut** "glowed like the sun" *See* CARRIER & RAYED MOTIF & SUN YOUNG -30b EGYPT \NEUt

Figure 98

• A mural on the west wall of the king's bedroom at Karnak depicts successive images of lion-headed figure of **Bes** holding a ring motif and a snake *See* BABY BOY & CARRIER & MARRIAGE & PATH & REGENERATION & RING MOTIF & RULER & WEST ORIENTATION -29a EGYPT, KARNAK *Figure* 99

Figure 99

• A row of stone sphinxes is at the same site, each with a miniature image of the king in its mouth *See* CARRIER & PATH & PROCESSION & REGENERATION & RULER -29a EGYPT, KARNAK *Figure* 100

Figure 100

• Painted wooden statues in Tutankhamun's tomb depict the king as the sun god **Osiris** carried on the back of a black leopard with gold ibex horns at its forehead. The color black represents the underworld *See* CARRIER & BLACK & GOLD & IBEX & RULER -13a EGYPT \EDVp *Figure* 101

• A gold-covered wood head of a leopard, attached to a leopard's skin, was buried with Tutankhamun *See* CARRIER & REGENERATION & RULER -13a EGYPT \EDVp

• A vase from the Tutankhamun tomb depicts the lion **Bes** with its paw on the "protection" symbol -13a EGYPT \EDVp

• Lion-headed **Sekhmet** was the underworld goddess of war and the patroness of Egyptian military campaigns. A statuette of the lion goddess depicts her holding the infant sun god Horus on her lap *See* HERO & SOCIETY AS AT THE AXIS MUNDI & SUN YOUNG & WAR -6a EGYPT \SMJp \LARp \BAPp

• A statuette depicting lion-headed **Bes** shows the figure holding a sword and a Roman shield *See* WAR -1a EGYPT, ROMAN *Figure* 102

Figure 101

• The prototypal young sun god's name **Apollo**, means "from the depth of the lion" *See* CARRIER & SUN YOUNG -20b GREEK \LARp \CIRt

Figure 102

• A cylinder seal depicts a lion accompanying the young sun god **Shamash** as he strides on the back of a rising feathered serpent *See* HERO & LEAP-UP & PATH -20b IRAQ, ACCADIAN \MUNp

• The Sphinx was the "custodian of the parting of the ways" *See* SUN YOUNG & TRINITY -19b IRAQ, ASSYRIAN \ELHp

• The drawing of a composite figure on an Olmec stone slab depicts a were-jaguar head on a fish's body which bears a large X symbol *See* FELINE & PATH & WHALE & X-CROSSING -15b MEXICO, LA VENTA *Figure* 103

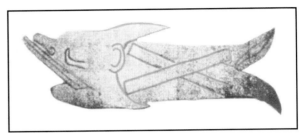

Figure 103

• A composite ground drawing facing to the east depicts a horned feline head on the body of a fish *See* ART & DEER & EAST ORIENTATION & IBEX & WHALE +1b PERU, NAZCA *Figure* 104

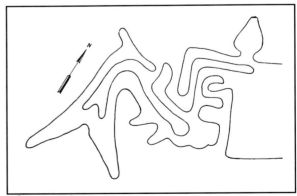

Figure 104

• The statue in a Javanese park of a lion with a fish's body represents the "komodo dragon" *See* DRAGON & HERO & PATH & SOCIETY AS AT THE AXIS MUNDI +19a INDONESIA, JAVA *Figure* 105

Figure 105

• A stone tablet from Mesoamerica's mother culture depicts a young lord [probably the young sun god] wearing a yoke said to be that of a ball player. He is seated on the coil of a feathered serpent and his face emerges from the mouth of a jaguar *See* CARRIER & DRAGON & GAME SPORT & PATH & SOCIETY AS AT THE AXIS MUNDI -15b MEXICO, LA VENTA *Figure* 106

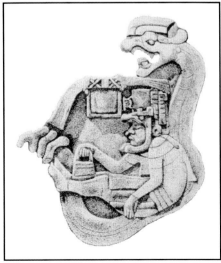

Figure 106

• Copper felines with upright rings on their backs [note similar Mayan figure] were discovered below the floor of a northwest chamber of the Nimrud Palace under the monumental figure of a winged man-bull found standing in its original position *See* BULL & CARRIER & HOUSE & PATH & RING MOTIF & SPRINGTIME SUNSET ORIENTATION & UNDERWORLD -13a IRAQ, ASSYRIAN \SAGt *Figure* 107

Figure 107

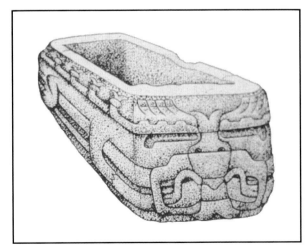

Figure 108

• The sides of a ruler's sarcophagus, supported on the backs of crouching lions, depicts the departed king seated on a feline-shaped throne in a field of lotus, where attendants salute the king with raised hands *See* CARRIER & DEATH &

HAND RAISED & LOTUS & REGENERATION & RULER -12a LEBANON, PHOENICIAN \PRIp

• A stone sarcophagus from one of the earliest ceremonial centers of Mesoamerica, was carved in the form of the were-jaguar *See* CARRIER & DEATH & REGENERATION -15b MEXICO, OLMEC *Figure* 108

• A bronze vessel from the period of the first emperor of China is in the form of **T'ao-T'ieh,** the feline who averts evil. Ring motifs are around the feline's eyes, entwined dragons cover its body, and a deer with a sequence of ring motifs on its body stands on the feline's back as the feline takes into its mouth a tranquil youth with large circular earplugs *See* BABY BOY & CARRIER & DEER & EARRING & EYE & PATH & RING MOTIFS IN SEQUENCE & SOCIETAL ASPECT -12a CHINA, SHANG \LEEt *Figure* 109

Figure 109

• In ancient Chinese iconography the tiger was the guardian of graves and the repeller of evil spirits *See* HERO & HUSK & SOCIETAL ASPECT & WAR -11b CHINA, CHOU \MUNt

• "Yahweh of armies who sits on the cherub (Hebrew for Sphinx)" II SAMUEL 6.2 *See* CARRIER & GOD & WAR -10b ISRAEL, JEWISH \SMKt

• A votive staff's bronze finial from a burial is in the form of a feline's head receiving a winged deity into its mouth *See* CARRIER & DEATH & PATH & REGENERATION & SOCIETAL ASPECT & STAFF & SUN YOUNG -10b IRAN, LURISTAN \ANBp \TELt

• An undeciphered golden bowl has a repousse lion with a star motif on its rump carrying a child on its back and treading on the figure of an aged man *See* BABY BOY & CARRIER & GOLD & TRINITY & WAR -9a IRAN, PERSIAN \GIRp

• A gold ornament depicts a running feline with its tail in the form of a snake; the figure of a young lord is embossed on its body *See* BABY BOY & CARRIER & PATH & SNAKE -8b PERU, CHAVIN \EMNp

• A large stone head of a jaguar with horns at its forehead was found in a ritual mound at an Olmecoid site near a string of volcanoes on the west coast of Guatemala *See* CARRIER & LEAP-UP & MOUND & VOLCANO & WATER & WEST ORIENTATION -5a GUATEMALA, MONTE ALTO \BERp

• A hammered gold plaque depicts a puma with snakes embossed on its body and a deity's head on its tongue *See* CARRIER & GOLD & PATH & SNAKE +2b PERU, MOCHICA *Figure* 110

Figure 110

• Pazuzu, represented in Mesopotamian art with a lion's head, gazelle's horns, and a feathered or scaly body, was the hero who protected newborn children from the demon **Lamashtu** when he came from the west bringing death. *See* BABY BOY & DEER & HUSK & PATH & UNDERWORLD & WAR -7a IRAQ, ACCADIAN \TELp

• A relief from the king's palace at Persepolis depicts a horned and winged lion. The lion attacking the bull was often associated in art with the king. *See* BULL & RULER & SOCIETY AS AT THE AXIS MUNDI & WAR -5a IRAN, PERSIAN \METt
Figure 111

Figure 111

• A radiant feline's head was the Mithraic symbol for the sun *See* CARRIER & RAYED MOTIF & SUN YOUNG -5b ITALY, MITHRAIC \CIRp

• Horses were buried in the tomb of a Scythian warrior chief, their harnesses decorated with tigers' heads *See* HORSE & REGENERATION & RULER & UNDERWORLD & WAR -5a RUSSIA, PAZYRYK \BRHt

• A war chariot attributed to an Etruscan burial has carved feline heads at the ends of its axle and yoke. An embossed shield on the chariot depicts a feline holding a fawn in its mouth *See* CARRIER & DEER & FELINE & HORSE & WAR -5a ITALY, ETRUSCAN \RIDp

• Bracelets found in burials often terminate with a lion's head holding a ball in its mouth **[Note:** Similar scenes were found in offering pits under the Aztec pyramids] *See* CARRIER & DEATH & REGENERATION & ROUND MOTIF & SOCIETAL ASPECT -5b ITALY, ROMAN \ARCp
Refer to *Figure 129*

• To the Hindu the lion is a solar image, described as a lion-monster of insatiable appetite. Balinese art depicts legendary lions with horns at their forehead and a rayed sun on their back *See* CARRIER & LEAP-UP & MOUTH & SUN -5b BALI, HINDU \WESp \AVDt \CIRt

• A stone ceiling panel represents the sun god **Vishnu** as a lion. The lion is the transient aspect of Vishnu but the cosmic serpent Ananta is Vishnu's permanent alter-ego *See* CARRIER & PATH & SERPENT ENTWINED & UNDERWORLD -5b INDIA, HINDU \MUNt
Figure 112

Figure 112

• An abandoned stock of lion sculptures, with the ring motif of the sun depicted on either their chest or their raised paw, remain at the pre-Buddhist shrine of Anuradhapura, "the house of great sacrifice" *See* CARRIER & HERO & HAND RAISED & RING MOTIF & SUN -5b SRI LANKA \HEVt

• A jade figure from a tomb depicts a young lord riding on the back of a feline whose tail is in the form of a snake *See* CARRIER & PATH -4a CHINA, CHOU \CHCp

• A fragmented Greek relief depicts the young god **Bellerophon** seated on a horse. He is assisted by the chimera in killing a bull which was originally part of the artifact *See* CHIMERA & HERO & HORSE & LEAP-UP & PATH & WAR -4a GREEK
Figure 113

Figure 113

• Scholars are puzzled by the bronze head-rest from an early tomb that depicts a feline biting the rump of a large bull which has a smaller bull emerging from its body *See* BRONZE & DEATH & HEAD & HERO & REGENERATION & SOCIETAL ASPECT & WAR   -1a CHINA, DIAN \MEUp *Figure 114*

Figure 114

• Marble statues of the young sun god, **Apollo**, with a griffin as his companion, often with its paw on the wheel of fortune, were found in Pompeiian garden shrines *See* GRIFFIN & HERO & HOUSE & SOCIETAL ASPECT & SUN YOUNG & WHEEL OF FORTUNE +1a ITALY, ROMAN \ISRp \ARCp

• A mosaic on the floor inside one of the villas in Pompeii depicts a winged child, with a series of ring motifs on his headband, riding on a lion *See* ANGEL & BABY BOY & CARRIER & RING MOTIF IN SEQUENCE +1a ITALY, ROMAN \KRBp

• Tintinnabulas depicting phallic figures hung from the ceilings of most Pompeiian villas. Typically, one depicts a child holding a ring motif in his hand as he rides on a feline which has the forepart of a winged phallus *See* BABY BOY & CARRIER & CASTRATION (CIRCUMCISION) & HOUSE & PATH & PHALLUS & RING MOTIF & WINGED +1a ITALY, ROMAN *Figure 115*

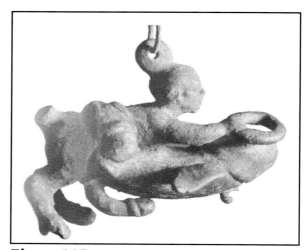

Figure 115

• A painted vessel from Callejon de Huales is in the form of a feline with a series of ring motifs along its body, holding in its paws a young lord with a painted series of round motifs on his earplugs and a cross motif on his chest [Compare to the Chinese T'ao T'ieh bronze vessel above] *See* BABY BOY & CARRIER & CROSS EAST & EARRING & RING/ ROUND MOTIF IN SEQUENCE +2b PERU, RECUAY *Figure 116*
Refer also to *Figure 110*

Figure 116

• The painted interior of a bowl depicts a winged feline on the path of a plumed serpent *See* CARRIER & SNAKE FEATHERED/ WINGED & VESSEL & WINGED +6a BOLIVIA, TIAHUACA *Figure* 117

Figure 117

• A Mayan figure vessel, discovered below the floor of a ritual house, depicts a young deity [probably the sun god] within the open mouth of a horned feline *See* CARRIER & DEER & HOUSE & SUN YOUNG & UNDERWORLD +9a BELIZE, SANTA RITA *Figure* 118

Figure 118

• This vessel was nested inside the open maw of a second vessel in the form of **Kukulkan**, the feathered serpent. When discovered, the nested vessels were within two large clay pots, one upright and one inverted and sealed mount-to-mouth *See* CALABASH & PATH & SNAKE FEATHERED/ WINGED & UNDERWORLD & VESSEL +9a BELIZE, SANTA RITA *Figure* 119

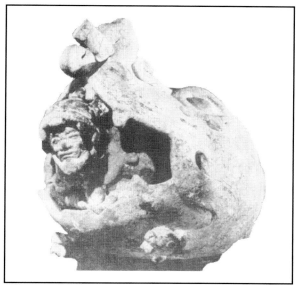

Figure 119

• The relief on a burial urn depicts a jaguar, its paws aggressively thrust forward, within the open maw of the feathered serpent *See* BURIAL & DEATH & HERO & PATH & REGENERATION & VESSEL & WAR +9a GUATEMALA, MAYAN *Figure* 120

Figure 120

• The detail of an embossed gold pectoral ornament depicts a feline with a series of ring motifs along its body treading on a serpent *See* GOLD & PATH & RING MOTIF IN SEQUENCE & SNAKE +14a COLOMBIA, SINU *Figure* 121

• Spanish conquerors reported that the natives believed the souls of those who died were transferred into jaguars *See* CARRIER & REGENERATION & SOCIETAL ASPECT & SOUL +16a COLOMBIA \AMNt

Figure 121

• Drawings made under the influence of hallucinogens depict a jaguar at "the house of the waters" and at "the house of the hill" in the underworld *See* HOUSE & MOUNTAIN & SOCIETY AS AT THE AXIS MUNDI & TRIANGLE MOTIF UPRIGHT & UNDERWORLD & WATER +19a COLOMBIA, TUKANO *Figure 122*

Figure 122

• A Mayan stone feline carries an unusually large stone ring on its back *See* CARRIER & RING MOTIF +12a MEXICO, MAYAPAN
Refer to *Figure 108*

• The relief on the wall of a Mayan temple depicts a young lord seated on a double-jaguar throne +3b MEXICO, PALENQUE \ROBp

• Paleochristian art discovered in the lower level of the Saint Seurin church depicts a youth with a fish's body riding on the back of a feline *See* CARRIER & HOUSE & PATH & WATER & WHALE +4b FRANCE, CHRISTIAN \WESp

• A drawing of the base of an early Christian cross depicts felines devouring a youth in the presence of snakes *See* BABY BOY & CARRIER & CROSS WEST & DEMYTHOLIZATION & PATH & SNAKE +4a IRELAND, CHRISTIAN *Figure 123*

Figure 123

• Figures of lions were often found at the entrance to tombs, in spite of the fact that lions were not native to the area *See* ART & DEATH & REGENERATION & WAR +6a CHINA, T'ANG \ARCt

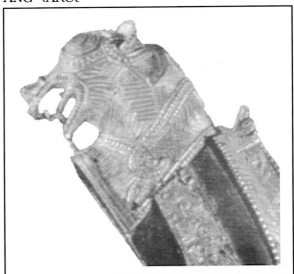

Figure 124

• The horse collar of a war-chariot found in a Viking burial terminates with the heads of horned felines, each holding a barely visible small bird in its mouth. **[Note** the small bird rising on a stick in the Well at Lascaux].

A series of ring motifs decorate the felines' horns and encircle their eyes *See* BIRD & CARRIER & DEATH & DEER & EYE & HORSE & REGENERATION & RING MOTIF IN SEQUENCE +9a SWEDEN, VIKING *Figure 124*
Refer also to *Figure 160*

• The main pyramid of the Aztecs had two temples at its top; one was the temple of their major deity **Huitzlipotli**, the young sun god, and the other was the temple of **Tlaloc** who was linked with the jaguar and the nighttime sun. Tlaloc, "he with the quality of earth", was represented by a jaguar face mask with large rings around the eyes *See* EYE & HERO & NIGHT & PYRAMID & TEMPLE & UNDERWORLD +13b MEXICO, TEMPLO MAYOR \AVDt *Figure 125* Figure 126

Figure 126

Figure 125

• Excavations at the stairway of the Templo Mayor uncovered the skeleton of a jaguar with a stone ball in its mouth and its head facing east. In an offering pit under the Templo, another skeletal head of the jaguar with a stone ball in its mouth was surrounded by seashells *See* CARRIER & CRUSTACEAN & EAST ORIENTATION & PATH & ROUND MOTIF & STAIRS INFERNAL & TEMPLE +13a MEXICO, AZTEC Figure 127 Figure 128

• Miguel Covarrubias, pioneer artist and art historian of Mesoamerica, traced the stylistic evolution of Tlaloc back to the Olmec were-jaguar [man-juguar] *See* BABY BOY & CARRIER & FELINE +13b MEXICO, AZTEC \MUNt

• Where the rainbow meets the horizon it makes a deep hole; in this hole one finds lions *See* ABYSS & RAINBOW +18a KENYA, CHAGA \PAQt

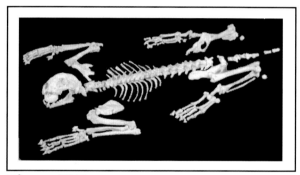
Figure 127

• Southeast Indians carried a copper-plated panther skull into battle *See* CARRIER & COPPER & SOCIETAL ASPECT & WAR +18a USA \WESp

Figure 128

• Embossed rodeo saddles of the Mexican cowboys depict a feline vanquishing a bull and a rising sun surrounded by flowers *See* BULL & FERTILITY & FLORA & GAME SPORT & HERO & SUN YOUNG & WAR +19a MEXICO \FONt

• During the *Long-haired Ones* folk dance, a participant portrays a boy-child with long golden hair riding on the back of a dancer wearing a feline mask carved with a sequence of rings *See* BABY BOY & CARRIER & DEMYTHOLIZATION & GOLD & RING MOTIF IN SEQUENCE & RITUAL +19a MEXICO *Figure* 129

Figure 129

• The highlights of the Chinese New Year parade are performers costumed as a dragon chasing a red ball and as the courageous lion who conquers evil *See* DRAGON & GAME SPORT & NEW YEAR & PATH & PROCESSION & RED & ROUND MOTIF & SEASON & WAR +19a CHINA \WESt

• A wooden ancestor-figure depicts a nude man sitting on a feline with a dead cockerel at his feet *See* ANCESTOR WORSHIP & BIRD & CARRIER & DEATH & REGENERATION +19a IVORY COAST \PAQp

• Under the water, wreathed in snakes, there is a lion and a family consisting of a man, woman, and baby *See* ABYSS & BABY BOY & MOTHER GODDESS & PATH & SOCIETY AS AT THE AXIS MUNDI & SUN OLD/ NEW & TRINITY & WATER +19a NIGERIA, IBIBIO \AFAt

• An important wooden stool carved from one tree trunk depicts a lion with its paw on a baby boy; the stool housed the owner's soul after his death *See* BABY BOY & CARRIER & HERO & PATH & REGENERATION & SOCIETAL ASPECT & SOUL & TREE & WAR +19a GHANA, AKAN
Figure 130

Figure 130

**See The Following Entries in Section Three
For Some Related Metaphors and Concepts**

- *carrier*
- *cat*
- *Cerberus*
- *chariot*
- *cherub*
- *chimera*
- *dog*
- *griffin*
- *hero*
- *jaguar*
- *leopard*
- *lion*
- *ocelot*
- *panther*
- *puma*
- *sphinx*
- *tiger*
- *vehicle*
- *werejaguar*
- *wolf*

War

war *The letter N of the Snake Ring Template.* The underworld conflict between the newborn sun and his jealous father-sun. The newborn sun was destined to assume the father-sun's entwined serpent path in the sky and bring on the new season of fertility. **a.** Upon leaving their homeland, symbolically the "center of the world", the members of a society metaphorically continue into the underworld along the new sun's path where they, like the new sun, must defeat the demonic forces of the underworld, actually the people outside of their homeland, for the good of the world. **b.** A societal endeavor to obtain victims, specifically the enemy leaders, for seasonal rituals of human sacrifice to inspire the death of the old sun. **c.** ***headhunting*** A societal endeavor to obtain human heads as an effigy of the old sun's head. The human heads would often be displayed at the top of the ritual house or on a pole. *Ref* CHAOS IN NATURE, HEAD, HOUSE, HUSK, PATH, RULER, SACRIFICE HUMAN, SOCIETIAL ASPECT, SOCIETY AS AT THE AXIS MUNDI, TRINITY, VERTICAL STICK .

• Explorers discovered many stenciled images of mutilated hands rising up the walls of Ice Age caves *See* HAND RAISED WITH MISSING DIGIT & HERO -350b FRANCE, GARGAS *Figure* 131

Figure 131

• The skeleton of a young man wearing a headdress of deer teeth was discovered in an Ice Age ritual burial with a stone knife in one hand *See* DEATH & DEER & REGENERATION & WEAPON -270 ITALY \MAQt

• A central theme of Mesopotamian mythology is the renewal of the forces of nature by the triumph of the season of fertility over evil and chaos. An uninterpreted plaque from the area likely depicts the hero knifing the bound old sun of chaos. The old sun is depicted by an aged figure with sagging chest, exposed ribs and an empty rhombus sign on his forehead for the container of the solar soul. A cylinder-seal impression from the same area may represent the victorious hero then running on the serpent path (with crossing lines along its body) through the underworld to rise in the eastern horizon as the new sun *See* CHAOS IN NATURE & EYE & PATH & SOUL & SUN OLD/ NEW & X-CROSSING *Figure* 132   *Figure* 133

Figure 132

Figure 133

• A scene painted on the wall of a shrine-room in the earliest city in the world, depicts a giant red bull being attacked by warriors -70b TURKEY, CATAL HUYUK \REAp

• According to the Rig Veda, our present world results from the victories by the gods over demonic forces which are defeated but never eradicated *See* REGENERATION & SEASON & TRINITY -19b INDIA, HINDU \MCCt

• A mythic scene of their recurrent wars depicts a sun-head figure riding on a horse *See* HERO, SUN YOUNG +18a USA, IROQUOIS \BUQp

• The dead become phantoms jealous of the living HUSK & SOCIETAL ASPECT & TRINITY +19 BRAZIL \LEVt

• A painting depicts the wife of the sun god **Shiva** mounted on a feline attacking a bull. Her ten arms carry the attributes of Shiva such as a solar ring, a bell, a trident, and a sword. She attacks the dark horned demon carrying sword and shield, who rises from the torso of the decapitated bull *See* BULL & FELINE & GODDESS & HUSK & MUSIC & REGENERATION & RING MOTIF & TRIDENT -5b INDIA, HINDU
Figure 134

Figure 134

**See The Following Entries in Section Three
For Some Related Metaphors and Concepts**

- *escape*
- *fight*
- *gambling*
- *game board*
- *game sport*
- *Gemini*
- *hand raised; missing digit*
- *knight*
- *lance or spear*
- *psychology child*
- *shield*
- *twins*
- *victory*
- *war*
- *warrior*
- *weapon*

Raised Hand,
Leaping Animal

hand raised *The letter O of the Snake Ring Template.* A metaphor for the new sun ascending with the solar soul through the eastern horizon to begin the new season of fertility. *Ref* GAME SPORT, WAR.

• Scholars are unable to explain the meaning of raised hands, the earliest and the most numerous of Ice Age cave wall decorations *See* BIRTH & CAVE & REGENERATION -350b \MAZt \GAXt

• The image of a hand raised to angles which may represent water is engraved on a bone artifact from an Ice Age cave *See* EAST ORIENTATION & LEAP-UP & WATER -350b FRANCE, LE MORIN *Figure* 135

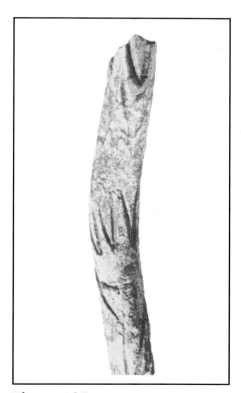

Figure 135

• An Ice Age engraved bone has the images of an arm and hand ascending from below to a great fish *See* EAST ORIENTATION & FISH & LEAP-UP & WATER -350b FRANCE, LAUGERIE BASSE *Figure* 136

Figure 136

• The raised hand is a hieroglyph for "Ka", the soul. A statue from the tomb of a king depicts hands rising from the ruler's head *See* FUNERAL & HEAD & REGENERATION & RULER & SOUL -30b EGYPT *Figure* 137

Figure 137

• Hands raised in the priestly blessing is a cosmic symbol in Jewish mysticism. In this drawing it is bringing forth wheat from the fields *See* FLORA & LEAP-UP & RITUAL & SEASON 19a JEWISH, KABALA *Figure* 138

The tenth letter of the English alphabet, the letter "J", corresponds to the tenth letter "yod" of the Hebrew alphabet from the word for "hand". Its symbol was originally an arm with a raised hand *See* LETTERS & WRITING -10b ISRAEL, JEWISH \ENDt

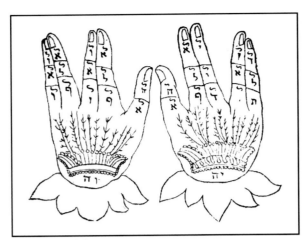

Figure 138

• The carving of an arm, wearing a bracelet consisting of a series of ring motifs, surmounts a mountain outcrop covered with images carved in the Olmec style, which included dragons with fish attributes and horned felines trampling bearded figures. A large Christian cross was erected by the Church near this carving *See* DEMYTHOLIZATION & DRAGON & CROSS EAST & FELINE & JEWELRY & PATH & RING MOTIF IN SEQUENCE & SOCIETAL ASPECT & WAR & WHALE -9b MEXICO, CHALCACINGO *Figure* 139

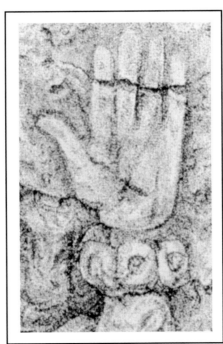

Figure 139

• **Itzamna**, the young sun god, was represented as a raised red hand *See* RED & SUN YOUNG +3b MEXICO, MAYAN \LARt

• At dawn, Southeast Indians raise their hands to the sunrise *See* LEAP-UP & SUN +18a USA, CHEROKEE \WESt

• They impress their hand prints on the roof beams of their kiva when they pray for rain *See* BIRTH & CAVE & HOUSE & RITUAL & SEASON & RAIN & SUN YOUNG +18a USA, HOPI \NABt

• Some California Indians regard the appearance in the sky of a constellation which they call "hand" as the beginning of the year *See* NEW YEAR +18a USA, KUMEYA \HEEt

• A raised hand was stencilled on the chest of the Plains Indians warrior chief *See* SOCIETAL ASPECT & SUN YOUNG & WAR +18a USA, MANDAN INDIANS \TUQp

Figure 140

• Burials were found in and around many of the Indian ritual mounds in the United States. An engraved stone disk from one of the mounds located on the Black Warrior River in Alabama depicts encircling serpents around a raised hand with an eye motif in its palm *See* DEATH & EYE & HAND RAISED & MOUND & PATH & REGENERATION & SOCIETY AS AT THE AXIS MUNDI & UROBORUS & WATER *Figure* 140

• To the Plains and Eastern Woodland Indians, the pictograph of an arm and raised hand represents the rising sun +19a USA, SIOUX, OJIBWAY \TOMt

• The hieroglyph of a raised hand with a ring motif in its palm was often associated with a sky-sign *See* LEAP-UP & RING MOTIF & WRITING +3b MEXICO, MAYAN \THNp

• Stencilled raised hands are common in the Mayan temples, scholars are puzzled by the many hand-signs in the Red Hand temple at Rio Bec *See* HOUSE & RED & REGENERATION +3b MEXICO, MAYAN \WESt

• Scholars are puzzled by the meaning of an early Christian cross with entwined serpents coiling up the remnants of its vertical arm. A child's head is within each of the serpent's coils, and at their top is a raised hand within a rayed ring motif *See* BABY BOY & CROSS EAST & DEMYTHOLIZATION & GUILLOCHE & LEAP-UP & PATH & RAYED MOTIF & RING MOTIF & SERPENT ENTWINED +9a IRELAND, CHRISTIAN *Figure* 141

raised hands, and bird-headed figures whose raised hands have their fingers curled into the ring motif *See* ABYSS & ART & BIRD & DESCENDING MOTIF & MOUNTAIN & REGENERATION & RING MOTIF & SOCIETAL ASPECT & SUN OLD & WATER & WRITING +15b EASTER ISLAND, ORONGO \ARCp
Figure 142

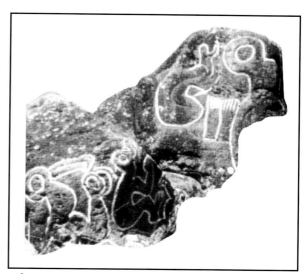

Figure 142

Figure 141

• Petroglyphs are inscribed inside a water-filled volcano at a sacred location on the west coast of the island, depicting ring motifs above

Figure 143

• Nail fetish figures have round mirror inserts in their stomach. The fingers of their raised hand are often coiled to form a ring motif *See* BLADE & DEATH & MIRROR & REGENERATION & RING MOTIF +19a ZAIRE, NKONDE *Figure 143*

• Starting approximately ten months old, deaf babies of deaf parents make the O.K. hand sign, indicating the infant's capacity for language *See* INFANT MENTALITY & PATH & RING MOTIF +19a LAURO PETITTO *Figure 144*

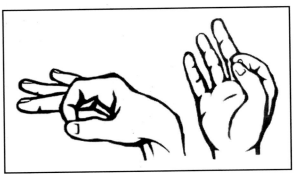

Figure 144

• Scholars are unable to explain the significance of the stencilled hands which the aborigines use to decorate their sacred rock shelters and caves *See* ART & CAVE & STONE +19a AUSTRALIA \CAIt

deer *or* leaping animal *The letter O of the Snake Ring Template.* A metaphor for the eastern horizon ascent of the new sun born to the old sun and mother goddess in the western underworld. *Ref* HAND RAISED, LEAP-UP, PATH.

• Engraved on the wall of an Ice Age cave in France is an ibex with a large ring motif depicted on its back *See* IBEX & LEAP-UP & RING MOTIF -100a FRANCE, SALLERLES-CABARDES *Figure 145*

• On an Ice Age cave wall the figure of a leaping deer is painted with human hands in the place of its front hooves; a path of dots is painted along its body *See* HAND RAISED & ROUND MOTIFS IN SEQUENCE -350b FRANCE, LES TROIS FRERES \GIEp

• The raised hand was the most common symbol and the earliest wall decoration of the Ice Age caves; some formed by the artists pressing their hands in the glacial clay of the cave walls *See* FLOOD & SUN YOUNG -350b \MAZt \MGDt \MUNt

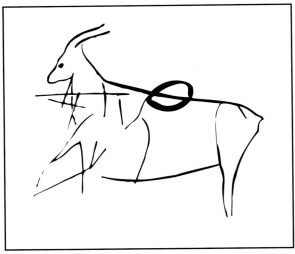

Figure 145

• A rock painting shows a horned phallic figure with his tail shaped as a paddle and an antelope leaping from his stomach; beside him is the image of a reclining pregnant female with upraised arms *See* BABY BOY & MARRIAGE & REGENERATION & SUN OLD & WATER -60b ALGERIA, TASILI-N-AJJER \NATp

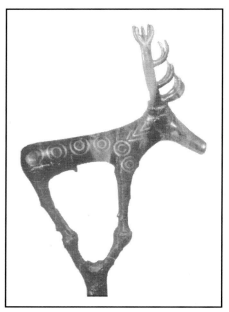

Figure 146

• A painted vessel depicts the goddess **Gaea** rising from the underworld holding the infant sun god **Dionysus** wrapped in a deerskin *See* BABY BOY & LEAP-UP & PATH -20b GREEK \LEIt

• The top of a carved staff from a burial depicts a stag with a series of ring motifs along its body -20a TURKEY, HATTIAN *Figure 146*

• Scholars are puzzled by a child's throne discovered in king Tutankhamun's tomb with gold side panels depicting an ibex and a leafy sprig *See* BABY BOY & FERTILITY & LEAP UP & REGENERATION & RULER & SOCIETAL ASPECT -13a EGYPT *Figure 147*

Figure 147

• Scholars cannot interpret the panels from a quiver which include scenes of a winged man attacked by a feline and, in a central panel, guardian felines with rayed ring motifs on their flanks holding one paw up to a marine bird and the other down to a youth holding an antelope in one hand and an ibex in the other *See* CARRIER & FELINE & HERO & LEAP-UP & MARINE BIRD & REGENERATION & SUN OLD/ YOUNG & WAR -7a IRAN, LURISTAN *Figure 148*

• A vessel depicts a young lord within the mouth of a serpent with deer ears in place of his own; accompanying glyphs refer to the deer as the sun +3b MEXICO, MAYAN \RODp

• The skin of a deer was stuffed with produce just before Spring, and then elevated on a pole at sunrise *See* FERTILITY & SUN YOUNG & VERTICAL LINE/ SHAPE +15a USA, TIMUCUA \CAIp

Figure 148

• During a folk dance performed on Easter and dedicated to the deer, the dancers sing, "comes the light of day, the sun is high and the rains come" *See* DEMYTHOLIZATION & LEAP-UP & SUN YOUNG +19a MEXICO \FONt

• Hohokan Indians at Eastertime perform a Deer Dance in honor of the infant Jesus *See* DEMYTHOLIZATION & LEAP-UP & SUN YOUNG +19a USA, PIMA \TUQt

• During the initiation rites boys dance in imitation of a deer; at the conclusion of the dance cassava bread is thrown into the rafters *See* FERTILITY & LEAP-UP & SOCIETAL ASPECT & SUN YOUNG +19a COLOMBIA, TUKANO \HUGt

**See The Following Entries in Section Three
For Some Related Metaphors and Concepts**

- *antelope*
- *arm*
- *ascension*
- *astrology*
- *beetle*
- *body paint*
- *butterfly*
- *chevron pointing up*
- *crime*
- *cross east*
- *east orientation*
- *fawn*
- *finger*
- *gazelle*
- *hand raised*
- *head*
- *ibex*
- *ladder celestial*
- *leap-up*
- *lore*
- *lotus*
- *ornamentation*
- *Pisces*
- *primate*
- *psychology dreams*
- *Sagittarius*
- *sheep (male)*
- *sociobiology*
- *stag*
- *T-upright*
- *vertical line/ shape*
- *zodiac*

Levels Celestial

levels celestial *The letter P of the Snake Ring Template.* The path of the seven visible planets in the sky, each planet placed at an equidistant level, through which the serpent path of the sun must pass up and down each day from dawn to sunset. The sun's steps through these levels are numbered; "one" is where the sun ascends through the eastern horizon, then up six steps to "seven" where it reaches its zenith in the sky. The sun then descends six steps again to "thirteen" where it seasonally dies and regenerates in the mountain-house of the western horizon waters *Ref* LEVELS, SEASON.

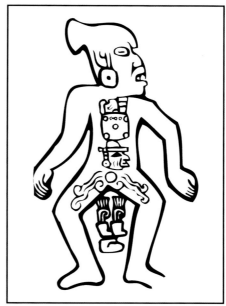

Figure 150

Figure 149

• In a 19th Century print, the sun god **Vishnu** reclines with his consort **Lakshmi** on the coils of the seven-headed serpent Ananta of the cosmic sea. From Vishnu's groin rises the deity **Brahma** on the lotus of Vishnu's dream *See* GODDESSES & LOTUS & PATH & REGENERATION & SNAKE & SUN OLD / YOUNG & WATER -19b INDIA, HINDU *Figure* 149

• A feature of Monte Alban, a mountain-top ceremonial center, is the "danzantes", a group of ancient carved stone panels on the western wall which, for the most part, depict castrated males with their eyes closed. Scholars are puzzled by the glyphs for "water", "light" and "thirteen" prominently embossed on a statue of a youth from the site *See* ART & BABY BOY & HOUSE & CASTRATION & DEATH & MOUNTAIN & RAYED MOTIF & REGENERATION & SOCIETY AS AT THE AXIS MUNDI & SUN OLD / YOUNG & WATER & WEST ORIENTATION +3b MEXICO, ZAPOTEC *Figure* 150 *Figure* 151

• The number seven appears frequently in Bible stories related to Jericho, in the legend of Atlantis, and in the numerical equivalents of knots on the quipus, the knotted strings placed in Andean burials **[Note:** All as allegories of the western horizon location where the sun descended to its death through seven levels and was reborn] *See* BURIALS & DEATH & DEMYTHOLIZATION & PATH & REGENERATION & ROPE & SOCIETY AS AT THE AXIS MUNDI \BREt \ENDt \MASt

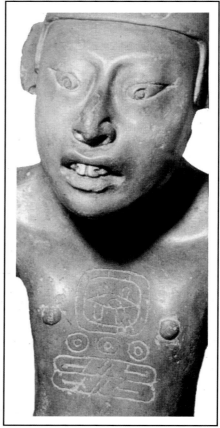

Figure 151

See The Following Entries in Section Three
For Some Related Metaphors and Concepts

- *bell*
- *celestial*
- *Day of Rest*
- *flute*
- *harp*
- *hemisphere motif*
- *lyre*
- *mathematics*
- *music*
- *number*
- *planet*
- *poetry*
- *Sabbath*
- *science*
- *seven*
- *twelve*
- *week*
- *whistling*
- *zenith*

Raptor

raptor *The letter Q of the Snake Ring Template.* A metaphor for the ascent of the sun to the highest level of the serpent path. *Ref* CARRIER, BIRD, CELESTIAL, WAR.

• The painted wall of a shrine room in the earliest true city in the world, above a ritual burial with its head painted red, depicts red vultures with round symbols in their body ascending above headless figures *See* CARRIER & HEAD & LEAP-UP & PATH & RED & REGENERATION & ROUND MOTIF & SOCIETAL ASPECT -70b TURKEY, CATAL HUYUK *Figure 152*

Figure 152

• A sun-disk flanked by falcon wings carved over the doorway of the mortuary temple of Dendur, personifies the sun god **Horus**, whose name translates to "sun" and "lofty" *See* CARRIER & REGENERATION & SOCIETAL ASPECT & SUN YOUNG -30b EGYPT \MUNt *Figure 153*

• Scholars wonder why figures of gold vultures and serpents were often placed under the wrappings of royal mummies, usually near to the head *See* CARRIER & GOLD & HEAD & PATH & REGENERATION & RULER -13a EGYPT, TUTANKHAMUN \EDVt

Figure 153

• A stone carving depicts the young sun god **Vishnu** carried by the sun-bird **Garuda** on an entwined snake path *See* CARRIER & PATH & SUN YOUNG & SERPENT ENTWINED +10a INDIA, HINDU *Figure 154*

• The eagle was a solar symbol. Aztecs referred to the morning sun as "the eagle that ascends", and the afternoon sun as "the eagle that falls" *See* CARRIER & SUN OLD/ YOUNG +15b MEXICO, AZTEC \ARUt \MAXt

• During sacred Maleku rites, an executioner called "the face of the sun" and "the lord of the above" fluttered his arms in imitation of a hawk and suddenly jerked up the victim's head with a noose. An elderly boar, selected because his tusks had grown in the form of circles, was then killed and laid on the body of the victim *See* DEATH & HEAD & PIG & RING MOTIF & SACRIFICE ANIMAL/ HUMAN & SUN OLD +18a NEW HEBRIDES \CAAt

• The griffin was consecrated to the young sun god **Apollo,** and was often depicted with its paw on the wheel of fortune *See* CARRIER & EAGLE & FELINE & PATH & SUN YOUNG & WHEEL +2a ITALY, ROMAN \ISRp \ARCp

Figure 154

• A raptor's claw made of mica from an Indian burial mound holds a round motif *See* CARRIER & DEATH & MICA & REGENERATION & ROUND MOTIF -10b USA, HOPEWELL *Figure* 155

• A Plains Indian myth tells that the snake wheel was once tied to a tipi pole over a grave. The snake wheel flew away and returned as an eagle *See* DEATH & EAGLE & PATH & SOCIETAL ASPECT & UROBORUS & VERTICAL STICK +19a USA, ARAPAHO \DOPt

• The eagle feathers medicine men used in their rituals represented the "heaven of the sun" +18a USA, MANDAN INDIANS \RAUt

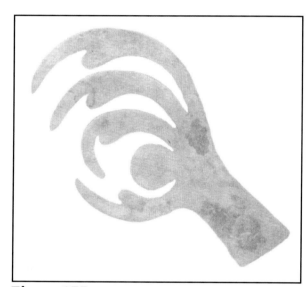

Figure 155

**See The Following Entries in Section Three
For Some Related Metaphors and Concepts**

- *condor*
- *eagle*
- *falcon*
- *feathered*
- *Garuda bird*
- *griffin*
- *hawk*
- *sandals winged*
- *sparrow hawk*
- *vulture*
- *winged*

Society as at the Axis Mundi

art *The letter* ***R*** *of the Snake Ring Template.* Originally a language to the sun, consisting of symbols, figures, rituals and colors, created by Ice Age tool-makers to correct a period of extreme climatic chaos and starvation. *Ref* CHAOS IN NATURE, FERTILITY, REGENERATION, SEASON

• In the Plains Indians' sun Dance they pray to the "man above" to give more light for vegetation, for their stock and for themselves, pleading that "this lodge be the painting that brings prosperity" *See* FAUNA & FLORA & HOUSE & RITUAL & SUN +19a USA, ARAPAHO \DOPt

• Starting about 35,000 years ago the glaciers that almost buried the Alps, Pyrenees, and Dordogne mountains melted, causing the greatest floods in geological history. The waters from the melting glaciers rushed through the caves, leaving clay which was drawn on while still wet *See* CAVE & FLOOD -350b \BRFt \BULt

• An engraving of a bull on glacial clay has a painted arrow through its chest and round motifs on its body *See* BULL & CELESTIAL & DEATH & ROUND MOTIF -350b FRANCE, CALBIERE \BRFp

• Preserved in the glacial clay on the floor of a cave around a raised prominence bearing the modeled clay bas-relief of a male bison, or bull, mounting a female bison are impressions of the feet of Ice Age people dancing on their heels in imitation of the hooves of beasts *See* BULL & CAVE & COW & DANCE & FOOT & MARRIAGE & PATH & SOCIETAL ASPECT -350b FRANCE, TUC D'AUDOBERT **Refer to** *Figure 68*

• Cave art continued for some 20,000 years; longer than the period from then until now. The speed of execution of the images made the activity a type of ceremony. Many pigments used for the colors were mixed of three or more ingredients obtained from several miles away. Some minerals were heated to provide color variations -350b \CAIt \NYTt \NATt \SCIt

• According to Claude Levi-Strauss, certain images presented together may have been an attempt to introduce initial order into the universe. The Tukano Indians of Colombia

believe that their art saves mankind from chaos. Taoist art is to induce harmony in nature \PHYt \RAWt \REJt

• An Ice Age ritual baton is inscribed with images of a snake, a salmon with a spur on its lip which appears when salmon spawn at springtime, and a male and female seal couple who mate at springtime [**Note:** signs of the springtime regeneration essential to the flora and fauna, and the serpent path along which it occurs] *See* BATON & CHAOS IN NATURE & PATH & SPRINGTIME -350b FRANCE, MONTGAUDIER *Figure 156*

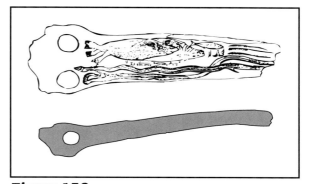

Figure 156

• The depths of the almost three hundred European art caves were holy places with no habitation, difficult to access and often with a series of red dots at the approach to the paintings. The dots and concentric circles were a common motif in the caves themselves *See* CAVE & RED & RING/ROUND MOTIF IN SEQUENCE -350b \LAUt \RAUt \NATp \WHJt \BRFt \SCOt

• Leaping bulls are painted on the ceilings of the French cave of Lascaux, France, high from the ground where it was difficult for the artists to reach. Charging and dying bulls are also on the ceiling of the Spanish Ice Age cave of Altamira *See* BULL & CELESTIAL & ROUND MOTIF & SACRIFICE ANIMAL -350b \BRFp \CAAt \NATp \CONt

• In the Ice Age cave of Motespan in France a clay figure of a headless bear had been dealt sharp blows; a bear's skull was found on the floor between its paws. A painting in the Ice Age cave of Trois Freres in France depicts men dancing around bears which have been killed

or decapitated *See* BEAR & DANCE & HEAD & SACRIFICE ANIMAL -350b FRANCE \CAIt \MUNt

• Female Venus figures appeared in Ice Age art 29,000 to 20,000 years ago in a zone from western France to the Ural mountains, following a period of extreme starvation and malnutrition evidenced in the dental remains of human fossils. Many of these figures, such as the Venus of Willendorf, are faceless and have emphasized pubics *See* BABY BOY & CHAOS IN NATURE & FERTILITY & GODDESSES & HAT/HEADRESS & MARRIAGE -350b AUSTRIA, WILLENDORF \SMJt *Figure* 157

Figure 157

• Women at the entrances to the deep caves often had parted legs and emphasized pubics. These Venus figures are acknowledged to be fertility symbols; but scholars are puzzled at their purpose since the last thing needed was more mouths to feed. Mircea Eliade believed that there was a connection between these Venus figures and the moon *See* CAVE & GODDESSES & MOON & REGENERATION & TRINITY -350b \SMJt \NWSt \ELIt \RAUt

• Many female genital symbols are on Ice Age blocks and slabs *See* REGENERATION & VAGINA -350b \BRFt \LEXt

• An upper-paleolithic monolith in Siberia was carved with a rayed sun-face, a bifid on its forehead, and decorated with serpents and series of round signs *See* PATH & ROUND MOTIF IN SEQUENCE & SUN YOUNG & TRINITY & VERTICAL LINE SHAPE -100a RUSSIA, SIBERIA *Figure* 158

Figure 158

• An Ice Age cave painting depicts three figures: the one on the right is a phallic anthropomorphic male bison with a symbol emanating from its nose. [**Note:** the symbol from the nose representing the breath, or soul, as it passes via a phallus to a vagina form on the engraved bone from La Madeleine]. He approaches the rear of a composite female figure depicted with the head of a female bison and the rump of a deer; on the left is a leaping deer resulting from this union, with a series of dots on its body and front hoofs represented as human hands *See* BULL & COW & DEER & HAND RAISED & HEAD & LEAP-UP & MARRIAGE & PHALLUS & ROUND MOTIF IN SEQUENCE & SOUL & VAGINA -350b FRANCE, TROIS FRERES *Figure* 159 *Figure* 160

• The world temperature underwent a period of warming after the Ice Age art began. After 9,000 B.C. when more rain fell and the climate finally became comparable to the present climate, men abandoned the art caves to decorate and worship in sacred houses -350b \SCOt \NWSt \SANt \NATp \MIDt

Figure 159

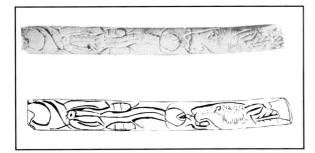

Figure 160

society as at the axis mundi *The letter R of the Snake Ring Template.* Symbolic designation of a society as located in the vertical segment of the serpent path which encloses the mythic mountain at the western horizon waters, the "center of the world", where each new sun of the successor season is born. *Ref* HOLE, HOUSE, MONOLITH, MOTHER GODDESS, MOUNTAIN, PYRAMID, SERPENT ENTWINED, SOCIETAL ASPECT, TREE, VERTICAL LINE/ SHAPE.

• The Desana people settled where the mythic staff "a shaft of sunlight" casts no shadow, at the central point where the sky meets the earth *See* AXIS MUNDI & PATH & SUN OLD & VERTICAL LINE/ SHAPE/ STICK & AXIS MUNDI +19a COLOMBIA, TUKANO \AVDt

• Most scholars believe the languages of Europe are variants of a single language that spread together with agriculture from the area of present Turkey. At the time they emanated, the first true cities in the world appeared in Turkey, with shrine rooms containing images of raised hand and ring motifs, bulls, felines, raptors, mother goddesses, and with large pilasters covered with serpent patterns (virtually identical to the metaphors of the Snake Ring) *See* AGRICULTURE & HOUSE & LETTERS & SNAKE & SPEECH & SOCIETAL ASPECT & TRANSCULTURAL SIMILARITY -80b TURKEY, ANATOLIA \SMKp \NYTp \ARCt

• The first culture centers in the New World contained images of raised hands, ring motifs, serpents, felines, and many deities, myths, rituals, and calendrical notations that spread throughout Mesoamerica. These appeared without precedent in such sites as San Lorenzo and La Venta, where a large stone-clad artificial mountain was its central focus *See* FELINE & GODDESSES & GODS & MOUNTAIN & SNAKE & STONE & TRANSCULTURAL SIMILARITY -15b MEXICO, OLMEC \MUTt \COEp

• The city of Larsa was the "home" at the junction between heaven and earth *See* HORIZON -35b IRAQ \ELIt

• Each major city was said to be at the sacred location where the mountain emerged from the primordial waters *See* CHAOS IN NATURE & FLOOD -30b EGYPT \EDUt

• Mount Olympus, the legendary abode of the sun gods, was in Thessaly, Crete, Carpathos Island, and Turkey *See* CAVE & GODDESSES & SUN OLD/ YOUNG & TRINITY -20b GREEK \WEBt

• Mount Meru is at the "center of the world" -19b INDIA, HINDU \ELIt

• The Ka'aba meteorite is the "center of the world" *See* STONE (MOUNTAIN) +5 SAUDI, MUSLIM \ELIt

• Calvary was the sacred hill at the "center of the world" *See* MOUND & MOUNTAIN 0b ITALY, CHRISTIAN \ELIt

• Images of serpents were placed over the

doorknobs and portals of the cities *See* HOUSES & PATH -19b IRAQ, ACCADIAN \MUNt

• Moses, who was referred to as "the rod", parted the Red Sea in the Exodus. The Hebrews went through to God's own mountain in the land of Canaan *See* ABYSS & DEMYTHOLIZATION & GOD & MOUNTAIN & VERTICAL LINE/ SHAPE & WATER -10b ISRAEL, JEWISH \ENDt

• In both Jewish and Islamic tradition, Mt. Moriah in Jerusalem is the Center or Navel of the World. On its flattened top was built the First and Second Temples, and now holds the Dome of the Rock. **[Note:** In *house* of Section Two the sacredness of mountain caves and of temples on tops of pyramids, mountains and mounds] *See* ABYSS & HOUSE & MOUNTAIN & PYRAMID & STONE & TRANSCULTURAL SIMILARITY - 10b ISRAEL, JEWISH \ENDt

• Official buildings had reliefs of pumas and serpents on the doorways *See* FELINE & HOUSE & PATH +14a PERU, INCA \STHt

• A nail holds the sacred mountain at Tidar, called "the mountain of the nail", fixed to the sea *See* BLADE & VERTICAL STICK & BLADE +5 JAVA \EXQt

• Natives refer to their island as the "center of the world" *See* VOLCANOES & WATER & WEST ORIENTATION +8a EASTER ISLAND \HEWt

• The Black hills are the "center of the world" +18 USA, SIOUX \BRPt

See The Following Entries in Section Three
For Some Related Metaphors and Concepts

- *agriculture*
- *alchemy*
- *alcoholic beverages*
- *animal worship*
- *animism*
- *astrology*
- *astronomy*
- *behaviorism*
- *chief*
- *communication*
- *cosmogony*
- *creation*
- *crown*
- *devil worship*
- *drink alcoholic*
- *drug*
- *effigy*
- *ethics*
- *fairy tale*
- *family of man*
- *funeral*
- *game board*
- *game children*
- *garment or clothing*
- *government*
- *hallucinogen*
- *hat or headdress*
- *head flattening*
- *horoscope*
- *hypnosis*
- *image*
- *infant mentality*
- *initiation rite*
- *jewelry*
- *justice*
- *king*
- *law*
- *letters*
- *machine*
- *magic*
- *mask*
- *metaphor*
- *Minstrel*
- *moon*
- *morality*
- *myth*
- *nudity*
- *occult*
- *orientation*
- *personification*
- *playing cards*
- *power*
- *precinct*
- *priest*
- *psychology child*
- *psychology contemporary problems*
- *psychology quantity*
- *religions contemporary*
- *religion primordial*
- *rite*
- *rite of passage*
- *ritual*
- *sacredness of life*
- *secret*
- *shaman*
- *speech*
- *string game*
- *superstition*
- *tarot pack*
- *tattoo*
- *theater*
- *throne*
- *tool-making*
- *toys*
- *trance*
- *transcultural similarity*
- *verb*
- *writing*

Ring Motif

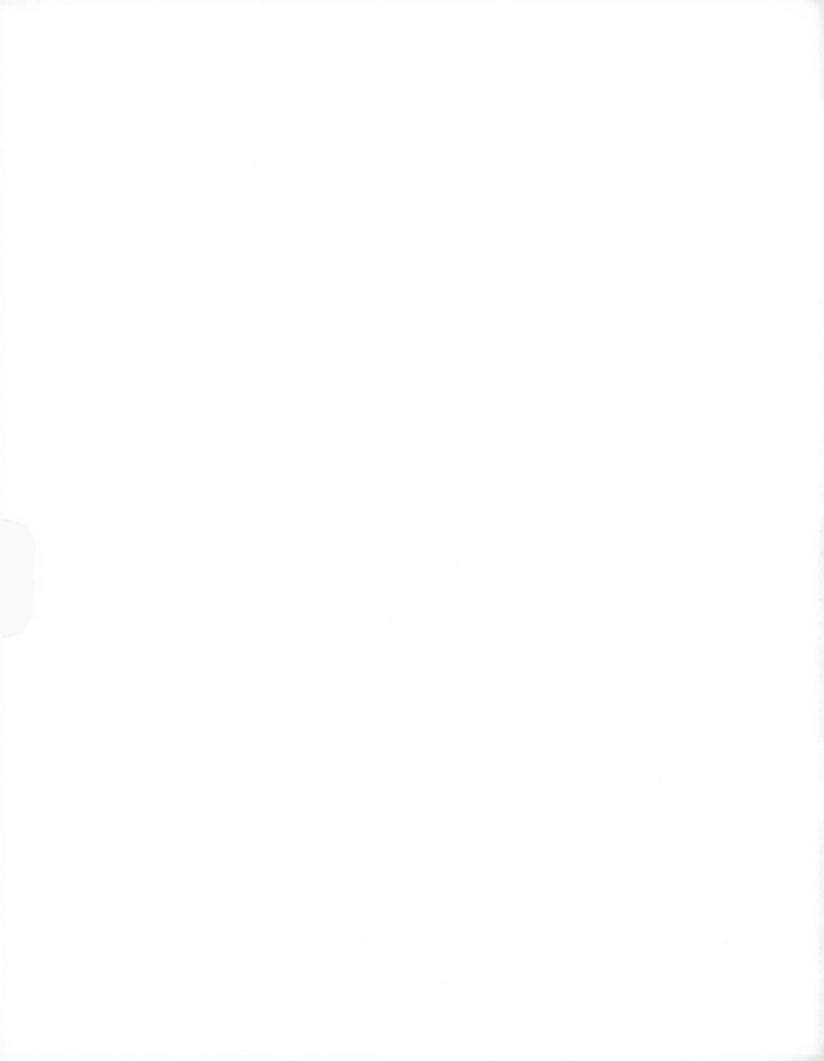

sun *The letter S of the Snake Ring Template. The luminous celestial body from which the earth receives light and heat.* The central focus of terminal Ice Age art and ritual, and of the religions which followed. Its personifications corresponded to the seasonal variations. *Ref* DEMYTHOLIZATION, FERTILITY, METAPHOR, RING/ ROUND MOTIF, SOUL, SUN OLD/ YOUNG, TRINITY.

ring motif *The letter S of the Snake Ring Template.* A metaphor for the sun and also for its path around the cosmos in the uroborus. *Ref* JEWELRY, MARRIAGE, PATH, ROUND MOTIF, SOCIETAL ASPECT.

• At the grave of a man in the Ice Age cave of Breno in Czechoslovakia there was a stone disk with a large hole in its center, which has been interpreted as a solar disk *See* CAVE & DEATH & REGENERATION & WHEEL -350b CZECHOSLOVAKIA, BRENO \MAQt

• A bas relief displays a ring motif painted on the stomach of a mother goddess figure who is giving birth *See* BABY BOY & MOTHER GODDESS & REGENERATION -70b TURKEY, CATAL HUYUK \REAt *Figure 161*

Figure 161

• The circle of the carved wood snake ring placed above the altar in their Sun Dance ceremony represents the sun and the entire

cosmos *See* ALTAR & SUN & UROBORUS & WHEEL +18a USA, ARAPAHO \AVDt
Refer to *Figure 76*

• A carved stone disk from the floor of a ceremonial ball-court depicts the ring motif in series contained within a larger ring motif *See* GAME SPORT & PATH & RING MOTIF IN SEQUENCE +3b MEXICO, MAYAN *Figure 162*

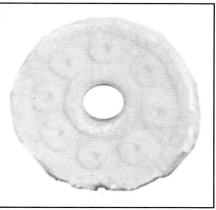

Figure 162

• An early Christian cross has entwined serpents up its vertical member with a series of children's heads within its coils, culminating at its top with a raised hand within a rayed circle motif *See* BABY BOY & CROSS EAST & DEMYTHOLIZATION & HAND RAISED & PATH & RAYED MOTIF & REGENERATION & SERPENT ENTWINED +9a IRELAND, CHRISTIAN
Refer to *Figure 142*

• The sun is represented as a ring motif over Cortez' shoulder in a painting secretly sent to the Emperor Montezuma depicting Fernando Cortez when he arrived to begin his conquest +15a MEXICO, AZTEC *Figure 163*

• Champollion began his interpretation of the Rosetta stone, which led to the decipherment of Egyptian hieroglyphics, with the discovery that the ring motif represented the sun god **Ra** +18a EGYPT \WESt

• The goddess **Nut** was often painted on or in sarcophagi with a series of ring motifs along her body representing the sun which entered her mouth in the underworld at sunset and was born from her womb at daybreak
See DEATH & MOTHER GODDESS & PATH &

REGENERATION & RING MOTIF IN SEQUENCE & SOCIETAL ASPECT -30b EGYPT \BRAp

Figure 163

• In parts of Africa where sun worship still exists, cave engravings of concentric rings represent the sun *See* RAYED MOTIF & SUN +19a ZIMBABWE \LARt *Figure* 164

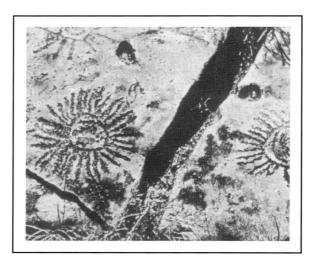

Figure 164

• A carved stella depicts the sun god, within a radiant ring motif, in the open maw of the celestial feathered serpent. Below him stands a youth wearing the ball players' yoke carved in the form of a feline, as he holds upwards a heart symbolizing his sacrifice to the sun on the ball-court *See* FELINE & GAME SPORT & PATH & RAYED MOTIF & SACRIFICE HUMAN & STELLA & SUN YOUNG & TRINITY & WAR +6a GUATEMALA, MAYAN *Figure* 165

• Descendants of a people conquered by the Aztecs still wear palm leaves woven into the shape of a ring to represent the sun in their ceremonial dances *See* DANCE & SUN +19a MEXICO, OTOMI \AVDt

Figure 165

• Paintings made of yarn of different colors impressed in wax or honey are traditional among certain Mexican Indians. In one of these a deer rises to a double-headed snake in the sky, above a house with a radiant ring motif sun over its doorway where a woman sits *See* DEER & HOUSE & LEAP-UP & MOTHER GODDESS & RAYED

MOTIF & SERPENT ENTWINED & THREAD +19a
MEXICO, HUICHOL \NASt *Figure 166*

Figure 166

Figure 167

• Priests in India, Sri Lanka, and the Maldives, identify ring motifs in old paintings and carved into ancient stones as sun symbols *See* DEMYTHOLIZATION & SUN -19b \HEVt

• Carved at the top of a pointed stele from Carthage is a ring motif sun joined with the moon. Symbols of the harvest are above a child who is standing on the gable of a house holding a thrysus and a wreath *See* BABY BOY & FERTILITY & HOUSE & MARRIAGE & MOON & PINE-CONE & REGENERATION & STAFF & STELE & WREATH -15b TUNIS, PHOENICIAN *Figure 167*

• A prominent petroglyph among the thousands of rock figures at the site called Toro Muerto, "dead bull", depicts a snake with a series of ring motifs along its body. The sun is a rayed ring motif between two llamas, one lean and one fat, representing the change in seasons *See* BULL & DEATH & FAUNA & PATH & RAYED MOTIF & RING MOTIF IN SEQUENCE & SEASON & SNAKE & STONE (MOUNTAIN) +8a PERU, HAURI \COSt *Figure 168*

• In the wall paintings of their sunken kivas, Southwest Indians represent the sun as a rayed ring motif *See* ART & HOUSE & RAYED MOTIF & UNDERWORLD +18a USA, HOPI \BOWp

Figure 168

**See The Following Entries in Section Three
For Some Related Metaphors and Concepts**

- *armadillo*
- *aureole*
- *avatar*
- *bead*
- *celestial
  observation*
- *chain*
- *cross circled*
- *crystal*
- *deities: numerous*
- *diamond*
- *disk*
- *earring*
- *foot*
- *garland*
- *God*
- *gods*
- *gold*
- *halo*
- *head*
- *heart human*
- *light*
- *lozenge*
- *man*

- *mica*
- *mirror*
- *necklace*
- *orb*
- *psychology
  contemporary*
- *radiance*
- *rayed motif*
- *ring motif*
- *ring motif in
  sequence*
- *round motif*
- *round motif in
  sequence*
- *Rosary*
- *ruler*
- *saint*
- *star motif*
- *sun old*
- *theogony*
- *torque*
- *yellow*
- *youth and old
  man*

Horse

horse *The letter T of the Snake Ring Template.* A metaphor for the speed of travel required for the sun to apparently traverse the underworld and the sky in one day. *Ref* CARRIER.

Figure 169

• A panorama carved in relief in the wall of an Ice Age shelter oriented east-west depicts a group of horses running in the eastward direction from a large round horned face at the wall's western extremity. One of the horses carries a ring motif on its back *See* CARRIER & CAVE & EAST ORIENTATION & HUSK & PATH & RING MOTIF & TRINITY & WAR -350b FRANCE, CAP BLANC \DORp

• The painted lower level of an Ice Age cave wall depicts running horses surrounded by black stenciled raised hand signs *See* BLACK & CARRIER & CAVE & HAND RAISED -350b FRANCE, PECH MERLE \DORp

• A golden horse-cart from a ceremonial burial in a bog which was a lake at the time, carries a large sun disk *See* FUNERAL & GOLD & REGENERATION & SOCIETAL ASPECT & WATER -14a DENMARK, CELTIC \ARCp

• A Scythian burial preserved in the frozen tundra contained fully tacked and ceremonially decorated war horses *See* CARRIER & DEATH & REGENERATION & UNDERWORLD -5a RUSSIA, PAZYRYK \BRHt

• An early Christian cross depicts an elderly man in a conical hat pointing with his hand and with a crozier to a feline with a ring motif on its rump who snarls at swine-like demons. Below this, a youth runs away carrying a pack on his back. The reverse of the cross, shown on the right, depicts a pattern of entwined bands above a youth on a horse departing from a house-top *See* BABY BOY & CARRIER & CONE & CROSS EAST/ WEST & CROZIER & DEMYTHOLIZATION & FELINE & GUILLOCHE & HERO & HOUSE & LEAP-UP & PATH & PIG & RING MOTIF & TRINITY & UNDERWORLD & WAR +4b IRELAND, CHRISTIAN *Figure 169*

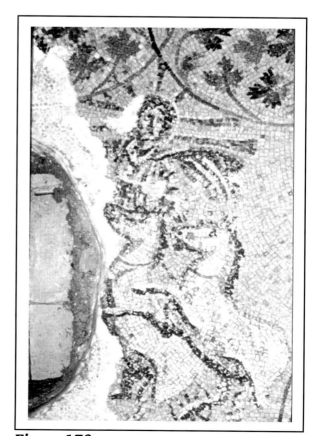

Figure 170

• The earliest mosaic of Jesus depicts Him as **Helios** in a chariot, rising to the sky *See* DEMYTHOLIZATION & HORSE & PATH & SUN YOUNG +2a ITALY, CHRISTIAN \BIBt *Figure 170*

**See The Following Entries in Section Three
For Some Related Metaphors and Concepts**

- *ass*
- *centaur*
- *chariot*
- *steed*

SECTION THREE

*The Encyclopedia
of Metaphors and Concepts
Associated with
The Snake Ring Story*

abortion *The letter I of the Snake Ring Template.* A perceived dangerous metaphor to the mother goddess not to give birth to the new sun or mother goddess which she carries. *Ref* BABY BOY/ GIRL, BIRTH, CHAOS IN NATURE, ETHICS, MENSTRUATION, MOTHER GODDESS, PREJUDICE, REGENERATION, SOCIETAL ASPECT.

abyss *The letter G of the Snake Ring Template. Ref* HOLE.

• A snake in relief is entering into a hole on the columnar body of a Canaanite incense burner *See* COLUMN & INCENSE & PATH & SNAKE -15b ISRAEL, CANAANITE *Figure 171*

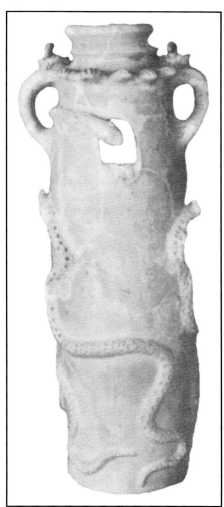

Figure 171

• **Ememqut**, the hero-son of **Big Raven**, went down a hole into an underground house; where he found and vanquished **Triton-man**, a demi-god of the sea *See* BIRD & HERO & HOUSE & TRINITY & UNDERWORLD & WAR & WATER +19a RUSSIA, KORYAK \CAIt

acorn *The letter E of the Snake Ring Template.* A metaphor for regeneration of the sun along the tree path into the western horizon. The acorn descending to the earth brings forth new birth. *Ref* BABY BOY, DESCENDING MOTIF, PINE-CONE, SUN YOUNG, TREE.

• In a region of Israel noted for its hot baths, the excavated floor mosaic of the Greco-Roman synagogue Beth Alpha, "house of the bull", depicts lion cubs devouring acorns at each side of the synagogue's ark. **[Note:** The young sun god **Apollo's** name means "from the mouth of the lion]**. The ark is shown as a house model, with a lamp hanging from its peak and marine birds treading on its steep pediment. At the opposite side of the floor, a mature lion with a sprig of a plant at hand confronts a bull **[Note:** The feline guardian-carrier of the new sun along its underworld path, from the house of the sun god's birth in the western horizon to its conflict in the underworld to, ultimately, its ascent at the eastern horizon, ages from infancy to maturity just as the young sun does along this path]**. In the center of the floor, the mosaic depicts signs of the zodiac surrounding **Helios**, the young sun god, who is ascending to the sky in his horse-drawn chariot *See* ART & BULL & CARRIER & CHARIOT & FELINE & FERTILITY & FIRE & HORSE & HOUSE MODEL & MARINE BIRD & PATH & SUN YOUNG & WAR & WATER & ZODIAC *Figure 172*

agriculture **1.** *The letter I of the Snake Ring Template :* FLORA. **2.** *The letter R of the Snake Ring Template.* A metaphor for the path of regeneration of the sun in the western horizon. The plow penetrates the earth; seeds follow, which mature in the underworld into new birth. *Ref* BABY BOY, BLADE, SOCIETY AS AT THE AXIS MUNDI & SUN YOUNG.

Figure 172

alchemy *The letter* **R** *of the Snake Ring Template. The pseudo-science of transforming base metals into gold.* A metaphor for the birth of the new sun in the underworld segment of the entwined serpent path. *Ref* GOLD, UNDERWORLD.

• The transformation of base metals represented redemption of the soul *See* FIRE & REGENERATION & SOCIETAL ASPECT & SOUL -3a GREEK \ARCt

• The symbol for alchemy was the uroborus, a snake apparently eating its tail *See* UROBORUS -20b GREEK \JUPt

• The production of metals was considered a birth from the underworld *See* BABY BOY -19b IRAQ, ASSYRIAN \HITt

• The Pope issued a bulletin forbidding the practice of Chemistry *See* DEMYTHOLIZATION & SCIENCE +3a ITALY, CHRISTIAN \ARCt

alcoholic beverages *The letter* **R** *of the Snake Ring Template. Ref* HALLUCINOGEN.

alligator *The letter* **A** *of the Snake Ring Template Ref* CROCODILE.

altar *The letter* **E** *of the Snake Ring Template.* riginally, a metaphor for the vertical serpent path of the virile old sun, from the sky to the underworld mountainhouse of the western horizon. *Ref* VERTICAL LINE/ SHAPE, WEST ORIENTATION.

• An illustration from the Fejevary-Mayer codex depicts a worshipper offering incense and a smoking pipe at a temple's altar, where there are flames and vertical entwined serpents at its top *See* FIRE & HOUSE & INCENSE & PATH & SMOKE & SERPENT ENTWINED & SOCIETAL ASPECT & TEMPLE +13b MEXICO, AZTEC *See* *Figure* 173

Figure 173

• Altars with bulls horns at their top were in the oldest true city known to man *See* BULL & BULL'S HORN & DEATH & PATH & REGENERATION & SOCIETY AS AT THE AXIS MUNDI -70a TURKEY, CATAL HUYUK *Figure* 174

• The top of the altar in Solomon's Temple was called "the Mountain of God"; its bottom, "the Bosom of Earth". Stone bull's horns were carved at each corner of its top. A snake was carved into its side, judged by the altar in the illustration, which is believed to be a duplicate of the atlar at Solomon's Temple, excavated at the Temple of

Beersheba *See* BULL & BULL'S HORN & DEATH & PATH & SOCIETY AS AT THE AXIS MUNDI   -7a JEWISH \ENDt *Figure 175*

• On top of the great altar of the sun god **Zeus** at the ancient Olympic Games, a mound was formed of the ashes of sacrificed bulls mixed with water from the nearby Alpheios river *See* DEATH & GAME SPORT & MOUND & PATH & REGENERATION & SACRIFICE ANIMAL & SOCIETY AS AT THE AXIS MUNDI & SUN OLD & WATER +1a GREEK, OLYMPUS \SWBp

Figure 174

Figure 175

• In a scene of sacrifice from the wall of the Temple of the Warriors, shown in a line drawing, the sacrificial altar is depicted along the body of the feathered serpent *See* HERO & PATH & SACRIFICE HUMAN +7a MEXICO, CHICHEN ITZA **Refer to** *Figure 339*

• The altars of the mountain-top ceremonial center, Machu Picchu, symbolized the sky, earth, and underworld bound together by the serpent Amaru, including the one at its top called "the Hitching Post of the sun", and the one inside a cave below one of its buildings, which were built of massive fitted stones *See* CAVE & MOUNTAIN & PATH & STONE & SOCIETY AS AT THE AXIS MUNDI & SUN OLD   +14a PERU, INCA \THTt *Figure 176*

• The Altar of the Dead is placed on the roof of the shrine house, where the worshippers dance. They move in the direction of the sun, crying "hotter, hotter" *See* DEATH & HOUSE & PATH & REGENERATION & SUN OLD/ YOUNG & UNDERWORLD +19a MALI, DOGON \GRKt

Figure 176

• At the culmination of the Christmas mass, the Pope circles the altar seven times, then kisses the altar as bells ring out *See* BABY BOY & LEVELS CELESTIAL & MARRIAGE & PRIEST 0b ITALY, CHRISTIAN \WESt

ancestor worship *The letter R of the Snake Ring Template.* Reverence for one's ancestors as metaphors for the old sun and the mother goddess, as we are metaphors for their children. *Ref* HAND RAISED, GODDESSES, SOCIETAL ASPECT, SUN OLD/ YOUNG.

anchor *The letter F of the Snake Ring Template. Ref* BOAT, CROSS WEST, WATER.

androgynous *The letter H of the Snake Ring Template. Ref* HERMAPHRODITE.

angel *The letter I of the Snake Ring Template.* A metaphor for the new born sun in the western horizon who will ascend to the sky in the eastern horizon. *Ref* BABY BOY. CHERUB, MOTHER GODDESS, TRINITY.

animal worship *The letter R of the Snake Ring Template.* Reverence for the animals which serve as metaphors for the sun within the Snake Ring path. *Ref* ART, BIRD, BULL, CARRIER, CROCODILE, DEER, ELEPHANT, FELINE, SNAKE.

animism *The letter R of the Snake Ring Template. Ascribes a soul to all natural objects.* An aspect of regarding a society as at the axis mundi, where all elements in the society's environment are permeated by the solar soul as it transfers along this axis mundi from the old sun to the soon to be reborn sun. *Ref* SOCIETY AS AT THE AXIS MUNDI, SOUL, STONE, TREE, TRINITY.

antelope *The letter O of the Snake Ring Illustration. Ref* DEER.

anvil *The letter D of the Snake Ring Template.* An element in the alchemical transformation of metals through the medium of fire. *Ref* ALCHEMY, BLACKSMITH, FIRE, TRINITY.

apple **1.** *The letter E of the Snake Ring Template.* A metaphor for the old sun at sunset along the vertical tree path into the western horizon. **2.** *The letter I of the Snake*

Ring Template. A metaphor for seasonal fertility. *Ref* FLORA, RED, ROUND MOTIF, TREE.

Aquarius *The letter F of the Snake Ring Template. The Water Bearer.* A metaphor for: **a**. The western horizon water. **b**.The flood waters resulting from the melting of the glaciers during the terminal Ice Age. *Ref* CHAOS IN NATURE, FLOOD, WATER, ZODIAC.

arch *The letter A of the Snake Ring Template.* A metaphor for the arching serpent path in the sky; the path of the old sun to its death, copulation and regeneration in the mountain-house of the western horizon. *Ref* DEATH, MARRIAGE, RAINBOW, REGENERATION, SOCIETY AS AT THE AXIS MUNDI, STONE.

• Concentric arches and serpent motifs are carved into many of the stones at the passage graves in Brittany *See* DEATH & HOUSE & REGENERATION & UNDERWORLD -45b FRANCE, GAVR'INIS \SMJp

• During present-day Mayan curing ceremonies, an arch is constructed over the entrance to the afflicted individual's room *See* HEALING & REGENERATION & SOCIETAL ASPECT +19a MEXICO, ZINACANTECO \VOGt

• The same arch is erected over the paths of newly married couples as over the paths of the deceased at funerals *See* FUNERAL, & MARRIAGE & SOCIETAL ASPECT & TRINITY +19a CHINA/ SWEDEN \ELIt

arch triumphal *The letter H of the Snake Ring Template.* An architectural metaphor for the departure from, and return to, the western horizon house at the axis mundi. *Ref* HOUSE, PROCESSION, SOCIETY AS AT THE AXIS MUNDI, STONE.

• A Mayan ceremonial arch has carved stone house models at each side of its center arch *See* ARCH & HOUSE & SOCIETY AS AT THE AXIS MUNDI +5b MEXICO, LABNA *Figure 177*

architecture *The letter H of the Snake Ring Template.* Design and symbols which impart a pleasing appearance and significance to a structure by associating it with the mountain-house of the western horizon waters. *Ref* ART, CAVE, COLUMN, FIRE, HOUSE, PYRAMID, SPIRE, SOCIETY AS AT THE AXIS MUNDI, STONE, WATER.

Figure 177

• The tomb of Zechariah was constructed in the form of a pyramid with columns below *See* COLUMN & DEATH & FUNERAL & PYRAMID & REGENERATION   -1a ISRAEL, MACABEES \ENDt

• Structures express a vision of the universe and man's place within it *See* SOCIETAL ASPECT +11a CHINA \WESt

• There were rock piles in many courtyards containing a cavern which was referred to as "the Mountain Home of the Immortals" *See* CAVE & MOUNTAIN & SOCIETAL ASPECT & TRINITY +11a CHINA \WESt

• The U. S. White House has pediments and scallop shells over its doorways and windows *See* CRUSTACEAN & PEDIMENT & RULER   +19a USA \TIMt

Aries *The letter* C *of the Snake Ring Template. The Ram. Ref* BULL, GOAT, ZODIAC.

arithmetic *The letters* K *&* P *of the Snake Ring Template. The art of computation by the use of positive real numbers. Ref* NUMBER.

• A carved relief from the wall of an Ice Age shelter depicts a faceless woman holding her left hand on her distended stomach; her right hand holds aloft a bull's horn inscribed with thirteen notches. Ice Age tally marks are the earliest evidence of counting *See* BABY BOY/ GIRL & BULL'S HORN & CAVE & LEVELS CELESTIAL & MOTHER GODDESS   -350b FRANCE, LAUSSEL \NYAt \ARCt
Refer to *Figure 43* SECTION TWO.

• The notched bones and batons found in terminal Ice Age caves were probably used for calendar counting [the word "tally" comes from the French word for "notch"] *See* BATON & TIME (CALENDAR) -350b FRANCE, LE PLACARD \NYAt *Figure 178*

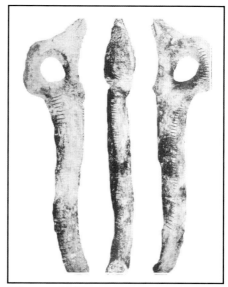

Figure 178

• An illustration in The Codex Vaticanus depicts thirteen steps through the seven layers of the sky and nine steps through the five layers of the underworld. The aged deity couple, parents of the gods, are in the 13th step *See* LEVELS CELESTIAL/ UNDERWORLD & MARRIAGE & PATH & REGENERATION & UROBORUS +13b MEXICO, AZTEC
Refer to *Figure 66* SECTION TWO.

• The god **Anu** was represented by the sacrificial heart of a bull in cuneiform script. Its pictograph was used for the number one *See* BULL & DEATH & LETTERS & REGENERATION -35b IRAQ, SUMERIAN \SANt

• Numbers are the keys to understanding myths *See* LEVELS CELESTIAL & UNDERWORLD +19a GIORGIO DI SANTILLANA \MCCt

• Integers appeared as ordered, not one-by-one *See* ART & CHAOS IN NATURE & LEVELS +19a JEAN PIAGET \PIBt

• Mathematics is the result of mysterious powers which no one understands *See* INFORMATION DESTROYED OR SECRET +19a MARSTON MORSE \NYTt

• The ibis-headed god of counting and writing, **Thoth**, is depicted in a coffin painting holding the "West" sign facing the sun god **Osiris** who is seated on a throne before a beheaded bull hanging head down from a staff. Statues of this same headless bull were at the west end of corridors in king Tutankhamun's tomb, with oars laying to the east direction on the floor before them. In the coffin painting, above the heads of the deity couple Osiris and **Isis,** a serpent emerges from a four-stepped underworld represented as eight cobras facing west and east *See* BULL & DEATH & LEVELS UNDERWORLD & MARINE BIRD & MOTHER GODDESS & PATH & REGENERATION & RULER & SNAKE & SOCIETAL ASPECT & STAIRS INFERNAL & SUN OLD & WATER & WEST ORIENTATION & WRITING -30b EGYPT \BAJt *Figure 179*
Refer also to *Figure 204*

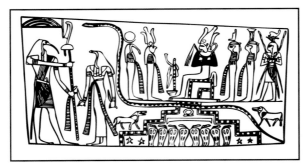

Figure 179

• The entire universe consists of the numbers and letters of the Hebrew alphabet -10b ISRAEL, JEWISH (KABALA) \OCTt

• The sun god **Indra** is the model for everything numbered or named. Numbers are associated with every line, junction and space in the uroborus-mandala *See* LETTERS & LEVELS & UROBORUS -19b INDIA, HINDU \MCCt

• The seven celestial and five underworld levels of the Mayan universe were a common idea throughout Mesoamerica. In the Mayan counting system, a shell-glyph represented the numerical zero [a metaphor for the horizon waters, where #1 of the celestial levels and #1 of the underworld levels meet] *See* CRUSTACEAN & LEVELS -6b MEXICO, MAYAN \MUTt *Figure 180*

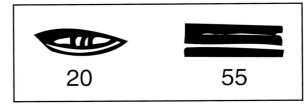

Figure 180

• Atlantis was an island surrounded by seven rings at the western horizon. The fallen sun god **Poseidon** mated with **Klito** there by surrounding her with "the numerate equivalent of marriage" *See* LEVELS CELESTIAL & MARRIAGE & SUN OLD & WATER & WEST ORIENTATION -4a GREEK, ATLANTIS \BREt

• Rosary beads (ending in the Cross) are used in counting the decades of prayers to the Virgin Mary, each group of prayers preceded by Our Father [God] *See* BEAD & CROSS WEST & GOD & MOTHER GODDESS & NUMBER & PATH & ROUND MOTIF IN SEQUENCE & SOCIETAL ASPECT & VIRGIN 0b CHRISTIAN \WEBp

• Scholars are puzzled by the quipus, colored strings with knots found in many graves. The knots have been deciphered as a numeric system [but why in burials?] Number seven appears most often of all the numbers *See* DEATH & LEVELS CELESTIAL & PATH & REGENERATION & ROPE +9b PERU, INCA \MASp

• The abacus has very ancient roots in the Far East, where it is still used for addition and subtraction. Beads above the horizontal bar are called "heaven" and the beads below the horizontal bar are called "earth" *See* AXIS MUNDI & BEAD & HORIZON & LEVELS CELESTIAL/ UNDERWORLD & RING MOTIF IN SEQUENCE +15a CHINA \DISp

• In the occultic universe there are seven planes of existence, of which the earth is the lowest *See* LEVELS CELESTIAL & OCCULT & TRANSCULTURAL SIMILARITY +19a \OCTt

• The 13th card generally depicts a skeleton entitled Death. This card does not foretell an end but rather a change *See* DEATH & GAME BOARD & REGENERATION \TL1t
Figure 181

ark *The letter F of the Snake Ring Template. A retained memory of the Ice Age chaos in nature and the flood. Ref* BOAT, CHAOS IN NATURE, FLOOD.

arm *The letter O of the Snake Ring Template. Ref* HANDS DOWN AND UP.

armadillo *The letter S of the Snake Ring Template. A nocturnal animal that curls itself into a ball. Ref* UROBORUS.

arrow *The letter E of the Snake Ring Template.* A metaphor for the sun's path from the eastern horizon to its penetration of the western horizon. *Ref* ARCH, BLADE, CELESTIAL, PATH.

art *The letter R of the Snake Ring Template. See* SECTION TWO.

ascension *The letter O of the Snake Ring Template. Ref* LEAP-UP.

ashlar *The letter G of the Snake Ring Template. A squared stone. : Ref* STONE.

Figure 181

astrology 1. *The letter I of the Snake Ring Template.* As the characteristics of a new sun, different for each season, are determined by the particular coil of the entwined serpent on the day of its birth, so it is with people. *Ref* BABY BOY/ GIRL, REGENERATION, SOCIETAL ASPECT **2.** *The letter R of the Snake Ring Template.* A practice of predicting human characteristics or experiences determined by the day of one's birth in the western horizon house as though within a specific coil of the entwined serpent path. *Ref* DEMYTHOLIZATION, HOUSE, HOROSCOPE, SERPENT ENTWINED, SOCIETAL ASPECT.

• A papyrus text relates that those honored by the sun god **Re** have a birthday when Re is born and enter into the serpent known as "Life of the Gods" *See* BIRTH & SOCIETAL ASPECT & SUN YOUNG -30b EGYPT \MUNt

• The astrology book *Venus and Mars* by Maternus was forbidden by the Church *See* DEMYTHOLYZATION +3a ITALY, CHRISTIAN \MAWt

• One's will is ruled by the position of the sun at the time of one's birth *See* BIRTH & SUN YOUNG +19a IRAQ, ZODIAC \CRUt

astronomy *The letter R of the Snake Ring Illustration.* *Ref* CELESTIAL OBSERVATIONS.

aureole *The letter S of the Snake Ring Illustration.* *Ref* HALO.

avatar *The letter S of the Snake Ring Illustration. Incarnation of a deity.* *Ref* CARRIER, PATH, REGENERATION.

axis mundi *The letter E of the Snake Ring Template.* *Ref* WORLD AXIS.

baby boy *The letter I of the Snake Ring Template.* The newborn sun who was conceived by the old sun and the mother goddess in the mountain-house at the western horizon waters. *Ref* HOUSE, MARRIAGE, MOTHER GODDESS, SEASON, SOCIETAL ASPECT, SUN OLD/ YOUNG, WATER, WEST ORIENTATION.

• A religious hymn relates that the sun god **Amon** gave birth to the sun god **Re** *See* REGENERATION & SUN OLD/ YOUNG -13a EGYPT \PRIt

• **Huitzlipochtli**, the young sun god, was born to the great water goddess in the west *See* MOTHER GODDESS & SUN YOUNG & WATER & WEST ORIENTATION+13b MEXICO, AZTEC \CAMt

• A great fish rubbed against a woman in the surf causing her to give birth to a son. Her son was carried by the great fish to the east, where he became the sun *See* MARINE CARRIER & SUN YOUNG & WATER & WHALE +19a PAPUA \COTt

baby girl *The letter H of the Snake Ring Template.* A newborn mother goddess who was conceived by the old sun and the mother goddess in the mountain-house at the western horizon waters in the western horizon. *Ref* GODDESSES, HOUSE, MARRIAGE, SUN OLD, WATER, WEST ORIENTATION.

badger *The letter I of the Snake Ring Template. A burrowing mammal.* A metaphor for the regeneration of the sun in the western horizon underworld. *Ref* HOLE.

banking *The letter I of the Snake Ring Template. Ref* COMMERCE, MONEY.

baptism *The letter H of the Snake Ring Template. Ref* BABY BOY/ GIRL, SOCIETAL ASPECT, WATER.

basilisk *The letter A of the Snake Ring Template. Gr. A legendary reptile who can cause death. Ref* DEATH, DRAGON, PATH, SUN OLD.

bat *The letter H of the Snake Ring Template.* A metaphor for one of the old suns of the past seasons, remaining in the mountain-house [cave] of the western horizon after solar regeneration. *Ref* BIRD, CAVE, TRINITY.

bath *The letter F of the Snake Ring Template.* As a ritual, a metaphor for the sun god and/or mother goddess in the waters of the western horizon. *Ref* GODDESSES, HEALING, SOCIETAL ASPECT, SUN OLD/ YOUNG, WATER.

baton *The letter E of the Snake Ring Template. A short staff often with an orb or ring at the top.* A metaphor for the vertical segment of the sun's snake path at the horizon; possibly used to inspire the sun on its path. *Ref* HORIZON, PATH, RING/ ROUND MOTIF, STAFF, SUN OLD/ YOUNG.

• An Ice Age baton shaped as a phallus has fish engraved on its surface *See* MARRIAGE & PHALLUS & WATER -350b FRANCE, BRUNIQUEL \GIEp

• Ice Age batons were so abundant they were possibly used by every man. Their fragility and the fact that the only sign of wear was on the handles, suggest that the batons were used in dances and rituals rather than for utilitarian purposes -350b \GRJt

• A staff with a ring motif at its top and a twisting snake along its length with a sequence of round motifs along its body, was carved on a boulder beside a path descending to the water *See* ROUND MOTIF IN SEQUENCE & SNAKE & SOCIETY AS AT THE AXIS MUNDI -30b ISRAEL, HAR KA MI \BIBp

• At the right edge of the roll-out of a cylinder seal, the baton-like staff with a ring at its top symbolizes the gatepost to the house of the goddess **Innanna**. The ring is connected to the head of a celestial snake whose body coils seven times, associated with winged bull-horned deities whose hands terminate in scorpions *See* BULL & HOUSE & LEVELS CELESTIAL & MARRIAGE & MOTHER GODDESS & SCORPION & SNAKE & WINGED -23a IRAQ, ACCADIAN
Figure 182

Figure 182

• The carved stone sides of a trough-like vessel from the city of Warka (Uruk) depict lambs and calves, representing springtime fertility, emerging from the house of the goddess **Innanna** with its baton-like gateposts *See* FAUNA & SPRINGTIME & VESSEL -30b IRAQ, SUMERIAN *Figure* 183

Figure 183

• A ceremonial scepter once carried by the Chinese ruler, has a PI disk at the top of its

vertical segment. A scene inscribed at the bottom of the arm depicts a mound surrounded by water *See* MOUND & PATH & RING MOTIF & RULER & SOCIETY AS AT THE AXIS MUNDI -15b CHINA \RAWt

• The emperor Montezuma carried a staff with a ring motif at its top *See* RING MOTIF & RULER +13b MEXICO, AZTEC \HAIp

bead *The letter S of the Snake Ring Template.* *Ref* JEWELRY, ROUND MOTIF IN SEQUENCE.

bear *The letter C of the Snake Ring Template.* *Ref* BULL.

• Near a fire hearth at the west end of an Ice Age cave nine bears' skulls in a row were covered by stone slabs buried in the red earth. The cave named Drachenloch, "dragon's lair", high up on a mountain, also contained the ritual burial of a bear skull with a thigh-bone shoved through it *See* BEAR & BURIAL & CAVE & DEATH & DRAGON & FIRE & HEAD & LEVELS MOUNTAIN & PATH & UNDERWORLD & RED & REGENERATION & RITUAL & STONE & WEST ORIENTATION -350a SWITZERLAND, NEANDERTHAL \CAIp *Figure* 184

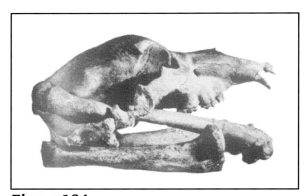

Figure 184

• An Ice Age engraved bone depicts a symbol emanating from the nose of a skeletal bear and entering into one end of a double-headed phallus, whose other end enters into a vulva-form *See* HEAD & MARRIAGE & PHALLUS & REGENERATION & SOUL -350b FRANCE, LA MADELEINE *Figure* 185

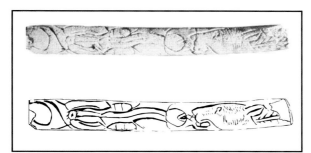

Figure 185

• A mosaic on the floor of a sixth century church depicts a youth fighting a bear with a sun-burst on its shoulder. The upper panel of this mosaic, not shown, depicts a lion defeating a bull. The ring sign of the sun-burst on the bear also designates the sun above a tree in this scene *See* BULL & DEMYTHOLIZATION & FELINE & HOUSE & PATH & RING MOTIF & SUN OLD & WAR +5a ISRAEL, CHRISTIAN *Figure 186*

Figure 186

• The bear symbolizes the clan's mythic ancestor *See* ANCESTOR WORSHIP +18a USA, WINNEBAGO \NABt

beaver *The letter I of the Snake Ring Template.* A metaphor for the sun born in the house beneath the western horizon waters. *Ref* BABY BOY.

• A beaver is depicted within the ceremonial houses with its paws raised. Its head is often surrounded by the rays of the sun *See* BABY BOY & HAND RAISED & RAYED MOTIF & SUN YOUNG +18a ALASKA, TLINGIT
Refer to *Figure 57* SECTION TWO.

bee *The letter I of the Snake Ring Template.* A metaphor for springtime fertility. *Ref* FLORA, SPRINGTIME.

beetle *The letter O of the Snake Ring Template.* A metaphor for the new sun rising from the waters of the eastern horizon. *Ref* LOTUS.

• Scarab beetles enter the lotus plant at night to eat the inside of the flower, and emerge at dawn when the petals open *See* EAST ORIENTATION & LOTUS & SUN YOUNG & WATER +19a \SMJt

• The scarab beetle and the beetle god **Khepri** represent the rising sun *See* SUN YOUNG -30b EGYPT \LARt \MUNt

behaviorism *The letter R of the Snake Ring Template.* The rituals that began culture during the terminal Ice Age, as efforts to avert extreme chaos in nature at the time, have been reinforced and perpetuated ever since by their apparent success. *Ref* CHAOS IN NATURE, PSYCHOLOGY CHILD, SOCIOBIOLOGY.

bell *The letter P of the Snake Ring Template.* *Ref* MUSIC.

bird 1. *The letter B of the Snake Ring Template.* 2. *The letter O of the Snake Ring Template.* See SECTION TWO.

birth *The letter I of the Snake Ring Template.* *Ref* BABY BOY/ GIRL, SOCIETAL ASPECT.

black *The letter K of the Snake Ring Template.* A metaphor for the underworld serpent path of the sun. *Ref* ART, DEATH, FELINE, LEVELS UNDERWORLD, NIGHT, UROBORUS.

• One of the earliest neolithic pots is decorated with a uroborus whose top half is painted white and its bottom half painted black *See* UNDERWORLD -45a CHINA, YANG-SHAO \MUNt

• Statues from Tutankhamun's tomb depict the ruler as the sun god **Osiris** carried on the back of a leopard with gold ibex horns at its forehead. The black paint of the leopard symbolizes the underworld *See* CARRIER & FELINE & IBEX & REGENERATION & RULER & SOCIETAL ASPECT -13a EGYPT \EDVt
Refer to *Figure 102* SECTION TWO.

• During circumcision rites, part of the initiates' bodies are painted black to represent the underworld *See* CIRCUMCISION & PUBERTY RITE & UNDERWORLD
+19a AUSTRALIA, WALBIRI \BRBp

blacksmith *The letter D of the Snake Ring Template. Ref* ANVIL.

Figure 187

blade 1. *The letter E of the Snake Ring Template.* A metaphor for the vertical segment of the snake path as it penetrates the western underworld. 2. *The letter D of the Snake Ring Template.* A metaphor for the death of the old sun within this path. *Ref* DEATH & SACRIFICE HUMAN, SUN OLD, VERTICAL LINE/ SHAPE.

• An Ice Age stone knife is carved with the image of an inverted bull inscribed with a snake. Dots connect the inverted bull to an antelope *See* ANTELOPE & BULL & DEATH & PATH

& REGENERATION & ROUND MOTIF IN SEQUENCE -150b CZECHOSLOVAKIA, PEKARNO \MAQp

• A knife associated with the shrine rooms of the oldest true city in the world has a handle formed of an entwined snake with a series of dots along the snake's body *See* HOUSE & PATH & ROUND MOTIF IN SEQUENCE & SERPENT ENTWINED -70b TURKEY, CATAL HUYUK
Figure 187

• Another knife, this one with traces of red pigment remaining on the blade, also has its handle in the form of entwined serpents. It was discovered at the bottom of a ceremonial cenote held sacred by Mayan, Toltec and Itza cultures *See* CENOTE & PATH & RED & SOCIETY AS AT THE AXIS MUNDI & TRANSCULTURAL SIMILARITY +7a MEXICO, CHICHEN ITZA
Figure 188

Figure 188

• The bronze scabbard of a sword is embossed with a frog in the mouth of a snake *See* HERO & FROG & PATH & SOCIETY AS AT THE AXIS MUNDI +8a NIGERIA, NOK \EYOp

• A chief's "sword", actually a staff, is pointed by subjects to heaven and then to earth as they pledge their loyalty. On its handle is a cut-out sun; on the staff itself is a seven coiled snake leading to a turtle *See* HERO & LEVELS CELESTIAL & PATH & RULER & SOCIETY AS AT THE AXIS MUNDI & TURTLE +19 a GHANA, ASHANTI \PAQp

blood *The letter I of the Snake Ring Template.* A metaphor, evidenced by the blood of virginal deities and of childbirth, for the passage of the solar soul through the mother goddess. *Ref* RED, SOUL, TRINITY.

• The symbol for water was also the symbol for sperm and conception *See* BIRTH & MARRIAGE & WATER -35b IRAQ, SUMERIAN \ELIt

• During the Bacchanalian women's mystery rite on the night of the winter solstice, nude women with snakes wound around their arms lashed at each other with knives. Their bleeding was the sun god within them. If a man stumbled on the rites he or an animal was sacrificed *See* CHRISTMASTIDE & DEAF & NIGHT & PATH & REGENERATION & SACRIFICE ANIMAL/ HUMAN & SNAKE & SUN OLD/ YOUNG -20b GREEK \DUSt

• Women are impure during their menstruation [loss of the solar soul] *See* PREJUDICE (ABORTION) & SOCIETAL ASPECT +19a BRAZIL \LETt

• During a woman's menstrual period she is a peril to the society *See* CHAOS IN NATURE & PREJUDICE (ABORTION) & SOCIETAL ASPECT +19a USA, YANA \KROt

• A woman is impure during her menstrual period; she must, at the conclusion, immerse herself in the mikvah, ritual bath, before her husband can approach her *See* MARRIAGE & PREJUDICE (ABORTION) & SOCIETAL ASPECT & WATER +19a ISRAEL, JEWISH \MIAt

• The joining of the great spiral serpent which envelopes the universe with its rainbow wife, animates the blood which passes through all male testes to create

semen *See* MARRIAGE & PATH & RAINBOW & SNAKE & SOCIETAL ASPECT & SPIRAL +19a HAITI, VOODOO \DATt

• According to present-day Maya, the soul existing in the blood of each person is transferred to the unborn embryo *See* MARRIAGE & PATH & SOCIETAL ASPECT & SOUL +19a MEXICO, ZINACANTECO \VOGt

• Red is a sacred color because it represents the blood from the joining of the sky god **Rangui Nui** with the earth goddess **Papa-tu-a-nuku** as they lie together *See* MARRIAGE & PATH & RED +19a NEW ZEALAND, MAORI \CAMt

boar *The letter C of the Snake Ring Template.* *Ref* BULL.

boat *The letter F of the Snake Ring Template.* A metaphor for the sun's path at the western horizon waters. *Ref* WATER.

• The sun enters the mountain of the west on its passage into the realm of death where it lands on a boat *See* DEATH & MOUNTAIN & SUN OLD & TRANSCULTURAL SIMILARITY & WATER & WEST ORIENTATION -30b EGYPT \ELHt

• The word "mni" that means "marriage" also has the meaning "to moor a boat" *See* MARRIAGE & WATER -30b EGYPT \PATt

• In death we join the sun at dusk on a boat in the west *See* DEATH & NIGHT & PATH & SOCIETAL ASPECT & SUN OLD -30b EGYPT \ARCt

• Dead are buried in a canoe at the center of the ritual house. The top ridgepole of the house is the path of the sun across the sky; the posts and walls of the house are the mountains at the edge of the world, and the house itself represents the center of the world *See* DEATH & HORIZON & HOUSE & MOUNTAIN & SOCIETY AS AT THE AXIS MUNDI & SOCIETAL ASPECT & WEST ORIENTATION & UNDERWORLD +19a COLOMBIA, TUKANO \HUGp **Refer to** *Figure 90* SECTION TWO.

body paint *The letter O of the Snake Ring Template.* Colors and symbols which designate the wearer as a metaphor for the regenerating suns or mother goddesses. *Ref* ART, RITUAL, SOCIETAL ASPECT.

• The skeleton of a youth was found in an Italian mountain-burial with a stone knife held in his hand. He wore a cap formed of strings of seashells hung with deers' teeth. A daub of yellow ochre was painted under the youth's chin, and his body was covered in red ochre. Batons inscribed with female figures were placed near his chest *See* CRUSTACEAN & BATON & DEER & HAT (CAP) & MARRIAGE & MOTHER GODDESS & PATH & RED & REGENERATION & RITUAL & UNDERWORLD & WAR & WATER & YELLOW (GOLD) -350b ITALY, ARENE CANDIDE \MAQt

• The yellow zig-zag lines painted on Sun Dancers' hands and feet symbolize the "serpent of the wheel" *See* DANCE & WHEEL & YELLOW & ZIG-ZAG MOTIF   +18a USA, ARAPAHO \DOPt

• A raised hand was painted on the warrior chief's chest *See* HAND RAISED & HERO & WAR +18a USA, MANDAN \BRBp

• A warrior's stiffened hair is formed into a horn, and painted with black rings. On his left cheek is painted a vertical snake, and on his right a black sun. *See* BLACK & BULL'S HORN & PATH & RING MOTIFS IN SEQUENCE & SUN OLD & TRINITY & WAR +18a USA, THOMPSON \BRBt

• Male children's feet are sometimes painted yellow at nighttime and the word "wang", king, is daubed on their forehead [**Note:** To assure their well-being in the hazardous nighttime journey] *See* PATH & RULER & SOCIETAL ASPECT & YELLOW   +19a CHINA \MUNt

• Designs of snakes, caves, rainbows, and spears are painted on men to assure the growth of plants for food *See* BLADE & BODY & CAVE & FERTILITY & PAINT & PATH & RAINBOW & REGENERATION & SOCIETAL ASPECT   +19a AUSTRALIA, WALBIRI \BRBt

bow *The letter E of the Snake Ring Template. Ref* ARROW, PATH, WAR.

bower *The letter H of the Snake Ring Template. A shelter or retreat.* A metaphor for the mountain-house of the western horizon in which the new sun, the bringer of fertility and its' apparent prosperity, is born. *Ref* FERTILITY, HOUSE, TREE.

branch *The letter E of the Snake Ring Template. Ref* TREE.

brass *The letter I of the Snake Ring Template. Ref* COPPER, SUN.

bronze *The letter I of the Snake Ring Template. Ref* COPPER, SUN.

bucentaur *The letter C of the Snake Ring Template. Gr. A fabulous monster, half bull, half man. Ref* BULL, TRINITY.

bucranium *The letter C of the Snake Ring Template. Gr. A skull of a bull. Ref* BULL, DEATH.

bull *The letter C of the Snake Ring Template.* See SECTION TWO.

bullroarer *The letter D of the Snake Ring Template. A hollow cone which emits a bleating or moaning animal sound when air passes through it, usually by swinging the instrument on a rope through the air.* A metaphor for the death of the virile old sun at the western horizon. *Ref* BULL, MUSIC, SUN OLD, TRINITY.

• Instruments resembling bullroarers were found in Ice Age caves *See* CAVE -350b RUSSIA \SMJt

• An aboriginal rock painting depicts a figure, crowned with the sun, who is apparently emanating from a swung bullroarer *See*

• The sound of the bullroarers used in the rituals of many African secret societies is the "voice of dead spirits." Bullroarers are also sounded when a notable of the village dies *See* BULL & DEATH & RITUAL & SOCIETAL ASPECT +19a KENYA, NANDI \PAQt

• During aboriginal circumcision rites, bullroarers are pressed on the wounds of the initiates and also hung on a high pole over the ceremony. An image of the bullroarer is painted on the initiate's chest, and a ring motif is painted on his back. **[Note:** The initiate symbolically suffers the trinitarian aspects of solar death and regeneration at the axis mundi. (See the trinitarian Ice Age painting in the Well at Lascaux, with its emasculated bull)**]** *See* CIRCUMCISION & REGENERATION & RING MOTIF & SOCIETY AS AT THE AXIS MUNDI +19a AUSTRALIA, ARNHEM *Figure* 189 **Refer also to** *Figure* 77 SECTION TWO.

Figure 189

• Bullroarers were known to have been used in the Greek initiation rites. It was reported that "bulls' voices roared" during the Greek ritual orgies *See* MARRIAGE & TRINITY -20b GREEK, ORPHIC \ELIt \CAAt

• An Anasazi bowl with a kill hole in its center shows a man using a bullroarer *See* OBJECTS RITUALLY BROKEN & VESSEL +6b USA, MIMBRES *Figure* 190

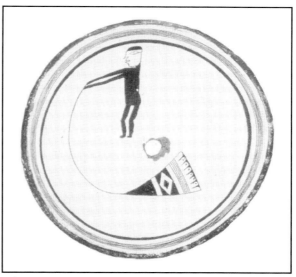

Figure 190

bundle of rods *The letter E of the Snake Ring Template.* Symbolic designation of a society as at the multiple crossings of the horizon by the snake path of the sun. *Ref* COMB.

• The fasces, a bundle of rods containing a battle ax, was carried in battles and placed before magistrates as a badge of authority *See* ETHICS & LAW & RULER & WAR + ITALY, ROMAN \WEBp

burial *The letter D of the Snake Ring Template. The ritual interment of the dead, which began with Ice Age Homo sapiens.* A metaphor for the death of the old sun in the western underworld. *Ref* DEATH, REGENERATION, RITUAL, UNDERWORLD.

butterfly *The letter O of the Snake Ring Template.* A metaphor for the ascent of the new sun at springtime. *Ref* BIRD.

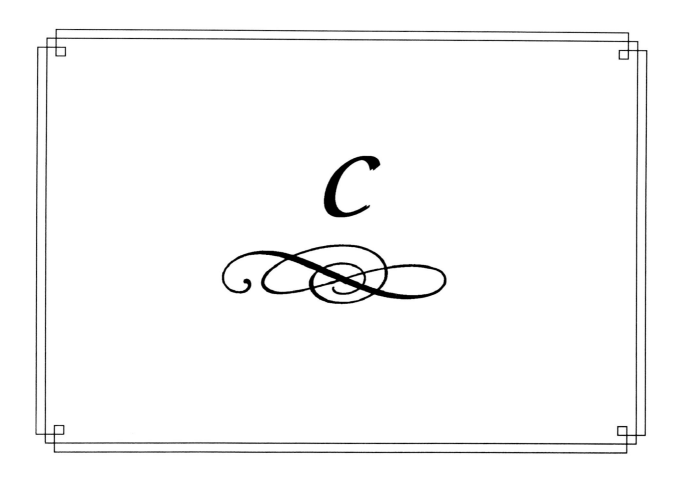

caduceus *The letter E of the Snake Ring Template. An insignia, usually with wings or a bird at its top, designating a physician.* A metaphor for the entwined serpent path of the sun, down from the sky along the axis mundi to its regeneration. *Ref* BIRD, HEALING, SERPENT ENTWINED, SOCIETAL ASPECT, STAFF, SUN OLD/ YOUNG, WINGED.
Refer to *Figure 13* SECTION TWO.

calabash *The solar orbit. A gourd.* A metaphor for the globe formed by the network of the sun's apparent path around the earth. *Ref* ARCHITECTURE, DOME, PATH, VESSEL, X-CROSSING.

• The calabash represented the dome of the sky and the inverted dome of the underworld, which contained the world's parents lying on top of each other *See* ANCESTOR WORSHIP & MARRIAGE -30b EGYPT \NEUt

• Heaven and earth were the respective halves of a cosmogonic egg in Phoenicia, Polynesia, Indonesia, India, Iran, Greece, Finland, Central America, and on the west coast of South America. *See* TRANSCULTURAL SIMILARITY -15b \ELHt

• Sacred calabashes in sanctuaries are painted with snakes which "carry the god wherever he wants to go". The top half of the calabash represents the dome of the sky and the bottom half represents the underworld, containing the oceans with the earth floating in their center. The horizons are where the top and bottom halves of the calabash join *See* DOME & PATH & SNAKE & SUN & VESSEL +19a NIGERIA, YORUBA \PAQt *Figure 191*

• An unexplained spherical gold vessel from the mother culture of South America is covered with embossed serpents. It is separated into two halves, so it could not have been used for utilitarian purposes *See* GOLD & SNAKE & TRANSCULTURAL SIMILARITY -8b PERU, CHAVIN *Figure 192*

• The Barasana believe that the sky is like the top of a gourd; the sky meets the earth at the horizon where there is a waterfall to the world

below *See* HORIZON & WATERFALL +19a COLOMBIA, TUKANO \AVDt

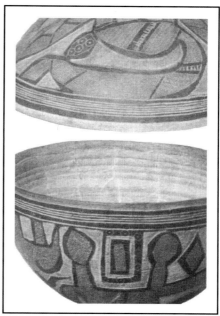

Figure 191

• A sacred calabash rattled during ceremonies is covered with a network formed of strung beads and snake vertebrae *See* BEAD & DEATH & MUSIC & PATH & ROUND MOTIF IN SEQUENCE & SNAKE & X-CROSSING +19a HAITI, VOODOO \DATt

Figure 192

calendar *The Solar Orbit Illustration. Ref* TIME, YEAR.

Cancer *The letter H of the Snake Ring Template.* *The Crab.* A metaphor for the threshold of the western horizon. *Ref* ABYSS, WATER, ZODIAC \CIRt

candle 1. *The letter D of the Snake Ring Template.* A metaphor for regenerative death of the old sun along the axis mundi. *Ref* DEATH, FIRE, ROMANTIC LOVE, SOCIETAL ASPECT.

canopy *The letter H of the Snake Ring Template.* A metaphor denoting an occurrence under the western horizon. *Ref* HORIZON, MARRIAGE, RULER.

capricorn *The letter C of the Snake Ring Template. The Goat; L. goat + horn, with a fish tail.* A metaphor for the descent of the virile old sun into the western horizon waters. *Ref* CORNUCOPIA, GOAT, WATER, ZODIAC.

carrier *The letter M of the Snake Ring Template.* A metaphor for transport within the designated carrier path. *Ref* ALLIGATOR/ CROCODILE, DRAGON, FELINE, HORSE, PATH, RAPTOR, WHALE.

• A stone bas relief depicts the sun god **Zeus** appearing to his worshippers in the form of a great, upright snake *See* PATH & SNAKE & SUN OLD & VERTICAL LINE / SHAPE -3a GREEK \CAMt *Figure* 193

carrier; machine *The letter M of the Snake Ring Template.* The fascination with automobiles, for example, as a metaphor for the transporter of the newborn sun through the perilous serpent path below the horizons. *Ref* FELINE, MACHINE, SOCIETAL ASPECT.

castration *The letter D of the Snake Ring Template.* A metaphor for the death of the virile old sun in the western horizon. *Ref* CIRCUMCISION, PHALLUS.

castle *The letter H of the Snake Ring Template.* A metaphor for the mountain-house in the western horizon waters. *Ref* HOUSE, RULER.

Figure 193

cat *The letter M of the Snake Ring Template.* *Ref* BLACK, FELINE, SUPERSTITION, SUN OLD/ YOUNG.

catastrophe *The letter I of the Snake Ring Template.* Originally attributed to a society's failure to inspire the sun to stay on the serpent path and seasonally regenerate itself, i.e., by ritual or victory in war. *Ref* CHAOS IN NATURE, ECLIPSE, ETHICS, PATH, REGENERATION, SOCIETAL ASPECT, WAR.

cauldron *The letter K of the Snake Ring Template. A large kettle for boiling water.* A metaphor for the boiling water at the fire of the western horizon. *Ref* FIRE, OCCULT, VESSEL, WATER.

celestial *The letter P of the Snake Ring Template.* The dome of the sky containing the seven celestial levels. *Ref* DOME, CELESTIAL LEVELS.

celestial observation *The letter R of the Snake Ring Template.* Originally to predict eclipses and to determine when to perform rituals to inspire the regeneration of a new sun. *Ref* CATASTROPHE, ECLIPSE, SEASON.

• Edzna in the Yucatan, one of the oldest and largest Mayan ceremonial centers, had a lunar observatory whose purpose was to predict the eclipses of the sun *See* ECLIPSE -1a MEXICO, MAYAN \TEOt

• Astronomers were mostly concerned with the phenomena occurring at the western horizon *See* HOUSE & REGENERATION & WEST ORIENTATION -35b IRAQ, SUMERIAN \MCCt

• The time of festivals was determined by solar observations at the rim of a volcanic crater on the western edge of the island *See* RITUAL & VOLCANO & WEST ORIENTATION +15 EASTER ISLAND \HEUt

cenote *The letter G of the Snake Ring Template. A sinkhole in limestone having a pool at the bottom. Ref* ABYSS, SOCIETY AS AT THE AXIS MUNDI, UNDERWORLD, WELL.

celibacy, priests' *The letter R of the Snake Ring Template.* A negation of previous practice after the solar path was demytholized and, with it, the idea of inspiring solar regenerations. *Ref* DEMYTHOLIZATION, MARRIAGE, PRIEST.

centaur *The letter T of the Snake Ring Template. Gr. A fabulous figure, half man, half horse. Ref* CARRIER, HORSE.

center of the world *The letter E of the Snake Ring Template. Ref* SOCIETY AS AT THE AXIS MUNDI.

Cerberus *The letter M of the Snake Ring Template. Gr. A three headed dog at the entrance to Hades. Ref* DOG, TRINITY.

chain *The letter S of the Snake Ring Template.* A metaphor for the path of the sun. *Ref* NECKLACE, RING MOTIF IN SEQUENCE.

chaos in nature *The letter I of the Snake Ring Template. Extreme catastrophe in nature; specif. seasonal irregularities, flooding, and*

terminal Ice Age. Ref CATASTROPHE, FERTILITY, FLOOD, SEASON.

• As the glaciers withdrew there was a death toll of animal life like never before. Retreat of the glaciers removed Ice Age man's main food, as the reindeers did not migrate south. Human dental remains of 35,000 to 30,000 years ago indicate malnutrition diseases and vast starvation. Hoofed animals moved towards northern Asia and beyond in great herds. These were followed by the Cro-magnon hunters, really us, developing a strategy for survival *See* ART & CATASTROPHE & RITUAL & SOCIETAL ASPECT -350b \ARCt \CAAt \CAIt \BULt \SMJt

• Homo sapiens had lived for hundreds of thousands of years before that time in almost featureless settlements. As the mammoth game began to disappear, Neanderthal bear and human internment rituals began. After the terminal Ice Age catastrophe, modern man was established as the sole human species, with our same gift of problem solving. Mankind created the reaping knife, harpoon, spear thrower, fishing hook and bow and arrow, all necessary for survival as the game diminished. In that tiny space of time, human consciousness shaped human culture by what some thought a lucky fluke. The Ice Age changed men from hunter- gatherer nomads to the inventor of the first musical instruments; the first trade; artificial lighting; the first beads, rings, and anklets; and the first art. The notched bones found in the Ice Age caves were probably the first instances of calendar counting *See* ART & BEAR & BURIAL & CAVE & FAUNA & HOUSE & JEWELRY & MUSIC & NUMBER & TOOLMAKING -350b \HAWp \SMJt \NEUt \NYAt \REAt \NWSt

• Homo sapien sites spread to South Africa, the Middle East, China, and across the Bering passage to what is now called Alaska. Aurignacoid myths, rites, and art spread to the Americas with a burst of culture -350b \NATp \CAIp \SCOt

• Venus figures appeared in the terminal Ice Age art following the period of extreme malnutrition *See* FERTILITY & MOTHER GODDESS & REGENERATION & SEASON -289a \SMJt

• The cosmos is in constant peril of cataclysm. The sun and the world had been destroyed four times; we are now in the period of the fifth sun *See* CHAOS IN NATURE & DEATH & SUN OLD/ YOUNG +13a MEXICO, AZTEC \AVEt

• If seasonal rituals are not done correctly the crops will fail *See* CATASTROPHE & FERTILITY & REGENERATION & SUN YOUNG +19a USA, HOPI \COSt

• If the rites to the sun are not properly performed, the universe will end *See* CATASTROPHE & REGENERATION & SOCIETAL ASPECT & SUN YOUNG +19a COLOMBIA, BARASANA \AVDt

chariot 1. *The letter T of the Snake Ring Template* : HORSE. **2.** *The letter M of the Snake Ring Template. Jewish Merkabah, the earliest throne mystery. The cherub is the chariot of God.* Ref BABY BOY, CARRIER, CHERUB, FELINE, SPHINX \OCTt \SMKt

checkerboard design *The letter K of the Snake Ring Template.* A symbol for the western horizon underworld. *Ref* BLACK, GAME BOARD.

• The god **Ptah**, placed a checkerboard on a man's head, causing him to sink into the underworld -30a EGYPT \SANt

• A checkerboard tapestry is hung on the house during mourning for the deceased +19a MALI, DOGON \GRKt

cherub 1. *The letter I of the Snake Ring Template.* A metaphor for the newborn sun. *Ref* ANGEL, BABY BOY. **2.** *The letter M of the Snake Ring Template. The cherub was represented in early Jewish art as a winged sphinx with a child's head. Ref* BABY BOY, CARRIER, FELINE, SPHINX.

chevron 1. Pointing down. *The letter D of the Snake Ring Template.* A symbol for the descent of the old sun into the western horizon. **2.** Pointing up. *The letter O of the Snake Ring Template.* A symbol for the ascent of the young sun from beneath the eastern horizon.

chicken *The letter D of the Snake Ring Template. Ref* ANIMAL SACRIFICE, BIRD.

chief *The letter R of the Snake Ring Template. Ref* RULER.

children *The letter I of the Snake Ring Template.* Societal metaphors for the progeny of the old sun and the mother goddess. *Ref* BABY BOY/ GIRL, SOCIETAL ASPECT.

chimera *The letter M of the Snake Ring Template. Gr. A fabulous lion with a snake for a tail and a goat's head rising from its back.* A metaphor for the feline carrier of the new sun through the underworld, to its leap-up in the east. *Ref* FELINE, GOAT, LEAP-UP, PATH.

Christmastide *The letter I of the Snake Ring Template. The annual church festival season in memory of the birth of Christ, celebrated generally from Christmas Eve until after New Years Day with special gifts. Ref* BABY BOY, GIFT GIVING, HEARTH, NEW YEAR, WINTER SOLSTICE.

Christmas tree *The letter E of the Snake Ring Template. Ref* HOUSE, SANTA CLAUS, SOCIETY AS AT THE AXIS MUNDI, TREE.

church *The letter H of the Snake Ring Template. Ref* HOUSE, TEMPLE.

circle motif *The letter A of the Snake Ring Template.* A metaphor for the path of the sun through the uroborus. *Ref* WHEEL.

circumcision 1. Male. *The letter D of the Snake Ring Template.* A metaphor for the death of the virile old sun into the waters of the western horizon, leading to union with the underworld mother goddess. *Ref* BLOOD, CASTRATION, PUBERTY RITE, SOCIETAL ASPECT, TRINITY. **2.** Female. *The letter H of the Snake Ring Template.* A ritual metaphor for the virgin goddess at the western horizon, where the old sun dies and passes to her, through coital blood, the solar soul is to be reborn as the sun of the next season. *Ref* BLOOD, COPULATION, GODDESSES, SOCIETAL ASPECT.

• A scene painted on the floor of the Well, a natural depression of the cave floor, depicts a castrated bull, a fallen bird-man, a small bird rising on a vertical line, and a leafed branch *See* ART & FERTILITY & TRINITY -350b FRANCE, LASCAUX \BRAp
Refer to *Figure 91* SECTION TWO.

• A carving from a tomb depicts a circumcision by priests called "mortuary priests" *See* DEATH -23a EGYPT *Figure 194*

Figure 194

• A relief of the El Tajin ball-court shows a figure with a barb in his penis. Blood from the wound flows to the face of a young deity who is within the mouth of a fish *See* BLOOD & GAME SPORT & MARINE CARRIER & PATH & REGENERATION & WHALE +14b MEXICO, EL TAJIN
Refer to *Figure 89* SECTION TWO.

• The prepuce is referred to as the sun *See* PHALLUS & RING MOTIF & SUN +19a MALI, DOGON \GRKt

• Ritual mutilation of the clitoris of young girls by their mothers followed by the sewing together of the girl's labia, is still practiced throughout Africa. The labia is resown each time after giving birth to a child *See* BLOOD +19a \NYTt

city *The letter R of the Snake Ring Template.* *Ref* SOCIETY AS AT THE AXIS MUNDI.

climate *The letter I of the Snake Ring Template.* The characteristics of nature brought on by catastrophe when unseasonal or when seasonal, by the birth of the new sun. *Ref* CATASTROPHE, SEASON.

clock *The letter A of the Snake Ring Template.* An instrument to measure the apparent movement of the sun through the sky and the underworld, within one coil of the serpent path. *Ref* PATH, TIME.

clover *The letter M of the Snake Ring Template.* A composite metaphor for the trinitarian aspects of the sun's springtime regeneration at the western horizon and the resultant fertility. *Ref* FERTILITY, SUPERSTITION, TRINITY.

clown *The letter L of the Snake Ring Template.* *Ref* JESTER.

cobweb *The letter A of the Snake Ring Template.* A metaphor for the crossing entwined serpent path. *Ref* WEAVING, X-CROSSING.

cock *The letter B of the Snake Ring Template.* *Ref* BIRD.

cockatrice *The letter B of the Snake Ring Template.* A legendary figure with the head, wings, and legs of a cock and the tail of a serpent. *Ref* BIRD, PATH.

coffin *The letter H of the Snake Ring Template* *Ref* SARCOPHAGUS.

collapse, mysterious *The letter R of the Snake Ring Template.* The unexplained collapse of civilizations; attributed to the loss of faith in the leaders' ability to insure the seasonal regenerations of the sun and its predictable path in the sky. *Ref* ECLIPSE, RULER.

• An Ugaritic tablet recounts the overthrow of the ruler due to a solar eclipse *See* ECLIPSE & RULER -12a SYRIA, PHOENICIAN \COSt

• The highland Mayan culture collapsed, probably due to religious revolts, at the same time that the eclipse forecast table failed to properly predict a solar eclipse **[Note:** Due to an error recorded in the Dresden Codex, in calculating the precision of the equinoxes] *See* CELESTIAL OBSERVATION & ECLIPSE & RULER +9a MEXICO, MAYAN \AVEt

column *The letter E of the Snake Ring Template. A supporting pillar often with a spiral or leafed top.* A metaphor for the vertical segment of the snake ring path from the sky to the underworld of the western horizon mountain-house. *Ref* ARCHITECTURE, HOUSE, SOCIETY AS AT THE AXIS MUNDI, SPIRAL, TREE.

• There are pillars connecting the sky to the earth -30b EGYPT \COTt

Figure 195

• At Abydos "where the head of **Osiris** rests", the sun god Osiris was worshipped as the evening sun. His head symbol is depicted on a pillar leading into a mountain glyph *See* HEAD & MOUNTAIN & SOCIETY AS AT THE AXIS MUNDI -13a EGYPT \NEUp

• A statue excavated in an ancient cemetery in Syria depicts the Greek goddess **Persephone** holding a vase. Her head is replaced by a column. Her headdress is a Graeco-Egyptian symbol designating fertility, with underworld associations *See* BURIAL & FERTILITY & MOTHER GODDESS & PATH & REGENERATION & VERTICAL LINE/ SHAPE & VESSEL & UNDERWORLD -20b SYRIA, GREEK \BRAt *Figure* 195

Figure 196

• A cross-shaped megalithic goddess from a Cyclades Island in the South Aegean Sea has an elongated featureless face *See* CROSS WEST & GODDESSES & VERTICAL LEVEL/ SHAPE *Figure* 196

• Some roofs of pyramid-temples were supported by stone columns carved to depict vertically descending serpents *See* PATH & HOUSE & PYRAMID (MOUNTAIN) +10b MEXICO, TULA/ CHICHEN ITZA *Figure* 197 *Figure* 198

• Snakes coil around pillars which connect the sky to the earth *See* HALLUCINOGEN +19a NIGERIA, YORUBA \PAQt

• Barren country women clasp the pillars of Saint Paul's Cathedral in order to bear children *See* BABY BOY/ GIRL & HOUSE & MARRIAGE & PATH & SOCIETAL ASPECT +18a ENGLAND \ELIt

comb *The letter E of the Snake Ring Template.* A metaphor for the daily descents of the sun to the mother goddess in the western horizon. *Ref* BUNDLE OF RODS, PATH, SOCIETAL ASPECT, VERTICAL LINE/ SHAPE.

commerce *The letter I of the Snake Ring Template. Originally the acquisition of items for ritual use to be used as metaphors to inspire the seasonal rebirth of a new young sun, the bringer of seasonal fertility, which resulted in prosperity.* **a**. The acquisition of items involving transportation. **b**. Use of something such as currency, as a medium of exchange. *Ref* BANKING, FERTILITY, GOLD, MONEY.

• A red painted shell, obtained from 120 miles away, was found on top of the trinitarian
images painted on the floor of a natural depression in the cave floor known as the Well. This is the earliest indication of items being obtained from a distant location for ritual use *See* ART & CRUSTACEAN & RED & TRINITY -350b FRANCE, LASCAUX
Refer to *Figure 33* SECTION TWO.

Figure 197

• Cowrie shells were imported from Maldive islands and used as a form of currency *See* COWRIE & CRUSTACEAN -15a INDIA \HEVt

Figure 198

• The people of the upper Volga region exchanged furs with Arab traders for cowries from the distant Maldives, where great mounds of them are visible under the clear water. The traders referred to the shells as "snake-heads" *See* FLOOD & MOUNT & PATH & SNAKE & WATER +6a RUSSIA, MARI \HEVt

• Certain cowrie shells are "snake-head" throughout the Indo-Pacific region. On Easter Island, specific other cowries are referred to "as dragon-head" +19a EASTER ISLAND \ABBp

• The cowries that were used in West African sacred icons were imported from the distant Maldive Islands *See* PATH & REGENERATION & WATER +19a NIGERIA \GARt

• Strings of shell, beads and wampum, were used by American Indians for currency, as well as for ceremonial pledges *See* REGENERATION & SEASON & SOCIETAL ASPECT +17a USA \NELt

• Solar images are displayed on the earliest coins *See* FERTILITY & PROSPERITY & SUN YOUNG -4b ISRAEL \ENDt

• In Roman times, and more recently in Peru and in France, coins had the image of the sun embossed on them *See* SUN YOUNG +18a \WEBt

communication *The letter R of the Snake Ring Template. Ref* SPEECH, WRITING.

condor *The letter Q of the Snake Ring Template. Ref* RAPTOR.

cone *The letter G of the Snake Ring Template.* A metaphor for the mountain home of the mother goddess in the western horizon. *Ref* MOUNTAIN, PYRAMID, TRIANGLE MOTIF UPRIGHT.

confluence of rivers *The letter F of the Snake Ring Template.* A metaphor for the western horizon waters. *Ref* WATER.

copper *The letter I of the Snake Ring Template. Ref* GOLD.

• In Western Africa, copper holds status equal to that of gold *See* GOLD +19a NIGERIA \GARt

• Gold was the younger brother of copper *See* ALCHEMY +19a MALI, DOGON \GRKt

• The twirling of the weaving spindle moves the copper spiral of the sun *See* PATH & SOCIETAL ASPECT & SPIRAL & WEAVING +19a MALI, DOGON \GRKt

copulation *The letter H of the Snake Ring Template. Human's copulation in private is unique in the animal world.* A metaphor for the underworld joining of the old sun with the mother goddess. *Ref* HOUSE, MARRIAGE, NIGHT, SOCIETAL ASPECT, UNDERWORLD.

coral *The letter E of the Snake Ring Template.* Often red in color, A metaphor for the composite images of tree and mountain under the western horizon water. *Ref* JEWELRY, MOUND, RED, TREE, WATER.

cornucopia *The letter I of the Snake Ring Template. Horn of plenty.* A metaphor for the fertility resulting from the old sun's sacrificial death and regeneration. *Ref* BULL, BULL'S HORN, FLORA, GOAT, GOLD, UNICORN.

cosmogony *The letter R of the Snake Ring Template. Gr. The creation of the world.* Metaphors of the Snake Ring, supposedly ending the terminal Ice Age's chaos in nature, were in evidence at the dawn of present
mankind, and in all creation stories thereafter. *Ref* ART, RITUAL, SEASON, RELIGIONS CONTEMPORARY/ PRIMORDIAL.

cosmology *The letter A of the Snake Ring Template. Metaphysics. The universe as an orderly system.* A proto-structure of the universe, which placed the world, its oceans, and the changes in the seasons within a serpentine path of the sun, forming the sky and the underworld. *Ref* CALABASH, DEMYTHOLIZATION.

cow *The letter H of the Snake Ring Template.* A metaphor for the mother goddess who joins with the old sun-bull in the western horizon to produce the new sun of fertility. *Ref* BULL, MOTHER GODDESS.

• The goddess **Neith** and the goddess **Hathor**, referred to as the cow who bore the sun, were linked with the primordial waters and with the serpent of many coils, the manifestation of the high god *See* BABY BOY & PATH & WATER -30b EGYPT \NEUt \MUNt

• In a detail of a tomb painting from the Papyrus of Ani, the cow-goddess **Hathor** is depicted waiting at the mountain of the west in a cluster of papyrus. She faces the young sun god **Horus** in his falcon form (not shown here). A structure with a cone-shaped roof is at the base of the mountain *See* DEATH & CONE & HOUSE & MOUNTAIN & PAPYRUS & RAPTOR & REGENERATION & SOCIETAL ASPECT & SUN YOUNG & WEST ORIENTATION -13a EGYPT *Figure* 199

crane *The letter B of the Snake Ring Template Ref* MARINE BIRD.

• A bull is engraved below a tree containing three cranes, representing the Celtic triple-gods, on the face of an altar from the site now occupied by the Notre Dame Cathedral *See* ALTAR & BIRD & BULL & DEMYTHOLIZATION & PATH & TREE & TRINITY -20b FRANCE, CELTIC \CAIp

• An elaborate wine vessel is decorated with the figures of a crane at its top and dragons on its sides *See* BIRD & FERTILITY & PATH & WATER -5b CHINA, SHANG \SMJp

Figure 199

crater *The letter G of the Snake Ring Template. Ref* ABYSS, HOLE, VOLCANO.

creation *The letter R of the Snake Ring Template. Ref* COSMOGONY.

cremation *The letter D of the Snake Ring Template.* A metaphor for the death of the old sun in flames at the western horizon. *Ref* DEATH, FIRE, SOCIETAL ASPECT.

crescent motif *The letter H of the Snake Ring Template. Ref* MOON.

crest *The letter A of the Snake Ring Template. The tuft on a helmet, or roach of hair on the head.* A metaphor designating the head of the wearer as within the arching snake path of the sun. *Ref* ARCH, HEAD, SOCIETAL ASPECT.

crime *The letter R of the Snake Ring Template.* **a.** Aberrations of the metaphors in the minds of a few. **b.** A diminution of the traditional metaphors previously prevalent in all societies which gave direction to, and confidence in, each individual's ritual life. *Ref* ETHICS, HAND RAISED, PSYCHOLOGY QUANTITY, SOCIETAL ASPECT, VIRTUAL REALITY.

• David Berkowitz known as the Son of Sam, killed more than six people, mostly young females, in late night hunts for victims. He left a final note before his capture with drawings of the biological symbols for male and female by either side of a cross and a snake symbol below *See* DEATH & CROSS WEST & MARRIAGE & PATH & RING MOTIF +19a USA \NWSp

• Ted Bundy killed more than twenty girls and had intercourse with the dead victims, claiming that he could not handle failures. He was consumed by forces he did not understand *See* DEATH & MARRIAGE +19a USA \MIBt

crocket *The letter H of the Snake Ring Template. An ornament of curved foliage on the sloping edge of a gable, spire, etc.* Designating a structure as a metaphor for the house at the western horizon where fertility in the form of a new sun of springtime is born. *Ref* ARCHITECTURE, FERTILITY, HOUSE.

crocodile *The letter A of the Snake Ring Template.* A reptilian metaphor for the snake path in the horizon waters. *Ref* ALLIGATOR, DRAGON, HORIZON, WATER.

• The Hebrew word for crocodile is the same as the word for dragon -10a ISRAEL, JEWISH \ENDt

• The young sun god **Horus** is sometimes depicted treading on the bodies of serpents or crocodiles *See* PATH -30b EGYPT \MUNt

• In a papyrus illustration, a solar barge is above the image of a coiled serpent ending at a crocodile *See* BOAT & HORIZON & PATH & REGENERATION -30b EGYPT \PIDp

• Live crocodiles were kept at the temples *See* HOUSE & WATER -30b EGYPT \CASt

• A Mayan stella is carved with the axial world tree in the form of a cross. At its top are a bird and snake. The roots at its bottom are depicted as a crocodile *See* BIRD & CROSS & SNAKE & SOCIETY AS AT THE AXIS MUNDI & STELLA & TREE -1.5a MEXICO, IZAPA \AVDp

cromlech *The letter E of the Snake Ring Template. Ref* DOLMEN.

crook 1. *The letter I of the Snake Ring Template. A shepherd's staff as in crook and flail.* A metaphor associating a deity or authority figure with the fertility of the crops and field, and thereby of the flocks. *Ref* FAUNA, FLORA, RULER, SEASON, SUN OLD/ YOUNG. 2. *The letter E of the Snake Ring Template. Ref* CROZIER.

cross circled *The letter E of the Snake Ring Template. Ref* SWASTIKA.

cross east *The letter O of the Snake Ring Template. Ref* CROSS. See SECTION TWO.

crossroad *The letter H of the Snake Ring Template.* A metaphor for the branching of the sun's path in the western underworld: the new sun to the east, the husk of the old sun to remain in the underworld. *Ref* HUSK, SOCIETY AS AT THE AXIS MUNDI, TRINITY.

cross west *The letter E of the Snake Ring Template Ref* CROSS. See SECTION TWO.

crow *The letter B of the Snake Ring Template. Ref* BIRD, BLACK.

crown *The letter R of the Snake Ring Template. Ref* DIAMOND, GOLD, RAYED MOTIF, RING MOTIF, RULER.

crozier *The letter E of the Snake Ring Template. Ch. A bishop's staff with a spiral top.* A metaphor for the path of the old sun, from the entwined serpent down into the western horizon. *Ref* CROOK, PRIEST, SPIRAL MOTIF,

STAFF, VERTICAL STICK.
Refer to *Figure 36* SECTION TWO.

Crucifixion *The letter R of the Snake Ring Template. Ch. The death of Christ on the cross, followed by his springtime resurrection. Ref* CHRISTMASTIDE, CROSS WEST, DEATH, EASTER, RESURRECTION, SPRINGTIME.

• The Crucifixion is often associated with fertility and fecundity, as in a sixteenth century drawing depicting the animals of the field gathered around the cross of the Crucifixion as it bears fruit *See* DEATH & FAUNA & FLORA & REGENERATION & SPRINGTIME +0b SWITZERLAND, CHRISTIAN \CAMp
Figure 200

Figure 200

crustacean *The letter F of the Snake Ring Template.* See SECTION TWO.

crustacean cowrie *The letter F of the Snake Ring Template.* A metaphor for the serpent path into the mountain house where the new sun is born to the mother goddess in the western horizon waters. *Ref* BABY BOY, CRUSTACEAN, HOUSE (CAVE), MARRIAGE, MOTHER GODDESS, MOUNTAIN, SOCIETAL ASPECT, SUN YOUNG, WATER.

• Reefs of cowrie shells appear as mountain peaks clearly visible beneath the Maldives' water, where all of the cowries used in Europe, Africa, India, the Middle East and Asia **[Note:** Cowrie shells' resemblance to a serpent's mouth led them to be called "snake-head"] were obtained for use in sacred art, rituals and for money *See* DANCE & FERTILITY & MONEY & MOUNTAIN & SNAKE & WATER +19a MALDIVES \HEVt \GARt

• Female statues had cowrie shells at their sexual centers *See* FERTILITY & MARRIAGE & WATER -20a JAPAN, JOMON \RAUt

• Female genitals were symbolized in art by cowrie shells -15b CHINA \MUNt

• Cowrie shells are abundant in the religious imagery of the New Guinea aborigines *See* ART & FERTILITY & RITUAL +19a NEW GUINEA, SEPIK \RAUt

• Statues of females with babies on their backs are embellished with strings of cowries, beads and coins *See* BABY BOY/ GIRL & GODDESSES & MONEY & PATH & ROUND MOTIF IN SEQUENCE & SOCIETAL ASPECT +19a NIGERIA, YORUBA \FAHp

crystal *The letter S of the Snake Ring Template. Occult. Associated with the spirit. Ref* DIAMOND.

cupid *The letter I of the Snake Ring Template. Ref* ANGEL, BABY BOY, WINGED.

cypress *The letter E of the Snake Ring Template. Gr. Sacred tree. A large swamp tree having red wood. Ref* RED, TREE, WATER.

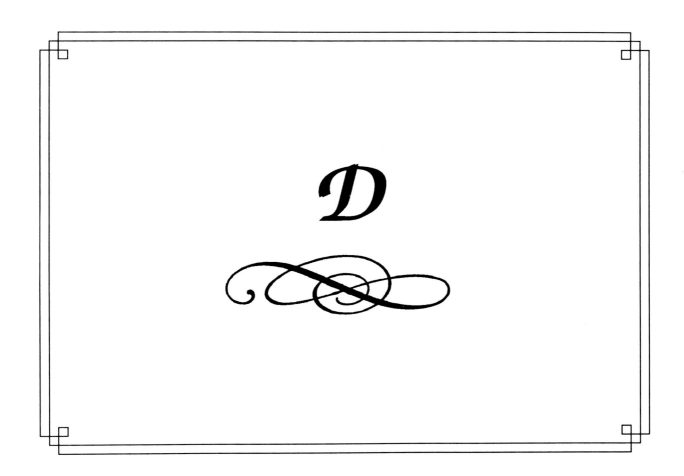

dance *The letter A of the Snake Ring Template.* A metaphor for the serpent path of the sun through the levels of the cosmos. *Ref* MUSIC, PATH, SOCIETAL ASPECT, WEST ORIENTATION.

• Human heelprints hardened in the glacial clay of an Ice Age cave floor suggest dancing was performed in a circle in imitation of the hooves of an animal, together with the impressions of sticks which were stamped by the dancers in the soft ground. This was performed around a raised prominence carved to depict a bison couple mating *See* BLADE & BULL & COPULATION & COW & PATH & STAFF -350b FRANCE, TUC D'AUDOUBERT \CAAp \RAUt **Refer to** *Figure 68* SECTION TWO.

• Dancing was part of the religious education dedicated to the worship of the sun god **Apollo** *See* REGENERATION & SUN YOUNG -20a GREEK \DUSt

• Medicine men holding live snakes dance around a large sacred rock in front of their tipi lodge. They wear red feathers on their heads and sashes made of shells *See* CRUSTACEAN & FEATHERED & HOUSE & PATH & PRIEST & RED & STONE +18a USA, HOPI \BOWp

• During dances in honor of their supreme deity **Upulero** they pray "Grandfather Sun come down and make our empty rice basket full" *See* DESCENDING MOTIF & FERTILITY & REGENERATION & SUN OLD +18a INDONESIA, SARMAT \ELIt

• The trunk of a large tree with a platform at its top is erected in the town square in preparation for a preconquest dance, where "voladeros" dressed as birds dance atop the structure. Dedicating themselves to the sun, they launch into the air with ropes tied around their waist which permit them to rotate either seven or thirteen times around the pole [depending on the height of the pole] until they descend to the ground. As they descend they sing songs to ensure the resurrection of the sun, seasonal rains, and an abundance of flora *See* BIRD & FERTILITY & LEVELS CELESTIAL & POLE & SPIRAL & RAIN & REGENERATION & RESURRECTION & ROPE & SOCIETY AS AT THE AXIS MUNDI & SUN OLD +19a MEXICO *Figure 201*

Figure 201

• During the Winalagilis dance, a board is presented depicting a double-headed serpent. A dancer identified with the sun is then lowered from the rafters of the ceremonial house wearing a raven mask *See* BIRD & HOUSE & PATH & SNAKE & SOCIETY AS AT THE AXIS MUNDI +19a CANADA, KWAKIUTL \CAIt \MUNt

• The shaman dances with a rattle staff decorated with the image of their mythic double headed serpent *See* MUSIC & PRIEST & SNAKE +19a ALASKA, TLINGIT \MUNt

• The Bear Dance is a mating dance, performed at Spring by men and women in a circle, within a circular enclosure. At the end of the dance, one of the bear dancers falls to the ground, then mating rituals are performed *See* BEAR & DEATH & MARRIAGE +19a USA, UTE \BAEt

• The Bushmen, one of the oldest continuous cultures (starting 20,000 B.C.), incorporate into their dances, images of the sun, fire and semen. Their dance is in five and seven beat phrases, at the conclusion of which they collapse in a simulated death. They say that when they dance they enter the earth where there is water *See* ABYSS & CELESTIAL/ UNDERWORLD & COPULATION & DEATH & FIRE & LEVELS & SUN OLD & WATER +19a SOUTH AFRICA, BUSHMAN \CAIt

• The Pygmies, with a culture almost as old as that of the Bushmen, dance in a long curling line simulating a serpent's movement +19a CONGO, PYGMY \CAIt

• "When we dance we become the god" *See* SOCIETAL ASPECT +19a HAITI, VOODOO \DATt

• A Shinto priest: "We don't have a theology we just dance" +19a JAPAN, SHINTO \WESt

• Female court dancers represent the snake woman who copulated with the ancestor king +19a CAMBODIA \NAUp

• In the ancient Hindu dance, **Deo**, which means god, the dancers represent their ancestor god who died from the dance and "did sex things". This dance was forbidden about twenty years ago by the Maldive authorities *See* DEMYTHOLIZATION +19a MALDIVES, HINDU \HEVt

• Although many of the rituals in the kivas are still held secret, it is known that priests paint their naked bodies black and tie their penis erect on a stick as they dance in a circle for a good season of crops *See* COPULATION & FERTILITY & HOUSE & PRIEST +19a USA, PUEBLO \RAUt

• The coiling dances and processions of the aborigines represent the movement of their magical snake, symbolizing their return along this path to "the source" *See* SOCIETAL ASPECT & SOCIETY AS AT THE AXIS MUNDI & UROBORUS +19a AUSTRALIA \RAUt

• Their bodies painted with the same designs that they paint on ritual skulls and on bullroarers, representing "a weedy swamp", the dancers perform with stamping tubes. **[Note**

the stamping sticks of the Ice Age dancers above and the stamping tubes of the Tukano dancers below]. At the conclusion of the dance, they turn to the east to greet the rising sun *See* DEATH & BULLROARER & REGENERATION & RUSHES & SUN YOUNG & STAFF +19a AUSTRALIA, ARNHEMLAND \ELHt *Figure* 202

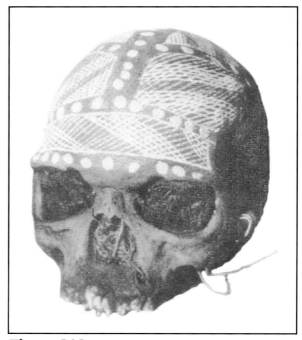

Figure 202

• Dancing maintains the continuity of all species *See* FAUNA & FLORA +19a AUSTRALIA, WALBIRI \BRBt

• Dances at the central area of their ritual house, called the center of the world, keep the cosmos moving. Their dancing replicates the east to west movement of the sun, transposing the vertical plane of the cosmos to the floor where they dance *See* HOUSE & PATH & SOCIETY AS AT THE AXIS MUNDI +19a COLOMBIA, BARASANA \AVDt

• In the Yaje Dance, dancers pound stamping tubes decorated with feathers on the earth to inspire the incestuous union of the sun-father with his daughter *See* FEATHERED & GODDESSES & INCEST & STAFF & SUN OLD +19a COLOMBIA, TUKANO *Figure* 203

Figure 203

darkness *The letter* **K** *of the Snake Ring Template. Ref* BLACK, NIGHT, UNDERWORLD.

Day of Rest *The letter* **P** *of the Snake Ring Template. Heb. The seventh day, the day the Lord rested.* A metaphor for the highest seventh layer of the sky, where the sun seems to pause at noon. *Ref* GODS, LEVELS.

death **a.** *The letter* **D** *of the Snake Ring Template. Tarot. The thirteenth enigma, representing not the end but a change. Ref* GAME BOARD, LEVELS CELESTIAL, REGENERATION, TAROT, TRINITY. **b.** *The letter* **D** *of the Snake Ring Template.* A metaphor for the death of the old sun in the western horizon waters. *Ref* FUNERAL, SOCIETAL ASPECT \TL1t

• After his death, the sun god **Osiris**, with the mother goddess **Isis**, conceived the young sun god **Horus** in the "Sea of Reeds" below the western horizon. This Sea of Reeds was synonymous with the Greek Elysian Field, an island in the western ocean-underworld, reached by a magical boat *See* ABYSS & BABY BOY & BIRTH & MOTHER GODDESS & REGENERATION & RUSHES & SUN OLD/ YOUNG & WEST ORIENTATION -30b EGYPT \EDWt

• Flowers were placed over the corpse and were worn at feasts *See* DEATH & FERTILITY & REGENERATION & SOCIETAL ASPECT -20b GREEK \CIRt

• Tombs of private burials had pyramids on their roof with a carved figure of the deceased adoring their sun god *See* PYRAMID & REGENERATION & SOCIETAL ASPECT & SUN OLD -15a EGYPT \EDWt

• At the western extremity of two narrow corridors in king Tutankhamun's tomb were golden figures of beheaded bovines hanging on a pole by their tail which wrapped around the pole. A series of oars were on the floor heading towards the east *See* BULL & PATH & REGENERATION & RULER & SACRIFICE ANIMAL & VERTICAL LINE/ SHAPE & WATER & WEST ORIENTATION -13a EGYPT *Figure 204 Figure 205*

Figure 204

• Miniature rafts and paddles were often placed in tombs *See* SOCIETAL ASPECT & WATER +2b PERU, MOCHICA \HEUt

• The dead were wrapped in buffalo hides and placed on scaffolds, or a buffalo hide was draped over the coffin at the burial *See* BULL & PATH & SOCIETAL ASPECT & VERTICAL LINE/ SHAPE +18a USA, MANDAN/ SIOUX \CATt \BRPt

• The Snake Wheel, a carved wooden uroborus decorated with eagle feathers, was sometimes tied to a tipi pole standing over the grave of the deceased *See* HOUSE & PATH & REGENERATION & SOCIETAL ASPECT & UROBORUS & VERTICAL LINE/ SHAPE +19a USA, ARAPAHO \DOPt

• The dead sink with the sun into the west +19a POLYNESIA \ELIt

• The soul goes back at death to the mythic waterhole for reincarnation *See* ABYSS & REGENERATION & SOUL & WATER +19a AUSTRALIA, UNUMBA \CAIt

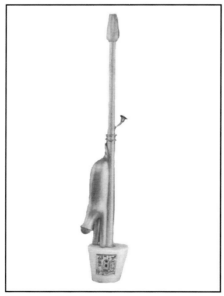

Figure 205

decapitation *The letter D of the Snake Ring Template.* A metaphor for removal of the old sun's head precluding the possibility of its reappearance in the sky. *Ref* HEAD, SOUL, WAR.

deer *or* **leaping animal** *The letter O of the Snake Ring Template. See* SECTION TWO.

deities, numerous *The letter H of the Snake Ring Template. Ref* BABY BOY/ GIRL, GODDESSES, SEASON, SUN OLD/ YOUNG, TRINITY.

deluge *The letter F of the Snake Ring Template. Ref* CATASTROPHE, CHAOS IN NATURE, FLOOD.

demon *The letter L of the Snake Ring Template.* The husk of an old sun of seasons past. *Ref* TRINITY, WAR.

demytholization **1.** *The letter A of the Snake Ring Template.* Revised perception of the nature of the sun and its earth-centered path, beginning after 7th century B.C. Ionian scientific revelations that the sun did not have human characteristics of birth and death, and did not circle the earth. *Ref* CALABASH. **2.** *The letter R of the Snake Ring Template.* Using interpretations of the basic metaphors to convert or replace other interpretations of the same metaphors. *Ref* INFORMATION DESTROYED OR SECRET, RELIGIONS CONTEMPORARY, WAR.

• Why is it that the worldwide solar elements seem to lack coherence to the modern mind? When civilizations were first on the march, the seasons were modes of the sacred and the sun was regarded as supreme +19a ELIADE, MIRCEA \ELIt

• Carnac Hill in Brittany, where thousands of megalithic monuments had been used over a period of twenty five hundred years for ritual burials, has been capped by a Christian chapel and renamed for Saint Michael the Dragon Slayer *See* DEATH & DRAGON & HOUSE & SOCIETY AS AT THE AXIS MUNDI & STONE -20a FRANCE, CARNAC \SEQt \SMJp

• In the ancient world, dragons were regarded as benevolent *See* FERTILITY & PATH 19a ANTHONY AVENI \AVDt

• The modern world began with the seventh century B.C. Ionian philosopher Thales of Miletus who, having achieved fame as the first to accurately predict a solar eclipse, pronounced that heavenly bodies were not deities. Subsequent Ionian philosophers were persecuted - Philolaus for claiming that the sun was on an independent orbit which did not go around the earth, and Anaxagoras for proclaiming that the sun was merely "a mass of red hot metal". In spite of these persecutions, the Hebrews, followed by Zoroaster and Buddha, rejected the sun as a god *See* PATH & SUN -6a GREEK, IONIAN \HITt \KIRt \NACt \WESt

• Statues of a large bronze serpent called Nehustan and the goddess **Astarte** had been in Solomon's temple for centuries but were removed by King Hezekeiah in the seventh century B.C. *See* DRAGON & HOUSE & MOTHER GODDESS -6a ISRAEL, JEWISH \ENDt \MUNt

• Deuteronomy, the core of the Torah, was written in the seventh century. It forbade the cult of the sun and the snake. Although many of the old ideas were retained in the biblical story of the Exodus, there is no archaeological evidence for human occupation of the Sinai during the generally accepted time for its occurrence -6a ISRAEL, JEWISH \BIBt \ENDt \SMKt

• Sampson whose name means "sun" was maimed in both legs and the seven locks of his hair were removed, before he destroyed himself and the Philistines by collapsing the columns of the temple of the sun god **Dagon**, father of the eastern bull god **Baal** *See* BULL & COLUMNS & FOOT & HOUSE & LEVELS CELESTIAL & PATH -6a ISRAEL, JEWISH \ENDt \NEUt

• Egyptian religious art collapsed within a century after the beginning of extensive trade with the Ionians *See* ART -5a EGYPT \CASt

• Greek art with divine and heroic themes fell apart after the middle of the fifth century B.C. Its collapse was linked to the growth of scientific thought in the Greek world *See* ART -4a GREEK \KIRt

• Olympic Games, the mother of sport contests, were dedicated to the young sun god **Zeus** in his fight against his father **Chronos**. They lost their religious significance in the fifth century B.C. as traditional religion faded. They had been held in an area surrounded by a channel of water at the foot of a hill where there was a married priestess halfway up called **Demeter of the Couch**. At the western extremity of where the races began, a

mechanism lowered a bronze dolphin and sent skyward a bronze eagle [the path of the uroborus]. The winner of the race was awarded a crown of leaves, and feted at a temple to **Zeus** which contained a snake and a rayed sun image *See* BRONZE & GAME SPORT & HOUSE & MARRIAGE & MOTHER GODDESS & MOUNTAIN (HILL) & PATH & RAPTOR & RAYED MOTIF & SNAKE & SOCIETY AS AT THE AXIS MUNDI & SUN OLD/ YOUNG & WEST ORIENTATION & WHALE -4a GREEK \SWBt \SANt \DUSt

• Revelations was a compendium of letters Saint John the Divine sent to Christian proselytizers in the pagan Pergamos. He decries the Red Dragon which "stood tall" where the "whore" associated with the moon, sat at the waters of the world. The Sun "clothed" the woman and she had a child who was to rule the world. But **God** took the boy to sit next to His throne before the dragon could swallow him. Michael forced from Heaven the great Dragon who had been deceiving the whole world, and threw it into the bottomless pit. As a result, thousands of male virgins were rescued from death [the sun of each season who died in the western horizon, copulated with the mother goddess and conceived the new sun of the successor season] *See* BABY BOY & DRAGON & GODDESS & MARRIAGE & MOON & PATH & PROSTITUTION & RED & REGENERATION & SUN YOUNG & VERTICAL LINE/ SHAPE & WATER +9a ITALY, REVELATIONS \MCCt \MERt

• Constantine, the third century A.D. Roman emperor, proclaimed **Jesus** as "the new sun" and celebrated his birth festival at the winter solstice, previously celebrated as the birth date of the Sol Invictus *See* BABY BOY & CHRISTMASTIDE & SOUTHWEST ORIENTATION & SUN YOUNG +2a ITALY, CHRISTIAN \ELIt

• A third century A.D. floor uncovered below the Vatican bears the earliest mosaic depicting **Jesus** as **Helios** the young sun god ascending to the sky in a chariot *See* HORSE & PATH & SUN YOUNG +2a ITALY, CHRISTIAN
Refer to *Figure 117* SECTION TWO.

• Muhammed, saying that "we wage war upon the serpent", departed from the many gods that were traditionally worshipped in his area to preach the concept of one **God** +5a IRAN, ISLAM \GEFt \MUNt

• The Viking plunderer of Christian monasteries, Felim of Munster, was related through marriage with the Celts previously Christianized by St. Patrick [who "chased the snakes" from a land which never had snakes] and the Romans. He had an ecclesiastical character and went about with a crozier in his hand [in a failed crusade to restore the old faith] +8a IRELAND, VIKING \HEPt

• The Teutons, until Christianized late in the first millennia, believed that there were seven skies plus the head and tail of a great serpent that encircled the world *See* LEVELS CELESTIAL & UROBORUS +15a GERMAN, TEUTONIC \MUNt \SANt

• To the Kabalists enlightenment meant "to strip off the skin of the serpent" +15a ISRAEL, JEWISH \NACt

• The Chilam Balam of Tizimin, a text written soon after the Spanish conquest, states that "once there was truth which we drew from the serpent in ancient days, from the heavens to the earth below" +15a MEXICO, MAYAN \AVDt

• Spanish conquerors tore down the Aztec shrine to Our Holy Mother **Tonantzin** and replaced it with the church to Our Lady of Guadelupe, the **Virgin Mary** *See* HOUSE & MOTHER GODDESS +15a MEXICO, CHRISTIAN \FONt \NYTt

• After suffering defeat at the battle of Wounded Knee, the Indians mourned that their sacred tree was now dead and their nation's hoop was broken, leaving them without a center *See* CIRCLE MOTIF & SOCIETAL ASPECT & SOCIETY AS AT THE AXIS MUNDI & TREE +18a USA, SIOUX \BRPt

• Plains Indians now chant the Rosary to the music they once sung in the honor of the sun *See* MUSIC & ROUND MOTIF IN SEQUENCE +18a USA, HOPI \BOWt

• Great Basin Indians refer to their Sun Dance lodge as a church. The lodge's center-pole represents the Crucifix, and the sun represents **God** *See* COLUMN & CROSS WEST & GOD & HOUSE & VERTICAL LINE/ SHAPE +19a USA, UTE \BAEt

• Images of the sun are placed above statues of saints in many churches of the present-day Inca of Peru. Christian and folk African religions fit well into their traditional beliefs +19a PERU, INCA \REVt

• Present-day Mayans pray to their Rain God as the Father, Son, and the Holy Ghost. They say that contemporary religions confuse only part of the truth with the whole truth *See* RAIN & REGENERATION & TRINITY +19a MEXICO, LACANDONES \BRUt \THLt

descending motif *The letter D of the Snake Ring Template.* A metaphor to inspire the descent of the old sun into the mountain-house of the western horizon. *Ref* ALTAR, TREE, VERTICAL LINE/ SHAPE.

devil *The letter L of the Snake Ring Template. Ref* SATAN.

devouring *The letter A of the Snake Ring Template. Ref* CARRIER, MOUTH.

devil worship *The letter R of the Snake Ring Template. Ref* FERTILITY, SUN OLD, TRINITY.

diamond *The letter S of the Snake Ring Template.* **a. ~ motif.** A metaphor for the eye. *Ref* EYE. **b. when radiant** [as in the jewel], a metaphor for the solar soul radiating from within the eye. *Ref* JEWELRY, RAYED MOTIF, SOCIETAL ASPECT.

disk *The letter S of the Snake Ring Template. Ref* ROUND MOTIF.

• The disks worn in the ears and lower lip are called Botogue, the name of their hero-deity *See* SUN YOUNG +19a BRAZIL, GE \LEVt

distaff *The letter E of the Snake Ring Template. The staff for holding flax in spinning.* A metaphor for the mother goddess at the axis mundi. *Ref* SOCIETAL ASPECT, VERTICAL LINE/ SHAPE, THREAD.

dog *The letter M of the Snake Ring Template.* A metaphor secondary to that of the feline for the companion and guardian of the new sun in its underworld path. *Ref* FELINE, HERO, SOCIETAL ASPECT.

• Dogs are the companions of the dead through the underworld *See* DEATH & REGENERATION & SOCIETAL ASPECT +1b MEXICO,COLIMA \SOVt

• A dog with a copper ring on its back was found in a running posture at the feet of a burial *See* CARRIER & COPPER & DEATH & REGENERATION & RING MOTIF & SOCIETAL ASPECT & UNDERWORLD +2a PERU, MOCHICA \NATp

dolmen *The letter E of the Snake Ring Template. Prehistoric. A horizontal stone supported by uprights.* A metaphor for the western horizon mountain-house. *Ref* ARCH, COMB, HOUSE, MONOLITH, SOCIETY AS AT THE AXIS MUNDI, STONE.

dolphin *The letter J of the Snake Ring Template. Ref* WHALE.

dome *The letter P of the Snake Ring Template.* A metaphor for the apparent dome-shaped path of the sun through the sky. *Ref* ARCHITECTURE, CALABASH, HOUSE.

door *The letter H of the Snake Ring Template.* A metaphor for the entrance into the mountain-house of the western horizon. *Ref* ARCHITECTURE, HOUSE, PEDIMENT.

dove *The letter B of the Snake Ring Template. Ref* BIRD, SUN OLD/ YOUNG.

dragon *The letter A of the Snake Ring Template. See* SECTION TWO.

dream *The letter R of the Snake Ring Template. Ref* DREAM, PSYCHOLOGY CHILD.

drink alcoholic *The letter R of the Snake Ring Template. Ref* HALLUCINOGEN.

drug *The letter R of the Snake Ring Template. Ref* HALLUCINOGEN.

drum *The letter E of the Snake Ring Template. Ref* MUSIC, TREE.

duality *The letter H of the Snake Ring Template.* Due to the solar regeneration within the *Snake Ring,* the same image may be a metaphor for either good or bad fortune to the old or new sun, depending upon whether it is oriented to the east or west, and whether shown ascending or descending. *Ref* EAST/ WEST ORIENTATION, FERTILITY, GAMBLING, REGENERATION, SUPERSTITIONS.

duck 1. *The letter F of the Snake Ring Template.* A metaphor for the western horizon water. *Ref* WATER. 2. *The letter B of the Snake Ring Template.* A metaphor for the sun descending into the western horizon waters. *Ref* MARINE BIRD, SUN OLD/ YOUNG.

• The body of a child decorated with jewelry was placed with his head facing east. In the burial were ivory figures of flying geese and a duck *See* BABY BOY & EAST ORIENTATION & PATH -350b RUSSIA, MALTA \CAAt

• The hieroglyph of a duck with a ring motif on it's back, translates as "the son of **Ra**" [the ring] -30a EGYPT, KARNAK \GIEs

• An illustration in the Fejervary-Mayer Codex depicts a bearded and duck-billed figure descending into a water-filled cave where a nude goddess waits with her vagina exposed. In the following illustration, the same figure is within the maw of a feathered serpent which has penetrated through the vagina of this goddess now holding a spindle. In the third illustration the serpent emerges from her navel, passes through and ascends above a ball-court while carrying a deer's head in its mouth *See* BABY BOY & DEER & GAME SPORT & LEAP-UP & MARRIAGE & PATH & SPINDLE & UNDERWORLD +13a MEXICO, AZTEC *Figure* 206 *Figure 207 Figure 208*

Figure 206

• Duck feathers ornamenting the mouths of Plains Indians' medicine pipes, associate the ceremonial smoke with the ritual waters *See* SOCIETAL ASPECT & TOBACCO & WATER +18a USA, MANDAN \RAUt

Figure 207

dwarf *The letter L of the Snake Ring Template.* A societal metaphor for the spent old sun. *Ref* HUSK, JESTER, SUN OLD.

Figure 208

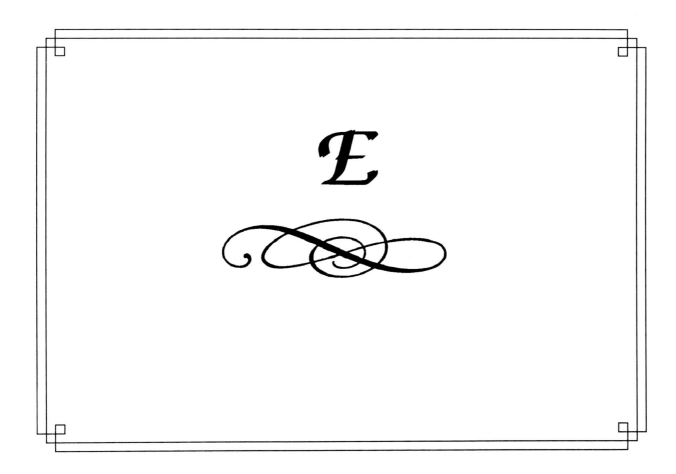

---

eagle *The letter Q of the Snake Ring Template.* *Ref* RAPTOR.

ear of corn *The letter I of the Snake Ring Template.* *Ref* FERTILITY, FLORA.

earring *The letter S of the Snake Ring Template.* A social metaphor denoting the wearer as the bearer of the solar soul. *Ref* JEWELRY, RING MOTIF, SOCIETAL ASPECT.

• During arguments one man might grasp his own penis while fingering his opponent's earring or bracelet and shouting: "give it" *See* BRACELET & PHALLUS & REGENERATION & SUN OLD/ YOUNG & WAR +18a BOLIVIA, NAMBIK \LETt

• Greater Southwest Indians pierce their infant's ears for earrings in their annual ceremonies to the sun for rain to awaken their crops. *See* BABY BOY/ GIRL & FERTILITY & RAIN +19a USA, HOPI \SINt

earth *The number 1 of the Snake Ring Template.* The common plane to both the celestial and infernal layers. *Ref* LEVELS.

earth mother *The letter H of the Snake Ring Template.* *Ref* MOTHER GODDESS, UNDERWORLD, WEST ORIENTATION.

earthquake *The letter I of the Snake Ring Template.* *Ref* ABYSS, CHAOS IN NATURE, SOCIETY AS AT THE AXIS MUNDI.

east orientation *The letter O of the Snake Ring Template.* A metaphor for the sun's passage through the perilous underworld, including its ascent at the eastern horizon. *Ref* LEAP-UP, PATH, SUN YOUNG.

• The Sphinx, facing away from the pyramid and to the east, was called **Horus** in the horizon *See* CARRIER & FELINE & HORIZON & PYRAMID & SUN YOUNG -25a EGYPT \SMJt
Figure 209

Figure 209

• At Palenque, a carved stone mural in the Temple of the Cross depicts on one of its panels an old deity with a long, limp penis who faces to the west. On the other panel, a young deity wearing an ornate headdress of a heron catching fish and a jaguar-head belt buckle faces to the east *See* BIRD & CIRCUMCISION & CROSS WEST & FELINE & HOUSE & PATH & PHALLUS & REGENERATION & SUN OLD/ YOUNG & WATER +3b MEXICO, MAYAN \ROBs

Easter *The letter I of the Snake Ring Template. Christ. A springtime church festival in memory of the resurrection of Christ. Ref* EGG, RABBIT, RESURRECTION, SPRINGTIME.

eclipse *The letter I of the Snake Ring Template.* A metaphor for the loss of the sun. If realized, it would be the end of all life. *Ref* CHAOS IN NATURE, FERTILITY.

• A Ugaritic tablet relates that the ruler was overthrown when an unforseen solar eclipse occurred *See* COLLAPSE MYSTERIOUS & RULER -12a SYRIA, PHOENICIAN \COSt

• The Dresden Codex's solar eclipse forecast table, in one of the few books remaining from the preconquest Maya, used the phases of the moon to that end *See* CELESTIAL OBSERVATION & COLLAPSE MYSTERIOUS +3b MEXICO, MAYAN \AVEp

• Emperor Ming issued a declaration following a solar eclipse that the eclipse evidenced he had not carried out "the great work of civilization" +2a CHINA, MING \CAAt

effigy *The letter R of the Snake Ring Template. A representation.* Ref ART, OCCULT, METAPHOR, SOCIETAL ASPECT, WRITING.

egg *The letter I of the Snake Ring Template.* **a**. A metaphor for the newborn sun. **b**. **~ hunt** A societal metaphor to inspire the newborn sun to rise from the hidden underworld. *Ref* EASTER, GAME CHILDREN, SPRINGTIME.

• Statues found in tombs depict the young sun god **Dionysis** holding an egg. To the Orphics, **Phanes-Dionysis**, the sun, was born of an egg [as birds are] *See* BIRD & SUN YOUNG -20b GREEK \ELIt \WIIt

• In prehistoric times, eggs were decorated at springtime and were later placed in burials *See* FUNERAL & REGENERATION & SOCIETAL ASPECT +13b LITHUANIA, BALTIC \FEJt

• The seal of the Chinese Emperor depicts a feline with the body of a dragon guarding the egg, symbol for the sun *See* FELINE & HERO & PATH & RULER & SUN YOUNG & WAR +17a CHINA, CHING \NYMp

• Bronze snakes with an egg in their mouths, coil down bronze ritual staffs *See* BABY BOY & BRONZE & PATH & REGENERATION & RITUAL & STAFF +8a NIGERIA, NOK \EYOp

• The egg does not symbolize birth, but a return *See* REGENERATION & SEASON & SUN YOUNG +19a INDIA, HINDU \ELIt

elephant *The letter E of the Snake Ring Template.* A composite metaphor for the vertical segment of the serpent path from the sky represented by the its trunk and the elephant's body as a metaphor for a cloud.

• An Ice Age cave painting depicts mammoths with multiple serpentine trunks at each end of a ten foot-long snake *See* CAVE & CELESTIAL & PATH & SNAKE & SOCIETY AS AT THE AXIS MUNDI -350b FRANCE, BAUME-LATRONE \MUNp

• The body of a mammoth formed of ivory is embossed with a series of X-bands *See* X-CROSSING -350b GERMANY \HAWp

• **Airavata**, a white elephant with seven trunks, was the steed of the sun god **Indra**. It was a cloud condemned to walk on earth *See* LEVELS CELESTIAL & PATH -19b INDIA, HINDU \LARt \WESt

Figure 210

• A bronze vessel is in the form of an elephant covered by dragons in relief. Its trunk is decorated with a tiger and with a small bird which has a ring motif for its head *See* BIRD & BRONZE & DRAGON & FELINE & PATH & RING MOTIF -13a CHINA, ANYANG *Figure 210*

• In spite of elephants having been extinct in the area for more than 2,000 years before the earliest Mesoamerican culture, fantastic elephant-like heads with a series of ring motifs along their trunks were at the upper facade of many Puuc-style Mayan structures *See* CELESTIAL & HOUSE & INFANT MENTALITY & PATH & RING MOTIF IN SEQUENCE +7a MEXICO, CHICHEN ITZA, UXMAL *Figure 211* *Figure 212*

• Elephants are often paraded during festivals in India with flowers painted on their body and images of cobras on their trunks *See* FERTILITY & PATH & PROCESSION & SNAKE +19a INDIA, HINDU \WESp

Figure 211

Figure 212

• A bronze pendant depicts an elephant's head covered with X-bands formed by a series of round motifs. The bands become spirals on the elephant's trunk *See* ROUND MOTIFS IN SEQUENCE & SPIRAL & X-CROSSING +8a NIGERIA, NOK *Figure* 213

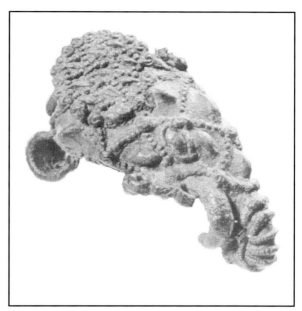

Figure 213

• Stone carvings of the water god **Makhara**, with a trunk like that of an elephant, are placed at ritual fountains near the entrances to Hindu temples *See* HOUSE & PATH & WATER +19a INDIA, HINDU \HEVt

• Bridegrooms ride on elephants at marriage ceremonies *See* MARRIAGE & PATH & SOCIETAL ASPECT +19a INDIA, HINDU \WESt

entwined motif in axis mundi.
Ref GUILLOCHE, SERPENT ENTWINED.

escape *The letter N of the Snake Ring Template.* A metaphor for the flight of the young sun from the underworld conflict with the husks of past seasons. *Ref* PSYCHOLOGY CHILD/ CONTEMPORARY/ DREAM, TRINITY, WAR.

eternity *The Solar Orbit Illustration.* A metaphor for the eternal passage of the solar soul back and forth from solstice to solstice. *Ref* SERPENT ENTWINED, SOUL, TIME.

ethics *The letter R of the Snake Ring Template.* The moral responsibility of a society and its members to present themselves as suitable metaphors of the sun-family's activities, to assure continuity of the seasons. *Ref* SOCIETAL ASPECT, SOCIETY AS AT THE AXIS MUNDI, WAR.

• To Christian reconstructionists, their activities represent those of the Kingdom of **God**; resulting in a morality that overrides government authority   +19a BILL MOYER \WESt

• The chief ethic, including an attitude on death, was Maat, whose purpose was to maintain the harmony of the world *See* FUNERAL & SEASON & SOCIETAL ASPECT -30b EGYPT \CASt

• Mankind must fulfill his or her dharma, the moral obligation to contribute to the harmony of the cosmos *See* SEASON & SOCIETAL ASPECT -19b INDIA, HINDU \NYTt

• Talmud Aggadah: Ethics are required to preserve the order of the world *See* SEASON & SOCIETAL ASPECT -5a ISRAEL, TALMUD \ENDt

• Virtue is the supernatural power exerted by a divine being *See* SOCIETAL ASPECT +19a ESKIMO \CAIt

eye *The letter S of the Snake Ring Template. Ref* DIAMOND MOTIF, RING MOTIF.

• The eye is the window of the soul *See* HEAD & SOCIETAL ASPECT & SOUL +15a LEONARDO DA VINCI \BOPt

• The circle of the iris is "the sun in the mouth" *See* HEAD & MOUTH & RING MOTIF & SOCIETAL ASPECT & SUN YOUNG   -30b EGYPT \CIRt

• The young sun god **Helios**, who presides over the seasons, was the eye of the old sun-god **Zeus** *See* SEASON & SUN YOUNG -20b GREEK \CIRt

• Ring motifs down the pillars of Tlaloc's temple at Templo Mayor may represent the large rings around the feline Tlaloc's eyes *See* CARRIER & FELINE & PILLAR & RING MOTIF IN SEQUENCE -13b MEXICO, AZTEC \MAXp

• In proto-Caananite script the letter "ayn" was an eye; which later changed to a ring motif. [The symbols were apparently equivalent]. The first and last letters of the Greek aplhabet, alpha and omega, derive from the proto-Caananite glyphs for "bull" and "ring motif" respectively, as do the English letters "A" and "O" [the same as the metaphors for the beginning and end of solar regeneration in the Snake Ring] *See* BULL & LETTERS & REGENERATION & RING MOTIF -10b ISRAEL, JEWISH \ENDt

• Dancers wear straw circles around their eyes *See* DANCE & RING MOTIF   +18a BOLIVIA, BORORO \LETt

• Irezumi tattooers place the eyes of the dragon in last, saying that they represent the spirit carried within the dragon *See* PATH & SOCIETAL ASPECT & SOUL & TATTOO +19a JAPAN \TATp

• The sun is the "eye of **Krren**" their supreme deity *See* PATH & SOUL & SUN   +19a ARGENTINA, TIERRA DEL FUEGIAN \ELIt

• The diamond-shape designs painted on bodies of the sun-lodge dancers represent the eyes of the sun *See* DANCE & REGENERATION & SOUL +19a USA, ARAPAHO \DOPp

• An engraved disk from a ritual mound depicts a raised hand surrounded by serpents with a large eye in its palm *See* HAND RAISED & MOUND & PATH & SOUL & SUN   +12a USA, MOUNDVILLE \CAMp

Refer to *Figure 163* SECTION TWO.

fairy tale *The letter* R *of the Snake Ring Template.* A story told to children, of events often ascribed to legendary figures or animals, but actually from the Snake Ring animals. A fairy tale is distinguished from a dream in that it usually has a happy ending. *Ref* PSYCHOLOGY CHILD / DREAM.

• Childhood folklore contains important clues to the workings of the collective memory *See* INFANT MENTALITY

• Children at all levels of intelligence find that fairy tales are their most satisfying stories. As yet, there has been no comprehensive analysis of fairy tales from a psychoanalytic point of view. Successful tales are told and re-told from generation to generation because they meet unconscious requirements. In many fairy tales, a child outwits a giant who threatens his or her life. Every fairy tale represents the workings of the psyche, speaking in a language of symbols representing unconscious content *See* BABY BOY & HERO & INFANT MENTALITY & WAR +19a \BEUt

• Fairy tales give symbolic expression to rites of passage. In a study of children approximately ten years old, aggressive fairy tales decreased their aggressive behavior *See* RITE OF PASSAGE & WAR +19a M ELIADE \BEUt

• In fairy tales, the gender is not important. Male and female figures appear in the same roles in different versions of the same tale. A girl can identify with "Jack And The Beanstalk" and a boy with "Rapunzel". [However, TV children adventure series with female lead characters were canceled after it was determined that girls would watch a male lead, but boys would not watch a female lead] *See* BABY BOY & HERO & INFANT MENTALITY & WAR. +19a \BEUt \NYTt

• Cinderella had a long oral history before it was written down in China in the ninth century, followed by Perrault in the seventeenth century, and by Grimm brothers in the past century. In some versions, an ash boy becomes the king ["Cendillon", the French name for Cinderella, has a masculine ending; the French "Le Petit Chaperon Rouge", or Little Red Riding Hood, is a masculine piece of apparel]. In other versions, a ring takes the place of a slipper. In the Chinese version, fish bones are kept in the child's room in the house *See* BABY BOY & DEATH & FIRE & HOUSE & INFANT MENTALITY & REGENERATION & RING MOTIF & WATER. +8a CHINA \BEUt

• In "East of the Sun and West of the Moon", a Norwegian fairy tale, a husband joins with his wife in the form of a bear. In the morning he turns into a handsome young prince who must then leave her *See* BEAR (BULL) & INFANT MENTALITY & MARRIAGE & MOON & PATH & REGENERATION & SUN OLD/ YOUNG +19a NORWAY \BEUt

• In the fairy tale called "The Enchanted Pig", a princess cuts her finger to make the last rung of a ladder which she used to rescue her pig-husband who "suffered many things". The spell broken, he assumes form and reigns as king *See* HAND RAISED WITH MISSING DIGIT & LADDER CELESTIAL & MARRIAGE & PIG (BOAR) & PSYCHOLOGY CHILD & REGENERATION +19a ROMANIA \BEUt

• The Grimm brothers' fairy tale, "The Frog King", was taken from a sixteenth century tale, "The Well At The World's End", where a princess' gold ball falls into a well. The frog returns the ball to the princess; they marry and he turns into a prince *See* ABYSS & FROG & GOLD & HORIZON & MARRIAGE & PSYCHOLOGY CHILD & REGENERATION & ROUND MOTIF & UNDERWORLD +15a SCOTLAND \BEUt

• Hansel and Gretel were led to the Gingerbread House by a white bird who, while singing, landed on its roof. Another white bird led the children to safety across the "big water". The wicked witch of the house was burned to death *See* BIRD & CROSSROAD & DEATH & FERTILITY & FIRE & HOUSE & MUSIC & PATH & PSYCHOLOGY CHILD & WATER +18a GERMAN \BEUt

• "Jack And The Beanstalk" was one of a series of "Jack" fairy tales with gold playing a role. Jack defeated a cannibalistic ogre and took his gold; Jack had a hen that laid a golden egg. In the main scene of the tale's title, Jack defeats his father and climbs a bean tree to heaven *See* CELESTIAL & EGG & GOLD & HERO & HUSK & PSYCHOLOGY CHILD & TREE & VERTICAL LINE/ SHAPE & WAR +18a ENGLAND \BEUt

• Versions of "The Sleeping Beauty" by the writers Perrault and Grimm, were preceded by an older form of the story by Baile called "The Sun, Moon and Italia" [the mother of the Sun and Moon], where love restores the maiden from a death-like trance *See* GODDESSES & INCEST & MARRIAGE & MOON & PSYCHOLOGY CHILD & RESURRECTION & SUN OLD/ YOUNG +16a FRANCE \BEUt

• "Puss In Boots" arranged for the hero's success through trickery. [Puss is one of many "tricksters" in world folklore. Able to triumph by guile rather than battle over the past seasons' husks in the underworld, Puss may be from "collective memory" as the feline-hero-companion to the new sun along the Snake Ring. Wearing boots symbolizes that Puss is travelling along this path. Then, "The Little Old Lady Who Lives In A Shoe" is within this path, as the metaphor for the mother goddess at the axis mundi in the western horizon. Together with the old suns of seasons past, "she has so many children she doesn't know what to do"; regenerations of the forthcoming seasonal suns and mother goddesses within the eternal serpent path] *See* FELINE & HERO & PSYCHOLOGY CHILD & SHOE (BOOT) +18a \BEUt

• In the popular tale, "The Three Little Pigs", the wolf falls down the chimney into boiling water. The oldest of the children, in some versions the youngest, becomes the victor. [Only one child can become the new sun. Note the similarity of this story to Santa Claus descending the chimney when the birth of **Christ** is celebrated, at the time when it was previously believed, the young sun god **Helios** was annually reborn; and when, currently, the baby of the New Year is born. Following the above analogy regarding Puss' boots, the traditional row of Christmas stocking stuffed with gifts on the fireplace mantle is the crossing path of the regenerated new sun to the eastern horizon, restoring the world's well-being, after the old sun has descended to the house of the western horizon in the red fire of sunset]. *See* CHRISTMASTIDE & CROSSROAD & DEATH & DESCENDING MOTIF & FIRE & GIFT GIVING & HOUSE & PSYCHOLOGY CHILD & REGENERATION & SOCIETAL ASPECT & WAR & WATER +18 \BEUt

falcon *The letter Q of the Snake Ring Template.* *Ref* RAPTOR.

family of man *The letter R of the Snake Ring Template.* Mankind all over is united by similar images and metaphors, suggesting a common underlying meaning to their lives. *Ref* PSYCHOLOGY CHILD, SOCIETAL ASPECT, SOCIETY AS AT THE AXIS MUNDI.

fan *The letter R of the Snake Ring Template.* A societal metaphor denoting the person as being at the western horizon of the arching serpent path. *Ref* ARCH, MOTHER GODDESS, RULER, RAINBOW, SOCIETAL ASPECT.

father *The letter C of the Snake Ring Template.* **a.** A societal metaphor for the old sun who begets the new sun *Ref* PSYCHOLOGY CONTEMPORARY, SOCIETAL ASPECT, SUN OLD/ YOUNG. **b.** ~ *Ref* GOD, HAND RAISED.

fauna *The letter I of the Snake Ring Template.* *Ref* FLORA.

fawn *The letter O of the Snake Ring Template.* A young deer. *Ref* DEER.

feathered *The letter P of the Snake Ring Template.* A metaphor which associates the figure, animal, object or symbol with the path of the sun in the past, present and future. *Ref* BIRD, DANCE, RAPTOR, SOCIETAL ASPECT, WINGED.

feline *The letter M of the Snake Ring Template.* See SECTION TWO.

fertility *The letter I of the Snake Ring Template.* A metaphor denoting seasonal sufficiency of flora and of fauna, usually represented as floral since the fauna is also largely dependent upon flora. *Ref* RAIN, SPRINGTIME.

fight *The letter N of the Snake Ring Template.* *Ref* WAR.

finger *The letter O of the Snake Ring Template.* **a.** A metaphor for the emergence of the new sun from the underworld. **b.** When amputated, in whole or in part, a metaphor for injuries suffered by the new sun in the perilous underworld struggle. *Ref* HAND RAISED, HAND RAISED WITH MISSING DIGIT, WAR.

fire *The letter D of the Snake Ring Template.* See SECTION TWO.

fireworks *The letter D of the Snake Ring Template.* A metaphor for the nighttime death of the old sun into the western horizon. *Ref* DEATH, REGENERATION, SOCIETY AS AT THE AXIS MUNDI.

fish **1.** *The letter F of the Snake Ring Template.* **a.** A metaphor for the sea. *Ref* WATER **b.** When depicted on the ceiling it represents the structure as below the sea. *Ref* ABYSS, HOUSE, UNDERWORLD. **2.** *The letter J of the Snake Ring Template.* As a carrier it denotes the underworld passage of the new sun from the waters of the western horizon. *Ref* MARINE CARRIER, WHALE.

Figure 214

• The shaft of a wooden ceremonial double axe passes between two blades inscribed with images of fish, continuing into the head of a nude female figure *See* ABYSS & LABRYS & PATH & MOTHER GODDESS & VERTICAL STICK & WATER +18a NIGERIA, YORUBA
Refer to *Figure 32* SECTION TWO.

• Painted wooden fish are worn on the clothing of Holy Week dancers before Easter *See* DEATH & RESURRECTION & SPRINGTIME & WATER & WEST ORIENTATION +19a MEXICO, CHRISTIAN *Figure 214*

• The mythic feathered serpent from which the pyramid Quetzlcoatl gets its name, is depicted coiling within seashells and fish on the surfaces of the pyramid still standing. The collapse of the culture in the 8th to 9th centuries has never been satisfactorily explained *See* COLLAPSE MYSTERIOUS & CRUSTACEAN & DRAGON & MOUNTAIN & PATH & PYRAMID -1b MEXICO, TEOTIHUACAN
Refer to *Figure 40* SECTION TWO.

Figure 215

• Anthropomorphic stone fish were found near the altars of one of the world's earliest cities *See* ALTAR & MARINE CARRIER & PATH & RITUAL & SOCIETY AS AT THE AXIS MUNDI & WATER -60b YUGOSLAVIA, LEPENSKI VIR *Figure 215*

• A dance mask of the Northwest Coast Indians depicts a demon with fishtails in his mouth within a house whose gable is formed of opposing serpent images. *See* DANCE & DEMON & HOUSE & PATH & PEDIMENT & WATER +18a ALASKA, HAIDA *Figure 216*

five *The letter K of the Snake Ring Template.* A numerical metaphor for the path of the sun to the nadir of the underworld. *Ref* LEVELS UNDERWORLD.

Figure 216

flag *The letter A of the Snake Ring Template.* A composite metaphor for the sinuous movement of the sun within the celestial serpent path to the axis mundi. *Ref* POLE, RIBBON, SOCIETY AS AT THE AXIS MUNDI.

• Flagstaffs at temples were in the form of dragons *See* DRAGON & HOUSE & RIBBON & VERTICAL LINE/ SHAPE +6a CHINA, T'ANG \TL9p

• The new ruler was covered with gold dust and carried on a raft, accompanied by music and flags, to the center of the lake, where the flags would be lowered and a quantity of gold dumped into the water *See* DESCENDING MOTIF & GOLD & MUSIC & REGENERATION & RULER & SOCIETY AS AT THE AXIS MUNDI & WATER +6b COLOMBIA, MUISCA \AMNt

• Feathers and seashells were attached to the flagpole protruding from the rooftop entrance to the kivas *See* HOUSE & PATH & SOCIETY AS AT THE AXIS MUNDI & UNDERWORLD & VERTICAL STICK & WATER +18a USA, HOPI \BOWp

• It is traditional, yet unexplained, to place a flag and tree at the top of major buildings during construction **[Note:** As though the building is in the underworld] *See* HOUSE & PATH & SOCIETY AS AT THE AXIS MUNDI & SUPERSTITION & TREE & UNDERWORLD +19a USA \TULp

• Flags are placed at altars to herald the spirits coming to the altar *See* ALTAR & PATH +19a HAITI, VOODOO \WESt

flame *The letter D of the Snake Ring Template. Ref* FIRE.

flood *The letter F of the Snake Ring Template.* The melting of the vast Ice Age glaciers produced flood waters which exposed mountains and caves previously concealed under the ice. *Ref* CHAOS IN NATURE.

• When the glaciers which had covered most of the Alps and Pyrennees melted, the result was one of the greatest floods in geological history. The melting waters rushed through the mountain caves, leaving clay on which the first art of the world was created *See* ART -350b \BULt \BRFt

• Everywhere in creation myths there is a pregenital flood symbolism +19a ERICH NEUMANN \NEUt

• Deluges' tradition: one era is abolished and a new era begins. Some people await a repetition of the same catastrophe +19a MIRCEA ELIADE \ELIt

• A change of only a few degrees in the mean temperature of the world would again generate droughts, freezes, and floods like those of the terminal Ice Age *See* FERTILITY & RAIN -350b \DISt

• The Book of the Dead, ascribed to the First Dynasty, describes a flood "in the beginning" -30b EGYPT \NEUt

• The mythic Atlantis flood resulted from the heavenly bodies straying off of their proper course *See* CHAOS IN NATURE & PATH & SERPENT ENTWINED & SUN -20b GREEK \GAWt \BREt

• The young sun god **Apollo** was a god of the axis. He first appeared after the great flood which covered the earth. He healed the sick, was the god of Spring who annually brought the crops, and his name means "from the depth of the lion". A Roman statue of the sun god in the British museum, believed to be a copy of the statue that once stood in the Temple of Apollo at Cyrene, depicts the deity holding a lyre. He is accompanied by a large coiled snake *See* CARRIER & CAVE & FELINE & FLORA & HEALING & MARINE BIRD & MUSIC & PATH & REGENERATION & SNAKE & SOCIETAL ASPECT & SOCIETY AS AT THE AXIS MUNDI & SPRINGTIME & SUN YOUNG & TREE -20b GREEK \CIRt \ELIt \GAWt \LARt \LEIt WESp

• According to legend, the Anahuarque mountain at Cuzco rose from the waters of the mythic flood, saving the Inca ancestors *See* MOUNTAIN & SOCIETY AS AT THE AXIS MUNDI & WATER +9b PERU, INCA \AVDt

• Before the Okipa Sun Dance ceremony began, a performer descended to the lodge from a bluff in the west saying that he was the only person saved from the great flood, from whence he now came to open the medicine lodge *See* HOUSE & MOUNTAIN & RITUAL & WEST ORIENTATION +18a USA, MANDAN \CAIt

• Indians from the interior of Bolivia, who had never experienced a flood have the legend of a great flood *See* TRANSCULTURAL SIMILARITY +18a BOLIVIA, BORORO \LETt

• Once when spring was approaching, it snowed so hard that the whole earth was covered. When the snow melted, the whole earth was flooded and only the very lucky reached mountain peaks above the waters *See* CHAOS IN NATURE & FERTILITY & SPRINGTIME +19a CHILE, YAMANA \CAIt

flora *The letter I of the Snake Ring Template.* *See* SECTION TWO.

flower *The letter I of the Snake Ring Template.* *Ref* FLORA.

flute *The letter P of the Snake Ring Template.* *Ref* MUSIC.

Fool *The letter L of the Snake Ring Template. Tarot. The final enigma, distinguished from the others because it is un-numbered.* A metaphor, until demytholization, for the old sun who remains in the underworld. *Ref* CLOWN, DEMYTHOLIZATION, JESTER, SUN OLD, TAROT PACK, TRINITY.

• The [court] fool wore a horned head-dress and carried a knobbed staff, often in the shape of a phallus with huge testicles. On the courts, the fool sang erotic songs and engaged in lecherous horseplay, but the performance became more subdued when he became the harlequin of an 18th century theater. **[Note:** Similarity to the Bull dancer in the Plains Indians' Sun Dance. He was seized by laughing spectators and his enormous wooden penis broken off. The audience at Mexico's pre-conquest Little Old Men dance also with laughter as actors portrayed old man with ribbons streaming from their heads, poking their canes under the dresses of any nearby women] *See* BULL & CASTRATION & DEMYTHOLIZATION & HUSK & MARRIAGE & PALACE & RIBBON & RULER & TRANSCULTURAL SIMILARITY & THEATER & TRINITY +14a \EUROPE \RPUt **Refer to** *Figures 20 and 79* SECTION TWO.

• Clowns, important in Pueblo kiva ceremonies, wear costumes painted in alternate black and white stripes. They have soft horns at their headdress and seashells tied around their ankles. When a clown dies, there is happy singing, because it is believed that he will be reborn as a baby. **[Note:** Like the Old Men Dance of Mexico, likely a humorous depiction of the husks in the underworld, the virile old suns who die in the western horizon water house to be reborn as the sun of the next season] *See* BULL & BLACK & CRUSTACEAN & HOUSE & RESURRECTION & SEASON =19a USA, HOPI \AMWp

foot *The letter A of the Snake Ring Template.* A metaphor for a path, *specif.*, the path of the sun within the entwined serpent path. *Ref* PATH, SHOE OR STOCKING.

forest *The letter E of the Snake Ring Template.* A metaphor for the successive daily descents of the sun into the western horizon, associated in myths and fairy tales with a cottage. *Ref* HOUSE, TREE.

fountain *The letter F of the Snake Ring Template.* A metaphor for the waters of the western horizon. *Ref* ARCHITECTURE, SOCIETY AS AT THE AXIS MUNDI, WATER.

fowl *The letters B and D of the Snake Ring Template.* When used in ritual and sacrifice, a metaphor for the descent and death of the old sun. *Ref* BIRD, SACRIFICE ANIMAL.

frog *The letter H of the Snake Ring Template. Frogs mate and bear their young in the water.* A metaphor for the springtime regeneration of the solar soul in the western horizon waters. *Ref* REGENERATION, WATER.

• Frogs croak on the first day of rainy season, when they mate exuberantly and give birth in the water *See* BIRTH & MARRIAGE & RAIN & WATER +13b MEXICO, AZTEC \CENp \SIFt \MAXt

• A burial near the present Lake Geneva contained thousands of bones of frogs and toads *See* FUNERAL & REGENERATION & WATER -350b SWITZERLAND, VEYRIER \NATt

• Frog sculptures were found at the rim of the sacred cenote at Chichen Itza *See* REGENERATION & SEASON & WATER & WELL +3b MEXICO, MAYAN \COIt

• Large stone frogs stand on the platform of the pyramid-temple in Mexico City, which was named Coatepec after the sacred mountain of the western waters where the new sun god was born *See* BABY BOY & HOUSE & PYRAMID & SOCIETY AS AT THE AXIS MUNDI & SUN YOUNG +13b MEXICO, AZTEC *Figure 217*

• Closely woven baskets containing sea-shells and water, and decorated with images of frogs

and tadpoles were placed at the Snake Dance altar *See* ALTAR & PATH & REGENERATION & WATER +18a USA, HOPI \BOWt

Figure 217

fruit *The letter I of the Snake Ring Template.* *Ref* FLORA.

funeral *The letter D of the Snake Ring Template.* Apparently discrepant death ceremonies, i.e. cremation, ashes spread upon the water, burials in trees, in boats, below cairns or at menhirs, in mounds or in pyramids, on mountains, in caves, below the ground or below the floors of churches and houses are various aspects of the fiery death of the old sun down the vertical serpent path, through the abyss in the western horizon waters, into the mountain house where the solar soul is regenerated. *Ref* ABYSS, BOAT, CAVE, FIRE, HOUSE, MOUNTAIN, MONOLITH, PYRAMID, REGENERATION, SOCIETAL ASPECT, STONE, UNDERWORLD.

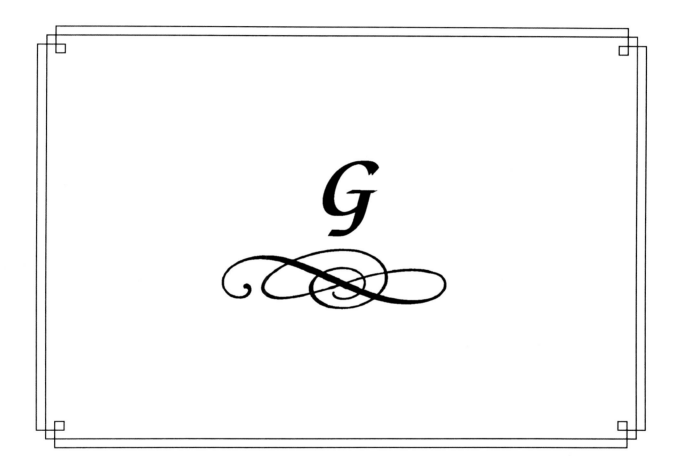

gambling *The letter N of the Snake Ring Template.* A metaphor for the element of chance in the survival of each new sun, including the hazardous west to east passage of the new sun through the underworld. *Ref* ECLIPSE, PATH, SOCIETAL ASPECT, WAR.

game board *The letter R of the Snake Ring Template.* A metaphor for the sun's passage through the layered cosmos, including the element of chance. *Ref* LEVELS, NUMBER, SNAKE, SOCIETAL ASPECT.

• A game board from a royal burial is carved in the form of a segmented spiral serpent along which a marble was rolled from the snake's mouth to its tail. The game was intended for the spirit of the dead Pharaoh to seek freedom from the dangers lurking in the netherworld *See* DEATH & GAME CHILDREN & PATH & REGENERATION & ROUND MOTIF & RULER & SPIRAL & UNDERWORLD & WAR. -40a EGYPT \MUNt
Figure 218

Figure 218

• The Senet board game found in several Pharaoh tombs was an allegorical journey of the dead through the underworld. Only the last five squares of the board were decorated, in the last one of which was the ring motif for the sun *See* CHECKBOARD DESIGN & DEATH & LEVELS UNDERWORLD & REGENERATION & RING MOTIF & RULER. -30b EGYPT *Figure* 219

Figure 219

• The messenger of the gods, **Hermes**, was the patron of gamblers. His staff was the entwined serpents of the caduceus *See* GAMBLING & GODS & HEALING PATH & HERMES & SERPENT ENTWINED -20b GREEK \WESt

• The gods in the Rig Veda were said to move like casts of the dice *See* GAMBLING & GODS & LEVELS & NUMBERS & PATH -19b INDIA, HINDU \SANt

• The Romans who were highly religious, cast lots in order to predict the future *See* NUMBER & PATH & SOCIETAL ASPECT -5b ITALY, ROMAN \REVt

• The game of I-Ching was to "bring man in accordance with the change of the past seasons" *See* GAMBLING & OCCULT & PATH & SEASON & SOCIETAL ASPECT & SUN YOUNG -5a CHINA \OCTt

• Games such as dice, knucklebones, and ball games were played when there was a great scarcity of food *See* FERTILITY & GAME SPORT & PATH & REGENERATION & WAR -4b EGYPT, LIBYAN \HEAt

• Although the 8th century domiciles of the religious centers vanished long ago, some of their floors still remain, bearing crude inscriptions of snakes on which the game of patolli, similar to the pachisi of present-day Egypt, Africa, Southern Asia, etc., was played *See* TRANSCULTURAL SIMILARITY -1b MEXICO, TEOTIHUACAN \MUTt \WEBt *Figure* 220

Figure 220

• When lots were cast, the player would say either "sun!" or "creature!". The same word "quih" meant both "sun" and "fate" *See* HUSK & LEVEL & NUMBER & SUN YOUNG & WAR +8a GUATEMALA, MAYAN \RECt

• The Indian game known as Planetary Battles was played until medieval times throughout Europe. It was similar to chess but had no Queen, and the move of the player was determined by the roll of dice *See* CHECKBOARD DESIGN & NUMBER & PATH & WAR +15a INDIA, HINDU \SANt \NAT

• The women make a coat of reindeer skins for the deceased during funeral rites, while the men play cards on the corpse *See* DEER & FUNERAL & GAMBLING & LEAP-UP & REGENERATION & SOCIETAL ASPECT & WAR +19a RUSSIA, KORYAK \SMJp

• Symbols on their gaming wheels correspond to the designs carved into the wood Snake Ring of their Sun Dance *See* GAMBLING & PATH & REGENERATION & SUN & UROBORUS +19a USA, ARAPAHO \DOPt

game children *The letter* ℛ *of the Snake Ring Template.* Remnants of mankind's ritual activities to inspire the regeneration and survival of the young sun. *Ref* FAIRY TALE, PSYCHOLOGY CHILD, SOCIOBIOLOGY.

• Children's games and toys were once sacred +19a MIRCEA ELIADE \ELIt

• Abandoned ritual tableaus became fairy tales and games +19a SIR JAMES FRAZER \FRBt

• A children's show is ritually performed in the kivas of the Greater Southwest Indians. Curtains depicting the sun are parted by hand puppets in the form of large water serpents to reveal painted images of thunder and rain *See* DEATH & HOUSE & PATH & REGENERATION & RITUAL & RAIN & SNAKE & SUN OLD/ YOUNG & THEATER & WATER +18a USA, ZUNI \NABt

• African people whose rock art has been carbon dated to 20,000 B.C. have a tradition of forming string images between their raised hands *See* HAND RAISED & STRING & WEAVING +19a SOUTH AFRICA, BUSHMAN \CAIp \MADt *Figure* 221

• Other cultures, including aboriginal, refer to the string game today by many names such as "ladder", "cats cradle", "calabash net" and "canoe" *See* BABY BOY & BOAT & CALABASH & FELINE & LADDER CELESTIAL & TRANSCULTURAL SIMILARITY & PSYCHOLOGY CHILD & X-CROSSING +19a NEW GUINEA\ AUSTRALIA\ POLYNESIA\ ESKIMO\ CHINA \CAIp \MADt

Figure 221

• The Greater Southwest Indians associate the string game with their war gods *See* PATH & WAR +19a NAVAHO, ZUNI \CAIp \MADt \WESt

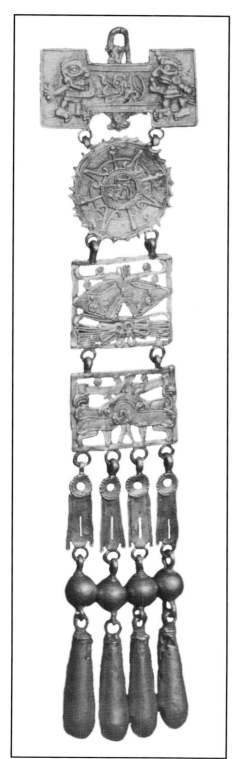

Figure 222

• A leader stood up and performed the string game, as a team of natives demonstrated to Heyerdahl how the colossal heads had been "walked" to their platforms *See* HORIZON & PATH & SUN OLD +19a EASTER ISLAND \HEUt

• The string game was taught them by their serpentine ancestor, the **Seventh Nommo** *See* ANCESTOR WORSHIP & GODS & LEVELS CELESTIAL & PATH & SOCIETAL ASPECT +19a MALI, DOGON \AFAt

• Children avoid stepping on cracks in the sidewalk, chanting "step on a crack, break your mother's back". In hopscotch, children hop a maze *See* ABYSS & ANCESTOR WORSHIP & MAZE & MOTHER GODDESS & SOCIETAL ASPECT & SOCIETY AS AT THE AXIS MUNDI +19a USA \DISt \WESt

• Parents attributed scores of their children's suicides and murders to the children playing the game Dungeons and Dragons. Dice are rolled to determine the outcome of battles with demons, one of which is a minotaur in the underworld *See* BULL & DEATH & DRAGON & GAMBLING & HOUSE & NUMBER & PATH & SACRIFICE HUMAN & SOCIETAL ASPECT & SUN YOUNG & UNDERWORLD & WAR +19a \WESp

game sport **1**. *The letter T of the Snake Ring Template.* A metaphor for the sun's speedy travel required to complete its passage between the horizons on the day when the seasons change : PATH. **2**. *The letter N of the Snake Ring Template.* A metaphor for the contest between the new and old suns in the hazardous west to east passage through the underworld. *Ref* WAR.

• A pectoral formed of a series of gold plaques, from a tomb of the Mixtec ceremonial center constructed on the flattened top of a mountain, depicts from bottom to top, balls and feathered ring motifs, a stylized feline-toad at the bottom of the pendant, an open-mouthed flint knife, a sun disk with a skull at its center and a ball-court within which players stand at each side of a skull similar to the skull   symbol for **Smoking Mirror** [illustrated below] the fallen sun god who has to be held down for the new sun to rise in the sky *See* DEATH & FEATHERED & FELINE & FROG & GOLD &   MOUNTAIN & RAYED &

REGENERATION & RING MOTIF & SKULL & WAR +9b
MEXICO, MONTE ALBAN \COTt \LARt \FURt
Figure 222   Figure 223

Figure 223

• The Hieros Gamos started at the annual Akitu festivals, approximately 2500 B.C. The games represented the renewal of the forces of nature by triumph over evil and chaos. In the Sumerian flood myth, the name of the demon of primeval chaos was **Kingu**, the same name as that of the bull thrown into a pit of bitumen at the annual festival *See* ABYSS & BLACK & BULL & CHAOS IN NATURE & DEMON & FLOOD & SACRIFICE ANIMAL & SUN OLD & TRINITY & WAR -25a IRAQ, ACCADIAN \MUNt

• Artifacts and wall paintings depict youths leaping over the heads of charging bulls *See* BABY BOY & BULL & SOCIETAL ASPECT & WAR -20b CRETE, MINOAN *Figure 224*

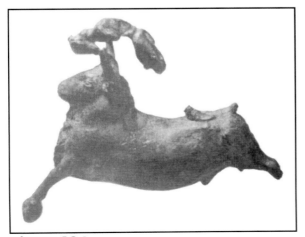

Figure 224

• In the Olympic Games, "race-in-armor", the runners carried shields depicting a rayed sun and a snake *See* HERO & PATH & SUN YOUNG & WAR -5a GREEK \SWBp

• Bronze discs from the site of the Olympic Games were dedicated as religious offerings in a spiral inscription addressed to the sun god **Zeus** *See* BRONZE & CELESTIAL & HERO & PATH & ROUND MOTIF & SUN YOUNG -5a GREEK \SWBp

• Religious ball games were performed by authority figures as a ritual to renew the crops after each winter and when there was a great scarcity of food *See* FERTILITY & REGENERATION & SEASON & WAR -4a EGYPT, LIBYAN \HEAt

• A pre-classic vessel in the form of a ball court is surrounded by serpents *See* PATH & SERPENT ENTWINED & VESSEL +2a GUATEMALA, MAYAN \BOQp

• Carved objects from Mesoamerican ballcourts often depict the cosmic serpent. A stone ring which had been mounted vertically near the top of a ball court wall was carved with an entwined feathered serpent through which the ball was impelled, and a carved palmate stone that was worn in a player's yoke during rituals at the games depicts a death's head figure descending on a feathered serpent *See* CELESTIAL & CIRCLE MOTIF & PATH & SERPENT ENTWINED & SKULL & STONE & SUN OLD & UNDERWORLD +6b MEXICO, MAYAN/ TOTONACAN *Figure 225   Figure 226*

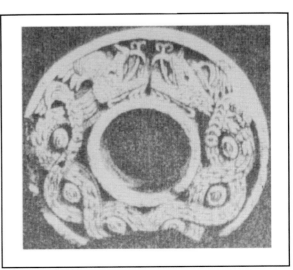

Figure 225

• The jaguar and the deer were often associated with the ritual ball game *See* DEER & FELINE & HERO & LEAP-UP +6a GUATEMALA, MAYAN \HEZt \RECt

• After the culture collapsed, the ball game was no longer played by the Maya *See* COLLAPSE MYSTERIOUS & RITUAL +9a GUATEMALA, MAYAN \THLt

• Spanish conquerors destroyed the many ballcourts that were being used in the ceremonial centers when they arrived because the ballcourts were "like a temple" *See* DEMYTHOLIZATION & RITUAL +15a MEXICO, AZTEC \STEt

• Ball players carved into stone slabs around a courtyard in the style of the Olmecs, the mother culture of Mesoamerica, are depicted on their hands and knees wearing entwined neck bands and protective headdresses with jaguar ears *See* FELINE & WAR -15b MEXICO, DAINZU *Figure 227*

Figure 226

Figure 227

• Scholars are puzzled by a painted vase which depicts seashells above two ball players. One ball player wears a headdress of a bird with a fish in it's mouth. The headdress of the other player represents a deer holding a flower suggesting that a contest takes place under the western horizon water, between the old sun who landed as a bird upon the water, and the young sun who leaps into the eastern horizon carrying the fertility of the new season *See* CRUSTACEAN & DEER & FLORA & MARINE BIRD & SUN YOUNG & UNDERWORLD +6a GUATEMALA, MAYAN \HEZp

• Stone sculptures in the ballcourts depicted the games' patron deity **Xochipilli**, the young sun god of flowers and food. The board game of patolli was also dedicated to him *See* FERTILITY & GAMBLING & GAME BOARD & SOCIETAL ASPECT & SPRINGTIME & SUN YOUNG & WAR +13b MEXICO, AZTEC \CAMp

• The word "ollin", describing the motion of the heavenly bodies, was also the name of the flying ball in the ball game *See* ROUND MOTIF & SUN +13b MEXICO, AZTEC \BOQt

• A detail from the carved stone panel flanking a ball-court depicts the ritual sacrifice of a figure wearing the regalia of a ball player *See*

HERO & OBJECTS RITUALLY BROKEN & SACRIFICE HUMAN +14b MEXICO, EL TAJIN *Figure* 228

Figure 228

• The sports center where contests and circuses were held was called "Euripus", which means "the navel of the sea". [Note: The names "Europe" and the goddess **Europa** are also derived from an ancient form of "the navel of the sea", suggesting that the sports contests, land and goddesses were similarly associated with the abyss at the western horizon water. Contestants made up to seven circuits around the center pyramid which was said to "belong to the sun" *See* ABYSS & GODDESSES & LEVELS CELESTIAL & PYRAMID & RITUAL & SUN OLD/ YOUNG & WEST ORIENTATION +11a ITALY, ROMAN \SANt

• The French game of La Soule, or "to raise up", was played before the door of the abbey on festival days of Christmas and Lent. Single men of the town were pitted against the married men in a struggle that was often bloody and sometimes fatal *See* CHRISTMASTIDE & HOUSE & LEAP-UP & MARRIAGE & REGENERATION & SOCIETAL ASPECT & SPRINGTIME & WAR +11a FRANCE \HEAt

• Ball games representing strife between Winter and Spring are played to bring on Spring *See* SPRINGTIME & TRINITY & WAR +18a MORROCCO \HEAt

• During the month of May, men costumed as tigers and bulls engage in desperate battles in churchyards, at times resulting in fatalities. Without their fight to "save the world", the sun will not rise and there will be no rain *See* BULL

& FELINE & HOUSE & RITUAL & RAIN & SOCIETAL ASPECT & SUN YOUNG & WAR +19a MEXICO *Figure* 229

Figure 229

• The oldest continuous sports festival in the U.S.A. is the Pueblo Race, with roots back to the Anasazi of the seventh century. It is run in an east-west direction on an unmarked track called the "sun road". The object of the race is not to win, but "to empower father sun" and bring rain *See* ANCESTOR WORSHIP & PATH & REGENERATION & RITUAL & RAIN & SOCIETAL ASPECT +19a USA, TAOS \AMWt

• During male initiation rites of aborigines living in the southern tip of South America, young men wrestle ominous figures wearing pyramidal head coverings similar to that worn today by the Ku Klux Klan. Upon winning, the initiate becomes a man *See* HUSK & PUBERTY RITE & PYRAMID & SOCIETAL ASPECT & TRANSCULTURAL SIMILARITY & UNDERWORLD & WAR +19a ARGENTINA, ONA \CAIp

• The Toreador who kills the bull in bullfights wears an emblazoned "suit of light" and a hat with cat-like ears. He carries a red cape with which to taunt the bull, although a bull cannot distinguish color. John Fulton, an American born matador, wore a "suit of light" depicting lions' heads superimposed on radiant suns. [Note: One of the bull's ears is sometimes cut off and displayed as a proud symbol of the bull's death, probably because the ear is near a horn and easier to excise] *See* ART & BULL & BULL'S HORN & FELINE & RAYED MOTIF & RED & REGENERATION & SUN YOUNG & WAR +19a SPAIN \WESp \ROMp

• One of the countless mysteries in our love of baseball is thrusting our arms upwards as we cheer. The high-five sign is also a symbol of victory in our other sports *See* CELESTIAL & HAND RAISED \AMWt

garden *The letter H of the Snake Ring Template. Ref* FLORA, SOCIETY AS AT THE AXIS MUNDI.

Garden of Eden *The letter H of the Snake Ring Template. Genesis: The garden where Adam, the proverbial first man, and Eve dwelled.* A metaphor for the western horizon, where the sun joins with the mother goddess to produce the new sun, bringer of fertility. **[Note:** Even after demytholization, mankind is the metaphor for the descendants of the creator couple]. *Ref* ANCESTOR WORSHIP, DEMYTHOLIZATION, HAND RAISED, SOCIETAL ASPECT.

• Scholars are puzzled by two contradictory accounts of creation placed one after the other in the Bible. The meanings of the Serpent and the other images in the Garden of Eden are problematic *See* DEMYTHOLIZATION & PATH & REGENERATION -6a ISRAEL, JEWISH \ENDt \NYTt

• Scholars find no acceptable explanation of the Tree of Knowledge. **God** said not to touch of it lest one die, but the serpent [the treatment of the serpent in Paradise amounts to desecration and demytholization, quite possibly intentional], advised that the one who touches it would be as **God**. After the couple touched the tree by eating its fruit, **God** said that "man became as one of us" and banished them *See* DEATH & DEMYTHOLIZATION & GOD & REGENERATION & SNAKE & TREE -6a ISRAEL, JEWISH \ENDt \LITt

• What was the Knowledge represented by the Tree in the Garden of Eden [written in the 8th to 7th centuries B.C.] that was so harmful, that this single tree would be out of bounds? *See* DEMYTHOLIZATION & SNAKE & TREE +19a ELAINE PAGELS \NYTt

• The Garden of Eden, also called the Garden of Yahweh and Garden of God, was at the "joining of rivers". According to Ezekiel, it was

the location of the "holy mountain" and "stones of fire", where Adam heard the voice of **God** while walking in the garden at evening *See* DESCENDING MOTIF & FIRE & GOD & JOINING OF RIVERS & MOUNTAIN & NIGHT & STONE & WATER -6a ISRAEL, JEWISH \ENDt \LITt

• Adam originally wore a garment of light. His was not at first a proper name; its etymology root is the color red. The Hebrew letters of the name are the pictographs for "bull", "fish" and "water", while the feminine form of Adam designates the earth. Hebrew letters for the name Eve are the pictographs for "ladder" and "vessel" *See* BULL & LADDER & RAYED MOTIF & RED & VESSEL & WATER -6a ISRAEL, JEWISH \ENDt \WESt

gargoyle *The letter F of the Snake Ring Template.* A metaphor for the fall of water at the abyss within the serpent path to the western mountain-house. *Ref* CHURCH, DRAGON, HOUSE, PATH, WATERFALL.

garland *The letter I of the Snake Ring Template. Ref* FLORA, WREATH.

garment *or* **clothing** *The letter R of the Snake Ring Template.* A part of the metaphors in the societal tableau inspiring the sun family to harmony in the seasons. *Ref* BODY PAINT, HAT, JEWELRY, SOCIETAL ASPECT, TATTOO.

• An American fashion expert: "Fashion is theater" *See* SOCIETAL ASPECT & THEATER +19a WENDY GOODMAN \WESt

• The hem was the most important part of a woman's robe, and was cut off in the event of her divorce *See* CROSS WEST & HORIZON & HORIZONTAL MOTIF & MARRIAGE & MOTHER GODDESS -20b IRAQ, ACCADIAN \ARCt

• The neck opening in the traditional blouses worn by many present-day Mayan women represents the sun, and the attached ribbons it's rays. Woven geometric motifs of the blouses are "the sun moving through the layers of the sky and underworld" *See* LEVELS & MARRIAGE & MOTHER GODDESS & PATH & RIBBON & SOCIETAL ASPECT & SUN OLD & WEAVING +19a MEXICO, MAYAN \WESp \ARCp

• Women decorate their dance costumes with the symbol of a horizontal rectangle, men with a tree or a cross. Both have flowers embroidered around these symbols *See* CROSS WEST & DANCE & FLORA & HORIZON & SOCIETAL ASPECT & THEATER & TREE +19a MEXICO, TZOTZIL \FONt

• **Samedi**, the god of death, is represented at cemeteries by wooden crosses draped with black coats and top hats *See* BLACK & CROSS WEST & DEATH & HAT & SOCIETAL ASPECT & SUN OLD & VERTICALITY +19a HAITI, VOODOO \RAUt

• To be naked is to be speechless +19a MALI, DOGON \GRKt

Garuda bird The letter Q of the Snake Ring Template. The carrier of the sun god Vishnu. *Ref* RAPTOR.

gateway The letter H of the Snake Ring Template. *Ref* HOUSE, PROCESSION, SOCIETY AS AT THE AXIS MUNDI.

gazelle The letter O of the Snake Ring Template. *Ref* DEER, LEAP-UP.

Gemini The letter I of the Snake Ring Template. Zodiac. The Twins. *Ref* TWINS.

ghost The letter L of the Snake Ring Template. A metaphor for the husks of the old suns, with emphasis on their ability to pass through the solid matter of the house as in the descent to the underworld. *Ref* HOUSE, OCCULT, PSYCHOLOGY CHILD, TRINITY.

giant The letter L of the Snake Ring Template. A metaphor for the old suns remaining in the underworld, with emphasis on their superhuman attributes. *Ref* FAIRY TALE, MYTH, TRINITY, WAR.

gift giving The letter I of the Snake Ring Template. *Ref* BIRTH, MARRIAGE, MATERIALISM, RITES OF PASSAGE, SEASON.

goat or *ram* The letter C of the Snake Ring Template. A metaphor for the virility of the old sun. *Ref* BEAR, BOAR, BULL.

• Images of an energetic bull and ram are sex symbols +19a PHILLIP RAWSON \RAUt

• The ram was the symbol of the sun god **Amon-Ra** -30b EGYPT \CIRt

• Before the second millennia B.C. the most common sacred male animal was the bull; after that it was the ram [corresponding to the shift in the vernal equinox star chart due to the precession of the equinoxes] *See* celestial observation -20b EGYPT \WETt

• The zodiac figure of Capricorn is a goat whose body ends in a fish tail. The image is said to refer to the abyss in the water and the heights of mountains *See* ABYSS & PATH & MOUNTAIN & SUN OLD & WATER & WEST ORIENTATION -20b \CIRp

• The goddesses **Aphrodite** and **Persephone** mated with goats and bulls. Persephone's son **Dionysus**, was portrayed in cult rituals as a virile goat or bull *See* INCEST & MARRIAGE & PATH & REGENERATION & RITUAL -20b GREEK \NEUt \RAUt \ARCt

• The bull-god **Bel**, successor to the deities **Anu** and **Enlil**, was also called "the great Ram" -19b IRAQ, ASSYRIAN \ELIt

• In the Rig Veda, the sun god **Indra** was "the leader of the other gods" and was represented at times as a bull or a ram *See* GODS -19b INDIA, HINDU \MCCt

• Rams are most often the animal being sacrificed in tribal art *See* DEATH & REGENERATION & SACRIFICE ANIMAL +18a NIGERIA, IFE \EYOp

• During the planting season, the village sanctuary is painted with the image of a ram "urinating". Its tail is in the shape of a serpent, and a calabash. The symbol of the sun's path is between its horns *See* ART & CALABASH & COPULATION & FERTILITY & FLORA & HOUSE & PATH & REGENERATION & SUN OLD +19a MALI, DOGON \GRKt

• Russian folklore describes the sun as a red ram with seven horns who enters into the underworld for its passage through the night *See* LEVELS CELESTIAL & PATH & RED & UNDERWORLD & WEST ORIENTATION +19a RUSSIA \ELHt

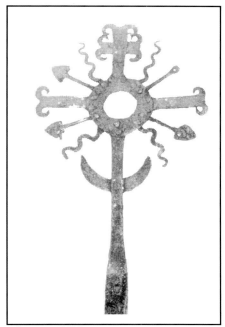

Figure 230

• Approximately 50,000 pre-Christian "iron crosses" remain at road crossings, cemeteries, sacred streams and holy groves, and on hills and trees. The crosses are often surmounting models of chapels and mounds of stones at these locations, in spite of objections by the Church. Rams' horns, heart motifs and snakes surround a ring motif of the sun which joins on the staff with a crescent moon *See* CROSSROAD & CROSS WEST & DEATH & HOUSE MODELS & MARRIAGE & MOON & MOUNTAIN & RING MOTIF & SNAKE & SOCIETY AS AT THE AXIS MUNDI & STONE & SUN OLD & TREE +13b LITHUANIA, BALTIC *Figure 230*

• A mosaic from the sixth century synagogue Bet Alef, "house of the bull", depicts Abraham's intended sacrifice of his son Isaac. On the mountain top is the burning bush where **God** spoke to Abraham, and the ram which was sacrificed in place of Isaac *See* BULL & DEATH & DEMYTHOLIZATION & FIRE & HOUSE &

MOUNTAIN & SACRIFICE ANIMAL/ HUMAN +5a ISRAEL, JEWISH *Figure 231*

Figure 231

• A Passover plate is marked for offerings of a roasted lamb shank representing death and sacrifice, parsley which is dipped in salt water to represent the sea, an egg symbolizing birth, and greens, herbs, apples and nuts, symbolizing springtime fertility. Passover was a pre-Judaic domestic ceremony [not a feast of the Exodus] celebrated by Canaanite herdsmen by smearing blood of sacrificed animals on the lintel and door posts of their houses at springtime before taking their flocks to the cultivated regions to graze *See* BIRTH & DEMYTHOLIZATION & EGG & DEATH & FERTILITY & FIRE & HOUSE & REGENERATION & RITUAL & SPRINGTIME & SOCIETAL ASPECT & SACRIFICE ANIMAL & WATER -10b ISRAEL, JEWISH \ENDt *Figure 232*

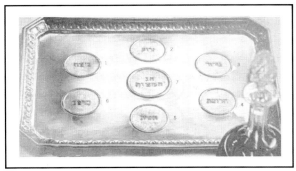

Figure 232

goblet *The letter K of the Snake Ring Template.* *Ref* CALABASH, VESSEL, WATER, WINE.

God *The letter S of the Snake Ring Template. The Being whom people worship as creator and ruler of the universe. Ref* DEMYTHOLIZATION, SUN OLD.

• In antiquity Yahweh was the sun -20b ISRAEL, JEWISH HANS LEISEGANG \AVDt

• God is in the making *See* DEMYTHOLIZATION +19a CLAUDE LEVI STRAUSS \LETt

goddesses numerous *The letter H of the Snake Ring Template.* Metaphors for the mother goddess of the western horizon water-house in her various incarnations of rebirth, together with her brother, the new sun, at the changes of the seasons. *Ref* BABY GIRL, HOUSE, HORIZON, INCEST, MOTHER GODDESS, PERSONIFICATION, SEASON, SOUL, WEST ORIENTATION, WATER.

• The daughter of "the woman horizontal" dwells in a house in the great water of the west, where she is visited by the sun at the end of his journey *See* DESCENDING MOTIF & HOUSE & HORIZON & MARRIAGE & SUN OLD & WATER & WEST ORIENTATION +18a USA, NAVAJO \COTt

gods *The letter S of the Snake Ring Template.* Metaphors for the sun in its various incarnations at the changes of the seasons. *Ref* BABY BOY, PERSONIFICATION, SEASON, SOUL, SUN OLD/ YOUNG, TRINITY.

• The sun of the wet season is different than the sun of the dry season *See* BIRTH & FERTILITY & REGENERATION & SEASON RAIN & SUN YOUNG +19a COLOMBIA, BARASANA \AVDt

• Aborigines living at Tierra del Fuego, the southern tip of South America, believe that there was an older sun-man in the sky. Then a younger sun-man took his place and the old father went away *See* CHAOS IN NATURE & REGENERATION & SUN OLD/ YOUNG +19a ARGENTINA, ONA \CAIt

• In Dogon mythology, typical of west coast Africa, their ancestor god's name is **Binu**, a contraction of two terms meaning "gone" and "come back" *See* PATH & REGENERATION & TRINITY +19a MALI, DOGON \GRKt

• Plains Indians pray, Grandfather sun, we have been saved to this day because your child, a young orphan, got the wheel from your grave when your foundation was blown down *See* CHAOS IN NATURE & DEATH & MARRIAGE & PATH & REGENERATION & SEASON & SUN OLD/ YOUNG & TRINITY & UROBORUS & WHEEL +19a USA, ARAPAHO \DOPt

gold 1. *The letter I of the Snake Ring Template.* A metaphor for the sun. *Ref* SUN OLD/ YOUNG. 2. *The letter S of the Snake Ring Template.* A metal of exceptional value resulting from the original belief that it was a residue of the sun which had been formed in the underworld. *Ref* ALCHEMY, DEATH, EARRING, JEWELRY, PSYCHOLOGY CHILD, RULER.

• The wearing of gold is a universal primitive urge *See* JEWELRY & SOCIETAL ASPECT & TRANSCULTURAL SIMILARITY +19A \TIMt

• In Hebrew the word for "light" is the Latin word for gold *See* LIGHT & RAYED MOTIF -10b ISRAEL, JEWISH \CIRt

• Gold is the image of solar light *See* LIGHT & SOUL & SUN +19a \CIRt

• Gold was associated with the rebirth of the sun and agriculture *See* AGRICULTURE & REGENERATION -10a PERU, CHAVIN \TL5t

• Gold hungry Spanish explorers were told that the source of gold was the setting sun [possibly one of the mysterious factors noted by Claude Levi-Strauss which drive societies westward] *See* BABY BOY & DEATH & REGENERATION & SUN & WEST ORIENTATION +15a MEXICO, MAYAN \BLBt

• A belief important to cosmology is that gold is the symbol of the sun *See* SUN YOUNG & TRANSCULTURAL SIMILARITY +19a GHANA, ASHANTI \AFAt

Golden Fleece *The letter C of the Snake Ring Template.* A metaphor for the regeneration resulting from the death of the old sun at the western horizon. *Ref* DEATH, GOAT, GOLD, REGENERATION, SHEEP MALE, TRINITY.

goose *The letter F of the Snake Ring Template.* *Ref* DUCK.

gopher *The letter K of the Snake Ring Template. A burrowing rodent. Ref* HOLE.

gorge *The letter K of the Snake Ring Template. Ref* ABYSS, VALLEY.

government *The letter R of the Snake Ring Template.* Authoritative direction or control to maintain an area, its ruler and/or inhabitants. Proper metaphors for the seasonal regenerations of the new sun. *Ref* ETHICS, LAW, RULER, SOCIETAL ASPECT, SOCIETY AS AT THE AXIS MUNDI.

Grail *The letter K of the Snake Ring Template. Knighthood. Goal of the quest for the cup used by Christ at the Last Supper.* A metaphor for heroes joining the underworld conflict. *Ref* DEMYTHOLIZATION, HERO, UNDERWORLD, VESSEL, WAR.

Great Mother *The letter H of the Snake Ring Template. Ref* MOTHER GODDESS.

griffin *The letters M & Q of the Snake Ring Template. Gr. A fabulous animal, half lion, half eagle.* A composite metaphor for the carriers of the sun through the perilous underworld and the lofty reaches of the sky. *Ref* CARRIER, FELINE, PATH, RAPTOR.

guilloche *The letter A of the Snake Ring Template. Interlaced bands with round devices in the openings. Ref* ENTWINED MOTIF, PATH, ROUND MOTIF IN SEQUENCE, SERPENT ENTWINED.

hallucinogen *The letter R of the Snake Ring Template. A substance that induces a perception of objects with no reality,* revealing metaphors of the Snake Ring path in the preconscious. *Ref* ALCOHOLIC BEVERAGES, DRUGS, PSYCHOLOGY CHILD/ DREAM.

• In a hymn of the Rig Veda, drugs are taken to "arrive at the light" *See* LIGHT +19a INDIA, HINDU \OCTt

• Smoking opium is called "tasting the dragon" +19a CHINA \WESt

• Opium is regarded as a supernatural adventure for healing *See* HEALING +19a INDONESIA \OCTt

• "Yaje snakes on houseposts" is a design made in sand paintings while under the influence of hallucinogens. When investigators imbibed the hallucinogens of the Yaje ritual under laboratory conditions, they had similar visions of snakes, as well as of felines and ring motifs. [The Yaje is a hallucinogenic vine that wraps around tree trunks in the jungle. Some patients in advanced societies who are being treated for substance abuse, also report seeing snakes wrapped around houseposts] *See* ART & COLUMN & HOUSE & INFANT MENTALITY & PATH & ROPE & SNAKE & SPIRAL & SOCIOBIOLOGY +19a COLOMBIA, TUKANO \REJt *Figure 233*

• Inhalation tubes for hallucinogenic substances were found in pouches around the necks of deceased in burials. The art on their surfaces depict felines and serpents with ring motifs along their bodies *See* BURIAL & DEATH & FELINE & REGENERATION & RING MOTIF IN SEQUENCE & SNAKE +5b CHILE, ATACAMENA \NUMp

•In tests similar to those performed in the Yaje rituals, investigators who imbibed the drugs used in primitives' initiation rites also experienced visions of snakes *See* INFANT MENTALITY & PATH & PUBERTY RITES & SNAKE +19a PERU, SHARAN \MUNt

• Hallucinogens provide access to the world that is portrayed in their myths *See* MYTHS +19a COLOMBIA, BARASANA \AVDt

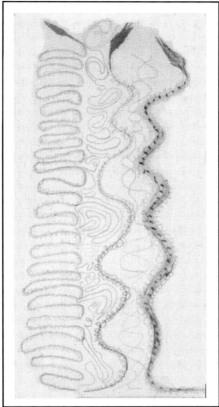

Figure 233

halo *The letter S of the Snake Ring Template.* A metaphor denoting a figure's head as the container for the solar soul. *Ref* DEMYTHOLIZATION, GODS, HEAD, RAYED MOTIF, RING MOTIF.

hammer 1. *The letter D of the Snake Ring Template.* A metaphor for transformation, or regeneration, using the anvil and fire as the medium. *Ref* ALCHEMY, ANVIL, BLACKSMITH, FIRE, TRINITY. 2. **~ vertical.** *The letter E of the Snake Ring Template.* A metaphor for the path through the western horizon. *Ref* ABYSS, CROSS WEST, HORIZON, LABRYS, REGENERATION, VERTICAL LINE/ SHAPE.

hand down *The letter D of the Snake Ring Template.* A metaphor for the sun descending into the western underworld. *Ref* DESCENDING MOTIF, HAND'S DOWN AND UP/ RAISED, REGENERATION.

hand raised **1**. *The letter O of the Snake Ring Template.* Raised hands are the most frequent images in the terminal Ice Age caves. See SECTION TWO.

hand raised with missing digit

The letter N of the Snake Ring Template. A composite metaphor for the young sun's triumph over the perils in the underworld, as he ascends with the solar soul in the east. *Ref* HAND RAISED, WAR.

• Mutilated hands were common in Ice Age art. 150 mutilated hands were imprinted on the walls of a single Ice Age cave in the Pyrenees mountains *See* ART & SOCIETAL ASPECT -350b FRANCE, GARGAS *Figure 234*

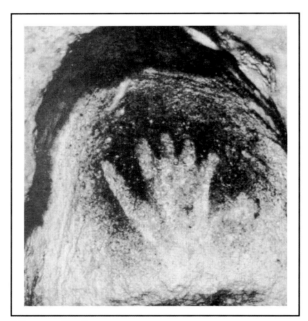

Figure 234

• Scholars are unable to decipher the earliest Greek writing. Heiroglyphs depicting raised hands with mutilated digits, bulls, birds, felines, fish, and flowers, were carved into the Phaistos disk in a spiral pattern of seven turns *See* LETTERS & LEVELS CELESTIAL & PATH & REGENERATION & SPIRAL & STONE & WRITING -19a CRETE, MINOAN *Figure 235   Figure 236*

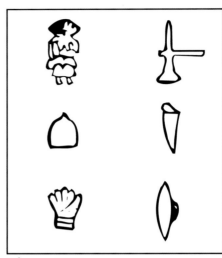

Figure 235

• A carved stone "hacha" associated with the Mesoamerican ball game, where players were ritually sacrificed, depicts a head with large circles around its eyes. A mutilated hand at its forehead has the ring motif in its palm *See* EYE & GAME SPORT & HEAD & HERO & RING MOTIF & SACRIFICE HUMAN +2a MEXICO, MAYAN \BOQp

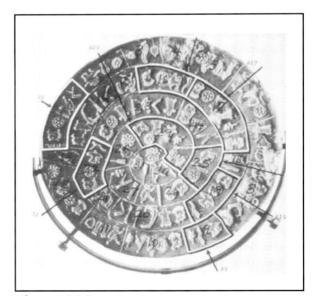

Figure 236

• In the raised hand salute to the ruler the index finger was bent as though mutilated *See* RULER & SOCIETAL ASPECT & WAR +3a IRAN, SASSANIAN \GIRt

• The mutilated hands of slaves captured in war and intended for human sacrifice were dipped in a dye and imprinted on the lintels and posts of the master's house *See* HOUSE & SACRIFICE HUMAN & WAR +15a MEXICO, AZTEC \CAJt

• In many of the puberty rites of American Indians finger joints were mutilated *See* PUBERTY RITES +18a USA \LETt

• George Catlin's painting of the Okipa Sun Dance ceremony depicts initiates hanging by ropes together with suspended buffalo skulls. The initiates hang in the center of the lodge from skewers piercing their flesh. In the front right corner of the painting, an initiate who has subsequently crawled on the ground until the suspended buffalo skulls were dislodged, now places his hand on a buffalo skull to have a digit amputated. After these sacrifices, the initiate is qualified to join the war parties *See* BULL & DEATH & HERO & PATH & PUBERTY RITES & REGENERATION & ROPE & SUN OLD/ YOUNG & WAR +18a USA, MANDAN \CAIp *Figure 237*

Figure 237

• A bloody raised hand was one of the oldest symbols once displayed on armor, is now used in heraldry *See* WAR +19a ENGLAND, MONARCHY \SMJt

• In the initiation rites of the mobsters called Yazuka in present-day Japan, they are tattooed with Irezumi images [typically a dragon] and a digit of the hand is amputated *See* PATH & PUBERTY RITE & PSYCHOLOGY CONTEMPORARY PROBLEMS & SOCIETAL ASPECT & TATTOO & TRANSCULTURAL SIMILARITY & WAR +19a JAPAN \NWSt

• The wife of a young Plains Indian chief cut off a finger of her hand as a sacrifice to the sun, so that her husband would be victorious in war *See* SUN YOUNG & WAR +19a USA, ARAPAHO \DOPt

• An Indian prayer: "I give you this joint of my finger so that I will strike one of the enemy, marry a good natured woman and have a tent of my own" *See* HOUSE & MARRIAGE & PATH & WAR +19a USA, CROW \CAAt

• At the death of a warrior, his widow cuts off part of his finger before taking the corpse to a mountaintop for funerary rites *See* DEATH & MOUNTAIN & PATH & REGENERATION & WAR +19a NEW GUINEA, SEPIK \COUt

• Stencils of hands with missing fingers have been found in many regions of Australia. Boomerangs are painted above the mutilated hands stenciled on Carnavon Mountain *See* MOUNTAIN & PATH & REGENERATION & WAR +19a AUSTRALIA \ARCp

hands down and up *The letter I of the Snake Ring Template.* A metaphor for the trinitarian path of the sun at the change in seasons. The father dies and descends to remain in the western underworld; the son rises in the eastern horizon. *Ref* TRINITY.

• A painting on the wall of an Ice Age cave in Spain depicts a prostrate bird-headed man next to a snake formed of round motifs. The lower part of the bird-man's body is formed of two opposing figures with their arms raised; one of the figures is upright and the other inverted *See* ART & BIRD & CAVE & CROSSROADS & PATH & ROUND MOTIF IN SEQUENCE & SNAKE -350b SPAIN, LA PILETA \BUMp

• An undeciphered shrine from the tomb of Tutankhamun depicts a solar disk within a uroborus held by a goddess between her arms. One of her hands is pointing down and the other hand is pointing up *See* CROSSROAD & DEATH & MOTHER GODDESS & PATH & REGENERATION & RULER & UROBORUS -13a EGYPT \EDVt

• Some deities are depicted with their hands pointing down and up, one hand in the "boon-bestowing gesture" pointing down and the other in the "fear-dispelling gesture" pointing up *See* DEATH & GODS & LEAP-UP & REGENERATION +5a INDIA, HINDU \CAMp

Hanged man *The letter D of the Snake Ring Template.* Tarot. *The twelfth enigma, the man, hanging in an inverted position.* A metaphor for the descent of the old sun to its death in the western horizon. *Ref* DEATH, DESCENDING MOTIF, LEVELS CELESTIAL, TAROT PACK, TREE.

hare *The letter H of the Snake Ring Template* *Ref* MARRIAGE, RABBIT.

harp *The letter P of the Snake Ring Template.* A metaphor for the passage of the sun through the celestial layers. *Ref* MUSIC.

hat *or* **headdress** *The letter R of the Snake Ring Template.* The wearer's head as a metaphor for: **a. round ~ (cap)** the round face of the sun, **b. top ~** the sun below the vertical segment of the serpent path at the western horizon, **c. feathered ~** the container of the solar sun that will ascend to the sky, **d. veiled** *or* **hooded** the underworld sun or goddess, **e. cone-shaped** the sun below the western horizon mountain. *Ref* FEATHERED, HEAD, MOUNTAIN, PSYCHOLOGY CHILD, ROUND MOTIF, SOCIETAL ASPECT, SUN OLD/ YOUNG, T-INVERTED, UNDERWORLD, WEST ORIENTATION.

• A gold-covered figure depicts the creator sky deity **Ptah** with a goat's beard and wearing a round cap. His cloak has feathers and wings, and his collar consists of seven rings. His staff, which has five horizontal elements including the ankh symbol for eternity, ends with a double-pronged bottom resembling a

snake holder **[Note:** Probably to hold to the eternal serpent path as he descends, via the axis mundi, from the seven-level sky to the five-level underworld**]** *See* ETERNITY & FEATHERED & GOAT & GODS & GOLD & HAT & LEVELS CELESTIAL/ INFERNAL & PATH & ROUND MOTIF & SNAKE & SOUL & VERTICAL STICK -13a EGYPT, TUTANKHAMUN *Figure 238*

Figure 238

• Colossal stone heads found in La Venta and other ceremonial centers of the oldest Mesoamerican culture, described as the mother culture, are carved in a spherical form. They wear a skull cap often decorated with ring motifs, jaguar paws and/or raised hand symbols. [Judging by the symbols, the colossal heads are metaphors for the seasonally reborn new suns] *See* FELINE & HAND RAISED & HAT & RING MOTIF & ROUND MOTIF & STONE & SUN YOUNG -9a MEXICO, OLMEC *Figure 239*

Figure 239

• Elders of the secret Poro society wear a skull cap *See* ROUND MOTIF & RULER +19a IVORY COAST, SENUFO \METt

• Skull caps were often found in graves along with nose rings and earrings *See* FUNERAL & JEWELRY & RING MOTIF & ROUND MOTIF +19a MALI, DOGON \ARCt

• Authority figures of the Ife mother culture delegate to the Yoruba king his right to wear a beaded skull cap *See* PATH & ROUND MOTIF IN SEQUENCE & ROUND MOTIF & RULER +19a NIGERIA, YORUBA \GARt

• Bronze panels which once sheathed the columns of the palace depict royal figures wearing skull caps +15a NIGERIA, BENIN \PAQp

hawk *The letter Q of the Snake Ring Template.* *Ref* RAPTOR.

head 1. *The letter S of the Snake Ring Template.* The visible part of the celestial sun; container of the everlasting solar soul. *Ref* ROUND MOTIF. **2.** *The letter R of the Snake Ring Template.* Part of the human anatomy used as a metaphor for the sun. *Ref* EARRING, GARMENT, HAT, SOCIETAL ASPECT.

• The pictogram for "soul" is a large head *See* SOUL +17a CHINA \BRAt

• Earrings and beads were placed in burials near the head, which was believed to be the carrier of the soul *See* JEWELRY & RING MOTIFS & ROUND MOTIFS IN SEQUENCE -30b EGYPT \WESt

• Cast marks on the forehead symbolize the head as the seat of the soul *See* BODY PAINT & ROUND MOTIF & SOCIETAL ASPECT -19b INDIA, HINDU \BRBt

• Homer described the dead as "empty heads" *See* HUSK & SOUL & TRINITY -6a GREEK \DUSt

• The roll-out of a painted cylindrical vase from a burial depicts an aged deity within the mouth of the feathered serpent Kukulkan. A serpent emanates from the old god's mouth to enwrap and possibly penetrate a nude goddess seated in a palace. [Death is a metaphor for the old sun's death along the serpent path into the mother goddess' western horizon house, where he transfers the solar soul to her by their copulation, and is reborn from her as the sun of the new season] *See* BURIAL & DEATH & HEAD & HOUSE & MARRIAGE & PATH & REGENERATION & SOCIETAL ASPECT & SOUL & VESSEL +3b MEXICO, MAYAN *Figure 240*

• The Inca represented the sun by a round face surrounded by rays *See* RAYED MOTIF & ROUND MOTIF +14b PERU, INCA \MASt

Figure 240

• The sun god **Siva's** necklace of heads represents his cycle of rebirths. A painting depicts a goddess carrying his sun-head while seated on a lion with a snake as its tail *See* CARRIER & FELINE & JEWELRY & PATH & REGENERATION & ROUND MOTIF IN SEQUENCE & SEASON & SOUL -19b INDIA, HINDU \SMJt *Figure 241*

Figure 241

Figure 242

• An offering tablet at the westernmost city of Egypt, where the god **Osiris** was worshipped as the evening sun, depicts his head at the top of a pillar that continues into the symbol for "mountain" *See* DESCENDING MOTIF & GODS & MOUNTAIN & PILLAR & SOCIETY AS AT THE AXIS MUNDI & WEST ORIENTATION -13a EGYPT, ABYDOS *Figure 242*

• A painted shrine wall of the earliest true city in the world depicts flying vultures with round motifs within their bodies, suggesting that they are carrying into the sky the heads of the beheaded male figures shown below *See* CARRIER & LEAP-UP & RAPTOR & ROUND MOTIF & SUN YOUNG -70b TURKEY, CATAL HUYUK \TILp **Refer to** *Figure 153* SECTION TWO.

• Human skulls covered in painted clay with cowrie shells for eyes, were imbedded in the walls and buried under the house floors of one of the oldest ceremonial centers in the world *See* CRUSTACEAN COWRIE & DEATH & HOUSE & REGENERATION & SOCIETY AS AT THE AXIS MUNDI -70a ISRAEL, JERICHO *Figure 243*

Figure 243

• The initiates in Aborigines' puberty rites pluck out their hair and beard in order to identify more closely with the appearance of the sun hero **Grogoragalloy**, son of the creator god *See* PUBERTY RITE & ROUND MOTIF & SOCIETAL ASPECT & SUN YOUNG +19a AUSTRALIA, WIRADJURI \ELIt

• Odd how many people go to extremes to remove their face hair +19a \BRBt

• The Plains Indians shaved all of their heads, sometimes leaving just a scalp-lock.

• Young Tchikrin boys of Brazil are designated as "the little ones" only after they have their eyebrows and eyelashes plucked.

• Southeast Indians of the U.S. also included their eyebrows when they plucked all of their face-hairs.

• The Hittites of the 2nd millennia B.C. in present-day Syria, shaved off their eyebrows as well when they shaved their faces.

• The explorers who arrived at Easter Island found that the natives' heads were close-shaven in emulation of their god, the sun, with a visible head "who needs no body."

• Buddhist priests with shaven heads burn incense and offer flowers to the Buddha *See* FLORA & HEAD & INCENSE & PRIEST & ROUND MOTIF & SOCIETAL ASPECT & SOUL \TUQp \BRBt \METt \HEWt \EXQp *Figure 244*

Figure 244

• The much earlier Sumerians of Iraq, shaved their faces.

• The Olmec and the Maya of Mesoamerica plucked out their facial hair, as did the nobles of Peru, the California Indian tribes, and the West Indians as the explorers noted when they arrived.

• The priests, deities, rulers, and males of ancient Egypt were generally depicted as clean shaven, although mortuary art sometimes depicted them wearing an artificial goat beard *See* GOAT & ROUND MOTIF & SOCIETAL ASPECT \PRIt \AMNt \HAIt \ARCt \KROt \LETt \ENDt \NEWt \EDVt

• The books of Deuteronomy and Leviticus forbade "rounding the corners of the face" as the other religions in the area did by shaving. According to Judges, when men permit their face hair to grow "they bless the Lord." **[Note:**

The wearing of skull-caps by Orthodox Jews, which rounded the face like shaving, began by with Jewish scholars in the sixteenth century in imitation of Babylonian scholars] *See* DEMYTHOLIZATION & HAT & ROUND MOTIF & SOCIETAL ASPECT -6a ISRAEL, JEWISH \ENDt \LITt

• The human heads acquired in headhunting represented the hornbill bird. **[Note:** "bird" as a metaphor for the sun] *See* BIRD & SUN OLD & WAR +19a NEW GUINEA, ASMAT \RAUt

• Head-hunting was once all over the world *See* ROUND MOTIF & SOUL & WAR +19a PHILLIP RAWSON \RAUt

head flattening *The letter R of the Snake Ring Template.* A ritual reshaping of the head as a metaphor for the head of the sun, to facilitate its passage, within the mythic serpent's body. *Ref* HEAD, PATH, SOCIETAL ASPECT.

• The mother culture of Mesoamerica began head-flattenning of infants, which became common throughout the area *See* BABY BOY -15b MEXICO, OLMEC \MUTt \LARt

• Skull flattening was common among the men +2b PERU, NAZCA \MASt

• Southeast Indians flattened their infants' heads until recent times +18a USA, NATCHEZ \TUQt

• Considering it an act of beauty, the Northwest Indians still flatten their infants heads on a cradle-board +19a CANADA \BUQt

• Skull flattening at infancy is practiced by some Amazonian tribes +19a COLOMBIA, TUKANO \HUGt

• An old Armenian custom, still practiced, is the cranial deformation of infants by binding them to a cradle-board +19a IRAQ, ARMENIA \FIEt

headhunting *The letter N of the Snake Ring Template. Ref* WAR.

healing *The letter* ***I*** *of the Snake Ring Template.* The human condition as a metaphor for the regeneration of the sun at the western horizon mountain-house within the serpent path *Ref* REGENERATION, SOCIETAL ASPECT.

• While exposing the sick part of the body to the smoke of a fiery cross, Bolivian Indians prick it with the tooth of a boa *See* CROSS WEST & DEATH & FIRE & PATH & REGENERATION & SNAKE & SOCIETAL ASPECT +18a BOLIVIA \LETt

• Live snakes were revered in the healing temples of Asclepios. At one of these temples, which were located near to springs, Hippocrates the father of modern medicine, was trained. According to legend, he was the son of the young sun god **Apollo**. Bulls were sacrificed at the temples. Patients slept in the bulls' hides and were fed mother's milk during the healing process, which was regarded as a period of incubation. Sterile women also went to the healing temples in the hope that the serpent god would "lay on their belly" and enable them to produce children. The symbol of modern medicine is the caduceus with entwined serpents *See* BABY BOY & BULL & CADUCEUS & DEATH & REGENERATION & SACRIFICE ANIMAL & SERPENT ENTWINED & SUN YOUNG & WATER -20b GREEK \MUNt \LEUt \OCTt *Figure 245* **Refer also to** *Figure 13* SECTION TWO.

Figure 245

• **Hygieia**, the Greek goddess of healing, is depicted in a Roman marble bas relief with a large serpent at her side. Above her are symbols of the young sun god **Apollo** [whose name means "from the mouth of the lion"], a snake emerging from a wine pitcher, and a basket containing a snake and the divine child. An infant is at her feet holding a bow *See* ARROW & BABY BOY & CARRIER & CUPID &

FELINE & GODDESSES & PATH & REGENERATION & SNAKE & SUN YOUNG & VESSEL & WAR +3 ITALY, ROMAN *Figure 246*

Figure 246

• In the Bible, Moses was also called "the rod" in commemoration of the rod he was holding which turned into a snake and his leprous hand was healed. According to lore, this snake was the winged serpent Nehustan, a statue which stood for almost four centuries in the Great Temple in Jerusalem, from the time the Temple was built until the statues of Nehustan and the mother goddess **Astarte** were removed in the seventh century B.C. *See* DEMYTHOLIZATION & HOUSE & MOTHER GODDESS & PATH & REGENERATION & SERPENT WINGED & SNAKE & SOCIETAL ASPECT & STAFF -10b ISRAEL, JEWISH \ENDt

• Indians say that the sick are in need of disentangling *See* PATH & REGENERATION & ROPE +19a MEXICO, HUICHOL \AVDt

• In Northwest Indians' healing ceremonies, the ill are cured by the use of a carved and painted double headed serpent staff "to capture souls" *See* PATH & REGENERATION & SOUL +18a USA, HAIDA *Figure 247*

Figure 247

• The leader points the stem of his pipe towards the rising sun then to the west when he prays over a patient in healing ceremonies, requesting help from "grandfather sun" to see the right road. During the same ceremony, he asks for rain for the vegetation *See* FERTILITY & REGENERATION & SEASON & SMOKE & SOCIETAL ASPECT & SUN OLD/ YOUNG +18a USA, ARAPAHO \DOPt

• Present-day Maya light incense at the foot of non-Christian crosses during the curing ceremonies. They bathe a black chicken in heated water from sacred holes before sacrificing the bird. After the patient drinks of its blood, the remains of the chicken are taken to the west side of a nearby mountain where it is placed in a hole, with its head facing east *See* BIRD & BLACK & BLOOD & CHICKEN & CROSS WEST & DEATH & FIRE & HOLE & MOUNTAIN & PATH & SACRIFICE ANIMAL & SOCIETAL ASPECT & WATER & EAST/ WEST ORIENTATION +19a MEXICO, ZINACANTECO *Figure 248*

• Villagers in upper Egypt sacrifice a goat to their resident snake to be cured from a disease *See* DEATH & GOAT & PATH & REGENERATION & SACRIFICE ANIMAL +19a EGYPT \MUNt

• For healing illnesses, some people offer sacrifices to their supreme deity, the sun *See* DEATH & REGENERATION & SUN OLD +19a INDONESIA \ELIt

• Snakes are the most common totem of Aborigine medicine men, who are both bark-painters and healers *See* ART & PATH & REGENERATION & SOCIETAL ASPECT +19a AUSTRALIA, ARNHEM LAND \MUNt \NATt

heart human *The letter R of the Snake Ring Template.* A physiological metaphor for the sun. *Ref* ALCHEMY, RED, ROMANTIC LOVE, ROUND MOTIF, SACRIFICE HUMAN, SOCIETAL ASPECT.

hearth *or* **fireplace** *The letter D of the Snake Ring Template.* Taken together with the house, a metaphor for the sun's fiery death leading to marriage and regeneration in the house of the western horizon. *Ref* ARCHITECTURE, FIRE, HOUSE, SOCIETAL ASPECT.

Figure 248

• At Christmastide, the winter solstice in the pre-Gregorian calendars, old St. Nick in his red suit descends the chimney to the hearth. A few days after his descent the New Year is born *See* BABY BOY & CANDLE & CHRISTMASTIDE & DESCENDING MOTIF & HOUSE & PATH & RED & REGENERATION & SOCIETY AS AT THE AXIS MUNDI & VERTICAL LINE/ SHAPE +19a CHRISTIAN \WESp

heaven *The letter P of the Snake Ring Template. Ref* CELESTIAL.

he-goat *The letter C of the Snake Ring Template. Ref* BEAR, BOAR, BULL, SHEEP.

helmet *The letter N of the Snake Ring Template. Ref* GARMENT, HAT, WAR.

hemisphere motif *The letters K & P of the Snake Ring Template.* Metaphors for the dome of the sky and the inverted dome of the underworld formed by the path of the entwined serpent. *Ref* CALABASH, LEVELS CELESTIAL/ UNDERWORLD.

herb *The letter I of the Snake Ring Template.* *Ref* FLORA.

herm *The letter E of the Snake Ring Template. Gr. A pillar usu. surmounted by a bearded head of Hermes.* *Ref* HERMES, STELE.

• Stone pillars often placed at Greek crossroads had the head of a bearded deity, or of **Hermes**, carved at its top. Rudimentary cross-arms were above a caduceus carved into its side, and prominent genitals were at its front surface *See* CADUCEUS & CROSSROAD & CROSS WEST & MARRIAGE & PATH & SERPENT ENTWINED & SOCIETY AS AT THE AXIS MUNDI & TRINITY & VERTICAL LINE/ SHAPE -20b GREEK *Figure* 249

Figure 249

hermaphrodite *The letter H of the Snake Ring Template.* A metaphor for the joined sun and mother goddess within the vertical segment of the entwined serpent path at the western horizon. *Ref* MARRIAGE, PATH.

Hermes *The letter A of the Snake Ring Template. Gr. Relig.; the messenger of the gods and conductor of the dead to Hades.* A metaphor for the entwined serpent path which guides the sun into the western horizon for its seasonal regenerations. *Ref* CADUCEUS, PATH.

Hermit *The letter L of the Snake Ring Template. Tarot. The ninth enigma: an old man carrying a lantern and a staff with a serpent entwined around it.* A metaphor for the old sun who is left behind in the nighttime underworld, after his son, the new sun, has taken his path in the sky. *Ref* LAMP, LEVELS UNDERWORLD, PATH, SERPENT ENTWINED, TAROT PACK, TRINITY, VERTICAL STICK.

hero *The letter N of the Snake Ring Template.* A societal metaphor for the young sun and his feline carrier and guardian, in their attempt to conquer the suns of the previous seasons, including the young sun's own father, who are obstructing the underworld serpent path to the east. *Ref* GAME SPORT, TRINITY, WAR.

• Myths of a hero are not changed in their essential form throughout the documented history of mankind. The hero enters a region of supernatural wonder, where fabulous forces are encountered and conquered +19a JOSEPH CAMPBELL \CADt

• The archetype of the hero is often in a sun myth, where the hero is either a god or the son of a god who kills his father +19a ERICH NEUMANN \NEUt

• The carved handle of a predynastic knife depicts a lion protecting a wary ibex by defeating a bull. On the upper register, a youth is standing between two heroic lions. The carving on the reverse of the handle depicts scenes from a conventional battle *See* BABY BOY & BULL & FELINE & IBEX & WAR -35a EGYPT *Figure* 250

• A painted vase depicts Achilles, the hero of the Trojan war, reclining on a bed inlaid with figures of a lion confronting a bull between two snakes. **[Note:** Among the enemies Achilles fought at Troy were Scamanders, bulls who arose from the Scamander River. The word "Troy" means "maze" or "to turn"]. Achilles' shield on the wall over his bed bears a gorgon head, closely resembling Egyptian representations of the feline hero, **Bes** *See* BULL & FELINE & MAZE & PATH & SNAKE & VESSEL & WAR & WATER -20b GREEK \DISt \ELIt *Figure* 251

• A common theme in Greek art depicts the young sun god **Apollo**, accompanied by a feline, killing giants *See* FELINE & GIANT & SUN YOUNG & TRINITY & WAR -20 GREEK \LARp

• An ancient seal remaining from the Holy Land issued by the warrior-king Jereboam II depicts a lion with a ring motif between its front paws *See* FELINE & RING MOTIF & RULER & SOCIETAL ASPECT & WAR -7a ISRAEL, JEWISH
Figure 252

Figure 252

• The task of the Knights was to "perfect the circle of the sun" *See* CIRCLE & PATH & WAR +7a ENGLAND, KNIGHTHOOD \CIRt

• The high deity, the sun, is the testing father as well as the terror of the young hero of Siberian tribal people. The same young hero who is their warrior model, is also the sun *See* SOCIETAL ASPECT & SUN OLD/ YOUNG & TRINITY & WAR +19a RUSSIA, BURIAT \CAIt

• The medal of the Order of the Sun and Lion, awarded for heroism, depicted a lion holding a sword before a blazing sun   +18a IRAN, PERSIAN *Figure* 253

heron The letter *B* of the Snake Ring Template. *Ref* MARINE BIRD.

hill The letter *G* of the Snake Ring Template. *Ref* MOUNTAIN.

Figure 250

• Heroes were called "subterranean ones." They existed within snakes *See* PATH & UNDERWORLD & WAR -20b GREEK \BRAt \LARt

Figure 251

Figure 253

hippopotamus *The letter H of the Snake Ring Template.* A metaphor for the sea goddess who gives birth to the new sun in the waters of the western horizon. *Ref* BABY BOY, COW, MOTHER GODDESS, WATER.

hole *The letter G of the Snake Ring Template.* A metaphor for the serpent path penetrating into the western horizon, forming the entranceway into the underworld and the mythic mountain-house. *Ref* ABYSS, SOCIETY AS AT THE AXIS MUNDI, WELL.

• The underworld land of the dead is associated with the concept of an abyss *See* DEATH & PATH & UNDERWORLD +19a \CIRt

• One of the strongest of the old ideas is that of a holy well *See* WELL +19a \MIEt

• The most significant art and ritual objects of the terminal Ice Age were found in the north-of-west chamber, "The Well", which depicts on its sunken floor, the trinity of the fallen and phallic bird-man, the small bird rising on a stick and the castrated bull. On the ceiling above The Well is a prehistoric tectiform sign, a compartmented rectangle, regarded as the symbol for "house" *See* ART & CAVE & HOUSE & PATH & SPRINGTIME SUNSET ORIENTATION & TRINITY & WELL -350b FRANCE, LASCAUX \CAIt
Refer to *Figure 165*

• Completely hidden by a horizontal six-foot stone slab inside a decorated Ice Age cave, a man-made mound contained burned organic matter and bones carved to represent serpents *See* CAVE & FIRE & HORIZON & MOUNTAIN & PATH & SNAKE & STONE & UNDERWORLD -350b SPAIN, EL JUYO \NAUt

• The ancient name Eridu, the seat of the gods in the Damuzi legend, means "the confluence of rivers" **[Note:** the "joining of rivers" at the Garden of Eden] where a whirlpool leads to the underworld *See* GARDEN OF EDEN & WATERFALL & WHIRLPOOL -35b IRAQ, SUMERIAN \SANt

• Present-day scholars are puzzled by two versions of the fate of the old sun god **Kronos**. In one, his son **Zeus** hurls him down into the pit of Tartaros, and in the other he sleeps eternally in a golden cave. **[Note**: the cave house in the underworld of the western horizon, where the trinity occurs] *See* CAVE & GOLD & PATH & TRINITY & UNDERWORLD & WAR -20b GREEK \SANt

• The goddess **Artemis** lived at a waterfall in Accadia which was the portal to the underworld *See* MOTHER GODDESS & WATERFALL -20b GREEK \LARt

• A Hindu myth tells of a lady who rises from the ocean to tell the hero Rama of a hole in the ocean leading to the underworld, where the "water of life" is located *See* HERO & REGENERATION & WATER -19b INDONESIA, HINDU \SANt

• Ahi Budhnya was the serpent of the watery abyss *See* AXIS MUNDI & PATH & SNAKE & WATER -19b INDIA, HINDU \MUNt

• The oldest Peruvian ceremonial centers had sunken courtyards at their center. These were later replaced with stone pyramids. **[Note:** their equivalence, representing the mountain at the abyss of the western horizon] *See* PATH & PYRAMID & SOCIETY AS AT THE AXIS MUNDI & STONE -18b PERU \TL5t

• A gigantic mask of the were-jaguar, formed of hundreds of pieces of serpentine stone, was discovered at the bottom of a deep pit in the mother culture site of La Venta *See* FELINE &

JADE & RITUAL & SOCIETY AS AT THE AXIS MUNDI & UNDERWORLD -15b MEXICO, LA VENTA
Figure 254

Figure 254

• In his search for immortality, Ulysses went to the whirlpool beyond the western limits of the world *See* HERO & REGENERATION & WEST ORIENTATION & WHIRLPOOL -8a GREEK \SANt

• All things come from the joining of yang and yin in a void. Called t'ai chai, the void is the womb of the universe *See* BABY BOY/ GIRL & FERTILITY & MARRIAGE & SEASON -5a CHINA, I-CHING \OCTt

• The kivas of Greater Southwest Indians have a hole in the floor called "the womb of mother earth". The hole links the kiva to the spirit world below *See* HOUSE & PATH & SOCIETY AS AT THE AXIS MUNDI +6a USA, PUEBLO \NATp \AMWt

• At the Grotto of Teutonic myth, the navel of the sea, water falls through a hole to the underworld *See* UNDERWORLD & WATERFALL +7b GERMAN, TEUTONIC \SANt

• Shakespeare derived his play "Hamlet" from a mythic dispute in a royal family over ownership of a fabulous mill. The mill created a whirlpool in the sea, leading to the land of the dead *See* DEATH & LORE & MILLSTONE & PATH & UNDERWORLD & WAR & WHIRLPOOL +9b DENMARK, FINNO-UGARITIC \SANt

• To the Maya, the sacred cave and well were both symbols of death *See* CAVE & DEATH & TRINITY & WELL +8a GUATEMALA, MAYAN \SCMt

• Scholars are puzzled as to why vertical stones were erected, and sharks and octopi depicted in the crater of the Mauna Kea volcano *See* FIRE & MENHIR & MOUNTAIN & SOCIETY AS AT THE AXIS MUNDI & STONE & WATER +12a HAWAII \ARCt

• A large serpent formed of stones was discovered underground in the area of the Great Serpent mound in Ohio. It is called the "sun serpent" because its tail is in the direction of the winter solstice sunset. Salient differences between the two images are that the "sun serpent" was built underground, faces to the east with nine flagstones placed in line on its tail, while the Great Serpent mound was built above ground, faces to the west, and has its body formed of seven coils. **[Note:** in the Snake Ring Template seven levels with thirteen steps in the sky, while in the underworld there are five levels with nine steps] *See* DRAGON & EAST/ WEST ORIENTATION & LEVELS CELESTIAL/ UNDERWORLD & PATH & STONE & UROBORUS +12a USA *Figure* 255
Figure 256

• An illustration of the steps through the celestial and underworld levels in the Nahuatl Codex Vaticanus depicts the old deity couple in the thirteenth step of the celestial levels, at the "navel of the world." A running feline is depicted at the ninth step of the corresponding underworld levels *See* AXIS MUNDI & FELINE & LEVELS CELESTIAL & MARRIAGE & WEST ORIENTATION +15a MEXICO, AZTEC
Refer to *Figure 78* SECTION TWO.

• The deity **Ometeotl** is in the region of the dead, below the "navel of the earth" *See* DEATH & SUN OLD & TRINITY & UNDERWORLD +13b MEXICO, AZTEC \CUPt

• Each ceremonial courtyard had a ritual pot buried at its center with only the hole of the neck visible *See* PATH & SOCIETY AS AT THE AXIS MUNDI & VESSEL +13a NIGERIA, IFE \GARp

• At the start of winter, a red cedar tree **[Note:** the tradition of a Christmas tree at the same time of the year]** was passed through the smoke-hole of the ceremonial house, connecting the sky to the underworld *See* CHRISTMASTIDE & FIRE & HOUSE & PATH & RED & & SMOKE & TREE +18a CANADA, KWAKIUTL \NABt

Figure 255

• The early Christians reused a pagan religious center at Goreme to carve nearly 3,000 churches into hills containing caves with shallow graves at their tops. This rich agricultural site in Cappadocia was also sacred to the Hittites. A fresco in one of the cave-churches depicts the Asia Minor mother goddess with the face of a man. The castrati who served her cult represented this image as bearded once a year *See* ART & CAVE & CASTRATION & DEMYTHOLIZATION & FERTILITY & MARRIAGE & MOUNTAIN & MOTHER GODDESS & PATH & PRIEST & REGENERATION & SEASON & SOCIETY AS AT THE AXIS MUNDI & SWORD -18b TURKEY, HITTITE \NYTt

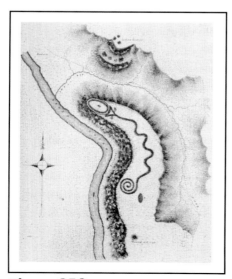

Figure 256

Figure 257

• A clay figure recovered from the bottom of Lake Maracaibo depicts a mother goddess with an elderly male figure apparently in her head. She holds her hands up, and a radiant sun appears on her loincloth *See* DESCENDING MOTIF & HAND RAISED & MOTHER GODDESS & PATH & REGENERATION & SOCIETY AS AT THE AXIS MUNDI & WATER +19a VENEZUELA *Figure 257*

• There is an invisible land below an abyss in the water *See* UNDERWORLD & WATER +19a HAITI, VOODOO \DATt

• Dancers in the Dreamtime ritual move along a serpentine trench to a circular moat referred to as "hole in the earth", where they jab their spears *See* BLADE & DANCE & PATH +19a AUSTRALIA, ARNHEM LAND \RAUp

• Aborigines paint red circles on the ground northwest of natural springs in their "sun ceremonies." They believe that the sun's ancestor lies beneath this hole where the sun originated, represented by the red circles *See*

BABY BOY & RED & RITUAL & SPRINGTIME SUNSET ORIENTATION & SUN OLD/ YOUNG & TRINITY & WATER +19a AUSTRALIA, ARANDA *Figure 258*

Figure 258

• **Kane**, the god of thunder, was thrust into the pit of Milu in the underworld, the "nethermost depths of night" *See* PATH & NIGHT & SEASON & TRINITY & WAR +19a HAWAII \COTt

• The vast Iguacu waterfall on the border between Argentina and Brazil is referred to by Indian natives as the "throat of the dragon". It has been described as "an ocean plunging into an abyss" *See* DRAGON & PATH & SOCIETY AS AT THE AXIS MUNDI & UROBORUS & WATERFALL +19a ARGENTINA \REVt
Refer to *Figure 80* SECTION TWO.

hollow *The letter G of the Snake Ring Template. Ref* VALLEY.

Holy Ghost *The letter L of the Snake Ring Template. Ref* DEMYTHOLIZATION, HUSK, TRINITY.

homosexuality *The letter G of the Snake Ring Template.* Possibly an innate avoidance, in some cases, of the dreamtime trauma in the underworld after coitus in the western horizon. [Many independent tests confirm that an individual is three times more likely to have a heart attack on awakening than at any other time. Taking a beta-blocker stress reducing drug on going to bed reduces the odds of having a heart attack on awakening] *Ref* BULL, CASTRATION, HERMAPHRODITE, PSYCHOLOGY CHILD/ DREAM, TRINITY, UNDERWORLD.

• Homosexuality may be from an innate source as a means to avoid the Oedipal trauma *See* INCEST & PATH & TRINITY & WAR +19a \NYT

• Coitus activates the fear of castration *See* CIRCUMCISION & DEATH & MARRIAGE +19a ERICH NEUMANN \NEUt

honey *The letter I of the Snake Ring Template. Ref* BEE, FERTILITY.

honeymoon *The letter H of the Snake Ring Template.* A societal metaphor for the mother goddess's joining with the old sun at the abyss in the western horizon waters to produce a new sun, the bringer of springtime fertility. *Ref* HONEY, MARRIAGE, MOON, SOCIETAL ASPECT, WATERFALL.

hood *The letter G of the Snake Ring Template. Ref* GARMENT, HAT, UNDERWORLD.

horizon *The letter F of the Snake Ring Template.* The supposed juncture of the dome of the sky and the inverted dome of the underworld; *specif.*, the western horizon where the old sun died and the new sun was born. *Ref* REGENERATION.

• The universe is like the sphere of a divided calabash, whose top half is the dome of the sky and whose bottom half is filled with the waters of the oceans with the flat earth floating inside. A divine snake, which is the path of the sun god establishing order, coils around these halves. The horizon is where the top and bottom halves meet *See* CALABASH +18a NIGERIA, BENIN \PAQt
Refer to *Figure 192*

• The sky is as a gourd. The horizon is where the sky meets the earth with a waterfall to the world below *See* CALABASH & WATERFALL +19a COLOMBIA, BARASANA \AVDt

• Atlantis was where the sky fused with the earth, the mythic western horizon land of **Poseidon** *See* SUN OLD & TRINITY & WATER & WEST ORIENTATION -20b GREEK, ATLANTIS \BREt

• King Akhenaton forbade all cults except the sun god **Aton's**, whose full name was **Re-Horus-of-the-horizon**. Akhenaton called his capital the "horizon of Aton" *See* SOCIETY AS AT THE AXIS MUNDI & SUN OLD/ YOUNG -13a EGYPT \ENBt \CASt

• A vertical stone pierced by a square hole stands before a stone bench at the foot of what was one of the largest pyramids in the world before the Spanish conquest. Sitting on the bench, one looks through the hole at a mountain framed on the western horizon, where the sun sets at the start of springtime. This mountain was sacred to the Toltecs as well as the Aztecs, who gave it the name of the mother goddess, "La Malinche." They gave the same name, perhaps sarcastically, to the mistress of the Spanish conqueror Hernando Cortez. They at first regarded him as the sun god from the east [which no doubt facilitated his remarkable triumph] *See* CELESTIAL OBSERVATION & MOTHER GODDESS & MOUNTAIN & PYRAMID & SOCIETY AS AT THE AXIS MUNDI & SPRINGTIME SUNSET ORIENTATION & SUN OLD +12a MEXICO, TOLTEC *Figure 259*

• In the Chinese abacus which has been in its present form for at least five centuries, and is still used widely for addition and subtraction, the counting bars above the horizontal are called "heaven", and the bars below are called "earth" *See* COUNTING & LEVELS CELESTIAL/ UNDERWORLD +15a CHINA \DISp

• Greater Southwest Indians call their mother goddess "the woman horizontal" *See* CROSS WEST +18a USA, NAVAHO \COTt

horizontal motif *The letter F of the Snake Ring Template.* *Ref* HORIZON.

Figure 259

horoscope *The letter R of the Snake Ring Template. Used in the practice of predicting human characteristics or experiences determined by the location of the stars, specif., the sun at a particular time.* *Ref* ASTROLOGY, SOCIETAL ASPECT.

horse *The letter T of the Snake Ring Template.* *See* SECTION TWO.

hour *The letter A of the Snake Ring Template.* One unit of the sun's apparent movement in a day, up and down through the seven levels in the sky and the down and up through the five levels in the underworld. *Ref* LEVELS CELESTIAL / UNDERWORLD, TIME.

hour-glass motif *The letter E of the Snake Ring Template.* A metaphor for the apparent passage of the sun between the celestial and the infernal hemispheres. *Ref* CALABASH, TIME.

house *The letter H of the Snake Ring Template.* *See* SECTION TWO.

house haunted *The letter H of the Snake Ring Template.* A composite metaphor for the house in the western horizon and the old sun devoid of his solar soul. *Ref* HOUSE, HUSK, OCCULT, TRINITY.

house model *The letter H of the Snake Ring Template.* Many have been found in worldwide burials, as a metaphor for the sun's regeneration in the mountain-house of the western horizon. *Ref* HOUSE, MOTHER GODDESS, SOCIETAL ASPECT, SUN OLD / YOUNG, UNDERWORLD.

• Miniature buildings with no apparent purpose were buried outside the walls of a mastaba, or funerary structure for royal burials, near the boat cavity at Saqqara. Scholars are puzzled by over 350 clay bull head with real horns placed on the terraces of the Saqqara mastaba, one of the earliest excavated to date. Later mastabas usually abutted the eastern walls of pyramids. **[Note:** The rulers' death as a metaphor for the sun's virile death into the mountain house of the western waters for regeneration] *See* BOAT & BULL & DEATH & HOUSE & PYRAMID & REGENERATION & RULER & UNDERWORLD & WATER & WEST ORIENTATION -27a EGYPT, SAQQARA *Figure* 260

Figure 261

Figure 260

• Scholars are also puzzled by the meaning of a house shrine with images of entwined serpents on the sides and floor, leading to the throne of a goddess. Round motifs are embossed in series along the bodies of the serpents *See* HOUSE & MOTHER GODDESS & PATH & ROUND MOTIF IN SEQUENCE & SOCIETAL ASPECT -27a IRAQ, ACCADIAN *Figure* 261

• A votive clay house model from the Temple of **Ishtar** at Assur is dedicated to her as the archetypal harlot. Serpents, with a series of round motifs along their bodies, are around its doorways, and doves are at the triangular windows *See* BIRD & GODDESSES & MARRIAGE & PATH & PROSTITUTION & ROUND MOTIF IN SEQUENCE & TRIANGLE MOTIF UPRIGHT -19b IRAQ, ASSYRIAN \MUNp

• A terra-cotta house model depicts a woman with her thighs spread apart at its window, probably the goddess **Astarte**. A man watches her from below, accompanied by a huge vertical serpent and a goat [the hooves are all that remains of the animal] *See* GOAT & GODDESSES & MARRIAGE & PATH & SNAKE & VERTICALITY   -15b ISRAEL, PHOENICIAN \MUNt

Figure 262

Figure 263

• House models were found in Chinese burials from early Neolithic times on, including elaborate four-story models from the second century Han dynasty *See* DEATH & REGENERATION & SOCIETAL ASPECT -15b CHINA *Figure 262*

• A rectangular house model probably the base of an incense burner from Beth Shamon, has a snake depicted vertically along its length, winding upwards to a female figure *See* FIRE & HOUSE & INCENSE & MOTHER GODDESS & PATH -10a ISRAEL, PHOENICIAN *Figure 263*

• The painted clay house model from a burial depicts a dead man at the top of a horizontal support for two small houses. Steps lead from his body to a lower level where a woman with ring motifs on her headdress sits with a dog nearby. Dogs were believed to be the companions of the dead through the underworld *See* DEATH & DOG & HORIZON & MOTHER GODDESS & PATH & RING MOTIF IN SEQUENCE & SOCIETAL ASPECT & STAIRS INFERNAL +1b MEXICO, COLIMA \SOUt *Figure 264*

Figure 264

• Scholars are puzzled by the many house shrines, called Sun Houses, found in the villas of Pompeii. They typically depict a ring motif and a bucranium, a bull's skull in their pediment, and a goddess within the house above a plumed snake *See* BULL & FERTILITY & DEATH & DRAGON & MOTHER GODDESS & PEDIMENT & RING MOTIF & SOCIETAL ASPECT +1a ITALY, ROMAN *Figure 265*

Figure 265

Figure 266

• Ceremonial structures at Uxmal have a native house, feathered serpents and images of crops carved over their doorways *See* FERTILITY & HOUSE & PATH & RITUAL +3b MEXICO, MAYAN **Refer to** *Figure 212*

• A snake is depicted descending to the roof of a shrine house on the body of a pot buried in the center of a shrine room's ceremonial courtyard, where only the pot's mouth is exposed. The neck of the pot has the symbol of an upright triangle with a ring motif at its center. The shrine room was furnished with the same ritual objects as those depicted on the pot. *See* HOLE & HOUSE & PATH & RING MOTIF & SNAKE & SOCIETY AS AT THE AXIS MUNDI & TRIANGLE MOTIF UPRIGHT & UNDERWORLD & VESSEL +18a NIGERIA, IFE *Figure 266* *Figure 267*

Figure 267

• Models of mbure, the men's house, are worshipped in private dwellings. The actual structures, built on high mounds and similarly covered with strings of seashells, serve as the center of religious ritual *See* CRUSTACEAN & HOUSE & MOUND & SOCIETY AS AT THE AXIS MUNDI & SOCIETAL ASPECT & UNDERWORLD & WATER +18a FIJI *Figure 268*

husk *The letter L of the Snake Ring Template.* A metaphor for the old sun remaining eternally in the underworld, after the transfer of its solar soul to the successor sun of the next season, as one of the group of former father-suns jealous of their sons replacing them in the sky. *Ref* CHAOS IN NATURE, DEMON, DEVIL, GHOST, GIANT, SUN OLD/ YOUNG, TRINITY.

hypnosis *The letter R of the Snake Ring Template.* A state of lowered consciousness when the preconscious mentality can be more readily accessed. *Ref* HALLUCINOGEN, PSYCHOLOGY CHILD/ DREAMS, SOCIOBIOLOGY.

Figure 268

I

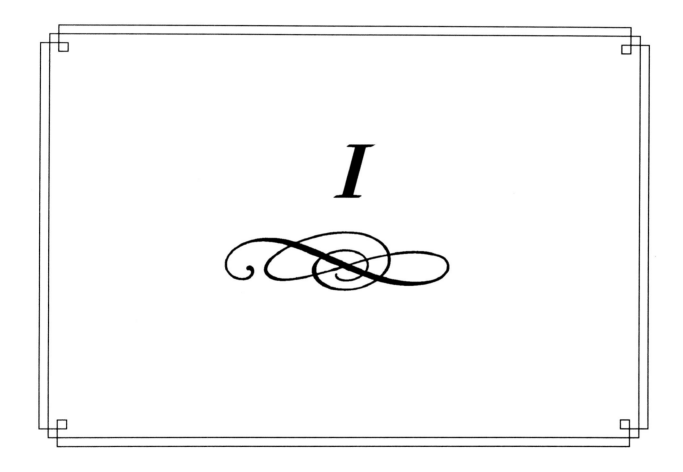

ibex *The letter O of the Snake Ring Template.*
A wild goat noted for its leaping characteristic.
Ref DEER.

ibis *The letter B of the Snake Ring Template.*
Ref MARINE BIRD.

Figure 269

• Ibises are "birds of disaster" *See* DEATH &
MARINE BIRD & WATER +16a NIGERIA, BENIN
\EYOt

image *The letter R of the Snake Ring Template.*
Ref ART, METAPHOR, RITUAL, SOCIETAL ASPECT.

incense *The letter D of the Snake Ring
Template. An odorous resin from a tree.* When
burned, a metaphor for the sunset death of the
old sun along the vertical serpent path to the
mother goddess' house in the western horizon.
Ref DEATH, FIRE, HOUSE, MARRIAGE, MOTHER
GODDESS, SOCIETAL ASPECT.

• The Pre-Columbian Fejervary-Mayer codex
depicts a goddess holding an incense bag as
she starts a fire along the body of the
feathered serpent. In a subsequent panel of
the codex, the goddess exposes her vagina to
a duck-billed deity who is entering her water-
filled cave. **[Note:** Refer to VAGINA for other
instances of goddesses exposing their vaginas].
In the next scene, the feathered serpent is the
path for the duck-billed deity passing through
her vagina, and in the last of this series the
feathered serpent emanates from her navel,
goes through a ballcourt and ascends with the
head of a deer in its mouth. **[Note:** that the
Snake Ring path from the west to the east
encompassed the sun-bird entering the cave
house of the mother goddess in the western
horizon water, copulating with her and then

remaining in the underworld, while the path
continues through the new sun's conflict in
the underworld represented by the ball game,
to the new sun's deer-like leap-up in the sky]
See BIRTH & DUCK & FEATHERED SERPENT & FIRE
& GAME SPORT & MARRIAGE & MOTHER GODDESS &
PATH & VAGINA +13b MEXICO *Figure 269*
Refer also to *Figures 207-209*

• Burial processions were always from the east
to the west, with the mourners dancing on the
way to the tomb. A carved stone depicts the
priest with a shaven head who usually wafted
incense as he led the burial procession. *See*
DANCE & DEATH & HEAD & PRIEST & PROCESSION &
ROUND MOTIF & WEST ORIENTATION & TOMB -30b
EGYPT \CASt *Figure 270*

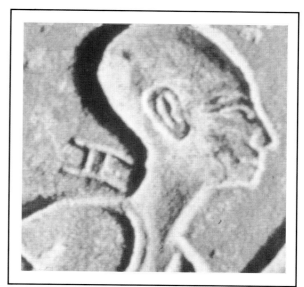

Figure 270

• A pottery incense stand has applied images
of small birds in its triangular windows.
Snakes wind upwards to where the incense
burner was supported *See* BIRD & FIRE & HOUSE
& PATH & SNAKE & TRIANGLE MOTIF UPRIGHT -10a
ISRAEL, PHOENICIAN *Figure 271*

• Another Phoenician incense stand bears
applied images of female figures holding one
hand to their breasts and the other to their
exposed vulvas *See* FIRE & MOTHER GODDESS &
PATH & REGENERATION & VAGINA -11a ISRAEL,
MEGIDDO
Refer to *Figure 74* SECTION TWO.

Figure 271

• The bronze statue of the feathered serpent Nehustan which stood in Solomon's Temple during the early Jewish period, was offered incense during healing rituals *See* BRONZE & DEMYTHOLIZATION & HEALING & HOUSE & PATH & REGENERATION & SOCIETAL ASPECT -10b ISRAEL, JEWISH \ENDt

Figure 272

• Many Chinese pottery and porcelain incense burners depict the legendary mountain on the

Island of the Immortals *See* FIRE & HUSK & MOUNTAIN & PATH & TRINITY & WATER -1a CHINA, HAN *Figure 272*

• Incense burners were thrown as offerings into lakes *See* FIRE & OFFERING & PATH & SOCIETY AS AT THE AXIS MUNDI & WATER +8a GUATEMALA, MAYAN \FOUt

• Scholars are puzzled by the statue of a goddess which was found lying on her back in an offering pit at Templo Mayor, the major Aztec pyramid-temple, with evidence of copal having been burned on her face *See* CROSS WEST & DEATH & FIRE & HORIZONTAL & MOTHER GODDESS & PATH & PYRAMID & UNDERWORLD +13b MEXICO, AZTEC \NYMp

• In Temple rites to the sun, the hearts of sacrificed captives were burned in braziers containing incense *See* FIRE & HEART HUMAN & HOUSE & SACRIFICE HUMAN & SUN OLD +13b MEXICO, AZTEC \TIMt

• Present-day Maya burn copal in rituals to "honor the sun" +18a MEXICO, YUCATAN \BOWt

• Incense is burned in their temples as a stairway for the gods to descend *See* FIRE & HOUSE & SNAKE & STAIRS INFERNAL & SUN OLD & TREE +19a BALI, HINDU \WESt

• Pygmy, next to Bushman the oldest continuous culture in the world, play a pipe instrument carved from a tree struck by lightning, and burn incense to their "father-god" in order to stop a storm **[Note** the oak tree, music and incense are metaphors for the path from the sky to the horizon, inspiring the old sun's death, and its regeneration into a new season] *See* DEATH & DESCENDING MOTIF & FIRE & MUSIC & OAK & REGENERATION & RITUAL & TREE +19a CONGO, PYGMY \CAIt

• Plains Indians believe that the incense which they burn is received by the sun *See* REGENERATION & RITUAL & SUN OLD +19a USA, ARAPAHO \DOPt

incest *The letter H of the Snake Ring Template.* The joining of the old sun with a member of his own sun-family in the western horizon, i.e. mother, sister, etc., to produce the sun of the next season. *Ref* GODDESSES, MARRIAGE, PATH, TRINITY.

• The incest in mythologies is not from sexual fixation to a person's mother, but it is instead a prefiguration of the sacred marriage; cave, earth, and tomb are its symbols *See* CAVE & DEATH & MARRIAGE & PSYCHOLOGY CHILD & UNDERWORLD +19a \NEUt

• The sun god **Enlil** separated his parents and copulated with his mother *See* MARRIAGE & PATH & PSYCHOLOGY SUMERIAN \COTt

• The sun god **Damuzzi** was slain and mourned by his mother who was also his lover. He was reborn through her *See* DEATH & PATH & MARRIAGE & REGENERATION -35b IRAQ, SUMERIAN \NEUt

• The sun god **Osiris** was also slain and mourned by his mother who was his lover as well and he was also reborn through her *See* DEATH & MARRIAGE & PATH & REGENERATION -30b EGYPT \NEUt

• Incest themes pervade the Rig Veda. The creation of the world was the result of incestuous activities between the original deities. **Usas** was the mother and the daughter of the sun *See* GODDESSES & PATH & TRINITY -30b INDIA, HINDU \MCCt

• Although the king and queen were often brother and sister, the king was regarded as the reincarnation of the sun god **Amon's** son and the queen as the reincarnation of Amon's wife *See* GODDESS & RULER & SUN OLD/ YOUNG -13a EGYPT \EDUt

• The creator sun god was the son as well as the husband of the creator goddess +6a COLOMBIA, MUISCA \COTt

• Creation took place in the underworld when the sun god exiled his father and copulated with his mother, who was also his sister *See* GODDESSES & WAR +19a ALGERIA, BERBER \COTt

• Dream Lover statuettes are made to represent spiritual spouses in the other world, whom one leaves at birth and rejoins at death. Individuals troubled by marital or child-bearing problems are helped by sleeping with their Dream Lover statuette one night a week *See* BIRTH & MARRIAGE & PATH & PSYCHOLOGY CHILD & SOCIETAL ASPECT +19a IVORY COAST, BAOULES *Figure 273*

• In order to save mankind from chaos, the sun father is seasonally induced to copulate with his daughter by suggestive dances performed while under the influence of the yaje hallucinogen *See* CHAOS IN NATURE & DANCE & FERTILITY & HALLUCINOGEN & PSYCHOLOGY CHILD +19a COLOMBIA, TUKANO \REJt

Figure 273

• In the Kote theater of west coast Africa, an actor depicts a blind man's wife who loses her vagina while she is in the river; her son thrusts his hand under her skirt to find it **[Note:** "blind" infers that her husband has transferred to her the solar soul, visible as the circle of the iris] *See* EYE & INCEST & THEATER & TRINITY & VAGINA & WATER +19a MALI, BAMANA \AFAt

infant mentality *The letter* ℛ *of the Snake Ring Template. Ref* PSYCHOLOGY CHILD.

infinity *The letter* 𝒜 *of the Snake Ring Template. Unlimited time or space.* A metaphor for the apparent path of the sun in the entwined serpent path, spiralling back and forth eternally between the solstice extremities. *Ref* MATHEMATICS, SERPENT ENTWINED.

information destroyed or secret *The letter* ℛ *of the Snake Ring Template.* **a**. Loss or reinterpretation of primordial beliefs. **b**. Knowledge unavailable due to aboriginal people keeping secret their primordial religion and its rituals. *Ref* DEMYTHOLIZATION, PRIMORDIAL RELIGION, PRIEST, RACIAL BIGOTRY, WAR.

• All myths are from the same old book, so to speak, of which all the earliest editions have been lost. The meanings behind terminal Ice Age cave art are still not solved *See* ART +19a \CAAt \CAIt

• The Philistines of the Bible left many stone altars with bulls' horns carved at their upper corners which may have been models for the similar altar in Solomon's Temple. Although the Philistines' religion was of central importance to their lives, no written language remains which might define it *See* ALTAR & BULL & DEATH & HOUSE -12b ISRAEL, PHILISTINES \TIMt
Refer to *Figure 176*

• There is nothing that remains of the sacred lore of the Druids, high priests of the Celts -14b ENGLAND, CELTIC \RAUt

• Few icons survived the missionaries destruction of Polynesian images +18a HAWAII \CAIt

• In the 7th century A.D., Emperor T'ang's library contained approximately 45,000 scrolls in the 7th century A.D. They included works on foreign religions and some of the earliest examples of printing. Most of these scrolls were destroyed by conquerors in the 9th century. The few remaining scrolls have since disappeared -15b CHINA \BOPt

• Paul convinced gentiles at the Greek city of Ephesus on the west coast of Turkey, to burn their "magic" books, valued at the time at 50,000 pieces of silver +0.9a \BIBt

• In the 1st century B.C the emperor Augustus burned 2,000 "magical" texts -5b ITALY, ROMAN \BIBt

• In the 4th century B.C., the library in Alexandria had assembled 750,000 original literary works from all of the known civilizations. The Romans sacked the library in the 1st century B.C. Crusaders destroyed many of the scrolls in the 4th century and all remaining scrolls were lost by the 7th century, supposedly burned by marauding Muslims -3a EGYPT \DEDt

• Christianized Roman emperors of the 4th century burned all non-Christian books 0b \DEDt

• Crusaders burned 100,000 Muslim books at Tripoli in the 12th century A.D. Cardinal Jiminez burned 24,000 Muslim books at Granada during the Inquisition +5b IRAN, ISLAM \DEDt

• The Conquistadors burned the boards with painted histories which they found in the Temple of the Sun, describing them as natives' "errors and folly" +9b PERU, INCA \HEUt \RAUt

• The original language of the Andean people of South America has since been lost +2b PERU, MOCHICAN \HEUt

• The Aztecs also burned the books (codices) of all the people they conquered +13b MEXICO, AZTEC \MUTt

• An unexplained cloth used in Fon rituals depicts a large, westernized Devil under a large plumed snake arching across the sky. Below him, other figures carry gongs, battle axes with blades of rams' heads and conventional snakes. **[Note** the uroboric snake in sky and underworld] *See* ARCH & DEVIL & DRAGON & HUSK & MUSIC & RAM & SNAKE & SOCIETY AS AT THE AXIS MUNDI & TRINITY & WAR +18a BENIN, FON
Figure 274

Figure 274

• The Polish astronomer Copernicus shocked the world in the 16th century A.D., by scientifically substantiating the revelations of the 7th century B.C. Ionians that the sun does not go around the earth. Galileo, the Italian astronomer, was forced to recant his support for Copernicus. In 1616, a Papal edict proclaiming that the sun goes around the earth, was issued and that those continuing to support Copernicus' astronomy would be burned at the stake *See* CALABASH & DEMYTHOLIZATION 0b \MIAt \WEBt

• Scholars are puzzled by images on the Narmar palette, a vessel-shaped carved stone believed to represent a pre-dynastic victory of an early ruler. At the top of the palette, bulls' heads are at either side and the pictogram is of a blade and a fish. Below this, the "ruler" is in a procession led by minions bearing staffs with birds at their top and followed by a youth holding a flower. The procession is directed towards a bird in a boat on the right side of the palette. Below the boat are two columns of beheaded victims, five in each column. In the scene at the bottom of the palette, a youth is running from an attacking bull before a palace. At the center of the palette, minions

hold ropes tied to two felines whose serpentine necks entwine to form a large ring. **[Note:** the symbols knife+fish are hieroglyphs in Egyptian for the words "nar-mer." Therefore, the authority figure glorified on this palette is assumed to be a prehistoric ruler by the name of Narmer. However, these symbols are metaphors for the vertical path of the sun penetrating the waters of the western horizon, which is consistent with the images at the top of the palette of bulls' heads sinking into a vessel-shaped underworld. The ruler may be a pharaoh by the name of Narmer, as rulers are often depicted in the role of the sun, or he may be the old sun on his path into the western horizon. The latter interpretation appears to be reinforced by the accompanying images of birds on staffs preceding him and landing on a boat, and a youth following him bearing a flower, the symbol of seasonal fertility. Below the bird in the boat, the two double columns of five beheaded bodies in each corresponding to the path down and up the five levels of the Land of the Dead, below the western horizon waters. At the bottom of the palette, as at the nadir of the five underworld levels in the Snake Ring, a youth escaping from a charging bull would represent the underworld conflict between the young sun and the husk of the once virile old sun. The central scene of the palette depicts felines' necks forming the ring motif of the sun, representing the young sun carried within the feline guardians, and the felines' attendants would be societal heroes helping to assure the emergence of each new seasonal sun into the sky. The reverse of this palette is not shown here, but continues the theme of the young sun vanquishing an enemy, whose head is below a field of rushes with its mouth being pried open. It is a familiar ritual in numerous Egyptian tomb paintings, of the soul being released from the dead. In this case, it is the solar soul of the father being released to his son, who, after vanquishing him, will take his place in the sky] *See* BIRD & BLADE & BOAT & BULL & CARRIER & DEATH & FELINE & FISH & HERO & HUSK & HOUSE & LEVELS UNDERWORLD & PATH & PROCESSION & RING MOTIF & RULER & RUSHES & SOUL & STAFF & STONE & TRINITY & VESSEL & WAR & WATER & WEST ORIENTATION -32a EGYPT
Figure 275

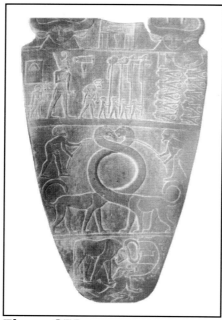

Figure 275

• Stars are sometimes shown along the goddess **Nut's** body, which has led scholars to conclude that she is a sky goddess. However, her image appears primarily in sarcophagi art, as the underworld goddess with a path of ring motifs along her body. The sun entered Nut's mouth at its sunset death and was reborn from her womb at dawn *See* ART & BURIAL & DEATH & MOTHER GODDESS & MOUTH & PATH & REGENERATION & RING MOTIF IN SEQUENCE & UNDERWORLD & UROBORUS -30b EGYPT \BAJt
Figure 276

• The Harappian script of the Indus valley civilization, at its prime covering an area greater than either Egypt or Mesopotamia, is still undeciphered -25b INDIA \HAWt

• The earliest original Greek writing remaining is of the 5th century B.C. Homer's original meanings were lost long before that time due to the Ionian demytholizations *See* DEMYTHOLIZATION -6a GREEK \ARCt \CAAt \SANt \WOOt

• None of the runic inscriptions has yet been deciphered. Most were found carved inside of the stave of churches. *See* ART & HOUSE & PATH & WRITING +7b NORWAY, VIKING \EXQt

Figure 276

• The glyphs at Teotihuacan, site of the great pyramids near Mexico City, "haven't even been sneezed at" They include snakes with ring motifs along their bodies *See* PATH & PYRAMID & RING MOTIF IN SEQUENCE & SNAKE & WRITING +7a MEXICO, TEOTIHUAHAN \TEOt

• The Tierra del Fuegians put to death anyone who reveals to outsiders the secrets of the Kina festival +19a CHILE, YAMANA \NEUt

• In Utiqiavik, Alaska, participants entered the karigi through a whale's skull and were enclosed by a structure formed of whales' ribs. Present day Eskimos will not discuss with outsiders the rituals and religion that were practiced in the karigi, a ceremonial house built on a mound overlooking the ocean *See* HAND RAISED & HOUSE & MOUNTAIN & SOCIETAL ASPECTS & SOCIETY AS AT THE AXIS MUNDI & WATER & WEST ORIENTATION & WHALE +14a ALASKA, ESKIMO \ARCp

• Members of the Lukasa secret societies are told to lie to outsiders about the meanings of the images which they use in their rituals +19a ZAIRE, LUBA \AFAt

• Present-day Mayas exclude outsiders from the caves where their most important rituals are conducted *See* CAVE +19a MEXICO, MAYAN \ARCt

• The utmost secrecy still surrounds the Greater Southwest Indians' kivas, religious beliefs and practices +18a USA, PUEBLO, TAOS \NABt

• Hopi keep secret the Soyal ceremony in their "sun-hill" kiva; they claim that the meaning of the body paint which they use in these ceremonies is largely forgotten *See* BODY PAINT & HOUSE & MOUNTAIN & SOCIETAL ASPECT & SUN OLD +19a USA, HOPI \BRBt \SINt

• The Mohave Indians will not explain to outsiders why they run through a maze near a sixty-five foot-long snake carved into the California desert rock. They also will not discuss the cremation rituals which are performed nearby *See* DEATH & FIRE & GAME SPORT & MAZE & PATH & REGENERATION & SOCIETAL ASPECT +19a USA, MOHAVE \NABp

• The meanings of the designs and colors which the Plains Indians paint on their tipi are kept secret from outsiders *See* ART & HOUSE & TRIANGLE MOTIF UPRIGHT +18a USA, ASSINIBOIN \NABp

• The inscriptions of priests' secret lore, including entwined feathered snake images, is still held secret from outsiders *See* SERPENT ENTWINED/ FEATHERED & WRITING +19a INDONESIA, SUMATRA \VOOp

• The aborigines claim they have lost the meaning of their Dreamtime story. They say that the rainbow snake and the sacred tree are merely fragments remaining from the unknown story *See* ARCH & DEMYTHOLIZATION & PATH & PSYCHOLOGY DREAM & SNAKE & TREE +19a AUSTRALIA \NATt

• Masked actors from various cults participate in the Dema feasts which are based on myths kept secret from those outside the culture +19a NEW GUINEA, MARINO \ELIt

initiation rite *The letter R of the Snake Ring Template.* *Ref* PUBERTY RITE, RITE OF PASSAGE.

integer *The letters P & K of the Snake Ring Template. A whole (not fractional or mixed) number; a figure first represented graphically by tally marks in terminal Ice Age art.* A metaphor denoting the sun's steps through one of the cosmic levels during the sun's apparent entwined serpent path around the earth. *Ref* NUMBER, MATHEMATICS, PATH.

intersection *The letter H of the Snake Ring Template. Ref* CROSSROAD, CROSS WEST, PATH, TRINITY.

invisibility *The letter K of the Snake Ring Template.* A characteristic of those who are resident below the horizons. *Ref* HUSK, GHOST, UNDERWORLD, VEIL.

island *The letter H of the Snake Ring Template.* A metaphor for the mother goddess's home in the western horizon waters. *Ref* FLOOD, WATER.

ivy *The letter I of the Snake Ring Template. Ref* FLORA.

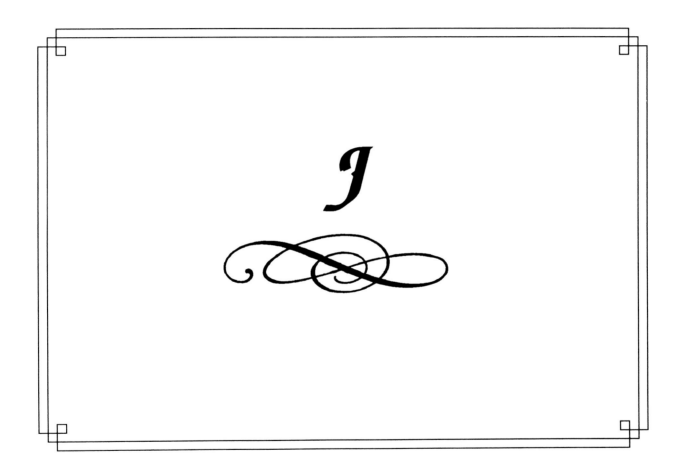

jade *The letter J of the Snake Ring Template.* A metaphor for the western horizon waters containing the mountain house of solar regeneration. *Ref* MOUNTAIN, REGENERATION, STONE, WATER.

• Aztecs associated jade with water. In a related way, the Maya always colored their water glyphs green +13b MEXICO \GATt \CENt

• Carved jade plaques on house altars depict a house standing on mountain peaks surrounded by water. Often these house-plaques are framed in wood by the carved figure of a dragon with the tail of a fish *See* DRAGON & HOUSE & MOUNTAIN & PATH & SOCIETAL ASPECT & WATER +18a CHINA \WESp

• A jade circle motif, the Chinese "pi" symbol, was placed on the back of some individuals when they were buried. Jade objects from royal burials were also in the form of tigers, dragons, and batons *See* BATON & CIRCLE MOTIF & DEATH & FELINE & PATH & REGENERATION & RULER & SOCIETAL ASPECTS -15b CHINA, SHANG \CIRt \RAWt

• Many jade figurines from the mother culture of Mesoamerica depict the were-jaguar, a human baby with the features of a jaguar *See* BABY BOY & CARRIER & FELINE & REGENERATION & UNDERWORLD & WATER -15b MEXICO, OLMEC \MUTt

• Scholars are puzzled by the quantity of jade beads found in Mayan burials and recovered from the sacred well at Chichen Itza *See* BURIAL & DEATH & HOLE & PATH & ROUND MOTIF IN SEQUENCE & SOCIETAL ASPECT & SOCIETY AS AT THE AXIS MUNDI +4a MEXICO, MAYAN \EXPt \WIKt

• Some of the jade and greenstone figures of fish and snakes found in offering pits at the Templo Mayor were painted with tar *See* BLACK & OFFERING & PATH & PYRAMID & UNDERWORLD & WATER +13b MEXICO, AZTEC \NUNp

• Southwest Indians placed small pieces of shell and/ or turquoise (which they used the same as jade) beneath the door of their hogan to link it to the "first hogan", which was said to have been modeled after a mountain called Heart of the Earth *See* CRUSTACEAN & HOUSE & MOUNTAIN & SOCIETAL ASPECT & UNDERWORLD & WATER +18a USA, NAVAJO \NABp

jaguar *The letter M of the Snake Ring Template. Ref* FELINE.

Janus *The letter H of the Snake Ring Template. Rom. God of doorways, represented with two opposite faces.* A metaphor for the branching of the sun's path in the mountain-house of the western horizon; the young sun passing to the east, the husk of the old sun remaining in the underworld. *Ref* CROSSROAD, TRINITY.

jester *The letter L of the Snake Ring Template.* A metaphor for the once virile old sun of the western horizon house who has been vanquished in the underworld struggle with the new sun and need no longer be feared. *Ref* CLOWN, DEMYTHOLIZATION, DWARF, TRINITY, PALACE, SOCIETY AS AT THE AXIS MUNDI.

jewelry *The letter R of the Snake Ring Template.* Designates the wearer as a societal metaphor for the sun, old or young, or the mother goddesses within the serpent path of the sun. *Ref* GOLD, MARRIAGE, RAYED MOTIF, RING MOTIF, ROUND MOTIF IN SEQUENCE, SOCIETAL ASPECT.

• Beads, rings, and anklets were found in terminal Ice Age burials and were depicted in Ice Age cave art. They had not appeared before in over two million years of human history. There was no gradual development, no earlier primitive efforts *See* CHAOS IN NATURE & TOOL-MAKERS -350b FRANCE/ ITALY/ SPAIN/ RUSSIA \SMJt \SCOt

• In an Ice Age burial, a necklace with a stone pendant in the form of a flying bird was found on a child buried in the fetal position, with his head facing to the east. A medallion also on his body had three sinuous serpents inscribed on one side, and a spiral with seven turns formed of dots inscribed on the reverse *See* BABY BOY & BIRD & EAST ORIENTATION & LEVELS CELESTIAL & PATH & ROUND MOTIF IN SEQUENCE &

SOCIETAL ASPECT & SPIRAL & TRINITY & UNDERWORLD -350b RUSSIA, MALTA \CAIp

• Gold bracelets of entwined snakes were very popular with the ancient Greeks, who thought they had the power to heal *See* BRACELET & CIRCLE MOTIF & GOLD & HEALING & PATH & REGENERATION & SOCIETAL ASPECT -2a GREEK \HEHt

• On every feast day, the Hopi of Arizona hung beads of seashells on the son of a widow. **[Note:** The widow is a metaphor for the mother goddess whose husband, the old sun, dies into the western horizon waters, and who there gives birth to the new sun of springtime fertility, represented by her son] *See* BABY BOY & CRUSTACEAN & DEATH & FERTILITY & REGENERATION & SOCIETAL ASPECT & WATER +18a USA, HOPI \BOWt

• A figured finger ring depicts a nude couple standing on a crocodile, the woman holding the man's penis *See* CIRCLE MOTIF & CROCODILE & MARRIAGE & PATH & PHALLUS & SOCIETAL ASPECT & WATER +18a MALI, DOGON \RAUp

• Many wood dolls of the Ashanti people depict a female figure hung with beads, horizontal stubs for her arms, and a over large, round face. **[Note:** refer to the gender sign for "female", consisting of the solar ring-motif at the top of a cross]. Tribal women wear these figures under their skirts to have healthy children *See* BABY BOY/ GIRL & CROSS WEST & RING MOTIF & ROUND MOTIF IN SEQUENCE & SOCIETAL ASPECT +19a GHANA, ASHANTI \PAQp

• Roman women put on a necklace of pearls before going to bed. [Refer to the Ice Age artifact of a woman wearing a necklace as she greets her bull spouse] *See* BABY BOY/ GIRL &

CRUSTACEAN & MARRIAGE & PATH & RING MOTIF & ROUND MOTIF IN SEQUENCE -5b ITALY, ROMAN \SMJt **Refer to** *Figure 50* SECTION TWO.

• In the wedding ceremonies of the ancient Egyptians and Greeks, the groom placed a ring on the finger of the bride. In more recent times, supposedly in France, the practice started of the bride throwing her bridal bouquet; the bridesmaid catching it will be the next married. **[Note:** Regenerating mother goddesses in the western horizon, who successively birth a new sun child of seasonal fertility] *See* BABY BOY/ GIRL & FERTILITY & GODDESSES & MARRIAGE & SOCIETAL ASPECT \HEHt \MIAt \WESt

joining of rivers *The letter F of the Snake Ring Template.* A metaphor for the waters of the western horizon. *Ref* FLOOD, WATER.

journey *The letter R of the Snake Ring Template. Ref* PATH, PROCESSION.

justice 1. *The letter R of the Snake Ring Template. The proper application of law.* A moral responsibility to all members of society, as metaphors of the sun family. *Ref* ETHICS, SOCIETAL ASPECT, SOCIETY AS AT THE AXIS MUNDI. 2. *The letter H of the Snake Ring Template. Tarot. The eighth enigma, the masked Empress holding in one hand a sword and in the other an unbalanced scale.* A metaphor for the trinity at the house of the mother goddess in the underworld, the penetration of the western horizon by the old sun, the husk of the old sun descending into the underworld and the new sun going up into the sky. *Ref* BLADE & HANDS DOWN AND UP, MOTHER GODDESS, TAROT PACK, TRINITY, VEIL.

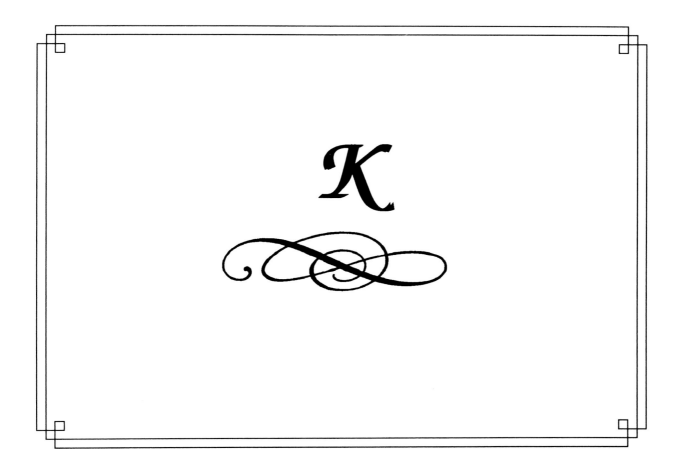

key *The letter H of the Snake Ring Template.* *Ref* HOUSE.

king *The letter R of the Snake Ring Template.* *Ref* RULER.

knife *The letter E of the Snake Ring Template.* *Ref* BLADE, WAR.

knight *The letter N of the Snake Ring Template.* *Ref* HERO.

knot *The letter H of the Snake Ring Template.* **a.** *A ~ in a single strand.* The interruption of the sun's passage at a cosmic level of the entwined serpent path. **b.** *A ~ joining two strands.* The joining of the celestial and underworld segments of the entwined serpent path. Ref ROPE.

labyrinth *The letter K of the Snake Ring Template. Gr. The same root as the word "labrys". Ref* MAZE.

labrys *The letter E of the Snake Ring Template. Gr. Cretan sacred double axe.* A metaphor for the passage of the old sun through the abyss of the western horizon into the underworld. *Ref* CROSS WEST, VERTICAL LINE/ SHAPE.

• The frequency of the labrys in Minoan art is puzzling to scholars. Often it has a bird at its top, as in the detail of a sarcophagus painting depicting the labrys at the left of the upper panel and musicians in the panel below, where a spotted bull is on an altar trussed for sacrifice *See* BIRD & BULL & MUSIC & SACRIFICE ANIMAL & ALTAR & DEATH & REGENERATION & SOCIETAL ASPECT -14a CRETE, MINOAN \ARCt*Figure 277*

Figure 277

• The ceremonial double axe often has its blades, at its top, inscribed with a cross or fish, and its handle below penetrating into the head of a nude female. *See* ABYSS & CROSS WEST & HORIZON & MOTHER GODDESS & PATH & WATER +19a NIGERIA, YORUBA \LARs \PAQt

ladder celestial *The letter P of the Snake Ring Template.* A metaphor for the ascent of the young sun through the layered cosmos. *Ref* LEAP-UP.

• Raised images on an incense burner from Qustul depict a ladder, youth and deer together with a feline in a boat *See* BABY BOY & CARRIER & DEER & FELINE & INCENSE & LEAP-UP & PATH & REGENERATION & WATER -3b EGYPT \ARCt

ladder infernal *The letter H of the Snake Ring Template.* A metaphor for the descent of the old sun through the layered cosmos into the infernal regions. *Ref* DESCENDING MOTIF.

• Jacob saw in his dream a ladder leading down from heaven to where he was resting. He erected a stone pillar and poured a libation of oil at its top, calling it the House of God *See* DEMYTHOLIZATION & HOUSE & LIBATION OIL & MENHIR & SOCIETY AS AT THE AXIS MUNDI & STONE -10b ISRAEL, JEWISH \ELIt

• In the underground kivas of Greater Southwest Indians, the ladder through smoke holes in the roof symbolize a rainbow leading into the underworld *See* ARCH & HOLE & HOUSE & RAINBOW & SOCIETY AS AT THE AXIS MUNDI & WEST ORIENTATION +19a USA, HOPI \NATt \NABt

• Ritual rooms are referred to as "water filled", and the ladders which provide access to them as "water ladders" *See* HOUSE & SOCIETY AS AT THE AXIS MUNDI & WATER +18a USA, ZUNI \BEOt

• Carved balustrades of the steep stone staircases at the front of many Mesoamerican pyramids depict giant feathered serpents with their heads down *See* DESCENDING MOTIF & MOUNTAIN & PATH & PYRAMID & SOCIETY AS AT THE AXIS MUNDI & STONE -1b MEXICO \TEOp

lake *The letter F of the Snake Ring Template. Ref* WATER, SOCIETY AS AT THE AXIS MUNDI.

lamb *The letter I of the Snake Ring Template. Ref* BABY BOY, SHEEP (GOAT).

lamp **1**. *The letter D of the Snake Ring Template. Ref* FIRE. **2**. *The letter K of the Snake Ring Template. Ref* NIGHT.

lance or spear 1. *The letter* 𝒩 *of the Snake Ring Template. Ref* WAR. **2.** *The letter* 𝓔 *of the Snake Ring Template. Ref* BLADE.

language *The letter* 𝓡 *of the Snake Ring Template. Ref* SPEECH, WRITING.

lantern *The letters* 𝓓 & 𝓚 *of the Snake Ring Template. Ref* LAMP.

laurel *The letter* I *of the Snake Ring Template. Ref* FLORA.

law *The letter* 𝓡 *of the Snake Ring Template.* Originally guidelines for individuals' activities as suitable metaphors for the sun-family's activities at the western horizon. *Ref* SOCIETY AS AT THE AXIS MUNDI.

• The stele bearing Hammurabi's code, engraved with laws proclaimed by the ruler Hammurabi, depicts at its top the ruler receiving his ring motif and baton of authority from the sun god **Shamash**. The deity wears large round earplugs and a headdress of bull horns. Flames erupt from his shoulders as he sits on the symbol for a mountain *See* BULL & EARRING & FIRE & MOUNTAIN & RING MOTIF & RULER & SOCIETY AS AT THE AXIS MUNDI & STAFF & SUN OLD -17a IRAQ, AMORITE *Figure* 278

Leo *The letter* 𝓜 *of the Snake Ring Template The Lion Ref* FELINE, ZODIAC.

leaf *The letter* I *of the Snake Ring Template. Ref* FLORA.

leap-up *The letter* O *of the Snake Ring Template.* A metaphor for the ascent of the sun through the eastern horizon to the levels of the cosmos. *Ref* DEER, EAST ORIENTATION, HAND RAISED, LOTUS.

• The fifth sign of the zodiac, it corresponds to solar power *See* CARRIER & LEVELS UNDERWORLD & SUN YOUNG & WAR & ZODIAC +19a \CIRt

leopard *The letter* 𝓜 *of the Snake Ring Template. Ref* FELINE.

Lesbianism *The letter* 𝓗 *of the Snake Ring Template. Ref* GODDESSES, HOMOSEXUALITY.

Figure 278

letters *The letter* 𝓡 *of the Snake Ring Template.* Graphic metaphors originally created to inspire the regeneration of a new sun along the Snake Ring path. *Ref* ART, FERTILITY, WRITING.

• The Assyrian, Greek, Hebrew, Norse, English, Arabic, East Indian, and Korean alphabets are from a common source -20b \POMt \BALt

• The earliest alphabet began in Sumer and Susa, 7th millennia B.C. to 4th millennia B.C. in Iraq and Iran. Pictographs including a bull, fish, mountain, deer, raised hands, crops and a ring motif, were pressed into clay tablets. Before then, these individual images were in relief on clay tokens that were assembled either on a string or in a clay envelope to form a message. These tokens were found by the thousands throughout the Fertile Crescent by the 8th millennium. These same images had previously been important decorations in the Ice Age caves, whose art was abandoned after twenty millennia of use when the weather finally settled to approximately its present pattern *See* ART & BULL & DEER & FERTILITY & FISH & HAND RAISED & MOUNTAIN & RING MOTIF -70b IRAQ/ IRAN \ARCp

• The first and last letters of the Greek alphabet, alpha and omega, were inscribed on the figure of a serpent biting its tail. The letter alpha is the head of a bull, inverted in the English alphabet to form the letter "A". The letter omega is a ring motif. **[Note:** These are the metaphors in the *Snake Ring* for the beginning and the result of the process of solar regeneration] *See* BULL & PATH & REGENERATION & RING MOTIF -20b GREEK, MITHRAIC \LEIt \WESt

• A 10th century rock engraving depicts a long runic inscription within the body of a fantastic serpent. Mythic scenes above the serpent are of the legendary journey of Sigurd. The Germanic *furhark*, runic alphabet, consists of 24 inscribed symbols whose earliest appearance was in the third century A.D., originally used for religious or magical purposes. The first letter of the alphabet, for example, is the symbol for cattle and virility, i.e., bull, and the third is the symbol for monster or goblin. Earliest *futharks* are engraved on stone slabs placed inside of grave chambers, where they could not have been meant for general view. The great majority of known runic inscriptions, totaling around 5,000, are in Scandinavia. They continued there into the Middle Ages and, in attenuated usage, into modern times. Generally, the use of runes disappeared with the coming of Christianity *See* DEATH & DEMYTHOLIZATION & GHOST & LEVELS & MYTH & PATH & REGENERATION & SOCIETAL ASPECT & STONE & TRINITY +2a SWEDEN, GERMANIC \CAMs \PAHp

levels *The letters* K *&* P *of the Snake Ring Template. See* SECTION TWO

levels celestial *The letter* P *of the Snake Ring Template. See* SECTION TWO

levels underworld *The letter* K *of the Snake Ring Template.* See SECTION TWO.

libation *The letter* E *of the Snake Ring Template.* A pouring of a liquid, or the liquid poured, either on a strove , on the ground or on a victim of sacrifice, in honor of a deity. **a**. ~ *oil* To facilitate the entry. *Ref* DESCENDING MOTIF, STONE. **b**. ~ *wine* The path to regeneration. *Ref* BLOOD, WINE.

Libra *The letter* P *of the Snake Ring Template. The seventh sign of the zodiac, represented by a pair of scales.* A metaphor for the sun at its highest level, midway between the supposed movement of the sun up and then down its arching path *See* LEVELS CELESTIAL & HORIZON & ZODIAC \WEBt

light *The letter* S *of the Snake Ring Template.* A metaphor for the sun. *Ref* RAYED MOTIF.

lightning *or* **thunderbolt** *The letter* E *of the Snake Ring Template.* A metaphor for the descent of the old sun down the vertical segment of the entwined serpent path. *Ref* DESCENDING MOTIF, LIGHT.

• The symbols of the Teutonic sun god **Balder**, whose face shone with his own light, were fire and the oak tree, a tree that is struck by lightning more often than any other tree, probably due to its high moisture content *See* FIRE & HEAD & LIGHT & PATH & SUN OLD & TREE -7b SWEDEN, TEUTONIC \OCTt \CIRt \TLAt

lingam *The letter* E *of the Snake Ring Template. Ref* PHALLUS.

lion *The letter* M *of the Snake Ring Template. Ref* FELINE.

llama 1. *The letter* C *of the Snake Ring Template. Ref* BULL. 2. *The letter* I *of the Snake Ring Template.* ~ **lean and fat.** *Ref* FAUNA, SEASON.

lodge *The letter* H *of the Snake Ring Template. Ref* HOUSE.

lore *The letter* R *of the Snake Ring Template. A body of traditional knowledge or beliefs.* Episodes in the sun's seasonal regenerations ascribed to legendary figures, deities or the time of chaos in nature. *Ref* DEMYTHOLIZATION, MYTH.

• Solar heroes provide most of the world folklore, long after they are emptied of religious content. Flood myths are the most numerous of all myths, they are practically everywhere. "Sacred" is the activities of supernatural beings at "the beginning" *See* CHAOS IN NATURE & FLOOD & PSYCHOLOGY CHILD & SUN OLD/ YOUNG +19a MIRCEA ELIADE \ELHt \ELIt

• In creation myths, the young gods tame nature by defeating the old gods of chaos. The young sun god **Damuzzi** was different for each season *See* CHAOS IN NATURE & REGENERATION & SEASON & SUN YOUNG & WAR -35b IRAQ, SUMERIAN \BIBt \HITt

• The lion Narasimha was a transient aspect of the sun god **Vishnu**, but the cosmic serpent Ananta was Vishnu's permanent alter-ego *See* CARRIER & FELINE & PATH & UNDERWORLD & UROBORUS -19a INDIA, HINDU \MUNt

• Time is an immense web consisting of rolling change that does not of itself change. The Legion of Immortals rode this web on dragons. *See* DRAGON & HORIZON & PATH & SERPENT ENTWINED & TIME & TRINITY & X-CROSSING & WATER -1b CHINA, TAOIST \RAWt \SCGt

• Pygmy and Bushmen, until recently true stone age people, regard their myths as actual happenings. They associate the moon with their mother goddess and with their own childbirth *See* BABY BOY/ GIRL & MOON & MYTH & SOCIETAL ASPECT +19a SOUTH AFRICA, BUSHMAN \CAIt

• A recurrent myth among North American Indians tells of a child who becomes an adult in a short time *See* BABY BOY & CARRIER & NIGHT & TIME & UNDERWORLD +19a CANADA, NOOTKA \BUQt

• Some South American tribal people retain the same type of shamanism and belief in mythic serpents that is common among Siberian tribal people. They believe that they are descended from people who took refuge on a mountain that rose above the flood waters *See* CHAOS IN NATURE & DRAGON & FLOOD & MOUNTAIN & PRIEST & RITUAL & TRANSCULTURAL SIMILARITY & WATER +19a CHILE, AURACANIAN \MUNt

lotus *The letter O of the Snake Ring Template. Any of several water lilies represented in ancient art, which open their petals at dawn.* A metaphor

for the emergence of the young sun from the eastern horizon waters. *Ref* BEETLE, LEAP-UP, PATH.

• A painted wooden bust from Tutankhamun's tomb depicts the young king emerging from a lotus *See* DEATH & REGENERATION & RULER -13a EGYPT *Figure 279*

Figure 279

The sun bathes in the lily lake before starting its journey across heaven *See* LEAP-UP & SUN YOUNG & WATER -30b EGYPT \EDWt

• The lotus is a symbol for sunrise among the Egyptian, Mesopotamian, Hindu, Phoenician, and Greek cultures -20b GREEK \HEVt

• The sun gods were born from the lotus and the lord **Brahma** was born from a lotus *See* BABY BOY & REGENERATION & SUN YOUNG -19b INDIA, HINDU ELIt \HEVt

• In a Sassanian cave painting, the young sun god **Mithra** is depicted on a lotus holding a sword *See* LEAP UP & PATH & SUN YOUNG & WAR +3a IRAN, MITHRAIC \GIRt

• Many stone carvings depict young lords emerging from water lilies   -6b MEXICO, MAYAN *Figure 280*

Figure 280

• A sarcophagus of a ruler from Byblos depicts him seated on a feline-shaped throne holding a lotus. Portrayed on its sides are nobles raising their hands to the departed king. The sarcophagus rests on carved figures of crouching lions *See* CARRIER & DEATH & FELINE & HAND RAISED & LEAP UP & REGENERATION & RULER -12a LEBANON, PHOENICIAN \PRIt

• An ivory miniature from Nimrud depicts a standing noble with an uraeus (a small cobra) on his head, raising his hand as he stands before a lotus *See* HAND RAISED & HEAD & PATH & SNAKE -7a IRAQ, ASSYRIAN *Figure 281*

• A painted tile depicts the sun god **Shamash** standing on a pedestal before a staff with a lotus at its base and a rayed ring motif at its top. Shamash holds a rod and ring *See* BATON

& HOUSE & PATH & REGENERATION & RING MOTIF & STAFF & SUN YOUNG -7a IRAQ, ASSYRIAN \PRIp

• The Buddhist illustrated book, *Kozuko Bosatsu,* imparts sacredness to a figure by depicting him seated on a lotus which is carried on the back of a lion *See* AVATAR & CARRIER & FELINE & PATH   +19a JAPAN, BUDDHIST \LARt

Figure 281

• Lilies in the water are a Rosicrucian metaphor for the Virgin Mary and Child. White lilies are a symbol for the resurrection of Christ. *See* BABY BOY & MOTHER GODDESS & RESURRECTION & WATER 0b ITALY, CHRISTIAN \BIBt \OCTp

loving cup *The letter N of the Snake Ring Template.* A metaphor for the victory of the young sun **[Note:** in the underworld represented by the vessel**]** to join with the mother goddess at the end of his season and produce the sun of the next season. *Ref* GAME SPORT, MARRIAGE, SEASON, SOCIETAL ASPECT, VESSEL, WAR.

lozenge *The letter S of the Snake Ring Template. A diamond-shaped figure.* *Ref* DIAMOND MOTIF, EYE.

lyre *The letter P of the Snake Ring Template.* *Ref* HARP.

machine *The letter* R *of the Snake Ring Template.* A composite result of tool-making skills. *Ref* ART, RITUAL, SOCIETAL ASPECT, TOOL-MAKING.

magic *The letter* R *of the Snake Ring Template. A claimed mastery of the secret forces of nature.* Use of the metaphors involved in regenerations of the sun to inspire or suggest corresponding occurrences in nature or mankind. *Ref* OCCULT, TRINITY, WAR, WITCHCRAFT.

• Why are magic and religion so fervent, ubiquitous and persistent among all peoples of the earth? *See* FERTILITY & OCCULT & PSYCHOLOGY CHILD & RELIGIONS CONTEMPORARY SEASON +19a WESTON LABARRE \JAAt

• Ideas of the past have been discarded; why not magic? \OCTt

• What experiences lend plausibility to magic? \JAAt

• The main aim of magic is to assure an adequate food supply *See* CHAOS IN NATURE & FERTILITY & SEASON

• Paleolithic art is sympathetic magic \CONt

man *The letter* R *of the Snake Ring Template.* The societal metaphor for the regenerative aspects of the sun within its path. *Ref* HAND RAISED, SOCIETAL ASPECT.

mandala *The letter* A *of the Snake Ring Template. Skt. A circular symbol for the universe.* A metaphor for the snake ring surrounding the earth. *Ref* UROBORUS.

• The word "mandala" representing the uroborus, means both "a circle which surrounds" and "the center" *See* ABYSS & AXIS MUNDI & CALABASH & SOCIETY AS AT THE AXIS MUNDI & UROBORUS -5b TIBET, TANTRIC \ELIt \NEUt

• The mandala is a map of the cosmos rotating around its central axis, Mt. Sumeru. The sky rests on this mountain, whose roots are in the substratum *See* AXIS MUNDI & MOUNTAIN

UNDERWORLD & WHEEL -19b INDIAN, HINDU \CUPt

marble *The letter* G *of the Snake Ring Template. Ref* STONE.

marine bird *The letter* F *of the Snake Ring Template.* **a.** *pl.* A metaphor for the western horizon water. **b.** *sing.* A metaphor for the old sun arriving at the western horizon water for regeneration into the new sun of the next season. *Ref* BIRD, DUCK, WATER.

• A warrior's helmet from Pompeii is embossed with the images of two young birds, a Horn of Plenty and a stork holding a serpent in it's beak *See* BIRD & CORNUCOPIA & FERTILITY & PATH TRINITY & WAR -5b ITALY, ROMAN \MURp

• Folk people cover the cradles of the children with pelican skins *See* BABY BOY/ GIRL SOCIETAL ASPECT & STORK & TRINITY +18a MEXICO \NA

• Three ibises perched in a tree are embossed on a bronze plaque that was used in war rituals. The plaque was later fastened to a column of the royal palace. Natives call the ibis "birds of disaster" *See* BRONZE & DEATH HOUSE & IBIS & PATH & REGENERATION & RULER TREE & TRINITY & WAR +16a NIGERIA, BENIN \EYOt

• An ancient ritual knife has the sinuous body of a snake along its handle, from the gold figure of a water bird to its copper blade *See* BIRD & BLADE & GOLD & PATH & WATER +9b PERU *Figure 282*

• Some of the oldest mummies in the world were discovered in burials near the west coast of Chile. They were painted black and red, and covered with the skins of pelicans and sea lions *See* BLACK & BURIAL & DEATH & FELINE & RED & REGENERATION & SOCIETAL ASPECT & WATER & WEST ORIENTATION -60b CHILE, CHINCHURRO \NAUp

• The hieroglyph of a stork represented the "ba", the immaterial element of a body at death *See* DEATH & SOCIETAL ASPECT & STONE -30b EGYPT \EDWt

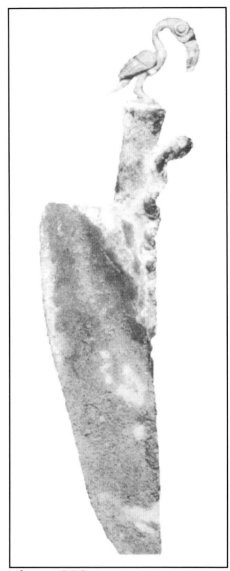

Figure 282

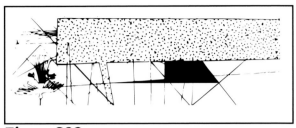

Figure 283

• Geese, in addition to bulls, were the usual animals sacrificed at the sun temples. **[Note:** that both aspects of the old sun's death were represented by these animal metaphors: a bird-like death from the sky into the western horizon waters, and virility at this death to produce the new sun of the next season] *See* BIRD & BULL & DEATH & GOOSE & HOUSE REGENERATION & SACRIFICE ANIMAL & SEASON & SUN OLD -24a EGYPT, USERKAF \EDWt

• An illustration in the Fejervary-Mayer codex depicts a bearded duck-mouthed figure descending into a water-filled cave, where a nude goddess waits with her vagina exposed. In the next illustration of the codex, the duck-figure is within the mouth of a feathered serpent that has penetrated under the goddess's skirt. In the third illustration, the serpent emerges from her navel, passes through and ascends above a ball-court while carrying a deer's head in its mouth *See* ART CAVE & BIRTH & DESCENDING MOTIF & DRAGON & DUCK & MARRIAGE & PATH & SNAKE-FEATHERED & VAGINA & WATER +13a MEXICO, AZTEC **Refer to** *Figures 207-209*

• A painted cylindrical vase of a type used only in burials, depicts a fantasy ball game between two players, one with a deer's headdress and the other with the headdress of a water bird. [The new sun who will leap up into the eastern sky, against the husk of the old sun who died from the sky into the western horizon waters] *See* DEATH & DEER & GAME SPORT & REGENERATION & SOCIETAL ASPECT & UNDERWORLD & VAGINA & VESSEL & WAR +3b MEXICO, MAYAN \FURp

• One of many huge ground drawings scraped into the red earth of a plain at the west coast of Peru, depicts a large water bird at the end of a broad path. The path is oriented to the sunset at the start of springtime [south of west in the southern latitudes] *See* ART & DESCENDING MOTIF & PATH & RED & SPRINGTIME SUNSET ORIENTATION & WATER +1b PERU, NAZCA *Figure 283*

• The soul of the dead return as sea birds *See* DEATH & SOCIETAL ASPECT & SOCIETY AS AT THE AXIS MUNDI -5b ENGLAND, CELTIC \NYTt

• A tile from a tomb depicts a crane at the top of a palace gate *See* DESCENDING MOTIF & DEATH & HOUSE & PALACE & SOCIETAL ASPECT -2a CHINA, HAN \SCGp

marine carrier *The letter J of the Snake Ring Template. Ref* CARRIER, FISH, WATER, WHALE.

marriage *The letter H of the Snake Ring Template. See* SECTION TWO.

mask *The letter R of the Snake Ring Template.* The wearers represent metaphors within the snake ring path, inspiring the suns or mother goddess to the requisite behavior for solar regeneration. *Ref* ART, DANCE, RITUAL.

materialism *The letter I of the Snake Ring Template.* Importance given to material goods, as metaphors for the seasonal fertility and prosperity brought on by the young sun. *Ref* COMMERCE, GIFT GIVING, GOLD, MONEY.

mathematics *The letters P & K of the Snake Ring Template. Application of numbers and counting to concepts of relationships.* Derived, as is music, from the complex passage of the sun within the eternal, crossing, serpentine path as it penetrates and re-penetrates the numbered levels. *Ref* ARITHMETIC, LEVELS, MUSIC, NUMBER, SERPENT-ENTWINED, X-CROSSING.

maze *The letter K of the Snake Ring Template.* A metaphor for the entwined serpent path of the new sun through the perilous underworld *Ref* LABYRINTH, SERPENT ENTWINED, UNDERWORLD.

• When the hero, Aeneas, arrived from Troy at the cave entrance to the underworld, a labyrinth was engraved into the rock. The demon Sybil taunted him until he pursued her into the underworld *See* CAVE & DEMYTHOLIZATION & GODDESSES & HERO & PATH STONE & UNDERWORLD -6a GREEK, TROY \CAAt

• An Etruscan jar painting depicts warriors emerging from a maze that is labeled with the name Troy. A similar Welsh word "troi" means "to turn". [Troy in present-day Turkey and Jericho in Israel, are similar in that no evidence has been found, in spite of archaeological investigations down to bedrock, for the great battles said to have been fought at either place. Greek lore suggests that Troy was at the axis mundi (its western location, surrounded by bulrushes, bull-men in the water, etc.), as did Jewish lore relating to Jericho (its western location, the parting of the water, the harlot found there, the seven circles, etc.). Each was a major religious center in its area when the new cultures arrived, which suggests that the "battles" were symbolic victories by the Greeks and Israelites over the indigenous faiths, in the process, taking over the indigenous models of the axis mundi locations as their own] *See* DEMYTHOLIZATION & HERO & SOCIETY AS AT THE AXIS MUNDI & UNDERWORLD & WAR -6a TURKEY, TROY \DISt

• The legendary and fearsome minotaur, half bull and half man, was in the labyrinth under the palace [actually, a mortuary temple] at Knossos *See* BULL & DEATH & DEVIL & HOUSE & REGENERATION & UNDERWORLD & WAR -20b CRETE, MINOAN \WOOt

• Passageways under some of the oldest Andean structures were in the form of a labyrinth -8b PERU, CHAVIN \STHt

• Worshippers follow a mosaic of a maze on the church floor, praying that they will not be ensnared by the devil *See* DEATH & DEMYTHOLIZATION & DEVIL & HOUSE & PATH & SOCIETAL ASPECT & UNDERWORLD & WAR +18a FRANCE, CHRISTIAN \DISp

• The soul of the dead travels across the great waters, where it encounters a woman sitting at the volcano-cave entrance to the underworld. Before one can approach her, she erases half of a drawing of the underworld labyrinth. Those who can complete the drawing may pass the land of the dead into the Sea of Life *See* CAVE & DEATH & GODDESS & HOLE(ABYSS) & REGENERATION & UNDERWORLD & WATER +19a NEW HEBRIDES, MALEKU \CAAt

• The Topock maze is eighteen acres of twisting furrows located near a sixty-five foot-long image of a twisting snake carved into the desert rock. To be spiritually restored, Mohave Indians run every mile of the maze. They will not discuss the ritual with outsiders *See* GAME SPORT & INFORMATION SECRET & PATH & SNAKE +12b USA, MOHAVE \NABp

• In the game of hopscotch, the child hops a maze *See* GAME CHILDREN & PSYCHOLOGY CHILD +19a \DISt

meander motif *The letter A of the Snake Ring Template.* A metaphor for the path of the sun through the cosmic serpent's twisting body. *Ref* FLAG, ROPE, SERPENT ENTWINED, VERTICAL LINE/ SHAPE.

• The spirals and meanders depicted on early European house models are said to represent serpents -50a RUSSIA, CUCUTEN \ARCp

• Meanders are depicted on the upper section of an attic vase, above abstract representations of women's heads. Below this is a scene of "Heracles" defeating a bearded centaur *See* PATH & VESSEL -20b GREEK \BOTp

• The wavy lines and ring motifs in the Indians' sand paintings, made under the influence of hallucinogens, are said to represent the thought of the sun-father towards fertilizing the Yaje woman. These designs are similar to the phosphenes produced by pressing on one's eyes *See* HALLUCINOGENS & MARRIAGE & PATH & SUN OLD +19a COLOMBIA, TUKANO *Figure 284*

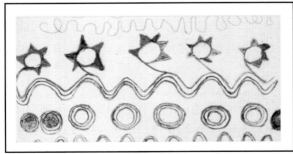

Figure 284

meaning of life *The letter R of the Snake Ring Template.* Within mankind's genetic heritage are metaphors for preserving fertility in the world by inspiring the sun's seasonal regenerations. These were created by tool-making mankind during the chaos of the

terminal Ice Age, and were apparently successful. One's life has to involve a certain minimum of these metaphors to have the special importance of being human. *Ref* ART, CHAOS IN NATURE, ETHICS, FERTILITY, METAPHOR, PSYCHOLOGY QUANTITY, RITUAL, SEASON, SOCIETAL ASPECT.

• The underlying anxiety of our time: What is the purpose of life? *See* DEMYTHOLIZATION & PSYCHOLOGY CONTEMPORARY/ QUANTITY +19a R WRIGHT \NYTt

• Civilization is a mechanism for the world's survival. **[Note:** If food becomes scarce, cellular slime molds, which normally slide independently on the forest floor engulfing food, cluster together into a tiny slug that inches toward heat or light seeking food] *See* CHAOS IN NATURE & FERTILITY & HOUSE & RITUAL & SOCIETAL ASPECT +19a \LETt \NYTt

• The great pyramid center near present-day Mexico City was called, "the city of weather magic" *See* PYRAMID & SEASON & SOCIETY AS AT THE AXIS MUNDI +7a MEXICO, TEOTIHUACAN \RAUt

• Our function is to maintain equilibrium in nature, or the world would collapse *See* CHAOS IN NATURE +19a BALI, HINDU \WESt

• Greater southwest Indians address the immortals for harmony in nature. The hierarchy of their groups match the hierarchy of the immortals. They say that there would be disaster if they failed to act properly *See* CHAOS IN NATURE & ETHICS & SOCIETAL ASPECT +19a USA, TAOS \TUQt

• For a festival before the rainy season, Mexicans dressed as felines and bulls, fought with sticks and whips in the church courtyards, at times with fatal results. They say that if they do not do this, the sun will not rise and the rain will not come *See* BULL & FELINE & GAME SPORT & HOUSE & PATH & RITUAL & SEASON(RAIN) & SUN OLD/ YOUNG & WAR +19a MEXICO \NATp
Refer to *Figure 230*

• Amazonian Indians say that their rituals save mankind from chaos *See* CHAOS IN NATURE & RITUAL +19a COLUMBIA, TUKANO

---

menhir *The letter E of the Snake Ring Template. Prehistoric. An upright rough stone. Ref* MONOLITH, SOCIETY AS AT THE AXIS MUNDI, STONE, VERTICAL STICK.

menstruation *The letter R of the Snake Ring Template.* An undesirable metaphor for the mother goddess' failure to birth a new sun or new mother goddess. *Ref* ABORTION, BLOOD, CHAOS IN NATURE, SOCIETAL ASPECT.

• American Indians, as with many tribal peoples of the world, believed that women during their " period" were a peril to mankind *See* BLOOD & CHAOS IN NATURE & SOCIETAL ASPECT +18a USA, YANA \KROt

menorah *The letter P of the Snake Ring Template. A candelabrum of seven branches that is in Jewish houses of worship.* A metaphor for the path of the sun through the celestial layers to the house of the western horizon. *Ref* FIRE, HOUSE, LEVELS CELESTIAL, LIGHT.

• Originally, the menorah was in the form of a 7-branched tree with flowers on its branches, standing on lions' paws *See* CELESTIAL LEVELS & FELINE & PATH & TREE & VERTICAL LINE/ SHAPE - 10b ISRAEL, JEWISH \ENDt

• The menorah in traditional synagogues must be located where the eastern sunlight falls on it. **[Note:** To guide the sun's arching path from east to west, through the levels of the sky to the tree path of the western horizon] *See* HOUSE & LEVELS CELESTIAL & PATH & SUN OLD +19a ISRAEL, JEWISH \WESt

Mercury *The letter A of the Snake Ring Template. Rom. Relig. Ref* HERMES.

• A Roman statue of **Mercury** depicts him running with wings at his head and feet and carrying the caduceus. The Messenger of the Gods was regarded as a penetration or sword. He made the sun god **Apollo's** lyre, and was the carrier of the infant sun god **Dionysus**. *See* BLADE & CADUCEUS & MUSIC & PATH & SERPENT ENTWINED & UROBORUS & WINGED +15a ITALY, ROMAN \JUPt \LARt \SANt \WESt
Figure 285

mermaid *The letter H of the Snake Ring Template.* A metaphor for the goddesses in the western horizon waters. *Ref* GODDESSES, MIRROR, MOTHER GODDESS, WATER.

Figure 285

metamorphosis *The letter H of the Snake Ring Template.* The change in solar form from the old sun to the new sun in the western horizon underworld. *Ref* ALCHEMY, GOLD, POLYTHEISM, SEASON, TRINITY.

metaphor *The letter R of the Snake Ring Template. A representation of an idea.* A graphic or ritual image used to inspire an activity of the sun based on Ice Age man's interpretation of the cosmos. *Ref* ART, CHAOS IN NATURE, PRIMAL ARCHETYPES, PRIMORDIAL RELIGION, SOCIETAL ASPECT, THEATER, TOOL-MAKING.

mica *The letter S of the Snake Ring Template.* A metaphor for the sun in the underworld. Just as the sun was believed to disappear into the underworld, the light of the sun reflected in mica exposed during the day is extinguished when the mica is placed in sacred caves or ritual burials. *Ref* BLACK, CAVE, DEATH, HOLE, RAYED MOTIF.

millstone *The letter A of the Snake Ring Template.* A metaphor for the coil of the entwined serpent path entering the mountain-house of the western horizon waters. *Ref* CIRCLE MOTIF, HOUSE, STONE, SERPENT ENTWINED, WEST ORIENTATION, WHEEL.

minaret *The letter E of the Snake Ring Template. Ar. A slender tower attached to a Mosque. Ref* HOUSE, TOWER, VERTICAL LINE/ SHAPE, SOCIETY AS AT THE AXIS MUNDI.

Minotaur *The letter L of the Snake Ring Template. Gr. A fabulous monster, half man, half bull, confined in the labyrinth.* A metaphor for the husk of the old sun in the perilous underworld. *Ref* BULL, MAZE, TRINITY, LEVELS UNDERWORLD, WAR.

Minstrel *The letter R of the Snake Ring Template. Tarot. The first enigma, wearing a hat in the form of a horizontal eight (the mathematical sign for infinity).* A metaphor for the entwined serpent path through the cosmic layers. *Ref* INFINITY, LEVELS CELESTIAL, MATHEMATICS, MUSIC, SERPENT ENTWINED, TAROT PACK, LEVELS UNDERWORLD.

mirror *The letter S of the Snake Ring Template.* Reflecting the sun's rays, the mirror serves as a metaphor for the sun itself. *Ref* DANCE, DEATH, FELINE, RAYED MOTIF, SOUL.

• The word ankh means "mirror", as well as "life" *See* SOCIETAL ASPECT -30b EGYPT \EDVt

• Aphrodite emerged from the sea holding a mirror with which to capture **Narcissus'**

reflection so she could seduce him *See* DEATH & GODDESS & MARRIAGE & MOTHER & TRINITY & WATER -20b GREEK \NEUt \SMJt

• The Egyptians associated the numerous mirrors they placed in burials with the sun *See* DEATH & REGENERATION & SOCIETAL ASPECT & SUN OLD/ YOUNG -30b EGYPT \ARCt

• Scholars are unable to explain the ritual function of mirrors worn as pendants and found in graves throughout the cultures of Mesoamerica *See* DEATH & REGENERATION & SOCIETAL ASPECT & TRANSCULTURAL SIMILARITY & SUN OLD/ YOUNG -15b MEXICO, OLMEC \MUTt

• Mirrors were regarded as figurative suns -6a CHINA, HAN \LEEt

• Shinto priests use mirrors in their rituals as representations of the sun *See* RITUAL -2b JAPAN, SHINTO \WESt

• When Magellan was killed by Mactan warriors in the Pacific, his fellow explorers mourned him as "our mirror, our light" *See* HERO & SUN YOUNG & WAR +15a PORTUGAL \BOPt

Figure 286

• Descendants of the Aztecs perform a battle-dance they call the Dance of the Moors and Christians, in which black-faced Moors are defeated by heroic Christians. Both groups wear red cloaks and have mirrors in their headdresses. Their faces are often shrouded by strings of beads which hang from their hats. Present-day Maya regard mirrors, particularly black ones, as reflections of the setting sun *See* BLACK & DEMYTHOLIZATION & PREJUDICE(DARK SKIN) & RED & SUN OLD/ YOUNG & VEIL +19b MEXICO *Figure 286*

• In a related battle-dance called el Pastorale, the dancer wearing the mask of a bull - demon and a youth with a flower on his headdress wear mirrors at their heads and on their costumes *See* BULL & FERTILITY & SUN OLD/ YOUNG & WAR +19a MEXICO *Figure 287*

Figure 287

mistletoe 1. *The letter E of the Snake Ring Template.* A metaphor for the sun at sunset, along the vertical tree path, to join with the mother goddess. *Ref* CHRISTMASTIDE, MARRIAGE, TREE, WEST ORIENTATION. **2.** *The letter I of the Snake Ring Template.* A metaphor for seasonal fertility. *Ref* APPLE, FLORA, MARRIAGE, RED, ROUND MOTIF, TREE, TRINITY, YELLOW.

money *The letter I of the Snake Ring Template.* **a.** A metaphor for the sun. **b.** A means to acquire metaphors for fertility and prosperity. *Ref* ART, BEADS, COMMERCE, CRUSTACEAN: COWRIE, FLORA, GOLD, MATERIALISM, ROUND MOTIF, RULER, SOCIETAL ASPECT, SOCIETY AS AT THE AXIS MUNDI.

monolith *The letter E of the Snake Ring Template.* A metaphor for the segment of the encircling serpent path penetrating the western horizon mountain-house where coital activities assure a new sun for the successor season. *Ref* COLUMN, MARRIAGE, MOUNTAIN, PATH, SEASON, SOCIETY AS AT THE AXIS MUNDI, STONE, UROBORUS, VERTICAL LINE/ SHAPE, WEST ORIENTATION.

• After his dream of the celestial ladder reaching from heaven to earth, Jacob erected a stone and anointed it with oil **[Note:** Oil as the lubricant, to facilitate the downward path of the sun], calling the location the "house of God" and the "gate of heaven" *See* DEMYTHOLIZATION & GOD & HOUSE & LADDER INFERNAL & SOCIETY AS AT THE AXIS MUNDI -10b ISRAEL, JEWISH \ELIt

• A massive stone pillar, with entwined serpents carved at its top and bottom, rests on a stylized tortoise. It is inscribed with writing referring to the pillar as the link between heaven and earth *See* TURTLE & SOCIETY AS AT THE AXIS MUNDI +18a CHINA, MING *Figure 288*

Figure 288

• The Great Father resides in menhirs (an upright stone) and the Great Mother in cromlechs (a circle of upright stones usually enclosing a dolmen or mound) *See* CROMLECH & DOLMEN & MENHIR & MOTHER GODDESS & MOUND PATH +19a INDIA, KHASIS \ELIt

---

moon *The letter H of the Snake Ring Template. Identified with the sea, the female menstrual cycle and the tides.* A metaphor for the mother goddess in the western horizon waters. *Ref* MARRIAGE, MENSTRUATION, MOTHER GODDESS, SOCIETAL ASPECT.

• A statue of **Apis**, the heavenly bull, has images of the sun disk and the uraeus between its horns, and a crescent shaped moon inscribed on its flank, "for procreation" *See* BULL & MARRIAGE & SUN OLD -30b EGYPT \ELHt *Figure 289*

Figure 289

• At a total eclipse, the moon appears as a dark cone which is approached by the sun before darkness falls. Less than seven minutes later, the sun reappears *See* DEATH & ECLIPSE & MARRIAGE & MOUND (MOUNTAIN) & NIGHT & REGENERATION & SUN OLD/ YOUNG \WESt

• The ancient Greeks and Celts knew of the link between the moon and the tides *See* WATER -20 GREEK, ENGLAND \ELIt

• The moon was the wife of the sun *See* MARRIAGE & SUN OLD & TRANSCULTURAL SIMILARITY +9b PERU, INCA \MASt

• To African Pygmies, the moon is the mother of fecundity *See* BABY BOY/ GIRL & FERTILITY MOTHER GODDESS +19a CONGO, PYGMY \ELIt

• Present-day Maya call the moon "our Holy Mother". They associate the moon with the Virgin Mary and the sun with God *See* DEMYTHOLIZATION & GOD & SOCIETAL ASPECT +19a MEXICO, ZINACANTECO \VOGt

• The moon calls the sun "my son" in stories by the Plains Indians *See* BIRTH & MOTHER GODDESS SUN YOUNG +19a USA, BLACKFOOT \CAIt

morality *The letter R of the Snake Ring Template. Ref* ETHICS, LAW, SOCIETAL ASPECT.

mother goddess *The letter H of the Snake Ring Template.* A metaphor for the unseen female below the western horizon who joins with the old sun in the mountain-house where the snake path enters the horizon waters. She gives birth to the new sun who will bring on the season of fertility. Her personification is regenerated in daughters by the old suns of the ebbing seasons *Ref* BABY GIRL, GODDESSES, HOUSE, INCEST, MOUNTAIN, SEASON, SERPENT ENTWINED, SIREN, VEIL.

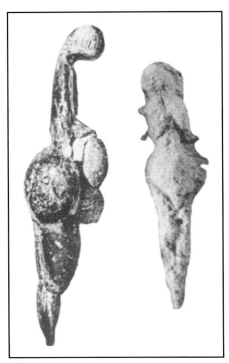

Figure 290

• In certain accounts, mythic mother and daughter figures are so closely identified that they appear to represent different aspects of the same goddess *See* GODDESSES +19a BRUNO BETTELHEIM \BEUt

• The underworld earth goddess **Papa** was the mother of the gods +19a HAWAII \COTt

• Carved venus figures from the Ice Age caves are frequently faceless and with bulbous rumps and stomachs *See* BIRTH & UNDERWORLD & VEIL -350b FRANCE *Figure 290 Figure 291*

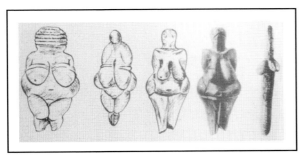

Figure 291

• Young ladies in their first communion dress as brides, complete with bridal veils, take part in the sacrament of wine during the Church ceremony *See* BABY GIRL & RITE OF PASSAGE & SOCIETAL ASPECT & VEIL & WINE +19a USA
Figure 292

Figure 292

• In accordance with Muslim law, Moroccan women dress in black and cover their faces with veils *See* BLACK & SOCIETAL ASPECT & UNDERWORLD & VEIL +19a MOROCCO, MUSLIM
Figure 293

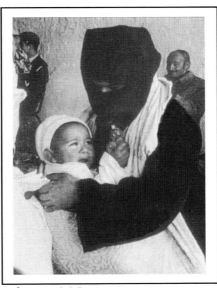

Figure 293

• A painted stucco relief on a wall of the first true city in the world depicts a mother goddess with a large ring motif at her navel and her legs spread widely apart. In an overall view of the shrine room, this goddess is seen giving birth. Below her is a sequence of three bulls' heads made of plaster. A figurine of the great goddess from a grain bin at the site depicts her sitting on a throne between two felines while giving birth *See* BIRTH & BULL & CARRIER & FELINE & FLORA & HOUSE & MARRIAGE & PATH & RING MOTIF & SOCIETY AS AT THE AXIS MUNDI & VAGINA -60b TURKEY, CATAL HUYUK
Figure 294 Figure 295 Figure 296

Figure 294

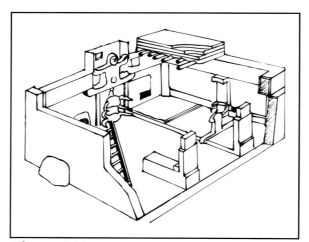

Figure 295

Figure 296

Figure 297

• A large clay figure of the earth mother **Ala** within her painted temple has prominent ring motifs painted on her elongated neck and on

her clothes. Her spouse, next to her, is mounted on a motorcycle and wears a European style sun helmet. Their son, a youth, walks before them *See* BABY BOY & HAT & HOUSE & MARRIAGE & RING MOTIF & SUN OLD / YOUNG & VEHICLE +18a NIGERIA, NOK

Figure 297   Figure 298

Figure 298

Figure 299

• The goddess **Coatlicue** was the goddess of life and death, wife and mother of the sun *See* BIRTH & DEATH & INCEST & MOON & PSYCHOLOGY & REGENERATION & SUN OLD/ YOUNG & TRANSCULTURAL SIMILARITY +13b MEXICO, AZTEC \NUNp \RAUt

• The goddess **Cybele** is seated between two lions as she holds a ring motif. **Note:** The felines wait to accompany her newborn sons through the perilous underworld to their ascent in the east] *See* CARRIER & FELINE & RING MOTIF -20b GREEK *Figure 299*

• A Cycladic goddess has a columnar head and a cross-form body *See* CROSS WEST & PATH & VERTICAL LINE/ SHAPE -25b SARDINIA, MEGALITHIC *Figure 300*
Refer also to *Figure 230*

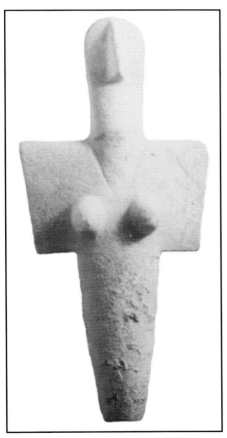

Figure 300

• Female statuettes from the city of Ur have snake heads and exaggerated shoulders *See* PATH & CROSS WEST & SNAKE -35b IRAQ, SUMERIAN *Figure 301*

• A female statue of the mother goddess **Coatlicue** from the main temple of the Aztecs in present day Mexico City, has snake heads in the place of her own. She birthed the young sun god **Huitzilipochtli** in the mythic mountain of the west, Coatepec "Serpent Mountain", the same name as the Templo

Mayor pyramid temple where the statue was found *See* BABY BOY & MOUNTAIN & PATH & PYRAMID & SNAKE & SOCIETY AS AT THE AXIS MUNDI & TRANSCULTURAL SIMILARITY & WEST ORIENTATION +13b MEXICO, AZTEC
Refer to *Figure 63* SECTION TWO.

Figure 301

• Depicted on a terracotta plaque, the goddess **Demeter** is accompanied by a plumed snake and holds a spike of wheat. In some versions of the myth, she birthed the sun god **Dionysus**. In others, he was birthed by Demeter's daughter, and alter ego, **Persephone** *See* BABY BOY & FLORA & GODDESSES & PATH & SEASONS & SNAKE FEATHERED & SUN YOUNG -20b GREEK *Figure 302*

Figure 302

• The painted native temple dedicated to the earth mother **Ala** depicts a female figure waiting in the doorway at the right side of the entrance. A male figure encircled by a snake approaches her from the other side of the temple entrance. The center post of this entrance is painted with a series of bands from top to bottom. The lintel at the top of this pole is hung with the skulls of sacrificed animals. **[Note:** For regeneration of the next season, the old sun must die at sunset along the vertical snake path into the mother goddess' house, as suggested by the sacrificed animals over this entrance, and by the goats' blood once spread on the door posts of the Passover domiciles] *See* ART & DEATH & DEMYTHOLINATION & HOUSE & PATH & POLE & REGENERATION & RING MOTIF IN SEQUENCE & SACRIFICE ANIMAL & SNAKE +18a NIGERIA, NOK *Figure* 303

Figure 303

Figure 304

• A painted figurine depicts a woman with a series of ring motifs down her headdress, and a large vulva painted on her chest. Her eyes are the heads of birds with large ring motif eyes, and her hands are occupied with spinning *See* BIRD & EYE & PATH & RING MOTIF IN SEQUENCE & VAGINA & WEAVING(SPINNING) +2b PERU, MOCHICA *Figure* 304

• The emblem of the goddess **Maya**, the eternal spinner, is a uroborus encircling a spider waiting in her web *See* DEATH & PATH & SPIDER & UROBORUS & WEAVING -5b INDIA, HINDU *Figure* 305

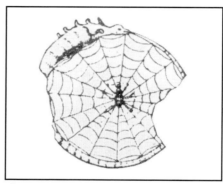

Figure 305

• Each creator god was called "bull of his mother". He was born from her in the world mountain, symbolized by the pyramid, and returned to her at death *See* BIRTH & BULL & INCEST & MARRIAGE & MOUNTAIN & PATH & PYRAMID PSYCHOLOGY -30b EGYPT \BAJt \CAMt

• The goddess **Usas** was born of the dawn. She was the mother as well as the daughter of the sun *See* GODDESSES & PATH & REGENERATION & SUN OLD -19b INDIA, HINDU \MCCt

• Statuettes from the palace [also a mortuary temple] at Knossos depict a bare breasted goddess holding snakes aloft. Her head is girdled by a series of round motifs and a small feline sits on her head *See* DEATH & FELINE & HOUSE & REGENERATION & ROUND MOTIF IN SEQUENCE & RULER -16a CRETE, MINOAN **Refer to** *Figure 85* SECTION TWO.

• Before entering their temples, Spartans and Greeks washed in enormous, elaborately carved water basins called *perirrhanteria*. These basins were carved of marble long before

marble was generally adopted for the arts. Typically, the basins were supported on the heads of female figures, the female figures sometimes standing on the backs of felines with rams' heads next to their own. **[Note:** The worshippers symbolically entered the western waters, a common orientation for ancient temples, before entering into the sacred house. Below this horizon mountain-house in the water are the goddesses, who join with the virile old sun as suggested by the adjacent ram's heads, to produce progeny. A boy-child will continue on this path through the underworld, with the protector feline, and rise up as the new sun in the dawn] *See* BIRTH & FELINE & GODDESSES & MARRIAGE & PATH & RAM & TEMPLE & STONE & UNDERWORLD & STONE (MARBLE) & WATER -6b GREEK, SPARTA
Figure 306

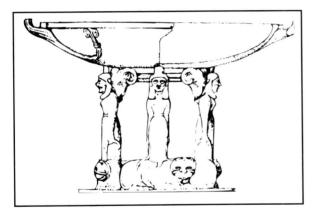

Figure 306

Figure 307

• The goddess **Manasa** is depicted in a stone carving with her seven-cobra emblem above her head. An aged deity is at her right side and a young deity at her left as she holds an erect cobra *See* PATH & REGENERATION & SNAKE & VERTICAL LINE/ SHAPE -5b INDIA, HINDU
Figure 307

• Stone carvings of aging women holding their vulvas open with their hands are above doorways of many early English and Irish churches *See* BIRTH & DEMYTHOLIZATION & HOUSE & MARRIAGE & REGENERATION & VULVA +3b ENGLAND, CHRISTIAN *Figure* 308

Figure 308

• A squatting goddess with her vulva exposed and wearing large ring motifs at her ears, and as a pectoral, is depicted on one of the stone slabs forming the boundary of a ceremonial ball-court. Ritual singing and dancing were performed at this site until the arrival of the Spanish conquerors in the fifteenth century +9a PUERTO RICO, TAINO *Figure* 309

Figure 309

Figure 310

• A small stone idol depicts the agony of the goddess **Tlazolteotl**, giving birth to the young sun god +13b MEXICO, AZTEC *Figure 310*

• A manuscript illustration depicts the Woman of the Primordial Water. A Phoenix bird, the embodiment of the sun god, is in flames in a pot on her head, while she stands in a boat on the water holding a honeycomb, the symbol of springtime fertility *See* BEE & PHOENIX BIRD & SPRINGTIME & WATER +17b FRANCE \CIRt \WEBt *Figure 311*

Figure 311

• According to Greater Southwest Indian lore, the mother goddess lives at the "mountain around which moving is done", guarded by huge snakes on the great water in the west, where she is visited by the sun at the end of his journey *See* MOUNTAIN & PATH & SNAKE & SUN OLD & WATER & WEST ORIENTATION & WHEEL +18a USA, NAVAJO \COTt \CAIt

• A dance mask depicts a woman, wearing large circular earplugs, entwined by a snake with round motifs along its body +19a IVORY COAST, BAULE *Figure 312*

mother goddess worship *The letter* ℛ *of the Snake Ring Template.* Ritual focus on the western horizon mother goddess who is joined by the old suns to seasonally produce a new sun *Ref* MARRIAGE, MOTHER GODDESS, SEASON.

mound *The letter* G *of the Snake Ring Template.* Ref MOUNTAIN.

• Megalithic chamber tombs were covered by earth mounds *See* DEATH & REGENERATION & SOCIETAL ASPECT -45b ENGLAND, MEGALITH \RAUt

Figure 312

• The stupa, a mound with a spire or umbrella at its top, is regarded as the world mountain and the home of the mountain mother of all life *See* DEATH & MOTHER GODDESS & MOUNTAIN & PATH & SOCIETY AS AT THE AXIS MUNDI & UMBRELLA & VERTICAL LINE / SHAPE +7a INDIA, BUDDHIST *Figure 313*

Figure 313

• All major cities of ancient Egypt were said to be the site of the primordial mound which rose from the flood waters at the birth of the world *See* CHAOS IN NATURE & FLOOD & INFANT MENTALITY & SOCIETY AS AT THE AXIS MUNDI -30b EGYPT \CASt

• The La Venta ceremonial center of the Mesoamerican mother culture was built on an island surrounded by a rush-filled swamp. It included a huge artificial mound and a ceremonial ball-court *See* GAME SPORT & PATH & RUSHES & SOCIETY AS AT THE AXIS MUNDI & WATER -15b MEXICO, LA VENTA \HAWt *Figure 314*

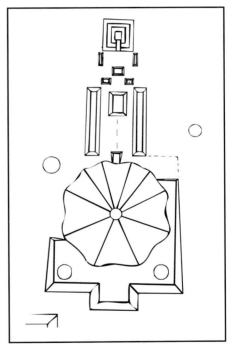

Figure 314

• Mississippian Indians constructed many ritual mounds, including one which covered approximately sixteen acres and measured one hundred feet in height +12a USA, CAHOKIA \TUQt

mountain *The letter G of the Snake Ring Template.* See SECTION TWO.

mouse *The letter K of the Snake Ring Template.* The holes rodents make in houses are taken as metaphors for the abyss from the western horizon house to the underworld, corresponding to the ritual holes made in the floor of American Indian kivas. The rodent going in an out of these holes becomes a metaphor for the sun god. In a similar manner, the beaver is sacred to the Northwest Coast Indians as a metaphor for the sun god for the reason that it is born in a house under the water. *Ref* BEAVER, HOLE, HOUSE, RAT.

• Framed photographs of Mickey Mouse are in Zen temples \TIMt

mouth *The letter A of the Snake Ring Template. Egypt. and Gr. Solar disks and sun gods are depicted in the mouth of fabulous animals.* A metaphor for the sun within the *Snake Ring* path and carriers. *Ref* CARRIER, FELINE, SERPENT ENTWINED, WHALE.

music *The letter P of the Snake Ring Template.* A metaphor for the complex passage of the sun within the eternal, crossing, serpentine path as it penetrates and re-penetrates the numbered levels. *Ref* LEVELS, MATHEMATICS, SERPENT ENTWINED, X-CROSSING.

• Many wonder why music and math are connected \NYTt

• The Bushmen, the oldest continuous culture in the world, dance in seven and five beat phrases *See* DANCE & DEATH & LEVELS CELESTIAL & LEVELS UNDERWORLD & PATH -200b SOUTH AFRICA, BUSHMEN \CAIt

• A reconstruction of a lyre from a royal burial has, at its front piece, the golden head of a bull with a blue beard. Another bull's-head lyre was recovered from a burial with the earliest music ever found, written in the diatonic scale used today *See* BULL & DEATH & GOLD & LEVELS CELESTIAL & REGENERATION & RULER -26a IRAQ, SUMERIAN *Figure* 315

• A silver lyre from a burial bears the figure of a leaping stag *See* DEATH & DEER & LEAP-UP & REGENERATION -35b IRAQ, SUMERIAN *Figure* 316

• A water insect is placed inside a new harp-lute only to escape through the sound holes. Members of the culture associate the insects escape with the resurrection of their creator deity *See* LEAP-UP & REGENERATION & WATER +19a MALI, DOGON \AFAt

Figure 315

• The Hindu and the Greek tone-mandala consisted of a diatonic scale, the same seven note scale as ours. Their scale falls, while ours rises *See* DESCENDING MOTIF & LEVELS CELESTIAL -20b GREEK, \MCCt

Figure 316

• Pythagoras: Friction between the seven moving spheres in the sky made music -4a GREEK, IONIAN \ABEt

• On the night of the Sun Dance ritual, the leader of the ceremonies entreats the people to make a joyful noise to attract the father above to the lodge where a wood snake ring is placed on a stick above a bull's skull painted with a series of red and black dots *See* BLACK & BULL & DEATH & NIGHT & PATH & RED & REGENERATION ROUND MOTIF IN SEQUENCE SOCIETY AS AT THE AXIS MUNDI & UROBORUS +19a USA, ARAPAHO \DOPt

Refer to *Figure 76* SECTION TWO.

• Tuning of the instruments is based on the diatonic scale +19a CHINA \MCCt

• When the Indian snake charmer plays music, it is not for the snake which has no ears, but for the audience *See* INFANT MENTALITY & PATH & SNAKE +19a INDIA \SMJp

• Flutes representing the mythic Anaconda are played by men dressed as the sun along an east to west axis of the ceremonial house. After the ceremony the flutes are returned to their hiding place in the river. The natives believe that if their rites are not performed, inspiring the Sun Father to copulate with the Yaje Woman, the universe will end *See* CHAOS IN NATURE & DANCE & MARRIAGE & PATH & RITUAL & SNAKE & SUN OLD & WEST ORIENTATION & WATER +19a COLOMBIA, TUKANO \AVDt

• In the form of an old man the loa "Legba" serves as the guardian of crossroads, he possesses the ability to communicate between the celestial spheres, and is invoked by the sound of drums and bells +19a HAITI, VOODOO \DATt

myth *The letter R of the Snake Ring Template. A story, the origin of which is forgotten.* Retained elements from the primordial religion, more recently ascribed to legendary figures, rulers, or animals. *Ref* RELIGIONS CONTEMPORARY/ PRIMORDIAL, DEMYTHOLIZATION, PSYCHOLOGY CONTEMPORARY/ CONTEMPORARY PROBLEMS/ DREAMS.

• Mythology is early astro-cosmic knowledge *See* CALABASH & CELESTIAL OBSERVATIONS & FERTILITY +19a KENNETH BRECHER \BREt

• Mythology is the product of the collective unconscious. It is the "self-rolling wheel", the creative principle of the uroborus *See* PATH & UROBORUS & WHEEL +19a \NEUt

• The meaning of the world's myths will emerge one day *See* DEMYTHOLIZATION & INFORMATION DESTROYED OR SECRET +19a \LETt

navel of the world *The letter G of the Snake Ring Template.* A metaphor for the penetration of the serpent path into the western horizon. *Ref* ABYSS, HOLE, SOCIETY AS AT THE AXIS MUNDI.

necklace *The letter R of the Snake Ring Template.* A societal metaphor denoting the wearer, particularly his or her head, as within the serpent path. *Ref* CINDER MOTIF, HEAD, JEWELRY, ROUND MOTIFS IN SEQUENCE, SOCIETAL ASPECT.

• Female figures in Ice Age art were nude, although they frequently wore bracelets and rows of beads *See* BEAD & JEWELRY & RING MOTIF IN SEQUENCE -350b ICE AGE
Refer to *Figure 50* SECTION TWO.

negro *The letter L of the Snake Ring Template.* Perceived as a metaphor for the husk of the old sun in the underworld *Ref* BLACK, PREJUDICE(DARK SKIN), SOCIETAL ASPECT, SOCIOBIOLOGY, WAR.

• The origin of castes is unknown. Only those of the lower caste, compelled to live outside the city gates, could dispose of the dead. The word for "caste" also means "color". Dark-skinned people are called "heathens". *See* PATH & SOCIETAL ASPECT & SOCIETY AS AT THE AXIS MUNDI -19b INDIA, HINDU \NAUt \TL5t

• There has always been a struggle between white and black man. It is the black men specifically who are attacked *See* WAR +19a M. JEFF \WESt

• All children, black or white, prefer to play with fair-skinned rather than dark-skinned dolls +19a \WESt

net *The letter A of the Snake Ring Template.* A metaphor for the entwined serpent path of the sun. *Ref* SERPENT ENTWINED, WEAVING, X-CROSSING.

New Year *The letter I of the Snake Ring Template.* A celebration of the new sun born at: **a.** The winter solstice when the old sun is at its weakest [the contemporary western Christmas-New Year interval]. **b.** The vernal equinox when a new sun brings springtime fertility [the archaic New Year]. *Ref* BABY BOY, CHAOS IN NATURE, CHRISTMASTIDE, FLORA, SEASON, SUN YOUNG.

• During the New Year celebration, dancers exorcise a demon represented by one of their members in the giant headdress of a one-horned beast. Children are given envelopes with money at the conclusion of the festival. [The demon is the old bull whose impotence is symbolized by a single horn and who must be vanquished in order for the sun of the New Year, represented by the children, to bring the next season and prosperity, represented by the money] *See* BABY BOY & BULL & FERTILITY & MONEY & UNICORN & WAR +19a ELLIS HENICAN \WESt

• The megalithic tomb at Newgrange is constructed with a slit above the doorway. The light of the sun penetrates the slit on the day of the winter solstice, which marked the beginning of the new year *See* DEATH & MOUND (MOUNTAIN) & REGENERATION & STONE -34b IRELAND \SEQt

• Dogs were sacrificed during the month of "Atemoztli" corresponding to the winter solstice, to assist the sun in it's passage across the underworld *See* BABY BOY & DOG (FELINE) & HERO & SUN YOUNG & UNDERWORLD +13a MEXICO, AZTEC \AVDt

• The winter solstice is viewed as a major crises point in the year, when the Indians perform crucial ceremonies to the sun *See* BABY BOY & DEATH & REGENERATION +18a USA, KUMEYA \HEEt

night *The letter K of the Snake Ring Template.* A metaphor for the time when the sun descends into the mountain-house of the mother goddess, and the next sun passes through the lower segment of the serpent coil to the east. *Ref* DEATH, EAST ORIENTATION, MARRIAGE, SUN OLD/ YOUNG, UNDERWORLD, UROBORUS.

• The Zinacanteco Indians believe that each person has a corresponding animal spirit companion which exists within a sacred mountain **[Note:** The feline hero for the daily nighttime passage from the western mountain] *See* FELINE & SOCIETY AS AT THE AXIS MUNDI +19a MEXICO, ZINACANTECO \VOGt

• Women fear that if they visit the chamber tombs at night they will become pregnant *See* DEATH & GODDESSES & MARRIAGE & SOCIETAL ASPECT & SOCIETY AS AT THE AXIS MUNDI +19a AUSTRALIA \RAUt

night-sea crossing *The letter F of the Snake Ring Template.* A metaphor for the marine passage of the sun from the waters of the western horizon in an eastward direction. *Ref* EAST ORIENTATION, UROBORUS, WATER.

nine *The letter K of the Snake Ring Template.* A numerical metaphor for the nine-step serpent path of the sun through the five levels of the underworld. *Ref* EAST ORIENTATION, LEVELS UNDERWORLD.

north orientation *The letter A of the Snake Ring Template.* A metaphor for the upper or sky portion of the snake path. *Ref* CELESTIAL, CIRCLE MOTIF, SOUTH ORIENTATION.

• When the great **Bodhisattva** was born, he took seven strides to the north and reached the top of the world. Buddha was very early identified with the sun *See* LEAP-UP & LEVELS CELESTIAL -5 CHINA, BUDDHISM \ELIt

• The entrance of the granary is to the north, where their ancestors come down from heaven *See* ANCESTOR WORSHIP & FERTILITY & HOUSE +19a MALI, DOGON \GRKt

• To the present day Maya, north represents the sun at its zenith. They have consistent symbols for east and west, but not for north and south +19a MEXICO, MAYAN \AMEt

• In the traditional Tibetan mandala north represents the sky and south represents the earth *See* CIRCLE MOTIF & UROBORUS -5b TIBET, TANTRIC \CUPt

• Daily the sun god rises from an opening in the north end of the mythic kiva in the eastern horizon, passes over the waters and descends to the mythic kiva of the goddess in the western horizon +19 USA \SINt

• To the Plains Indians, north is the sky and south is the earth +19a USA, OMAHA \NABt

• In the Woodland Prairie Indians' ritual houses, the wall post at the north is called "noon" +18a USA, SAUK \NABt

nudity *The letter R of the Snake Ring Template.* A metaphor for mankind's state before his use of symbols, i.e. before the primordial religion. *Ref* ART, BODY PAINT, GARMENTS, SOCIETAL ASPECT.

number *The letters P & K of the Snake Ring Template.* A metaphor denoting the location of the sun, with respect to the cosmic levels, during the sun's apparent entwined serpent path around the earth. *Ref* INTEGERS, LEVELS, MATHEMATICS, SERPENT ENTWINED.

nymph *The letter H of the Snake Ring Template. Gr. The word for bride; a female divinity.* The mother goddess who joins with the old sun in the mountain-house of the western horizon waters. *Ref* MARRIAGE, GODDESSES, SOCIETAL ASPECT, WATER.

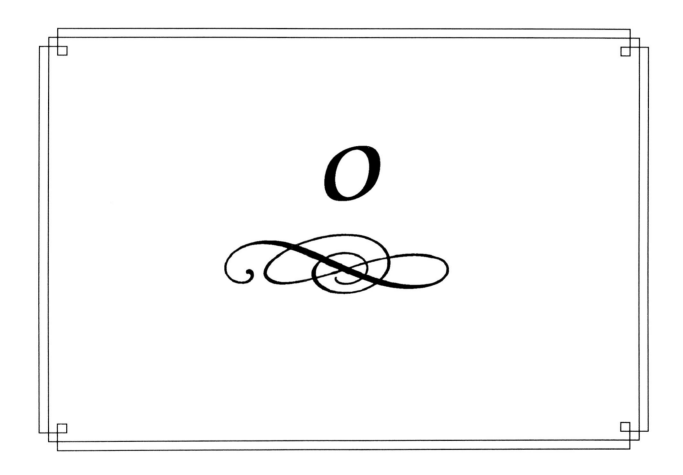

oak *The letter E of the Snake Ring Template.* *Ref* TREE.

oar *The letter F of the Snake Ring Template.* A metaphor for the passage of the old sun to or from the waters of the western horizon. *Ref* BOAT.

obelisk *The letter E of the Snake Ring Template. Egypt. A tapering pillar, terminating in a pyramid.* A metaphor for the vertical descent of the old sun at the mountain-house of the western horizon. *Ref* PYRAMID, STONE, VERTICAL LINE/ SHAPE.

object ritually broken *The letter D of the Snake Ring Template.* As a metaphor for death. So the object can enter the Land of the Dead under the western horizon. *Ref* DEATH, GOLD, HOLE, RULER, SEASON, VESSEL.

• Vases were deliberately broken at entrances to tombs *See* DEATH & UNDERWORLD & VESSEL -22a EGYPT \EDWt

• When rulers changed, pottery was smashed and fires were lit *See* DEATH & FIRE & REGENERATION & RULER -6 MEXICO, MAYAN \ARCt

• The ritual breaking of vessels is referred to in the Kabala as the "death of kings". **[Note:** The breaking of a glass by the groom with his feet in Jewish wedding ceremonies would seem to signify his death like the sun god into the western horizon, where he joins with his bride, who represents the unseen mother goddess in the underworld. This interpretation is apparently reinforced by the traditional "huppah", or canopy, under which the ceremony is conducted] *See* DEATH & MARRIAGE & RULER & UNDERWORLD & VESSEL -1b ISRAEL, JEWISH \ENDt

occult *The letter R of the Snake Ring Template.* *Ref* MAGIC.

ocelot *The letter M of the Snake Ring Template.* *Ref* FELINE.

octopus *The letter F of the Snake Ring Template.* A metaphor, suggested by a series of ring-like cups on its serpentine arms, for the serpent path of the sun into the horizon waters. *Ref* RING MOTIF IN SEQUENCE, SNAKE, WATER.

offering *The letter R of the Snake Ring Template.* Objects or activities ceremonially presented to deities to inspire their favorable activities.

ogre *The letter L of the Snake Ring Template.* *Ref* HUSK, PSYCHOLOGY CHILD, WAR.

olive branch/ tree *The letter I of the Snake Ring Template. An emblem of peace.* A metaphor suggesting that the war in the underworld is over. *Ref* DOVE, FLORA, TREE, WAR (NEGATION), WREATH.

omphalos *The letter G of the Snake Ring Template. Gr. Navel.* *Ref* ABYSS, NAVEL OF THE WORLD.

orb *The letter S of the Snake Ring Template.* A metaphor for the sun, often placed at the top of a vertical element such as a scepter or a flagpole. *Ref* FLAG, ROUND MOTIF, RULER, SCEPTER, SOCIETY AS AT THE AXIS MUNDI, VERTICAL LINE/ SHAPE.

orgy *The letter H of the Snake Ring Template. Gk. A riotous display.* A ritual metaphor to inspire the joining of the old sun and the mother goddess. *Ref* MARRIAGE, REGENERATION, SOCIETAL ASPECT.

orientation *The letter R of the Snake Ring Template.* Images and activities were oriented to the west (and sometimes north) as metaphors for the old sun, while others were oriented to the east (and sometimes south) as metaphors for the new sun. *Ref* ALTAR, ART, EAST ORIENTATION, RITUAL, SACRIFICE ANIMAL/ HUMAN, WEST ORIENTATION.

• The offerings and their positioning is a language that needs deciphering. They are different depending on which way they are facing +13a MEXICO, AZTEC(Templo Mayor) \MAXp

ornamentation *The letter O of the Snake Ring Template.* Symbols and motifs used to reinforce a metaphor. *Ref* ARCHITECTURE, BODY PAINT, GARMENTS, JEWELRY, SOCIETAL ASPECT.

oven or furnace *The letter D of the Snake Ring Template.* A metaphor for the fiery death in the western horizon, which begins the old sun's transference of the solar soul to a new sun. *Ref* ALCHEMY, FIRE, HOUSE, METAMORPHOSIS.

owl *The letter B of the Snake Ring Template.* A bird metaphor for the old sun in the nighttime. *Ref* BIRD, CIRCLE MOTIF, NIGHT.

• A bronze owl-shaped wine vessel has its wings outlined with serpents ending with feline heads. A face with goat's horns is on its chest *See* BIRD & GOAT & FELINE & PATH & SNAKE -12 CHINA, SHANG \CHFp

ox *The letter C of the Snake Ring Template.* *Ref* BULL.

paddle *The letter E of the Snake Ring Template.* *Ref* BOAT, VERTICAL STICK.

palace *The letter G of the Snake Ring Template.* *Ref* HOUSE.

palm 1. *The letter E of the Snake Ring Template.* A metaphor for the vertical tree path into the western horizon. *Ref* CROSS WEST, VERTICAL STICK. 2. *The letter I of the Snake Ring Template.* A metaphor for seasonal fertility. *Ref* FLORA, TREE.

panther *The letter M of the Snake Ring Template.* *Ref* FELINE.

papyrus *The letter E of the Snake Ring Template. Egypt. A tall sedge native to the nile region used as writing material.* **a.** A metaphor for the vertical segment of the serpent path penetrating the waters of the western horizon. **b.** When inscribed with heiroglyphs: a metaphor to inspire activities of solar regeneration within this vertical path. *Ref* RUSHES, VERTICAL STICK, WRITING.

paradise *The letter H of the Snake Ring Template. A place of bliss; sometimes the garden of Eden.* A metaphor for the mountain-house location within the vertical segment of the serpent path. The western horizon where the old sun dies and joins with the mother goddess to produce the new sun, bringer of fertility. *Ref* DEMYTHOLIZATION, FLORA, SNAKE, TRINITY, WEST ORIENTATION.

path *The letter A of the Snake Ring Template.* A metaphor for the path of the sun through the entwined serpent. *Ref* PROCESSION, SERPENT ENTWINED, SOCIETAL ASPECT.

• A huge dragon with its tail in its mouth exists outside the world, surrounding it completely *See* CALABASH & UROBORUS -20b GREEK, GNOSTIC \LEIt

• The sun's way across heaven's dome is a bridge as wide as the distance between the winter solstice and the summer solstice *See* ARCH & CALABASH & PATH +19a CANADA, BELLA COOLA \CAIt

• The sun wears the mask of the mythic serpent Sisiutl *See* PATH & SERPENT ENTWINED +19a CANADA, KWAKIUTL \MUNt

• Easter Island derives its name from its 18th century discovery on Easter Sunday by the Dutch admiral, Jacob Roggeveen, who noted that the people made fires and prostrated themselves before their colossal statues then raised their hands to the sun. [Other seafarers who stopped at this westernmost island for only a day or so did not observe this ceremony]. The huge stone "moais" were usually placed in groups of seven on top of platforms that were used for burials. One of these statues, abandoned before it was moved to its final location, has a boat carved on its chest with a rope leading below the boat to a turtle. *See* BOAT & DEATH & FIRE & HAND RAISED & LEVELS CELESTIAL & REGENERATION & RELIGIONS CONTEMPORARY & ROPE & SPRINGTIME & TURTLE & VERTICAL LINE/ SHAPE & WATER & WEST ORIENTATION +17a EASTER ISLAND \HEWt \HEUt *Figure 317*

Figure 317

• A great dragon was believed to connect the sky and the earth. Dragons were simultaneously aerial, aquatic, and subterranean -15b CHINA \CIRt

• Dance was part of the religious and military training and was an important part of worship of the sun god **Apollo** -20 GREEK \DUSt

• Many still believe that the cosmos is held together by the circling path of the sun +19 MEXICO \AVDt

• The sculpture of a deity with a series of ring motifs around his head is depicted within the mouth of the feathered serpent Kukulkan. It was once attached by a tenon into the upper corner of an Uxmal temple +7a MEXICO, MAYAN *Figure* 318

Figure 318

• Why is the Fijiian supreme sky divinity represented as a serpent in a cave? *See* CAVE & PATH & REGENERATION & SUN OLD +19a MIRCEA ELIADE \ELIt

peacock *The letter B of the Snake Ring Template.* A metaphor for the old sun descended from the sky: a concept reinforced by the fabulous appearance of the bird and the ring motif displayed on its fan shaped tail-feathers. *Ref* ARCH, BIRD, RING MOTIF.

pearl *The letter I of the Snake Ring Template.* **a**. A metaphor for the new sun born in the waters of the western horizon from the romantic union of the old sun and the mother goddess. **b**. *~ necklace* A composite metaphor denoting the new sun born in the waters of the western horizon within the encircling serpent

path. *Ref* BEAVER, CRUSTACEAN, FROG, JEWELRY, ROUND SIGNS IN SEQUENCE, ROUND MOTIF.

pediment *The letter G of the Snake Ring Template. Egypt. pyramid.* **a**. A gable or similar decoration designating the structure as a metaphor for the mountain-house beneath the abyss of the western horizon water. **b**. *cut ~* A metaphor for the abyss into the mountain-house of the western horizon. **c**. *cut ~ with volutes* A metaphor for the abyss into the waters of the western horizon with the mountain-house below. *Ref* ABYSS, ARCHITECTURE, HOLE, HOUSE, PYRAMID, VOLCANO, WATER.

pelican *The letter B of the Snake Ring Template. Ref* MARINE BIRD.

perfume *The letter I of the Snake Ring Template. A fluid preparation of the essence of flowers used for scenting.* A metaphor for the fertility brought on by the new sun, who was born from the romantic union between the old sun and the mother goddess at the western horizon. *Ref* FLORA, ROMANTIC LOVE, SOCIETAL ASPECT.

personification *The letter R of the Snake Ring Template. Representation of an inanimate object or a concept as endowed with personal attributes.* A group of metaphors endowing human characteristics to the sun to assure fertility, based on the observation that the sun penetrates the earth at sunset in a conceptual emulation of human copulation. Since all flora requires exposure to the sun to bloom, yet blooms only at springtime, the sun at springtime was a special sun born at this time of the conceived copulation. Other aspects of the sun as the father and of the earth or moon as the mother are similarly inspired by the use of human metaphors. *Ref* ART, DEATH, GODDESSES, GODS, MOON, MARRIAGE, RITUAL, SOCIETAL ASPECT, SUN OLD/ YOUNG.

phallus *The letter E of the Snake Ring Template.* A metaphor for the virile path of the old suns to their joining with the mother goddess to be taken, in turn, by each new sun of the next season. *Ref* MARRIAGE, SNAKE, VERTICAL LINE/ SHAPE, WATER.

• A cave painting depicts a phallic bison situated over a hole -250 SPAIN \GIEt

• There were many statuettes of men with enormous penises -7a EGYPT \BAJt *Figure 319*

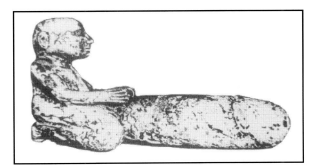

Figure 319

• To Shinto worshippers the phallus represented the "heavenly root", regarded as a symbol of solar energy -20 JAPAN \RAUt

• A composite representation of the sun god **Siva** depicts his feminine aspect or "Sakti", seated on the bull "Nandi" whose high domed head is carved in the form of a lingam +6 INDIA \LARt

• The holiest image in Hindu temples is a lingam, a stone effigy of the sun god **Siva's** phallus, kept in a room known as the "womb house." At an annual festival in honor of the marriage of **Siva**, thousands of lingams are bedecked with flowers and washed with milk and water *See* BIRTH & CASTRATION & CIRCUMCISION & FLORA & HOUSE & MARRIAGE & PHALLUS & STONE & SUN OLD & WATER -5 INDIA \COTt *Figure 320*

Figure 320

philosophy *The letter R of the Snake Ring Template. Ref* SCIENCE.

phoenix bird *The letter B of the Snake Ring Template.* A metaphor for the old sun dying in flames at the western horizon, to be regenerated into the newborn sun who will rise the following morning in the east. *Ref* BIRD, FIRE, REGENERATION, SUN OLD/ YOUNG.

• The phoenix bird represented the sun. It was usually depicted colored red *See* RED & REGENERATION \CIRt

• The phoenix bird symbolized the death and resurrection of the sun -30b EGYPT \ELHt

• The dragon and phoenix bird are common motifs in Tibetan sleeping mats *See* DRAGON & NIGHT & PATH & REGENERATION & SOCIETAL ASPECT +19a TIBET, TANTRIC \WESt

pig *The letter C of the Snake Ring Template. Ref* BOAR, SACRIFICE ANIMAL.

• **Set**, the enemy of the sun god **Osiris**, is identified with the sacrificial bull and the black boar -30 EGYPT \NEUt

• The Great Mother is shown killing a boar, the symbol of her son-lover -6b ITALY \NEUt

• The boar stands for licentiousness and suicide -5 INDIA \CIRt

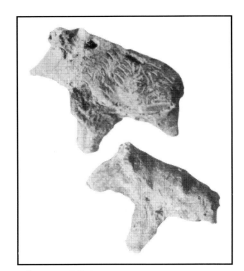

Figure 321

• Statues of bulls and boars show signs that they were intentionally broken as part of a ritual -70b TURKEY, CATAL HUYUK *Figure 321*

pilgrimage *The letter R of the Snake Ring Template.* Ref PROCESSION, WEST ORIENTATION.

pillar *The letter E of the Snake Ring Template.* Ref COLUMN.

• Scholars are puzzled by the pillar of one of the earliest excavated temples which was painted three times with a pattern that the discoverers have described as a red serpent-motif *See* HOUSE & RED & SOCIETY AS AT THE AXIS MUNDI & VERTICALITY -40a ROMANIA, KARANO *Figure 322*

pine *The letter E of the Snake Ring Template.* Ref TREE.

pine-cone *The letter E of the Snake Ring Template.* A metaphor for regeneration of the sun along the tree path into the western horizon; the pine-cone (the solar soul) descends to the earth where it is reborn. *Ref* ACORN, BIRTH, DESCENDING MOTIF, EGG, SOUL, SUN YOUNG, TREE.

• An icon of Nepal, adopted as the symbol of the Asia House in New York city, is a guardian feline carrying a pine-cone upon its head +17a NEPAL *Figure 323*

Pisces *The letter O of the Snake Ring Template. Tarot. The final enigma; The Fishes.* A metaphor for the new sun rising from the eastern horizon waters. *Ref* EAST ORIENTATION, HORIZONTAL MOTIF, WATER, ZODIAC.

pit *The letter G of the Snake Ring Template.* Ref HOLE.

planet *The letter P of the Snake Ring Template. Any of the seven apparently wandering celestial bodies, Jupiter, Mars, Mercury, the Moon, Saturn, the Sun, and Venus, as distinguished from the fixed stars. Ref* CELESTIAL OBSERVATIONS, LEVELS CELESTIAL.

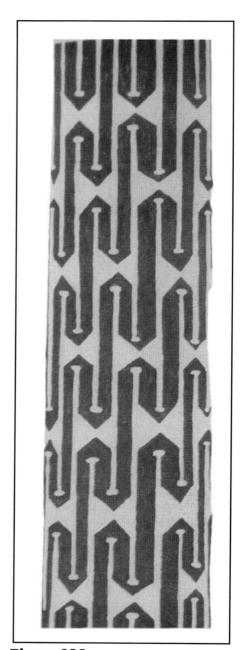

Figure 322

playing cards *The letter R of the Snake Ring Template. Used in playing games with their earliest expression in the enigmas of the tarot pack. Ref* ART, GAMBLING, GAME BOARD, TAROT PACK.

Figure 323

plow *The letter E of the Snake Ring Template.* A metaphor for the old sun's penetration of the earth within the vertical segment of the serpent path, the beginning of the process that results in fertility of the land. *Ref* BLADE, FLORA, TRINITY.

poetry *The letter P of the Snake Ring Template.* A versified metaphor for the path of the sun through the numbered levels of the cosmos. *Ref* LEVELS, MARRIAGE, MUSIC, PATH.

pole *The letter E of the Snake Ring Template.* A metaphor for the tree at the western horizon, a symbol of the descent of the old sun within the vertical segment of the entwined serpent path; often associated with the ritual house. *Ref* ALTAR, RITUAL HOUSE, SOCIETY AS AT THE AXIS MUNDI, TREE, TOTEM POLE, VERTICAL STICK.

polytheism **1**. *The letter S of the Snake Ring Template. Gr. Belief in a plurality of gods.* The various male deities are personified metaphors for: **a**. the sun of each season. **b**. for each seasonal sun aging from infant sun at the beginning of a season to old sun at the end of the same season when the old sun fathers the new sun of the next season. **c**. the collective old suns remaining as husks of the past seasonal suns in the underworld. **2**. *The letter H of the Snake Ring Template.* The various female deities, whether mother or daughter, are metaphors for the mother goddess, the personified western horizon spouse of the successive old suns who father the new suns. **3**. *The letters A, B, C, M, O, Q, T of the Snake Ring Template.* Fabulous animals are metaphors to inspire each successive sun to perform the correct activities from the beginning to the end of each successive season. *Ref* GODS, GODDESSES, HUSK, SEASON, SUN, TRINITY.

pomegranate *The letter I of the Snake Ring Template.* A metaphor for seasonal fertility resulting from the western horizon death, copulation and regeneration of the sun in the mother goddesses' mountain-house. *Ref* BLOOD, FLORA, HOUSE, RITUAL, TRINITY.

poplar *The letter E of the Snake Ring Template. Ref* TREE.

porpoise *The letter J of the Snake Ring Template. Ref* WHALE.

power *The letter R of the Snake Ring Template.* **a**. *temporal* ~ : by convincingly associating oneself with the sun. **b**. *clerical* ~ : by convincingly presenting rituals to inspire the sun. *Ref* CROWN, DEMYTHOLIZATION, PRIEST, RITUAL, RULER, SCEPTER, SEASON.

precinct *The letter R of the Snake Ring Template. An enclosed or otherwise limited grounds.* A metaphor denoting an enclosed area and/or structure as at the western horizon within the serpent path. *Ref* HOUSE, SOCIETY AS AT THE AXIS MUNDI, WALLED ENCLOSURE.

prejudice *The letter R of the Snake Ring Template.* A subconscious fear that the Ice Age chaos in nature will recur, directed against: **a**. ***foreign people/religion.*** Since all cultures and religions ritually designate themselves as at the axis mundi, those outside this location on the *Snake Ring* path are either "celestial gods," often visitors from more advanced cultures, or "underworld demons", applied to "others", particularly those of darker skins. **b**. ***dark skin*** Members of the demonic underworld forces, who threaten the path of the new sun. **c**. *semitism* Following Ionian demytholization, the Jews were the first to reject, or to modify those retained, basic metaphors that assured the regeneration of a new sun or new mother goddess. **d. *abortion*** A dangerous metaphor of the mother goddess' failure when pregnant to produce a new sun or new mother goddess. *Ref* ABORTION, BABY BOY/GIRL, BLACK, CHAOS IN NATURE, DEMYTHOLIZATION, FERTILITY, NEGRO, SOCIETAL ASPECT, SOCIETY AS AT THE AXIS MUNDI, SOCIOBIOLOGY, WAR.

priest *The letter R of the Snake Ring Template.* Originally a conductor of rituals to influence the sun's activities. *Ref* ALTAR, DEMYTHOLIZATION, GOD, HAND RAISED, HOUSE, RITUAL, SACRIFICE ANIMAL/ HUMAN, SEASON, SHAMAN, SOCIETY AS AT THE AXIS MUNDI.

• Druids, the priests of the Celts, were in contact with the supernatural "sidhe" and "banshee" beings who lived at the bottom of lakes or beyond the sea. They conducted ceremonies at the eve of May Day and in November, when cattle were ritually slaughtered *See* BULL & GHOST & SACRIFICE ANIMAL & SOCIETY AS AT THE AXIS MUNDI & SPRINGTIME & UNDERWORLD & WATER -14b IRELAND, CELTIC \SMJt

• Aztec priests performed human and bird sacrifices. Their hair was matted with blood. They painted themselves black and wore cloaks decorated with skulls and bones *See* BLACK & BLOOD & DEATH & REGENERATION & SACRIFICE ANIMAL/ HUMAN & UNDERWORLD +13b MEXICO, AZTEC \LEYt

• The shaman was asexual, serving as a contact between the upper and lower worlds *See* AXIS MUNDI & MOTHER GODDESS & SUN OLD +6b USA, INDIAN \RAUt

primate *The letter O of the Snake Ring Template.* An animal metaphor for the ascent of the new sun above the eastern horizon. *Ref* LEAP UP, TREE.

• A statue depicts lion-headed **Bes** with an eye on his chest. He is embracing a baboon, while a number of baboons ascend on his feathered headdress. **[Note:** The feline has successfully carried the regenerated solar soul within the new sun to the eastern horizon, where the primates inspire its continued upward path]

See CARRIER & EAST ORIENTATION & EYE & FEATHER & FELINE & PATH & SOUL -30b EGYPT \CASp

• Some painted vessels found in burials depict a monkey with the ears of a deer *See* DEATH & DEER & LEAP-UP & REGENERATION +3b MEXICO, MAYAN \RODp

primal archetypes *The images of the Snake Ring Template.* Retained images from the primordial religion. *Ref* PSYCHOLOGY CHILD/ CONTEMPORARY/ DREAMS, SOCIOBIOLOGY, SOCIETAL ASPECT.

• The consciousness seeks to wrest from the unconscious the archetypes that it needs *See* PRIMAL ARCHETYPES & PSYCHOLOGY CHILD & TOOLMAKING +19a \NEUt

• A theory about the complexity of the use and reuse of images can only result from the study of the images themselves *See* ART & PSYCHOLOGY CHILD +19a \MAQt

• An Ice Age engraved bone fragment from Raymonden depicts a skeletal bull entering into a vagina sign, and humanoid figures **[Note:** Sunset death followed by virile copulation between the old sun and mother goddess regenerate fertility which sustains human life] *See* BULL & DEATH & REGENERATION & VAGINA -350 FRANCE [Figure 324] **Refer also to** [Figure 185]

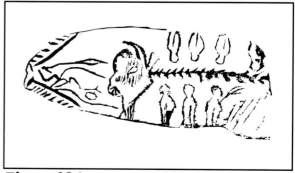

Figure 324

prime matter *The letter H of the Snake Ring Template.* A metaphor for the indeterminate matter in the underworld from which gold, representing a new sun, is formed. *Ref* ALCHEMY, GOLD, TRINITY.

prince *The letter I of the Snake Ring Template.* A metaphor in myth and legend for the young sun. *Ref* BABY BOY, FAIRY TALE, LORE, RULER, SUN YOUNG.

procession *The letter R of the Snake Ring Template.* A metaphor for the path of the sun. *Ref* EAST/ WEST ORIENTATION, PATH, SERPENT ENTWINED, SOCIETAL ASPECT.

• Elements included in the procession for the sun god **Dionysis** were wine, a he-goat, figs, and the "phallos." At the end of the festival, young men participated in a foot race *See* FLORA & MARRIAGE & PATH & REGENERATION -20b GREEK \DUSt

• Fortuna, the "wheel of the year", is derived from medieval processions focused on the sun during which wheels were borne on boats or chariots +15b \ELIt

• Runners participate in a ritual relay in the fall and in the spring to lend their strength to the sun so it will make it through to the next season +18a USA \NABt

prostitution *The letter H of the Snake Ring Template.* Originally, a ritual metaphor for the mother goddess stimulating the old sun's virility in the western horizon house. In coitus, he passes to her his solar soul, symbolized by a ring or round motif [like a wedding ring], for regeneration in their son of the next season. **[Note:** She differs from a "societal aspect wife" who, after coitus, gives birth to the old sun's children and with whom the husk of the old sun remains]. *Ref* COMMERCE, COPULATION, HARLOT, GODDESSES, FLORA, MONEY, RING/ ROUND MOTIF, PATH, SOCIETAL ASPECT, SUN OLD.

• Sacred prostitution was part of the cult of **Ishtar**, the archetypal harlot -35b IRAQ, SUMERIAN \MUNt \LARt

• Sacred prostitution was part of the worship of the goddess **Astarte** -20b IRAQ, BABYLON \RAUt

• In early historical times there was sacred prostitution by women portraying the wife of the deity -19b INDIA, HINDU \RAUt

• Priestesses were prostitutes in the temples -2b JAPAN, SHINTO \RAUt

• Sacred prostitution at their temple insured the fertility of the world +18a WEST AFRICA, EWE \ELIt

• The rhinemaidens of the Wagnerian "ring operas" were prostitutes *See* GODDESSES & MARRIAGE & RING MOTIF & WATER +18a GERMAN \DILp

• The spirit woman called "prostitute with a hole in her back" castrates those men who go to her *See* ABYSS(HOLE) & CASTRATION & HORIZONTAL(CROSS WEST) & MOTHER GODDESS & SOCIETY AS AT THE AXIS MUNDI +19a JAVA, MODJUK \GEFt

• Rahab, the harlot, was taken by Joshua from the Canaanite city of Jericho when its walls came down, to live thereafter among the Israelites *See* DEMYTHOLIZATION & MOTHER GODDESS & SOCIETY AS AT THE AXIS MUNDI & WAR -10b ISRAEL, JEWISH \BIBp

• In the Revelations of John, in which he castigates the Anatolians for their pagan beliefs, their "Kings of the World" have immoral relations with a notorious prostitute who sits by the waters of the world *See* DEMYTHOLIZATION & HORIZON & MARRIAGE & MOTHER GODDESS & SUN OLD & WATER +9a ITALY, CHRISTIAN \MERt \JUPt

psyche *The letter R of the Snake Ring Template. The human mental life, the soul.* Ref HAND RAISED, PSYCHOLOGY CHILD, SOUL.

psychology child *The letter R of the Snake Ring Template. Attributes of infant mentality; the Id.* A genetically retained language of metaphors to inspire regeneration of the sun, which, during the terminal Ice Age's chaos in nature, seemed to restore the harmony and fertility: **1.** Children's sense of themselves and their activities as though within the *Snake Ring* path, a concept which began with the numerous stenciled raised hands in the terminal Ice Age caves. *Ref* GAME CHILDREN, HAND RAISED, SOCIETAL ASPECT, SOCIOBIOLOGY. **2.** *The letter N of the Snake Ring Template.* Childhood fears of the dark and of the boogey man retained from the young sun's perilous nighttime passage through the underworld. *Ref* GHOST, HAND RAISED WITH MISSING DIGIT, HUSK, NIGHT, TRINITY, WAR. **3**. *The letter H of the Snake Ring Template.* Oedipal aspects of victory over the father sun in the perilous nighttime underworld passage by the young sun, followed later by return to the mother goddess in the mountain-house of the western horizon to procreate the sun of the next season. In another Freudian context, daughters and their mothers are co-existing goddesses in the western horizon, rivals for the father-suns' love *Ref* BABY BOY/ GIRL, FAIRY TALE, GODDESSES, INCEST, PSYCHOLOGY CONTEMPORARY, SEASON, SERPENT ENTWINED.

• Research into childhood folklore lends important clues to the workings of the collective memory +19a \NYTt

• The wholeness of child psychology is determined by the uroborus +19a \NEUt

• The childhood trauma of a "night space" of a "creepy room" *See* GHOST & HOUSE & NIGHT +19a \NEUt

• It is normal for children to have nightmares up to the age of six years +19a \WESt

• The psychic history of mankind is recapitulated in the ontogenetic history of each individual. As a result, transpersonal factors are evident in different cultures *See* TRANSCULTURAL SIMILARITY \NEUt

• The brain remembers past success \EDEt

• The psyche's enigma is limitless \JUNt

• The DNA's double helix structure is a library of information on how to survive. Certain areas of the DNA molecule are called "junk" DNA because their function is not clear. **[Note:** In the *Snake Ring* may lie the key to defining the psyche, and the key to its genetic transmittal may lie in the "junk" DNA**]** \SMJt

• Most experts believe that the genes carry messages early humans once needed for survival \TIMt

• Archetypes exist side-by-side in the collective unconscious, today known as self. **[Note:** the Freudian "Id"**]**. The consciousness seeks to wrest from this unconscious the archetypes that it needs \NEUt

• The snake often stands for unconsciousness itself +19a MILTON ADLER \MUNt

• Nightmares are a racial memory implanted in the genes a million [*sic*] years ago *See* PSYCHOLOGY DREAM +19a \JUNt \SMJt

• Religion is a tug of genes from earlier times. Celestial and underworld gods are dominants in man's unconsciousness *See* PATH & TRINITY & UROBORUS \DISt \NYTt

• Biology and culture are parts of the same system. Much of social behavior is biologically programmed *See* SOCIETAL ASPECT \DISt \NYTt

psychology contemporary *The letter S of the Snake Ring Template. Psychol. The Ego.* A melding of the realities of individual and society with the other reality of the childhood *Snake Ring* psychology. *Ref* ETHICS, GAME SPORT, MARRIAGE, PSYCHOLOGY CHILD, RELIGION, SOCIETAL ASPECT, WAR.

• The history of the current psychic life begins with the glacial epoch. As the Ice Age intensified, the food shortages led to the anxieties presently seen in infants and in human conflicts *See* WAR +19a SIEGMUND FREUD \NYTt

• Freud regretted that his ideas were made a preserve of medical science, and so emptied of the prehistoric past he discovered in everybody. Neurotics, he believed, were anchored somewhere in this prehistoric past. His study of neuroses and of dreams began as windows into this "baby mentality", as merely part of his effort to develop a general theory of the mind \APPt \BOPt

• Non-Jungians trace archetypes to the basic similarities of life situations rather than a collective unconscious. **[Note:** Why, then, are mythic serpents in widely separated areas where snakes never existed, and why the dreams of flying and falling which puzzled Freud?**]** *See* PATH & SNAKE & SOCIETAL ASPECT \MUNt

• The striking similarity in the myths, dreams and symbols of widely separated people led Jung to his theory of a collective unconsciousness \JUNt

• The symbols of unconscious are in the world's myths and fairy tales. Man is whole when his conscious is at peace with this unconscious \JUNt

• The archetypal images which exist in man's unconscious are as innate as the instincts in geese to migrate annually or the dance which bees perform to inform the community of the location for a food source +19a \JUNt

• Symbols prevent the life of the community and the collective unconscious from falling apart +19a \NEUt

• In the unconscious is not merely the serpent, but its circular configuration as the primal dragon, the wheel that rolls of itself *See* DRAGON & UROBORUS & WHEEL +19a \NEUt \MUNt

• Both genes and environment contribute to the development of behavior +19a E.O. WILSON \TIMt

• Women and men think differently. Women need human connections, whereas men value freedom *See* BABY BOY/ GIRL & GODDESSES & HAND RAISED & PATH & SOCIETAL ASPECT +19a C. GILLIGAN \TIMt

• Everything in human life is a simulation running on a truly universal machine +19a E. FREDKIN \TIMt

psychology contemporary problems *The letter R of the Snake Ring Template.* *Ref* MEANING OF LIFE, PSYCHOLOGY CONTEMPORARY/ QUANTITY, VIRTUAL REALITY.

• Archetypes are inherited. They are collective, not personal, structural elements of the human psyche, whose injury causes neurotic, even psychotic disorders \NEUt

• Primitive and ancient societies evidenced a network of symbols and structural forms that functioned like a computer generating rules for

behavior at every level of society *See* SOCIETAL ASPECT \VOGt

• The increase today in severe mental illness is believed due to the decrease in structure within contemporary society \PSYt

• There is widespread moral disarray because we are lacking the traditional universal code \TIMt

• By emancipating man from the natural unconscious, western culture has precipitated a crisis; the link with the unconscious becomes atrophied \NEUt

• We live a full life only when we are in harmony with the primordial symbols \CAAt

• We must rediscover the collective human aspect; the strata from which symbols derive is essential to cure the sick soul of modern man \NEUt

psychology dream *The letter O of the Snake Ring Template.* Metaphors from the experiences of the *Snake Ring* path, often triggered by societal situations. *Ref* PSYCHOLOGY CHILD.

• Dreams are private myths, and myths are public dreams *See* PSYCHOLOGY CHILD +19a \CAIt \OMNt

• Dreams are a superseded infantile mental life. They are the royal road to the unconscious mind *See* PSYCHOLOGY CHILD/ CONTEMPORARY +18a SIEGMUND FREUD \FRNt

• Dream images are universal in every culture. No one has solved the source of these dream images. According to Freud, they are archaic remnants \WESt \NYTt \JUNt

• The common dream symbol of a snake represents transcendence between heaven and earth. It is also first in the list of ominous dreams *See* UROBORUS & WAR \JUNt \MUNt

• In dreams of pursuit by wild animals, often bulls, the dreamer's father is represented by the wild animal. Bulls in dreams are archetypal sexuality. There is often a conjunction of sexuality and death in dreams *See* BULL & COPULATION & DEATH & TRINITY & WAR \FRNt \NEUt \NYTt

• The eye symbol is prominent in Oedipal dreams *See* MOTIF & SOUL & TRINITY \FRNt

• Dreamers are not afraid of dream-lions *See* CARRIER & FELINE & HERO \FRNt

• Recurrent archetypal dreams are beneficial. They give guidance in solving problems of both inner and outer life *See* MEANING OF LIFE & SOCIETAL ASPECT \OMNt \JUNt

psychology quantity *The letter S of the Snake Ring Template.* A minimum "critical mass" of metaphors required to give meaning to one's life. *Ref* RELIGIONS, SOCIETAL ASPECT, SOCIETY AS AT THE AXIS MUNDI, VIRTUAL REALITY.

puberty *The letter R of the Snake Ring Template. Ref* RITE OF PASSAGE.

puma *The letter M of the Snake Ring Template. Ref* FELINE.

pumpkin **1**. *The letter I of the Snake Ring Template. Ref* FLORA. **2**. *The letter L of the Snake Ring Template.* A metaphor for the husk of the old sun in the underworld. *Ref* FIRE, ROUND MOTIF. **3**. *The letter A of the Snake Ring Template.* A metaphor for the path of the sun around the dome of the sky and the inverted dome of the underworld. *Ref* CALABASH.

pyramid *The letter G of the Snake Ring Template. See* SECTION TWO.

quarters of the world *The letter A of the Snake Ring Template.* A horizontal metaphor for the north, south, east and west orientations of the vertical cosmic serpent coil at the axis mundi. *Ref* EAST/ NORTH/ SOUTH/ WEST ORIENTATION, SOCIETY AS AT THE AXIS MUNDI.

queen *The letter H of the Snake Ring Template.* Corresponding to the metaphor of her spouse, the ruler, as the sun, a metaphor for the mother goddess of the western horizon mountain-house. *Ref* MOTHER GODDESS, RULER, SOCIETY AS AT THE AXIS MUNDI.

questions by scholars *The letter K of the Snake Ring Template.* A consequence of demytholizations of the underworld serpent path of the sun. *Ref* DEMYTHOLIZATION, PATH, SERPENT ENTWINED, SUN OLD/ YOUNG.

• What is the source of early man's intellectual demands? *See* CHAOS IN NATURE & FERTILITY & TOOL-MAKING

• What is the meaning behind the Ice Age burials, where individuals were interred in beds of red ochre inside caves which were decorated in their entirety with the same substance? *See* CHAOS IN NATURE & CAVE & DEATH & RED & REGENERATION & RITUAL \LERt

• What was the connection between the sun and the snake in ancient sun worship, and why were seasons modes of the sacred? *See* PATH & REGENERATION & SNAKE \ELIt

• What is the purpose of the numerous erotic scenes found in the private homes and brothels at Pompeii? *See* HOUSE & MARRIAGE & PROSTITUTION & REGENERATION & SOCIETAL ASPECT & VOLCANO & WATER & WEST ORIENTATION \GRBt

• Why are goats which eat vegetation a symbol for the god of vegetation in European folk ritual? *See* GOAT (BULL) \FRBt

• Why did the Assyrian empire suddenly collapse in -626 while at the height of activity? *See* COLLAPSE MYSTERIOUS & ECLIPSE \TL5t

• Why should a single tree be off limits in the Garden of Eden? *See* GARDEN OF EDEN & SOCIETY AS AT THE AXIS MUNDI & TREE -7a ISRAEL NYTt

• No one has yet dated and placed the common location from which mythological items are derived *See* CHAOS IN NATURE & MYTH +19a \ELHt

• All things are hidden, obscure, and debatable if the cause of the phenomena be unknown, but everything is clear if this cause be known *See* SNAKE RING +18a LOUIS PASTEUR \DISt

quipu *The letter A of the Snake Ring Template. Knotted and colored strings placed in Andean burials. The knots have been deciphered as equivalents of numbers.* *Ref* DEATH & LEVELS & NUMBER & PATH & REGENERATION & ROPE.

rabbit *The letter H of the Snake Ring Template.* A metaphor for the virility of the old sun who regenerates the sun of the next season. *Ref* DEMYTHOLIZATION, REGENERATION, RESURRECTION, SEASON.

• A statue of a rabbit shows the animal with a skull at it's waist and the head of the sun god **Tonatiuh** emerging from a raptors mouth at it's groin *See* BABY BOY & DEATH & PATH & RAPTOR & REGENERATION +13 MEXICO \ELHt

radiance *The letter S of the Snake Ring Template.* A metaphor denoting the possession of solar characteristics. *Ref* CARRIER, HALO, HEAD, RAYED MOTIF.

rain *The letter I of the Snake Ring Template.* The seasonal rain required for the crops, specifically the rain brought on by the new sun at the start of springtime. *Ref* BABY BOY, FLORA, REGENERATION, SPRINGTIME.

• The Greater Southwest Indians perform Eagle, Buffalo, and Butterfly dances in their kivas, as well as engage in foot races at fall and springtime, for moisture to insure good crops *See* BIRD (BUTTERFLY) & BULL & DANCE & GAME SPORT & PATH & RAPTOR & REGENERATION +19 USA HOPI \SINt

• Cave and rock paintings represent dangerous "dreamtime" ancestral beings who control the seasonal rains, and consequently, the life of people and animals. Prior to the monsoons, the paintings are retouched by the ceremonial leader *See* ANCESTOR WORSHIP & ART & FAUNA & FLORA & PRIEST & SEASON +19a AUSTRALIA, ABORIGINAL \ARCt

rainbow *The letter A of the Snake Ring Template.* A metaphor for the serpent path of the sun in the sky from the eastern to the western horizon. *Ref* ARCH, SERPENT ENTWINED, TRINITY, UROBORUS, WEST ORIENTATION.

• The word "rainbow" is represented in ancient glyphs by the image of a serpent *See* ART & WRITING -15 CHINA \MUNt

• The mythic bridge Bifrost, meaning "rainbow", reached from the dwellings of the gods to those of man *See* ARCHITECTURE & SOCIETY AS AT THE AXIS MUNDI & WATER -7b SWEDEN \LARt

• The rainbow was believed to touch the place where the sacred mountain reached heaven +7b GERMANY \ELIt

ram *The letter C of the Snake Ring Template.* Ref BULL, GOAT.

raptor *The letter Q of the Snake Ring Template.* See SECTION TWO.

rat *The letter H of the Snake Ring Template. Ref* MOUSE.

rayed motif *The letter S of the Snake Ring Template.* A metaphor denoting the possession of solar characteristics. *Ref* RADIANCE.

• Among all peoples and religions, creation appears as the creation or emission of light \NEUt

• The god **Amida** is the "lord of boundless light" -20 JAPAN \OCTt

red *The letter D of the Snake Ring Template.* The red of sunset as a metaphor for the fiery death of the old sun into the western horizon waters, the blood-passage of its solar soul into the mother goddess, and, through her, to be regenerated in the new sun of the next season. *Ref* BABY BOY, DEATH, FIRE, REGENERATION, WATER.

• In Neanderthal burials the dead were interred with pots of red ochre *See* DEATH & REGENERATION & SOCIETAL ASPECT -990 FRANCE \BRBt

• During the terminal Ice Age, sea shells containing red ochre were placed in an art cave with vivid images of charging and dying bulls painted on its ceiling *See* BULL & CAVE & CRUSTACEAN & DEATH & PATH -350b SPAIN, ALTAMIRA \CONt *Figure 325*

Figure 325

• A lamp of finer manufacture than other similar artifacts was discovered in The Well with a seashell painted with red ochre *See* CAVE & CRUSTACEAN(WATER) & FIRE & HOLE -350b FRANCE, LASCAUX \SCIt
Refer to *Figure 21* SECTION TWO.

• To Taoist's the color red was holy and represented a furnace -5 CHINA \SCGt

Red (Reed) Sea *The letter F of the Snake Ring Template. Biblical. The sea that was parted by Moses during the Exodus of his people from Egypt on the way to the Promised Land.* A metaphor for the abyss in the western horizon waters, where the sun descends within the vertical segment of the serpent path into the mountain-house. *Ref* ABYSS, DEMYTHOLIZATION, RED, RUSHES, SOCIETY AS AT THE AXIS MUNDI, WATER, WEST ORIENTATION.

reed *The letter F of the Snake Ring Template.* *Ref* RUSHES, VERTICAL LINE/ SHAPE.

reef *The letter G of the Snake Ring Template.* A metaphor for the mountain under the waters of western horizon. *Ref* MOUNTAIN, UNDERWORLD, WATER.

regeneration *The letter H of the Snake Ring Template.* A metaphor for the transference of the solar soul, through the mother goddess, from the old sun who dies in the sunset at the end of the waning season to the newborn sun of the forthcoming season of fertility. *Ref* BIRTH, DEATH, MOTHER GODDESS, SEASON, SOUL, SUN OLD/ YOUNG, TRINITY, WEST ORIENTATION.

religions contemporary *The letter R of the Snake Ring Template.* Generally, systems of faith and worship that began after the Ionian demytholization of the original terminal Ice Age belief and rituals. Only Hinduism, one of the major religions, retains the essence of the primordial religion. *Ref* DEMYTHOLIZATION, LORE, RELIGION PRIMORDIAL, SNAKE, SOCIETAL ASPECT, SOCIOBIOLOGY.

• Present-day Maya still worship the sun, saying that Christians confuse their part of the truth with the whole truth *See* DEMYTHOLIZATION & GOD & RELIGIONS CONTEMPORARY +19a MEXICO, LACANDONE \BRUt \SCDt

• In matters of faith, science can never provide the ultimate answers +19a MICHAEL LEMONICK \TIMt

religion primordial *The letter R of the Snake Ring Template.* A system of belief and rituals begun in the terminal Ice Age to restore the harmony of the seasons, still retained by some tribal people. *Ref* CHAOS IN NATURE, FERTILITY, PSYCHOLOGY DREAM/ CHILD

• The foundation of the aboriginal belief system is the "dreamtime", which represents the time before supernatural powers transformed the earth into it's present form **[Note:** Actually, the *Snake Ring* path of the sun-family's regenerations before each current season] +19a AUSTRALIA \ARCt

reptile carrier *The letter A of the Snake Ring Template.* A metaphor for the serpent path of the sun. *Ref* PATH.

• The sun god **Re** was reborn inside the backbone of the serpent known as the "life of the gods" *See* REGENERATION & SNAKE & SUN OLD/ YOUNG -30b EGYPT \MUNt

• An image on rock art, RC[14] dated to at least 8,000 B.C. from some covering encrustations, depicts a youth and the sun on a serpentine

---

path *See* BABY BOY & SNAKE & SUN YOUNG -80a USA, CALIFORNIA \TURp

• Configurations of monoliths on the Avebury plain are in an east to west serpentine path, with a ring of stone situated as within the serpent's body *See* RING MOTIF & SNAKE & STONE & WEST ORIENTATION -45b ENGLAND *Figure 326*

Figure 326

• A preclassic vessel in the form of a ball-court has a double-headed serpent's body as the ballcourt's sides, and the serpent's heads at its ends *See* GAME SPORT & PATH +2a GUATEMALA,MAYAN \BOQP

resurrection *The letter I of the Snake Ring Template. Ref* DEMYTHOLIZATION, REGENERATION, SUN OLD/ YOUNG.

return *The letter A of the Snake Ring Template.* A metaphor for the returning path of the sun to the western horizon mountain-house, the allegorical "mother land" of one's birth, for seasonal regeneration. *Ref* DEATH, PROCESSION, SOCIETY AS AT THE AXIS MUNDI.

rhinoceros *The letter L of the Snake Ring Template.* A metaphor for the virile old sun remaining in the western horizon after its death, copulation and defeat in the underworld battle [symbolized by it now having only one horn]. *Ref* BULL, DEATH, MARRIAGE, SEASON, UNICORN, WAR.

• A rhinoceros is depicted leaving the trinitarian scene in The Well of the Ice Age cave, comprised of a fallen bird figure, a rising

bird on a stick, and a wounded bison *See* ABYSS & BIRD & CAVE & HUSK & TRINITY -350b FRANCE, LASCAUX \GIEt
Refer to *Figure 109* SECTION TWO.

• Powdered horns of rhinoceros and deer are used as aphrodisiacs *See* BABY BOY & DEER & HUSK & LEAP-UP & MARRIAGE & PSYCHOLOGY CHILD & SOCIETAL ASPECT +19a CHINA \WESt

ribbon *The letter A of the Snake Ring Template. Ref* FLAG, ROPE, PATH, SOCIETAL ASPECT, THREAD.

• Siberian shamans have ribbons in the form of serpents sewn to their robes. **[Note:** Because of the cold climate, snakes have never been indigenous to the area] *See* PATH & PRIEST +19a RUSSIA, ALTAI \MUNt

• The ribbons worn on the clothes of present-day Mayan women represent the rays of the sun. On men's clothes the ribbons represent feathers *See* FEATHER(CELESTIAL) & GARMENTS & MARRIAGE & PATH & SOCIETAL ASPECT +19a MEXICO, MAYAN \WESp \VOGt

• At the traditional Lent festival of Ypres, stuffed cats (once was live cats) with trailing ribbons are thrown from the belfry. Children in the audience are dressed in cat costumes *See* BABY BOY & CARRIER & DEMYTHOLIZATION & EASTER & FELINE & FERTILITY & HERO & HOUSE & PATH & RED & UNDERWORLD +19a BELGIUM \NYTp

Figure 327

• Ribbons are attached to the "tefillin", prayer boxes used in daily prayer by Orthodox Jews. The ribbons on the left arm are wrapped in a spiral of seven turns down the arm to the hand, where the ribbons are entwined to form the pictographs of the Hebrew letters "shen" [an inverted snake] and "dalet" [a fish] *See* FISH & HAND RAISED & LEVELS CELESTIAL & PATH & SNAKE & SOCIETAL ASPECT & WATER -10b ISRAEL, JEWISH *Figure 327*

• In burials, the ribbon band of the hat is cut as though it is a snake **[Note:** Signifying the end of one's life, allegorical of the sun's death within the serpent path] *See* DEATH & GARMENT & HAT & PATH & SOCIETAL ASPECT +19a MEXICO, MAYAN \VOGt

ring motif *The letter S of the Snake Ring Template.* See SECTION TWO.

ring motif in sequence *The letter S of the Snake Ring Template.* A metaphor for the movement of the sun, or the solar soul, through the serpent path. *Ref* JEWELRY, PATH, RING MOTIF, SOCIETAL ASPECT, SOUL, TRINITY.

Figure 328

• An archaeological reconstruction of a painted shrine relief room in the world's first true city depicts at its upper register, female breasts alternating with sculpted bull's heads. The bull's heads are painted with stylized crosses. In the middle band, ring motifs in series terminate in raised hand signs. The bottom panel is a field of raised hands. All of these images were painted or stenciled in red. *See*

BULL & CAVE & CROSS WEST & HAND RAISED & HOUSE & MOTHER GODDESS & SOCIETY AS AT THE AXIS MUNDI & SUN OLD -70b TURKEY, CATAL HUYUK *Figure 328*

• The carved image of a raised hand at the top of an outcrop of stone in Chalcacingo (above petroglyphs depicting a bull-horned captive carrying the were-jaguar infant on his back, the composite figure of a whale-dragon carrying a youth in its mouth, and horned felines trampling on an aged enemy) wears a bracelet comprised of a series of ring motifs **[Note:** Signifying the victorious leap-up of the young sun after a perilous underworld passage, including the conflict with his sun-father] *See* BULL & DRAGON & FELINE & HAND RAISED & WAR & WHALE -9b MEXICO, OLMEC

Refer to *Figures 106, 162* SECTION TWO.

• The relief carved into the top of the stone face of a temple at Dzibilchaltun depicts an entwined serpent with a series of ring motifs along it's body *See* HOUSE & PATH & SNAKE +7a MEXICO, MAYAN *Figure 329*

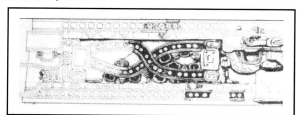

Figure 329

Figure 330

• A temple model from a Jama Coaque burial depicts a goddess seated in a temple on the upper levels of a pyramid. Both structures are decorated with ring motifs in series *See* DEATH & HOUSE & MOTHER GODDESS & PATH & PYRAMID (MOUNTAIN) & REGENERATION -5a ECUADOR *Figure* 330

• Feathers and ring motifs in series decorate the bullroarers used in the rituals of many South American Indians *See* BULL & BULLROARER & CELESTIAL & PATH +18a BOLIVIA, BORORO *Figure* 331

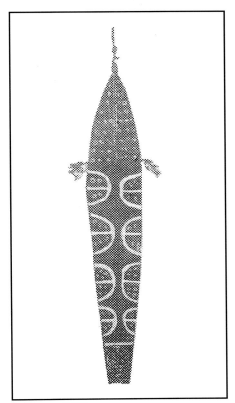

Figure 331

• Amazonian sand paintings of ring-shaped elements and wavy lines represent the fertilizing power of the sun father with his Yaje daughter *See* INCEST & MARRIAGE & MEANDER & PATH & RING MOTIF IN SEQUENCE & SUN OLD +19a COLOMBIA, TUKANO \REJt *Figure* 332
Refer to *Figure 88* SECTION TWO.

rite The letter ℛ of the Snake Ring Template. Ref PROCESSION, RITUAL, SOCIETAL ASPECT.

rite of passage The letter ℛ of the Snake Ring Template. A ritual that correlates a stage of

an individual's life with an event in the life cycle of the sun god or the mother goddess within the *Snake Ring*. *Ref* BAPTISM, CIRCUMCISION, DEMYTHOLIZATION, FUNERAL, GODDESSES, MARRIAGE, SOCIETAL ASPECT, SUN OLD / YOUNG, WAR.

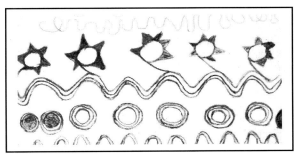

Figure 332

• At First Communion, young girls are dressed as a veiled bride *See* GODDESSES & MARRIAGE & SOCIETAL ASPECT & UNDERWORLD & VEIL +19a ITALY, CHRISTIAN \TIMs
Refer to *Figure 293*

ritual The letter ℛ of the Snake Ring Template. A performance to inspire the sun to an activity along the serpent path. *Ref* ART, BIRTH, DANCE, DEATH, EAST/ WEST ORIENTATION, GAME BOARD/ SPORT, HOUSE, INTEGERS, MARRIAGE, MUSIC, PRIEST, SACRIFICE ANIMAL/ HUMAN, SEASON, SOCIETAL ASPECT, THEATER.

• Their myths were reenacted at the main pyramid-temple, which bore the same name, Coatepec, as the mythic "snake mountain" where the sky, earth, and entrance way to the underworld crossed and where the new sun was born *See* BABY BOY & BIRTH & PYRAMID (MOUNTAIN) & SOCIETY AS AT THE AXIS MUNDI +13b MEXICO, AZTEC \MAXt

• During his ceremonies, the shaman chants about a mythic serpent while moving in a snake's sinuous path, symbolically following the course of the sun *See* PATH & PRIEST & PROCESSION & SNAKE +19 RUSSIA, EVENKI \MUNt

• At the rainy season their deity comes down a fig tree to make his wife, the earth mother, fruitful. A feast is held at that time, when a ladder with seven rungs is erected on a fig tree where the villagers offer sacrifices, sing, dance, and have a collective orgy. They pray to "the Lord, our grandfather sun" to come down and make the empty rice basket full *See* DANCE & FERTILITY & LADDER INFERNAL & LEVELS CELESTIAL & MARRIAGE & MOTHER GODDESS & MUSIC & RAIN & SUN OLD & SACRIFICE & TREE +19a INDONESIA, SARMAT \ELIt

• Before erecting the lodge for the sun dance ceremony, a prayer is offered to the "man above" to give more light for the vegetation and stock, with the wish that the ceremonies performed be a "painting" that brings prosperity *See* ART & FERTILITY & LIGHT & PROSPERITY & SUN OLD +19a USA, ARAPAHO \DOPt

• Double bladed paddles are carried by all important male figures at meetings and ceremonies *See* HOUSE & WATER +18 EASTER ISLAND \HEUt

ritual house The letter H of the Snake Ring Template.

river The letter F of the Snake Ring Template. Ref SOCIETY AS AT THE AXIS MUNDI, WATER.

rock The letter G of the Snake Ring Template. Ref STONE.

romantic love The letter H of the Snake Ring Template. A metaphor for the relationship between the old sun and the mother goddess at the western horizon. Ref MARRIAGE, SOCIETAL ASPECT.

room The letter H of the Snake Ring Template Ref CAVE.

rope The letter A of the Snake Ring Template. Ref PATH, THREAD.

• The Mayan word, "k'an", for cord and hammock also means "snake" and "sky" *See* PATH & SERPENT ENTWINED & SOCIETAL ASPECT & X-CROSSING +19a BELIZE, MAYAN \AVDt

• The word "rope" was also an expression for the serpent -20b GREEK \MUNt

• Snakes are called the "rope of the forest" +19a KENYA, LUO \MUNt

• Cartouches surrounding the names of rulers, and often carrying the sign for infinity or universality, were in the form of a rope in a loop *See* INFINITY & PATH & RULER -15b EGYPT \EDVt

• The **Norms**, daughters of **Erda** the earth goddess, spun the Rope of Fate *See* GODDESSES & PATH & REGENERATION +7a GERMAN, TEUTONIC \DILt

• Present day Mayans hang a rope from the center of their ceiling to mark the entry of the Lord to the earth below *See* HOUSE & PATH & SOCIETY AS AT THE AXIS MUNDI +19a MEXICO, ZINACANTECA \AVDt

• Fishermen tie knots in ropes to control the winds *See* CELESTIAL & PATH +19a SCOTLAND \CIRt

• A cylinder seal depicts a nude goddess seated on a recumbent bull below the arch of a rope with wings attached *See* ARCH & BULL & GODDESS & WINGED -20b SYRIA \GRAs

rosary The letter S of the Snake Ring Template. Christian. A string of beads, hung with a crucifix for counting prayers to the Virgin Mother. Each set of prayers is preceded by a Pater Noster. Ref BEADS, CROSS WEST, DEMYTHOLIZATION, GOD, MOTHER GODDESS, PATH, NUMBER, ROUND MOTIF IN SEQUENCE, SUN OLD.

• Southwest Indians chant the rosary to the music they once sung in honor of the sun *See* DEMYTHOLIZATION & MUSIC & PATH & SUN OLD

• Venezuelan Indians, in their annual "devil dance", wear devil masks, crosses pinned to their red costumes, and carry rosaries as they dance in front of the church until the sun goes down *See* DANCE & DEVIL & CROSS WEST & HOUSE & NIGHT(DEATH) & PATH & RED & SUN OLD +19a VENEZUELA \ATLt

rose The letter I of the Snake Ring Template. Particularly when red in color, a composite metaphor for the regeneration and fertility resulting from the romantic joining of the old sun with the mother goddess. Ref FLORA, MARRIAGE, RED, SUN OLD/ YOUNG.

round motif *The letter S of the Snake Ring Template.* A metaphor for the sun. *Ref* RING MOTIF.

• The ring or disc is frequently an emblem of the sun \CIRt

• In the Egyptian zodiac, stars were represented by small red dots. In their petroglyphs, the round dot or cupule stood for **Ra**, the sun god *See* RED & STONE & SUN OLD - 30b EGYPT \NYTt \GIEs

• An Ice Age cave painting depicts a bison composed almost entirely of red dots **[Note:** that the bull is a metaphor for the virility of the old sun in its seasonal regenerations] -350b FRANCE *Figure 333*

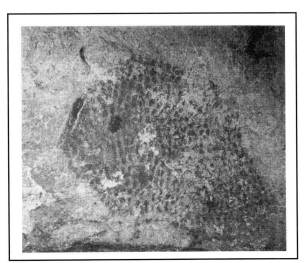

Figure 333

round motif in sequence *The letter S of the Snake Ring Template.* A metaphor for the path of the sun through the *Snake Ring*, producing regeneration of the seasons. This path includes the sun's bird-like path through the sky, and its bull-like virility in the western horizon house of sunset death. *Ref* JEWELRY, PATH, ROSARY, ROUND MOTIF.

• An engraved Ice Age cave artifact depicts a serpent with a series of dots along its body. Above and below the serpent is the path of a bird with enlarged eyes with sprigs of plants *See* BIRD & FERTILITY & PATH & SNAKE -350b FRANCE, LORTHET *Figure 334*

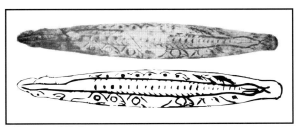

Figure 334

• One face of a boulder west of the Pyramid of the Sun is covered with petroglyphs in the form of concentric circles, that local people equate with the sun. The other side of the boulder has the petroglyph of a snake whose body is comprised of a series of dots +7a MEXICO, AZTEC \TEOt

• In a shelter located next to a dell with a spring, a series of cupules are engraved in the east-west direction on the underside of a stone covering a Neanderthal burial. A hole in the floor of the shelter contained ashes and the bones of a wild ox *See* BULL & CAVE & DEATH & FIRE & HOLE & PATH & SOCIETAL ASPECT & WATER & WEST ORIENTATION -990b FRANCE, LA FERRASSIE \RAUt *Figure 335*

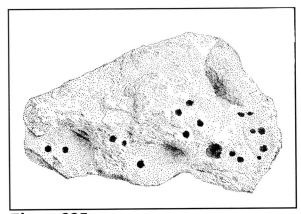

Figure 335

• A buffalo skull painted with a vertical series of red and black dots is one of the most important objects placed on the Sun Dance altar. It is regarded as the temporary home for the "Above One". Above the skull is a stick with a wooden snake formed into a ring at its top *See* ALTAR & BULL & DEATH & PATH & SUN OLD & UROBORUS +18a USA, ARAPAHO \DOCt **Refer to** *Figure 91* SECTION TWO.

• West Coast American Indians had many sunburst images in their rock art, with a ring at their center, which were important to their belief. Their boulders called "death stones" were engraved with cupules *See* DEATH & RING MOTIF & STONE(MOUNTAIN) & SUN OLD & WATER & WEST ORIENTATION +6b USA, KUMEYA *Figure* 336

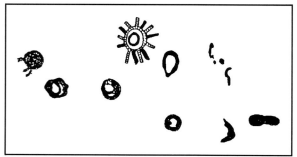

Figure 336

rudder or steering paddle *The letter E of the Snake Ring Template.* A metaphor for the vertical segment of the sun's serpent path into the waters of the western horizon. *Ref* BOAT, VERTICAL LINE/ SHAPE, SUN OLD, WATER.

• The painted rudder of a ship from a tomb depicts a teary eye and a cross where the rudder penetrates the water *See* BOAT & CROSS & DEATH & EYE & REGENERATION -30b EGYPT \GAUp

• In Oceanic ceremonies, the leaders carried paddles with feathers at the top above the painted head of a figure wearing earplugs *See* BOAT & EARRING & FEATHERED & PRIEST & VERTICAL LINE/ SHAPE +18a EASTER ISLAND \HEUp

ruler *The letter S of the Snake Ring Template.* A societal metaphor for the sun, reinforced by the gold crown and scepter, and royal succession through the blood line. *Ref* BLOOD, GOLD, HOUSE, RITUAL, SOCIETY AS AT THE AXIS MUNDI, VERTICAL STICK, WAR.

• The mystery of monarchy is its life \WYTt

• The first Inca rulers were "children of the sun" +9b PERU, INCA \RAUt

• Southwest Indians referred to their chief as "the great sun" +15a USA, NATCHEY \NELt

• The people regard their ruler as the sun +19a GHANA \PAQt

• When the pharaoh was alive he was associated with the young sun god **Horus**. After death he was represented as **Osiris**, the sun god in the underworld -30b EGYPT \COTt

• A plaque from Megiddo depicts at its top, below a winged sun disk, the ruler as the sun god with a scabbard and sword. Below this are men and women with bovine attributes and water birds. Figures of aggressive bulls stand on a wall at the bottom of the plaque *See* BIRD & BULL & HOUSE(UNDERWORLD) & WAR & WATER -13a ISRAEL, HITTITE *Figure* 337

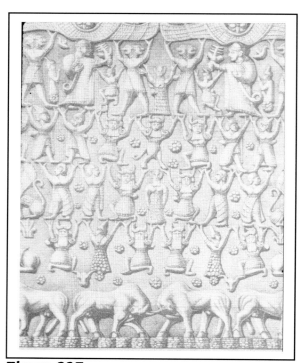

Figure 337

• During the coronation ceremony, the ruler-to-be holds a gold scepter surmounted by an orb on which a gold dove perches with outstretched wings, while the ruler is anointed with oil from the beak of a god eagle ampulla. After the ceremony, the ruler holds a scepter surmounted by an orb and a cross. At the opening of the final session of parliament, aids to the ruler are titled the Red Dragon and the Black Rod. A rampant lion is the symbol of the country, which the ruler takes as his own ceremonial theater with himself as its subject. After royal betrothals, the ruler plays the traditional betrothal ball game. If the birthday of a child born of the union falls on the thirteenth, the registration of the royal birth is ascribed to a later date. **[Note:** The thirteenth is a bad omen, particularly to one so closely identified with the metaphors of the *Snake Ring* path. The 13th level is where the sun dies, and baby deaths were a common occurrence in olden times] *See* BLACK & CROSS WEST & DRAGON & FELINE & GOLD & GAME SPORT & LEVEL CELESTIAL & MARRIAGE & PATH & RAPTOR & RED & ROUND MOTIF & SOCIETY AS AT THE AXIS MUNDI & STAFF & SUPERSTITION +19a ENGLAND \WESt \TIMp \SMJt

rushes *The letter F of the Snake Ring Template. Plants that are usually found in or near water.* A metaphor for the western horizon waters. *Ref* WATER.

• Stock tomb paintings often depict the family of the deceased at a body of water with an abundance of marsh reeds *See* DEATH & REGENERATION & WATER -30b EGYPT *Figure* 338

Figure 338

• After his death below the western horizon in the "sea of reeds", the sun god **Osiris** conceived with **Isis**, the new sun god **Horus** *See* BABY BOY & DEATH & MARRIAGE & MOTHER GODDESS & REGENERATION & SUN OLD/ YOUNG & UNDERWORLD & WEST ORIENTATION -30b EGYPT \EDWt

• The capital of the Toltec Empire was Tula, from the Nahuatl world "tollan", for the "place of reeds" where the sun god **Huitylipochtli** was born at Coatepec mountain to the mother goddess **Coatlicue** *See* BABY BOY & MOUNTAIN & SUN YOUNG & SOCIETY AS AT THE AXIS MUNDI & TRANSCULTURAL SIMILARITY +10b MEXICO, TOLTEC \FURt \EXQt

• The painted wall of the throne room at the Knossos Mortuary Temple depicts a griffin in a landscape of hills, water and rushes *See* DEATH & FELINE & MOUNTAIN & PATH & RAPTOR & REGENERATION & RULER -20b CRETE, MINOAN \WOOp

• King Sargon who established the first great empire in history, was said to have been found as a baby in the rushes at the side of a river *See* BABY BOY & BIRTH & RULER & WATER -23a IRAQ, ACCADIAN /TIMt

• The goddess **Cybel's** sanctuary was in the reeds by a river *See* MOTHER GODDESS & WATER -15b LEBANON, PHOENICIAN /COTt

• Moses was found as a baby floating in Egyptian bulrushes *See* BABY BOY & DEMYTHOLIZATION & WATER -10b ISRAEL, JEWISH /ENDt

• Each season the Eastern Woodland Indians rebuild their houses with marsh grass from bodies of water up to fifty miles away, making offerings of tobacco to the snakes they believe own the marsh *See* FIRE & HOUSE & PATH & SNAKE & SOCIETY AS AT THE AXIS MUNDI & TOBACCO & WATER +19a USA, KICKAPOO \NABt

Sabbath *The letter P of the Snake Ring Template. Christian. Sunday, the Lord's Day.* A metaphor for the seventh, highest level in the sky, where the sun appears to rest before it starts its descent. *Ref* DAY OF REST, GOD, LEVELS CELESTIAL, DEMYTHOLIZATION.

sacredness of life 1. *~ human The letter R of the Snake Ring Template. Ref* SOCIETAL ASPECT. **2.** *~ flora & fauna The letter I of the Snake Ring Template. Ref* FLORA.

sacrifice animal *The letter D of the Snake Ring Template.* The death of a solar metaphor, used as a ritual suggestion to the thought of the old sun for its own death. The old sun must die within the serpent path, for a change in nature, into the western horizon waters, where it will be regenerated in a new form. *Ref* BIRD, BULL, DEATH, GOAT, OBJECTS RITUALLY BROKEN, PIG, REGENERATION, RITUAL, SEASON, SUN OLD/ YOUNG.

• a 100-foot long model boat was buried at the south side of an altar where birds were sacrificed *See* ALTAR & BIRD & SOUTH ORIENTATION(UNDERWORLD) -24a EGYPT, ABU GURAB \EDWt

• **Kingu** the god of chaos was also the name given to the bull annually sacrificed by being thrown into a pit of hot bitumen. **[Note:** If the old sun in the sky was permitted to continue without seasonal regenerations, it would become too weak, as when daylight becomes shortest at the winter solstice. The other possibility was that the new flora would not have the necessary sunlight to grow, as required at the start of springtime. This aged sun was believed responsible for the chaos in nature during the terminal Ice Age] *See* BULL & BLACK & CHAOS IN NATURE & FIRE & HOLE -25 IRAQ, BABYLONIAN \MUNt

• In Dionysian rites held on the night of the winter solstice, nude women with snakes wrapped around their arms held knives and lashed about to the sound of cymbals, sacrificing any animal or man who stumbled upon the ritual *See* COPULATION (NUDE) & DEATH & MOTHER GODDESS & MUSIC & PATH & SACRIFICE HUMAN & SOCIETAL ASPECT & SNAKE & WINTER SOLSTICE -20b GREEK \DUSt

• The Barombi secret society sacrifices chickens to their ancestral god who, to the Kenyans, appears as a snake, at a crater lake *See* ANCESTOR WORSHIP & BIRD & HOLE & MOUNTAIN & PATH & SNAKE & SOCIETY AS AT THE AXIS MUNDI & WATER +19a \CAMEROON, BANTU \WATp \WESt

• A chicken with its wings cut off is tied to the neck of a wooden image of the **Mama Wata**, the goddess wrapped in a snake, before the pair is thrown into the water. An egg is then thrown into the water after them. **[Note:** The bird metaphor for the old sun who ends his serpentine path, joins with the mother goddess in the western water, to give birth to the new sun] *See* BIRD & EGG & MOTHER GODDESS & PATH & SNAKE & SOCIETY AS AT THE AXIS MUNDI & WATER +19a NIGERIA, IBIBIO \AFAt
Refer to *Figure 61* SECTION TWO.

• Quail, identified with their sun god, was the most frequent sacrifice *See* BIRD & DEATH & SUN OLD +13b MEXICO, AZTEC \MUTt

• When there is a drought, folk people of Mexico sacrifice a chicken and pour its blood on thirteen tortillas they refer to as "clouds" *See* DEATH & LEVELS CELESTIAL & PATH & RAINY SEASON & REGENERATION +19a MEXICO \NATt

• Socrates, at his suicide, asked that a cock be sacrificed *See* BIRD & DEATH & REGENERATION & SOCIETAL ASPECT -3a GREEK \ELHt

• Until this past century, folk people of Europe killed a wren on Christmas day and placed it on a pole *See* BIRD & DEATH & CHRISTMASTIDE & DEMYTHOLIZATION & PATH & REGENERATION & VERTICAL STICK +18a FRANCE \FRBt

• Doves were important sacrifices on the altar of Solomon's Temple *See* ALTAR & HOUSE -10b ISRAEL, JEWISH \ENDt

• On the high holy day of Yom Kippur, marking the start of the agricultural year in the Holy Land, a chicken is swung around the head and its entrails are placed on the roof of the house *See* BIRD & CELESTIAL & DEATH & FERTILITY & HOUSE & REGENERATION & SOCIETY AS AT THE AXIS MUNDI +19a ISRAEL, JEWISH WESt

• A sacrificed chicken was placed with a fish on the platforms of the colossal statues *See* BIRD & DEATH & FISH (WATER) & REGENERATION \HEUt

• The blood of a sacrificed rooster or pig [at one time it was the blood of a captive] is poured in the first posthole when a longhouse is being built *See* BIRD & BLOOD & DEATH & HOLE & HOUSE & PIG & POST & SACRIFICE HUMAN & SOCIETY AS AT THE AXIS MUNDI & WAR

sacrifice human 1. *The letter D of the Snake Ring Template.* The use of human death as a metaphor for the death of the old sun into the western horizon house within the serpent path, where its soul must be regenerated into a new form for a change in nature. *Ref* ALTAR, DEATH, HOUSE, REGENERATION, SOCIETAL ASPECT, SOCIETY AS AT THE AXIS MUNDI. 2. *The letter R of the Snake Ring Template.* Ritually breaking the human body so it may enter the land of the dead. *Ref* GAME SPORT, HERO, OBJECTS RITUALLY BROKEN, WAR.

• During the ceremonies the priest would tear out the heart of the victim and hold it up towards the sun; all victims were sacrificed by sundown +13b MEXICO, AZTEC \LEYt

• A sacrifice scene in the Mayan Temple of the Warriors at Chichen Itza depicts the sacrifice taking place on an altar along the body of the feathered serpent *See* ALTAR & DEATH & PATH & WAR +8a MEXICO, MAYAN *Figure 339*

• North American Indians performed human sacrifice at the annual "feast of fire" which was held "when the days are shortest" +18a USA, HOPI \BOWt

Sagittarius *The letter N of the Snake Ring Template. The Archer. A centaur shooting an arrow.* The young sun on his horse carrier. He must be victorious on his underworld path to the eastern horizon, where he begins the arching path through the sky. *Ref* ARROW, CARRIER, HORSE, WAR, ZODIAC.

sail *The letter F of the Snake Ring Template. Ref* BOAT, FLAG.

Figure 339

saint *The letter S of the Snake Ring Template. A beatified soul.* A mortal believed to possess one or more solar characteristics; as distinguished from societal behavior as a suggestion to the thought of the sun-family. *Ref* AVATAR, DEMYTHOLIZATION, HALO, SOCIETAL ASPECT.

salamander *The letter A of the Snake Ring Template. An amphibian superficially resembling a lizard; mythically associated with fire. Ref* DRAGON, FIRE, PATH.

salt *The letter F of the Snake Ring Template.* A metaphor for the western horizon oceans. *Ref* CRUSTACEAN.

sandals winged *The letter P of the Snake Ring Template.* A metaphor for the apparent path of the sun through the sky. *Ref* BIRD, FEATHERED.

Santa Claus *The letter C of the Snake Ring Template. The spirit of Christmas personified.* A metaphor for the old sun, whose descent to the mountain-house in the western horizon marks the end of the fall season, when daylight becomes dangerously shortened. The house chimney serves as a metaphor for this descent along the vertical serpent path into the mountain-house of the mother goddess, where the new sun of winter is born, assuring continued harmony in the seasons. *Ref* CHRISTMASTIDE, DEMYTHOLIZATION, GIFT GIVING, HEARTH, HOUSE, RED, SOCIETY AS AT THE AXIS MUNDI, VERTICAL LINE/ SHAPE, WINTER SOLSTICE.

Satan *The letter L of the Snake Ring Template. An archangel cast from heaven.* The adversary of **God** and of **Christ**, often depicted with a bull's horns and tail. *Ref* BULL, DEVIL, SUN OLD, TRINITY, WAR.

sarcophagus *The letter H of the Snake Ring Template.* A metaphor for the western horizon house where the old sun dies and is regenerated into the new sun of the next season. *Ref* DEATH, HOUSE, REGENERATION.

scale *The letter L of the Snake Ring Template.* *Ref* ETHICS, HANDS UP AND DOWN, JUSTICE.

scepter *The letter E of the Snake Ring Template.* A metaphor denoting the ruler as the sun within the vertical segment of the serpent path at the "center of the world". *Ref* RULER, SOCIETY AS AT THE AXIS MUNDI, STAFF, VERTICAL STICK.

science *The letter R of the Snake Ring Template. The observation of, and accumulation of knowledge pertaining to, the operation of the physical world.* Counting and writing, the rudimentary tools of later science, were based on observations begun in the Ice Age during a desperate time of starvation and climatic chaos. These were part of an effort to influence the sun to seasonal regenerations by metaphors along its apparent serpentine path around the world. By the much later time of Ionian demytholizations, the metaphors, apparently successful, were imbedded in the psyche and surfaced in later religions, and the then liberated methodology, based on observation and creative experimentation, was applied to other ends. *Ref* ART, CELESTIAL OBSERVATIONS, CHAOS IN NATURE, DEMYTHOLIZATION, FLORA, INTEGERS, LORE, SEASON, SOCIOBIOLOGY, TOOL-MAKING, WRITING.

Scorpio *The letter D of the snake Ring Template. The eighth sign of the zodiac.* *Ref* SCORPION.

• The sign which follows Libra, when a man's life lies under the threat of death *See* HORIZON & UNDERWORLD & WAR & ZODIAC \CIRt

scorpion *The letter D of the Snake Ring Template.* A metaphor for the old sun's defeat at the hands of the new sun in the underworld path, symbolized by the scorpion's venomous sting, and the path of round motifs along the scorpion's segmented tail. *Ref* DEATH, ROUND MOTIF IN SEQUENCE, SUN OLD/ YOUNG, WAR.

scythe *The letter D of the Snake Ring Template. An instrument for mowing, linked with allegories of death.* A metaphor for the death of the old sun, whose regeneration results in a bountiful crop. **[Note:** The 13th card in the Tarot pack, the skeletal Grim Reaper, indicates "death" as well as a forthcoming change. This is the level of the *Snake Ring* where solar death and regeneration takes place] *Ref* DEATH, FERTILITY, REGENERATION, SEASON, SUN OLD, TRINITY.

sea *The letter F of the Snake Ring Template.* *Ref* WATER.

Seal of Solomon *The letter E of the Snake Ring Template.* *Ref* STAR MOTIF SIX POINTED.

season *The letter I of the Snake Ring Template.* A change in nature resulting from the sun's regeneration within the entwined serpent path at the western horizon, where the solar soul is transferred from the sun of the previous season to its son, the new sun of the next season. The urgency for this occurrence was primarily at the start of springtime when a strong, new sun was to bring rain and fertility and at the winter solstice when a new sun was required to replace the sun which was weakening. *Ref* BABY BOY, FLORA, NEW YEAR, RAIN, RITUAL, SERPENT ENTWINED, SPRINGTIME, SUN OLD/ YOUNG, TRINITY, WEST ORIENTATION.

• According to the writer Posidonius, the sun calls forth the seasons *See* REGENERATION & SUN YOUNG -1a GREEK \LEIt

secret *The letter R of the Snake Ring Template.* *Ref* DEMYTHOLIZATION, INFORMATION DESTROYED OR SECRET, QUESTION.

serpent entwined *The letter A of the Snake Ring Template.* The sun appears to pass through the sky and the underworld each day, to rise again in the east. In the northern latitudes, the opposite applies to the southern latitudes, the sequence of these daily coils spirals northward during the first half of the year, from the winter solstice to the summer solstice. For the second half of the year, the sequence of these daily coils returns southward from the summer solstice to the winter solstice. These apparent paths of the sun, crossing each other at the eastern and western horizons, form an unending, entwined serpent-path of the sun's movement, encompassing infinite time and the entire universe. *Ref* CALABASH, CELESTIAL OBSERVATIONS, DRAGON, INFINITY, PATH, TIME, VESSEL, WEAVING, X-CROSSING.

• A painting from the Valley of the Kings burial site for royalty, depicts a winged snake with the cartouches for infinity and universality held protectively between its wings and carried as a symbol on its body *See* DEATH & PATH & REGENERATION & RULER & SUN OLD/ YOUNG -15a EGYPT *Figure* 340

• **Ninshibur**, the messenger, was the prototype for **Hermes** who carried the entwined serpent caduceus. He and his Roman counterpart **Mercury** were the paths of souls to the land of the dead in the underworld and also the paths of the souls' rebirth *See* BIRTH & CADUCEUS & DEATH & REGENERATION & SOCIETAL ASPECT & SOUL & UROBORUS -5b IRAQ \CAAt

• When prisoners of war were sacrificed in the bloody games of the imperial days, an attendant arrayed as **Hermes** dealt the death blow to the forehead of the victim *See* CADUCEUS & DEATH & HERO & GAME SPORT & PATH & WAR +4 ITALY, ROMAN \QUEt

Figure 340

• The aboriginal people believe they are descended from two snakes which travel around the world, leaving the souls of children where they stop *See* BIRTH & PATH & SOCIETAL ASPECT +19a AUSTRALIA, URABUN \ELIt

seven *The letter P of the Snake Ring Template.* The level of the sun at its zenith; it is the level transversed by the arching celestial serpent midway in its path from the eastern to the western horizon. *Ref* LEVELS CELESTIAL, NUMBERS.

shadow *The letter L of the Snake Ring Template.* A trinitarian aspect of primitive thought, corresponding to one's underworld ancestor. *Ref* ANCESTOR WORSHIP, BLACK, HUSK, SOCIETAL ASPECT, TRINITY.

shaman *The letter R of the Snake Ring Template.* A presenter of images and rituals based on the belief that it is mankind's responsibility to inspire the sun's regenerative activities within the vertical segment of the snake path at the western horizon. *Ref* HEALING, PRIEST, SOCIETAL ASPECT, SOCIETY AS AT THE AXIS.

sheaf *The letter I of the Snake Ring Template.* *A quantity of grain bound together. Ref* FLORA.

sheep (male) *The letter C of the Snake Ring Template. A genus allied to the goat.* *Ref* GOAT.

shell *The letter F of the Snake Ring Template.* *Ref* CRUSTACEAN.

shepherd *The letter I of the Snake Ring Template.* A metaphor for: **a**. The seasonal rebirth of nature. **b**. The reborn sun who brings fertility. *Ref* CROOK, DEMYTHOLIZATION, FAUNA, FLORA, SPRINGTIME, TRINITY.

shield *The letter N of the Snake Ring Template.* *Ref* HERO, WAR.

ship *The letter F of the Snake Ring Template.* *Ref* BOAT.

Figure 341

shoe or ***stocking*** *The letter A of the Snake Ring Template.* A metaphor for the path of the sun within the entwined serpent. *Ref* CHRISTMASTIDE, FAIRY TALE, PATH, PROCESSION.

siren *The letter H of the Snake Ring Template. Gr. A divinity associated with death and water; an enticing, dangerous woman.* A metaphor for the

mother goddess at the western extremity of the serpent path, who entices the old sun to lose its solar soul through death and copulation in the horizon waters, specifically, on the day the seasons change, thereby producing the new bearer of the solar soul the next season. *Ref* MERMAID, MOTHER GODDESS, SEASON, SOUL, TRINITY, WATER.

skeletal *The letter D of the Snake Ring Template.* A metaphor for the western horizon death of the old sun within the serpent path. *Ref* COPULATION, DEATH, SKULL.

skull *The letter D of the Snake Ring Template.* A metaphor for the western horizon death of the old sun within the vertical segment of the serpent path. Its head was the part of the sun god apparent in the sky, and the container of the solar soul. *Ref* DEATH, HEAD, SNAKE, SOUL, VERTICAL LINE/ SHAPE.

• An icon preserved in the bedroom of the Dali Lama's palace in Tibet, and regarded as most sacred, is an inverted human skull with silver rings around its eyes *See* DEATH & DESCENDING & HEAD & EYE MOTIF & RING MOTIF & RULER -5b TIBET, TANTRIC \NATs *Figure 341*

• A gold pin from a Mixtec tomb burial depicts two ball players, one on either side of a solar disk with the image of a skull at it's center +9a MEXICO, MONTE ALBAN *See* DEATH & GAME SPORT(WAR) & GOLD & PATH & REGENERATION **Refer to** *Figure 236*

• **Kirttimukha**, the "terrible face of God", is the skull aspect of the sun. He creates his children and then devours them. **[Note:** In all sun worshipping mythologies, the sun generates and devours his children] *See* HUSK & TRANSCULTURAL SIMILARITY & SUN OLD/ YOUNG & WAR +13b INDIA, HINDU \CAMt \ELIt

smoke *The letter D of the Snake Ring Template.* A metaphor for the fiery path of the old sun at the western horizon, descending to its death and regeneration. *Ref* FIRE.

• Oracles in the cave at Delphi inhaled smoke from burning laurel leaves. **[Note:** "Delphi" and "dolphin" are from the same Greek linguistic root, both mythologically associated with the mountain-house (cave) in the western horizon waters where the old sun dies and is regenerated. From there the new sun, in this case **Dionysus/Apollo,** similar to the story of Jonah in the Whale in Biblical demytholization, is carried to the east by a whale/dolphin] *See* CAVE & FIRE & GAMBLING (FORTUNE OR CHANCE) & HOUSE & TREE & WHALE -20b GREEK, \OCTt

• A codex illustration depicts an attendant offering a smoking pipe to a pair of entwined serpents, between the sky and the flames of a temple altar *See* ALTAR & FIRE & HOUSE & PATH +13b MEXICO, AZTEC \CAMs *Figure 342*

Figure 342

• To the Plains Indians the smoke from a pipe symbolized the union of the sky and the earth +18a USA, MANDAN \RAUt

• Southwest Indians used incense and pipe-smoking for the same purpose, to send a message to the sun in the sky *See* SOCIETAL ASPECT & SUN OLD & TOBACCO +19 USA, HOPI \BOWt \SINt

• Eastern Woodlands Indians sprinkled tobacco on fire to carry their prayers up to heaven +19a USA, IROQUOIS \NATt

• During the Sun Dance ceremony, a pipe was placed in the front of the buffalo skull, with its stem facing to the south *See* BULL & DANCE & DEATH & FIRE & SOUTH ORIENTATION (UNDERWORLD) & SUN OLD +19a USA, ARAPAHo \DOPt

snail *The letter 𝓚 of the Snake Ring Template.* A metaphor for the serpent path in the underworld. *Ref* PATH, TURTLE, UNDERWORLD.

snake *The letter 𝓐 of the Snake Ring Template.* See SECTION TWO.

snake feathered/ winged *The letter 𝓐 of the Snake Ring Template. Ref* DRAGON.

snake wheel *The letter 𝓐 of the Snake Ring Template.* A metaphor for the journey of the solar soul around the earth on the days the seasons change. *Ref* CIRCLE FORM, CIRCLE MOTIF, SEASON, UROBORUS.

society as at the axis mundi *The letter 𝓡 of the Snake Ring Template. See* SECTION TWO.

societal aspect *The letter 𝓡 of the Snake Ring Template.* Each society, its individuals and activities, is a metaphor to inspire the emergence of the new sun of the next season, thereby averting chaos in nature and maintaining harmony in the world. *Ref* HAND RAISED, RITE OF PASSAGE, SOCIETY AS AT THE AXIS MUNDI.

• Gen. 1:24 - God said, "Let us make man in our own image" *See* DEMYTHOLIZATION & GOD -10b ISRAEL, JEWISH \LITt

• Myths organize the daily life of South American tribal people *See* SOCIETAL ASPECT & SOCIETY AS AT THE AXIS MUNDI +19a S. HUGH-JONES \HUGt

• In traditional life, the creation myth is the model for everything done \ELIt

• There is a Muslim saying that "man is the eye through which God knows Himself" +19a SEYYED HOSSEIN NASR \LIFt

• The union of the sun with the earth goddess is the prototype for contemporary marriage ceremonies *See* MARRIAGE +19a \NEUt

society contemporary *The letter 𝓡 of the Snake Ring Template. Ref* SOCIETAL ASPECT.

• All societal life, including secular, theological, legal and economic, is oriented to the opposition between light and darkness.

[Note: "Oriented" to the western horizon, where the new sun is to be born from the sunset death of the old sun, and to the underworld victories of the new sun over the old sun, so harmony in nature and fertility will be perpetuated**]** *See* CHAOS IN NATURE & COMMERCE & ETHICS & PRIEST & RITUAL & RULER & SEASON & SOCIETY AS AT THE AXIS MUNDI & WAR. +19a CASSINER \NEUt

• According to a contemporary Confucian scholar, Wei Ming Tu, Imbedded in our human nature is the secret code for heaven's self-realization. Heaven needs our active participation to realize its own truth *See* REGENERATION & RITUAL & SOCIETAL ASPECT +19a CHINA \LIFt

• Similarities in the societal rituals and symbols of Mayan and Catholics permitted the belief system of modern day Maya to continue after the conquest *See* DEMYTHOLIZATION & TRANSCULTURAL SIMILARITY

sociobiology *The letter R of the Snake Ring Template.* The science of the inheritance, within the gene pool, of societal behavior essential to the survival of species. *Ref* ART, CHAOS IN NATURE, FLOOD, FLORA, HAND RAISED, PSYCHOLOGY CHILD, SOCIETAL ASPECT.

After years of bitter debate as to whether nature [biology] or culture plays the larger role in human behavior, the sociobiologist E.O. Wilson has won. Important behavior is concealed to be coded in the genes, including acquired behavior considered vital to the gene pool's survival. These characteristics are likely communicated from generation to generation in the molecular language of the DNA. The Darwanian dictate of "survival of the fittest" has to be modified from survival of the individual to survival of the gene pool. **[Note:** Heros sacrifice themselves in conflicts because the "conflict" image of the *Snake Ring* will contribute to the survival of their gene pool as well as the other "non-Darwinian" images and ideas derived from the terminal Ice Age**]** *See* CHAOS IN NATURE & CHILD & FERTILITY & PSYCHOLOGY CHILD & RITUAL & WAR \DISt \NYTt \PIAt \TIMt

• Most experts now believe that human genes carry messages which primitive humans once

needed for survival *See* ART & CHAOS IN NATURE & FLOOD & RITUAL & SEASON \TIMt

• The brain [genes] remembers past success [and threats to survival] *See* CHAOS IN NATURE & PSYCHOLOGY CHILD \EDEt

• There is a psycho-physiological basis to the formation of visual images in the brain. These fantasy figures and scenes are inherited; they are collective, not personal. Their injury causes neurotic, even psychotic, disorders *See* PSYCHOLOGY CRIMINAL/ CONTEMPORARY PROBLEMS & TRANSCULTURAL SIMILARITY \NEUt

• Religion is a part of the genes from earlier times *See* DEMYTHOLIZATION & RELIGION PRIMORDIAL \DISt

• Myths address themselves to the human nervous system [genes] *See* MYTH +19a \CAIt \OMNt

• Bees sting, after which they die, to save their gene pool *See* HERO +19a HAMILTON /WESt

• Chicks just hatched from the egg hide if a model of a chicken hawk is drawn forward on an overhead wire. The image of the enemy is lodged in their nervous system. They do not hide if the model is drawn backwards or if the model of a sea gull or a pigeon is used \CAIt \OMNt

• Biology and culture are part of the system. Yet most psychoanalysts are unaware of important biological factors in human behavior \NYTt

soul *The letter S of the Snake Ring Template. The animating principle of life is regarded as immortal and separable from the body at death.* A metaphor for the solar characteristics that continue through the successive deaths and births of the suns which bring on the changes of the seasons. *Ref* ETERNITY, PSYCHE, SEASON, SOCIETAL ASPECT, SUN OLD/ YOUNG, TRINITY.

• An Ice Age cave painting depicts three figures: A phallic bull-man expelling breath from his nose, behind a composite figure with the hind quarters of a deer and the forequarters of a female bison and the third figure of a leaping deer with its forefeet

represented as human hands and a series of painted dots along its body. **[Note:** The composite cow-deer at the center of the painting is an allegory of the mother goddess. She conveys the solar soul from the old bull-sun's copulation with her, to their deer-son, the new sun who leaps up into the path in the sky] *See* BIRTH & BULL & COW & DEER & HEAD & MARRIAGE & ROUND MOTIF IN SERIES -300b FRANCE, TROIS FRERES
Refer to *Figure 160* SECTION TWO.

• In the psychology of symbols, the spiritual soul descends from heaven. It is apportioned to the head, where it becomes concerned with the earthly world rather than the celestial *See* HEAD & SOCIETAL ASPECT & PSYCHOLOGY \NEUt

• **Ka** was the ghost-soul in the **Osiris** mystery where the young sun **Horus** was conceived after his father Osiris' death in the waters of the western horizon. The ghost-soul whose hieroglyph was the raised hand was the archetype of what is today known as "self" *See* DEATH & GHOST & HAND RAISED & REGENERATION & SOCIETAL ASPECT & SUN OLD/ YOUNG & WATER & WEST ORIENTATION -30b EGYPT \NEUt \BAJt

• All ritual centers were temporary dwellings for the soul of the dead although their main purpose was assuring fertility *See* DEATH & FERTILITY & HOUSE & REGENERATION & SOCIETAL ASPECT & SOCIETY AS AT THE AXIS MUNDI \ELIt

• **Megbe**, the solar soul, was passed from a dying father to his son, when the son put his mouth on that of his father *See* DEATH & REGENERATION & SOCIETAL ASPECT +19a CONGO, PYGMY \CAIt

• A print depicts the sun god **Vishnu** with his beloved **Lakshimi** reclining on their seven headed serpent of the cosmic sea. **Brahma**, possessor of Om, the eternal soul, rises on a lotus from Vishnu's body *See* BIRTH & LEVELS CELESTIAL & LOTUS & MARRIAGE & REGENERATION & TRANSCULTURAL SIMILARITY & SUN OLD & WATER +18a INDIA, HINDU
Refer to *Figure 150* SECTION TWO.

• In a dream, the father finds a child germ which was created by **Wondjina** under the water. The father projects this child-germ into his wife where it assumes a human form. At the human's death, the germ-child returns to

a waterhole and awaits reincarnation *See* BIRTH & DEATH & MARRIAGE & REGENERATION & WATER +19a AUSTRALIA \CAIt

south orientation *The letter K of the Snake Ring Template.* A metaphor for the lower or underworld portion of the snake path. In contemporary usage, one often says **"downtown"** when referring to the southern portion of a locale and **"uptown"** when referring to its northern portion. *Ref* CIRCLE MOTIF, NORTH ORIENTATION, SOCIETY AS AT THE AXIS MUNDI, VERTICAL LINE/ SHAPE.

• The "shen" glyph, meaning "circuit", placed at the south side of papyri illustrations denotes "night" *See* NIGHT & PATH & UROBORUS -30b EGYPT \PIDt

• The south direction represents the sun in the underworld. It is denoted by the left hand pointing down. South and North are regarded as "sides of the path of the sun" *See* HANDS DOWN AND UP +19a MEXICO, MAYAN \AMEt \VOGt

• Souls of the dead "journey to the south" after they "go to the mountain" *See* MOUNTAIN & PATH & SOCIETAL ASPECT & SOUL & UROBORUS +19a MALI, DOGON \GRKt

• Esbirnos as well as Mongols say that the Land of the Dead is "far to the south" \ELIt

southwest orientation *The letter R of the Snake Ring Template.* A ritual orientation to sunset on the day of the winter solstice in the northern hemisphere (the mirror image of this orientation applying in the southern hemisphere) when the sun is apparently at its weakest and the hours of daylight are shortest. At this urgent time, it was feared, the sun may be lost. Before this happened the old sun must be inspired to die in the western horizon and join with the mother goddess within the serpent path, producing a vigorous new sun containing the solar soul which will resume the annual cycle of the seasons. *Ref* BABY BOY, CHAOS IN NATURE, CHRISTMASTIDE, ECLIPSE, MARRIAGE, NEW YEAR, RELIGIONS CONTEMPORARY, RITUAL, SEASON, SOUL, TRINITY, WINTER SOLSTICE.

• Although the stone circle at Stonehenge has been proposed to be an astronomical observatory, more recent studies of Stonehenge's alignment, as well as those of other stone circles in Britain, reveal that Stonehenge's astral alignments were merely fortuitous. Its structures were built and changed for twenty centuries, over several periods from 3,100 to 1,100 B.C. From the earliest period there was a ceremonial avenue running westward from the River Avon, to a heel stone standing outside the entrance to the circular site, surrounded by a deep ditch. Sighting from this heel stone, one looks southwest to the center of the site and, on this same axis, to the sunset on the day of the winter solstice. Stones weighing up to 4 tons a piece were brought, around 2,100 B.C., from mountains on the west coast of Wales some 240 miles away, an astounding feat, worked and erected around the site's center. These were later surrounded by more durable sarsen stones and lintels from Avebury only 20 miles away, where huge blocks lie thickly on the surface. Carved on some of these various stones are ring motifs and symbols of daggers, axe-heads and mother goddesses, while lying within the ditch were the shoulder blades of oxen, i.e., bulls, and the antlers of deer. Cremated human bones had been placed in chalk-filled holes within the circle, which formed the centerpiece for the richest concentration of burial mounds in all of northwest Europe. **[Note:** The location of Stonehenge on the west side of the River Avon compared to the similar location of ancient Egypt's pyramids and royal burials on the west side of the River Nile. Also note the ritual significance of the winter solstice orientation of Stonehenge. This was the time when the young sun god Helios of the Greeks was annually reborn to take his father's place in the sky, and when Jesus Christ was purportedly born. Rituals conducted at Stonehenge were likely to inspire the old sun's flaming death at the time of the winter solstice into the abyss of the western horizon waters, where the mythical mountain-house of solar regeneration was located. The stone circle, itself, was a metaphor for the vertical serpent path surrounding the horizon mountain, with ritual significance comparable to the dragons bedecking Mesoamerican pyramids, atop Viking stave churches and ancient Japanese temples, down the gable of the Benin palace, and forming the carved rafters and columns of

some Northwest Indians' meeting houses] *See* ABYSS & ART & BABY BOY & BLADE & BULL & BURIAL & CHRISTMASTIDE & CREMATION & DEATH & DEER & HOUSE & MOTHER GODDESS & MOUNTAIN & MOUND & PATH & PROCESSION & PYRAMID & REGENERATION & RING MOTIF & RITUAL & SOCIETAL ASPECT & SOCIETY AS AT THE AXIS MUNDI & STONE & SUN OLD/ YOUNG & TRANSCULTURAL SIMILARITY & VERTICAL LINE/ SHAPE & WATER & WEST ORIENTATION -31b ENGLAND \ARCt \ATKp \DISt

• The light of the rising sun enters a slit of New Grange, a megalithic tomb under an earthen mound, on the day of the winter solstice. The beam of light successively illuminates ring motifs, spirals, and serpentine lines inscribed on the back wall, above burials in a cruciform chamber at the end of a long passageway. **[Note:** Possibly a message to the sun, on that day when it appears to be at its weakest, to descend on its spiraling serpentine path to the mountain, or mound, of the western horizon. There the cross-form chamber and the ritual burials are part of the message, to die where its path crosses the horizon]. *See* BURIAL & CROSS WEST & DEATH & MOUND & NORTH/ SOUTH ORIENTATION & PATH & RING MOTIF & SOCIETAL ASPECT & STONE & SPIRAL & WRITING   -31a IRELAND \TL4t \TIKp

• Earliest Mosques were oriented to the setting sun on the day of the winter solstice +19b SAUDI \AVDt

sparrow hawk *The letter Q of the Snake Ring Template. Ref* RAPTOR.

speech *The letter R of the Snake Ring Template.* A verbal means of communication, probably derived from sounds, emphasizing the *Snake Ring* images to the thought of the sun, corresponding to the manner in which the seven tones of music began as an auditory means of communicating the seven levels of celestial descent to the old sun-bull. The sounds of speech are constant and pervasive in spite of the many evolved and regional changes over the millennia, corresponding to the constancy of the alphabet throughout the evolution of writing. All are from the same toolmaking source. *Ref* ART, PSYCHOLOGY CHILD, MUSIC, TOOLMAKING, WRITING.

• Neurologists note that there is a connection between music and spoken language, but the mechanism is unknown \OMNt

• Language has a mysterious totality. Some sounds have the same meaning in all languages \WETt

• Linguistic universals are an innate mental endowment. How does the human mind have this innate property? N. CHOMSKY \WETt

• Toolmaking is from the left inferior temporal lobe of the brain. If it is damaged, it disturbs speech. This malfunction is not reproducible in apes LORENZ \CAIt

• Dance and language are from the unconscious mind \BOAs \WESt

• There is a sub-logic common to logic and languages \PIBt

• In the study of creole, there is evidence for the bioprogram of early childhood language /NWSt

• Languages have dead and petrified metaphors \RAUt

• Persisting linguistics are a mental sedimentation from the horizon of civilization \HUSt

• The copper spiral on the chieftain's drum is the channel propelling the Word of the sun. The sun's son, his rival, spoke his dance *See* COPPER(BRONZE) & DANCE & MUSIC & RULER & SPIRAL & SUN OLD/ YOUNG & WAR +19a MALI, DOGON \GRKt

• Throughout all of Polynesia, the word for the sun is "Ra", the same as the Egyptian name for the sun god +19a POLYNESIA \HEUt

• The Mayan grammar is very similar to our own -6b MEXICO, MAYAN \PHYt

sphinx *The letter M of the Snake Ring Template.* A metaphor for the victorious underworld passage to the east of the new sun from the mountain-house of the old sun's death. A ruler's head on a feline's body is often an allegory of the young sun on this journey. *Ref* CARRIER, DEATH, EAST ORIENTATION, FELINE, MOUNTAIN, PYRAMID, REGENERATION, RULER.

• The temple between the paws of the Sphinx is oriented to the sun's path on the day of the vernal equinox *See* CARRIER & FELINE & HOUSE & PATH & SPRINGTIME -25b EGYPT \SMJt

spider *The letter A of the Snake Ring Template.* A metaphor for the sun and/or goddess within the crossing paths of the entwined serpent at the horizons *Ref* DEATH, MOTHER GODDESS, SUN OLD/ YOUNG, WEAVING, X-CROSSING.

spindle *The letter A of the Snake Ring Template. The stick by which the thread is twisted in spinning.* *Ref* SPINNING.

spinning *The letter A of the Snake Ring Template.* A metaphor for the entwined serpent path at the western horizon, where the mother goddess awaits the old sun's descent. *Ref* SOCIETAL ASPECTS, SPINDLE, THREAD, WEAVING.

spiral motif *The letter A of the Snake Ring Template.* A symbol for the serpent path. *Ref* SNAKE.

• A paleolithic mammoth tooth is carved with snakes on one side and spirals formed of a series of cupules on the reverse *See* ROUND MOTIF IN SEQUENCE & PATH & SNAKE & -100a RUSSIA, MALTA *Figure 343*

• A dominant motif repeatedly found on old European house models from burials, is the meander or figurative representation of a snake, and its derivative spiraling lines *See* DEATH & HOUSE MODEL & PATH & REGENERATION & SOCIETAL ASPECT -50a RUSSIA, CUCUTENI \ARCp

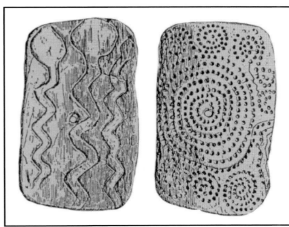

Figure 343

spire *The letter E of the Snake Ring Template.* A metaphor for the vertical segment of the serpent path to the mountain-house at the western horizon. *Ref* ARCHITECTURE, CHURCH, HOUSE, SOCIETY AS AT THE AXIS MUNDI, STONE, VERTICAL LINE/SHAPE.

springtime *The letter I of the Snake Ring Template.* A time for the seasonal regeneration of a new sun, which will result in the re-emergence of flora; the ending of the starvation and chaos in nature during the terminal Ice Age. *Ref* CHAOS IN NATURE, FLORA, REGENERATION, RITUAL, SPRINGTIME SUNSET ORIENTATION.

• At the spring festival members of the cult of the Eastern mother goddess **Artemis Ephesias** participated in self castration orgies and a bullfight was held *See* CASTRATION & GAME SPORT & MARRIAGE & MOTHER GODDESS & PATH -20b CRETE \GIEt

• The immortals become young each spring *See* ETERNITY & REGENERATION & SOUL -5b CHINA, TAOIST \WESt

• A Deer Dance is held at Easter, when the dancers sing, "comes the light of day, the sun is high, the rains come" +19a MEXICO \FONt

springtime sunset orientation *The letter R of the Snake Ring Template.* Orientation, slightly north of west of the viewer in the northern hemisphere, of art and ritual to the sunset on the evening when the season

of fertility is expected to begin. The new sun, born of the old sun who dies at that time and place, will bring fertility, thereby maintaining harmony in nature. *Ref* ART, BABY BOY, CHAOS IN NATURE, EASTER, FLORA, NEW YEAR, REGENERATION, RELIGIONS CONTEMPORARY, RITUAL, SEASON, SOUL, SPRINGTIME, TRINITY.

• Most ritual artifacts in the Ice Age cave at Lascaux were found in the Well, which was located in a cavern oriented slightly north of west of the main chamber -300b FRANCE, LASCAUX
Refer to *Figure 33* SECTION TWO.

• The constellation Gemini is called "creation time". The vernal equinox was in Gemini during the Andean golden age +9b PERU, INCA \SANt

• In the southern hemisphere, where the orientation of seasonal sunsets is a mirror image of those in the northern hemisphere, the men's house and the dance area were skewed slightly south of west *See* DANCE & HOUSE & SOCIETAL ASPECT +18a BOLIVIA, BORORO \LETt

square *The number 1 of the Snake Ring Template.* A symbol for the earth surrounded by water. The plane of the earth is considered common to both the celestial and underworld layers. *Ref* CALABASH, LEVELS, NUMBERS.

staff *The letter E of the Snake Ring Template.* *Ref* VERTICAL STICK.

stag *The letter O of the Snake Ring Template.* *Ref* DEER.

stairs celestial *The letter P of the Snake Ring Template.* *Ref* LADDER CELESTIAL, LEVELS CELESTIAL.

stairs infernal *The letter K of the Snake Ring Template.* *Ref* LADDER INFERNAL, LEVELS UNDERWORLD.

• The ziggurat of Nippur had a chamber at its summit to accommodate their sun god and a stairway for his divine descent -20b IRAQ \CAMt

• The afternoon sun on the day of the vernal equinox throws a shadow of the large carved snake on the balustrade descending the stairs of the pyramid *See* DESCENDING MOTIF & PATH & PYRAMID & SNAKE & SUN OLD +3a MEXICO \TLSt

• The roof combs of many Middle Eastern sacred houses were in the form of a descending double staircase; for example, at the tops of Solomon's Temple in Jerusalem and King Darius' shrine for the New Year festival *See* DESCENDING MOTIF & HOUSE -10b ISRAEL, JEWISH \HAWp -5a IRAN, PERSIA \PRIp

star and crescent motif *The letter H of the Snake Ring Template. The symbol of Islam.*

A metaphor for the joining of the old sun with the mother goddess in the western horizon. Compare **cross** and **star motif six pointed.** *Ref* MARRIAGE, MOON, STAR MOTIF, TRANSCULTURAL SIMILARITY, SOCIETY AS AT THE AXIS MUNDI.

star motif 1. *The letter S of the Snake Ring Template. A metaphor for an astral body. Ref:* SUN OLD/ YOUNG. **2. ~ six pointed.** *The letter H of the Snake Ring Template. Heb. Mogen David; Widely used as a symbol of Judaism.* Its intersecting downward and upward pointing triangles is a metaphor for the descent of the old sun into the mountain of the western horizon; *specif.*, the joining of the old sun with the mother goddess in the western horizon mountain-house. Compare **cross** and **star and crescent motif.** *Ref* CROSS WEST, HORIZON, MARRIAGE, SOCIETY AS AT THE AXIS MUNDI, TRANSCULTURAL SIMILARITY, TRIANGLE INVERTED/ UPRIGHT.

steed *The letter T of the Snake Ring Template.* *Ref* CARRIER, HORSE.

stele or *stella* *The letter E of the Snake Ring Template. A ceremonial, upright stone slab.* A metaphor for the vertical segment of the encircling serpent path penetrating the western horizon. Its stone material suggesting the horizon mountain-house, where the old sun's death and coital activities with the mother goddess produced a new sun for the following season. *Ref* COLUMN, FLORA, MARRIAGE,

MONOLITH, MOUNTAIN, RULER, SEASON, SOCIETAL ASPECT, SOCIETY AS AT THE AXIS MUNDI, VERTICAL LINE/ SHAPE, STONE.

• Stella covered with carved serpents were an essential symbol of the cult of the empire *See* PATH & SOCIETY AS AT THE AXIS MUNDI -30b EGYPT \MUNt

• Women set up Nagakals, stones depicting a serpent with a human head, when they desire offspring. When the carving of a stone is completed, it is immersed in a pond for six months then placed at the gateway to a temple or shrine *See* BIRTH & HOUSE & PATH & SOCIETAL ASPECT & WATER +19a INDIA, HINDU \COTt

• Large stelae erected over tombs served as "mansions for the spirit" *See* DEATH & PATH & RED & REGENERATION & UNDERWORLD & VESSEL +3b ETHIOPIA \GARt

• A carved stella at Piedras Negras shows a god seated in a niche formed by the bodies of celestial serpents. Above the seated god is a bird with a snake in it's mouth. The head of the serpent is depicted on it's wings. At the bottom of the stela is a scene of human sacrifice, and a woman wearing a jaguar headdress. Stelae of this type were the first monument erected at a given location *See* BIRD & FELINE & GODDESS & LADDER INFERNAL & PATH & SACRIFICE HUMAN & SERPENT FEATHERED & SOCIETY AS AT THE AXIS MUNDI & STONE +7b GUATEMALA \EXPp

stone *The letter G of the Snake Ring Template.* A metaphor for the mountain where the serpent path of the old sun penetrates the western horizon. *Ref* ART, CAVE, HOUSE, MONOLITH, MOUNTAIN, PYRAMID, SERPENT ENTWINED, SOCIETY AS AT THE AXIS MUNDI, STELA.

• Pyramids were the first structures for which stones were used. They were at the west side of the river situated near the capital, as an allegory for the site of the setting sun. A mound of stones was sometimes left in the center of the pyramid's construction, even though it made the layout much more difficult *See* PYRAMID(MOUNTAIN) & SOCIETY AS AT THE AXIS MUNDI & SUN OLD & WEST ORIENTATION & WATER -30b EGYPT \EDWt

• Southwest Indians ritually placed piles of stones where they prayed to the sun +19a USA, HOPI \BOWt

• In Maki ceremony, a boar is sacrificed on a high stone platform where a fire is lit. Reference is made to a mythological tower and fire, while actually pointing to a large volcano on the neighboring island of Ambrym that is known as the "happy land of the living dead" *See* BOAR(PIG) & FIRE & PATH & SACRIFICE ANIMAL & SOCIETY AS AT THE AXIS MUNDI & TOWER & TRINITY(HUSK) & VOLCANO +19a NEW HEBRIDES \CAAt

• In the 7th century, the church in Rome issued an edict excommunicating all stone worshippers. Charlemagne, in the following century, ordered the destruction of pagan stone monuments. Church leaders in recent times put up signs describing megalithic sites as "the debris of a bloody cult", and attempted to haul away their monuments *See* DEMYTHOLIZATION +6a ITALY, CHRISTIAN \SMJt

stork *The letter B of the Snake Ring Template.* A metaphor for the old sun's descent from the sky to the western horizon waters, carrying the solar soul that will be regenerated in the newborn sun of the next season. *Ref* BIRD, BIRTH, MARINE BIRD, REGENERATION, SEASON, SOCIETAL ASPECT, SOUL, SUN OLD/ YOUNG,

storm *The letter I of the Snake Ring Template* *Ref* CHAOS IN NATURE.

stranger *The letter C of the Snake Ring Template.* A metaphor for the old sun arriving at the western horizon house of the mother goddess. *Ref* SOCIETY AS AT THE AXIS MUNDI, SOCIETAL ASPECT, SUN OLD, TRINITY.

streamer *The letter A of the Snake Ring Template. Ref* FLAG, SNAKE.

• Serpent-shaped streamers, open at one end to be inflated by the wind, were carried by the Roman cohorts and the medieval armies of Europe *See* PATH & UNDERWORLD & UROBORUS & WAR -5b ITALY, ROMAN \WEBt

• The gatepost of the goddess **Inanna** had a streamer attached to the ring at its top *See* MOTHER GODDESS & HOUSE & VERTICAL LINE/ SHAPE & RIBBON & RING MOTIF & BATON & PATH -35b IRAQ, SUMERIAN *Figure* 344

Figure 344

string or **cord** *The letter A of the Snake Ring Template. Ref* GAME CHILDREN, ROPE, THREAD.

string game *The letter R of the Snake Ring Template.* A metaphor for the path of the sun through the coils of the entwined serpent, intersecting the celestial and infernal cosmic layers. *Ref* GAME CHILDREN, LEVELS, MAZE, SERPENT ENTWINED, STRING, TRANSCULTURAL SIMILARITY, X-CROSSING.

• The Seventh Nummo, who came down to earth in sinuous form, brought mankind the "cat's cradle" string game, and music to accompany the game *See* BIRTH & FELINE & MUSIC & PSYCHOLOGY CHILD & UNDERWORLD & X-CROSSING +19a MALI, DOGON \AFAt

• When preparing to move a twenty ton statue, the workers swayed with their string game to music +19a EASTER ISLAND \HEUt

string knotted *The letter A of the Snake Ring Template.* **a. ~ multiple knots.** A metaphor for the serpent path of the sun intersecting the cosmic levels. **b. ~ single knot.** A metaphor for the termination of the entwined serpent path of the sun. *Ref* LEVELS, NUMBERS, OCCULT, PATH, QUIPU, SOCIETAL ASPECT, STRING.

structuralism *The letter R of the Snake Ring Template. A theory of a universal structure in mental life.* The collective metaphors within the *Snake Ring* was used repeatedly during the recurrent crises of the terminal Ice Age and for millenia thereafter. It became a scheme of metaphors embedded in the human psyche by apparently restoring harmony of trhe seasons for our survival. *Ref* ART, CHAOS IN NATURE, FERTILITY, METAPHOR, PSYCHE, PSYCHOLOGY CHILD/ CONTEMPORARY, RITUAL, SERPENT ENTWINED, SOCIETAL ASPECT, SOCIOBIOLOGY, TOOL-MAKING.

sulphur *The letter D of the Snake Ring Template. Chem. A yellow element, occurring naturally, which burns in the air.* An alchemic metaphor for the flaming death of the old sun at the western horizon, in the regeneration of a new sun of the next season. *Ref* ALCHEMY, FIRE, YELLOW.

sun old *The letter S of the Snake Ring Template.* A metaphor for the sun at the end of a season. It **a**. descends on the snake path from the sky to its death in the western horizon, **b**. joins with the mother goddess in the mountain-house to produce the new sun of the next season, to whom it transfers its solar soul, **c**. remains in the underworld as the jealous enemy of this new sun who received the solar soul. *Ref* BABY BOY, BULL, CAVE, DEATH, FIRE, HOUSE, HUSK, MARRIAGE, MOTHER GODDESS, MOUNTAIN, SEASON, SERPENT ENTWINED, TRINITY, WAR, WEST ORIENTATION.

• A carved Babylonian plaque depicts the sun god knifing a bound, aged figure with a radiant sun for its head. At the forehead of the latter is a diamond motif *See* WAR & TRINITY & EYE & DIAMOND MOTIF -19a IRAQ, ACCADIAN **Refer to** *Figure 133* SECTION TWO.

• A wood box from a burial, contained the mummy of a snake. Its carved top depicts a cobra with the head of the old sun god **Aton** in place of its own *See* DEATH & PATH & REGENERATION & SNAKE & SOCIETAL ASPECT & SUN OLD -5a EGYPT *Figure 345*

Figure 345

• A carved stone slab depicts worshippers in attitudes of reverence to the old sun god **Zeus** when he appears in the form of a great snake *See* PATH & SUN OLD & SOCIETY AS AT THE AXIS MUNDI -3a GREEK **Refer to** *Figure 194*

• An illustration from the Dresden Codex depicts the old sun god copulating with a goddess above the mat symbol of entwined bands *See* HORIZON & MARRIAGE & MOTHER GODDESS & PATH & X-CROSSING +3b MEXICO, MAYAN **Refer to** *Figure 65* SECTION TWO

• The symbol of the fallen sun god **Smoking Mirror** was also the symbol for making war. It depicts a skull with a glyph on its head for a mirror on the water surrounded by flames. On the back of its head is a ring motif *See* MIRROR & FIRE & SKULL(DEATH) & WATER & TRINITY & WAR & RING MOTIF +13b MEXICO, AZTEC **Refer to** *Figure 224*

sun young *The letter S of the Snake Ring Template.* See SECTION TWO.

superstition *The letter R of the Snake Ring Template.* The metaphors within the serpent path on the day that the season changes. These metaphors are omens of bad fortune to the old sun. The same metaphors are omens of good fortune associated with the new sun. *Ref* BLACK, CAT, GAMBLING, LADDER INFERNAL, MIRROR, PSYCHOLOGY CHILD, SEVEN, SOCIETAL ASPECT, THIRTEEN.

• The most intelligent of African cultures are also the most superstitious. They make fetish houses when they fear a flood or inclement weather *See* FLOOD & HOUSE & MARRIAGE & MODEL & REGENERATION & SEASON +18a NIGERIA \RAUt

• In the Far East, old superstitions are used to exert control over society, as religious belief is used in some Western societies *See* ETHICS & LAW & SOCIETY AS AT THE AXIS MUNDI +19a JAPAN \NYTt

swallow *The letter B of the Snake Ring Template. Ref* BIRD.

swan *The letter F of the Snake Ring Template. Ref* MARINE BIRD.

• Arriving in a chariot drawn by swans, the sun god **Apollo** brought the springtime harvest and healed the sick *See* BABY BOY & BIRTH & FERTILITY & HEALING & STORK & WATER -20b GREEK \GAWt

• Scientists unearthed swan figures made of felt and stuffed with deer's hair in Scythian burials *See* DEATH & DEER(LEAP-UP) & SOCIETAL ASPECT & WATER -5a RUSSIA, PAZYRYK \BRHp

• A Roman wall painting depicts the goddess **Leda** copulating with the sun god **Zeus** manifested to her in the form of a swan *See* HOUSE & MARRIAGE & SOCIETAL ASPECT & WATER +1a ITALY, POMPEII \GRBp

swastika *The letter E of the Snake Ring Template.* A metaphor for the western horizon penetration of the sun within the circle of the entwined serpent path. *Ref* CROSS CIRCLED/WEST, PROCESSION, SOCIETY AS AT THE AXIS MUNDI.

sweat lodge *The Letter H of the Snake Ring Template.* A metaphor for the house in the western horizon water at the time of a change in season, when the sun is regenerated through the fire and heat of sunset into the new sun of the next season. *Ref* FIRE, HOUSE, REGENERATION, SOCIETAL ASPECTS, WATER

• The sweat house is still used by Plains Indian tribes particularly in their seasonal Sun Dance. The fire that supplies the heat for the lodge is called "the fire of no end". A buffalo skull is placed beside the entrance or on top of the lodge *See* BULL & DEATH & PATH & REGENERATION & SOCIETAL ASPECT +19a USA, CROW \NABt

• The Cantabrian valley was, at the start of the terminal Ice Age, filled by glaciers. Included in a walled enclosure of an Ice Age art cave was a man-made pond, the remains of a large fire, and lumps of red ochre *See* CAVE & CHAOS IN NATURE & FIRE & PATH & RED(REGENERATION) & WATER -350b SPAIN, EL JUYO \NUYt

• Scholars are puzzled by a bas relief depicting water nymphs at each side of the head of the sun god on the pediment of a Roman temple in front of which there was a perpetual fire and a nearby hot springs in an artificial grotto *See* CAVE & FIRE & GODDESSES & SOCIETY AS AT THE AXIS MUNDI & SUN OLD & TEMPLE & WATER +1a ENGLAND, BATH
Refer to *Figure 48* SECTION TWO.

• Fire, water and a spike of wheat were the symbols of the ancient, sacred Eleusinian rites. A chest containing a snake kept in a cave was presented to the assembly while initiates touched the effigy of a womb *See* CAVE & FERTILITY & REGENERATION & SNAKE -7a GREEK, ELEUSIUS \WIIt

swordfish *The letter D of the Snake Ring Template.* A metaphor for the death of the old sun in the waters of the western horizon. *Ref* BLADE, DEATH, FISH, RULER, SOCIETAL ASPECT, WATER, WEST ORIENTATION.

• The swordfish is one of the forms into which
the mythic Unicorn is capable of transforming
See TRINITY & UNDERWORLD & UNICORN & WATER
+19a \CIRt

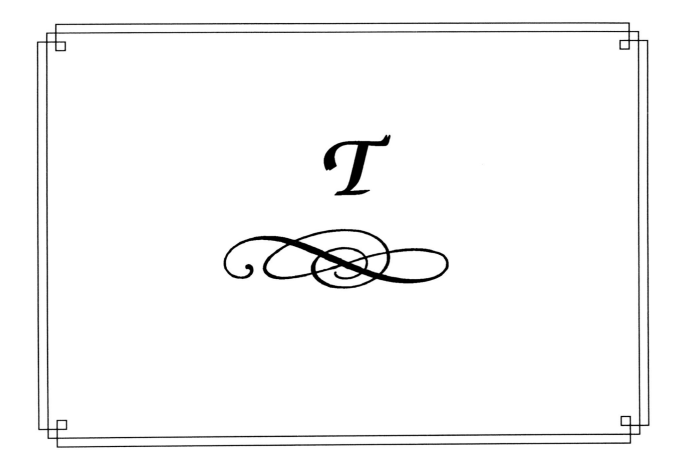

tarot pack *The letter R of the Snake Ring Template.* Ideograms of the terminal Ice Age *Snake Ring* used as metaphors in fortune telling, as though the subject is a member of the sun family. *Ref* GAME BOARD, MOTHER GODDESS, SOCIETAL ASPECT, SUN OLD/YOUNG.

tattoo *The letter R of the Snake Ring Template.* Designates the wearer as a member of the sun family within the *Snake Ring* path. *Ref* BODY PAINT, HAND RAISED, PATH, SOCIETAL ASPECT.

• Women at puberty are considered a sacred object after they are ritually scarred around their navel with a circle, a process which is believed to safeguard the welfare of the community *See* BIRTH & DRAGON & EYE & FERTILITY & MOTHER GODDESS & PATH & RING MOTIF & SOCIETAL ASPECT & SOUL & TRANSCULTURAL SIMILARITY +19a NIGERIA \BRBt

• Tattoo artists place the eyes in the dragon last, representing the spirit carried within the beast. **[Note:** The dragon is the most common of all tatoos**]** *See* DRAGON & EYE & PATH & SOUL & TRANSCULTURAL SIMILARITY +19 JAPAN \TATt

Taurus *The letter C of the Snake Ring Template. The Bull.* Ref BULL, ZODIAC.

temple *The letter H of the Snake Ring Template.* Ref HOUSE.

tipi or tent *The letter H of the Snake Ring Template.* A metaphor for the mountain-house of the western horizon. *Ref* CAVE, HOUSE, SOCIETAL ASPECT, TRIANGLE MOTIF, UPRIGHT (MOUNTAIN).

ternary *The letter L of the Snake Ring Template.* Ref TRINITY.

theater *The letter R of the Snake Ring Template.* Originally, metaphors presented in an allegory of the western horizon, at the "center of the world". *Ref* ALTAR, BIRTH, DANCE, DEATH, DESCENDING MOTIF, HOUSE, MARRIAGE, MUSIC, RITUAL, SACRIFICE ANIMAL/ HUMAN, SOCIETAL ASPECT, WEST ORIENTATION.

• Springtime festivals in honor of the sun god **Dionysus** were held in circular areas hollowed out in the side of a hill. A central altar was the focal point for performances including singing and dancing *See* ALTAR & CAVE & DANCE & MUSIC & SPRINGTIME & SUN YOUNG -20b GREEK \SOPt

• In performances of the ancient Tale of the White Serpent, a pilgrim marries a weeping girl who has a child. She turns into a serpent and devours the child *See* BABY BOY & PATH & SNAKE & STRANGER +19a CHINA \MUNt

• A "legendary" detail in writings of "Dio Cassius" recount that the populace of Pompeii was seated in the theater during the eruption of mount Vesuvius -5b ITALY, POMPEII \GRBt

theogony *The letter S of the Snake Ring Template. The generations of the gods.* Ref POLYTHEISM, REGENERATION, SEASON, SUN, TRINITY.

thirteen *The letter P of the Snake Ring Template.* A numerical metaphor for the death of the old sun at the mountain-house of the western horizon. *Ref* CAVE, LEVELS CELESTIAL, MARRIAGE, PROCESSION, WEST ORIENTATION.

thread *The letter A of the Snake Ring Template.* Ref ROPE, SPINDLE, WEAVING.

• Aboriginal women cut their pubic hair to weave into a long thread, which is said to capture people's soul when they sleep. When a medicine woman dances with the string, it becomes a snake. She puts it in the water where it becomes a "big dragon". The dragon becomes a cloud flying in the air, and finally becomes a snake again *See* CELESTIAL & DRAGON & GODDESS & SOUL & WATER +19a AUSTRALIA, PINDUPI \CAAt

• Granaries are modeled after a mythical one "where the ancestors came down", with the sun at the bottom. The bobbin at its top has a thread stretching to the sky *See* ANCESTOR WORSHIP & FERTILITY & FLORA & HOUSE & PATH & PYRAMID & STREAMER & SOCIETY AS AT THE AXIS MUNDI & VERTICAL LINE/SHAPE & WEAVING +19a MALI, DOGON *Figure 346*

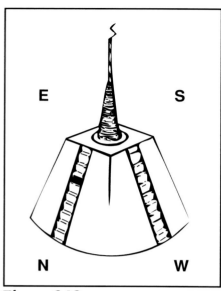

Figure 346

• When we dance, we enter the earth. After traveling a long way, we emerge climbing threads to reach God's place, then return and re-enter the earth *See* DANCE & GOD & PATH +19a SOUTH AFRICA, BUSHMAN \CATt

three *The letter L of the Snake Ring Template.* A numerical metaphor for the trinity. *Ref* TRINITY.

threshold *The letter H of the Snake Ring Template.* *Ref* HOUSE.

throne *The letter R of the Snake Ring Template.* A metaphor, often constructed with feline and/or dragon attributes designating the ruler as an allegory of the victorious young sun of the underworld serpent path. *Ref* CARRIER, DRAGON, FELINE, HERO, PATH, RULER, SOCIETAL ASPECT, WAR.

tiger *The letter M of the Snake Ring Template.* *Ref* FELINE.

time *The letter A of the Snake Ring Template.* A metaphor for the total movement of the sun within the entwined serpent: **a. day** The sun travels down and up within one coil of the entwined serpent, through the five infernal and seven celestial layers of the cosmos. **b. year** The sun's travels in these daily coils

from the winter solstice to the summer solstice and back again. **c. season** The old sun is regenerated within one of the daily coils into the new sun of the following season. *Ref* HOUR, INTEGER, LEVELS, LEVELS CELESTIAL/ UNDERWORLD, NEW YEAR, PATH, SEASON, SERPENT ENTWINED, SPRINGTIME.

• The dragon is a symbol of the year \JUQt

• The twenty-four hour day began at nightfall -30b EGYPT \COSt

• The Aztec belief system had the premise that space and time are co-terminus +15b MEXICO, AZTEC \AVEt

• For the ancient Babylonians the day began at midnight -7b IRAQ, BABYLON \NAUt

• One must rule space to master time +19a CHINA \SANt

• Time is not straight but a series of recurring cycles +19a BALI, HINDU \WESt

toad *The letter I of the Snake Ring Template.* *Ref* FROG.

tobacco *The letter D of the Snake Ring Template.* *Ref* FIRE, SMOKE, SOCIETAL ASPECT, TREE.

tomb *The letter H of the Snake Ring Template.* A metaphor for the sacred western mountain-house where the old sun died and was reborn each season. *Ref* DEATH, HOUSE, HOUSE MODEL, SARCOPHAGUS, SOCIETAL ASPECT.

tombstone *The letter E of the Snake Ring Template.* *Ref* DEATH, STELLA, STONE, VERTICAL LINE/ SHAPE.

tool-making *The letter R of the Snake Ring Template. Innate human attribute: Creation of an instrument as a means to an end and carrying it for future use.* Tools remained virtually unchanged for millions of years then with the advent of Homo sapiens became vastly improved. The creation of art and rituals meets all aspects of the above definition. It represented a sophisticated application of the unique human trait, under the most urgent circumstances *Ref* ART, CAVE, CHAOS IN NATURE, INTEGER, PSYCHOLOGY CHILD, RELIGION, RITUAL, SOCIETAL ASPECT, SOCIOBIOLOGY, STRUCTURALISM, TRANSCULTURAL SIMILARITY.

• Archaeologists often determine the evolutionary age of ancient human finds by the tools they left behind \ENBt

• The basic stone tool kit was unchanged for millions of years prior to Homo sapiens \NYTt

• Neanderthal's tools remained the same for more than 100,000 years. Innovation is the fundamental difference between us and them \NATt

• Cro-magnon man was capable of fishing, a skill which Neanderthal man never mastered \BULt

• Cro-magnon man developed the spear thrower and the bow and arrow to kill from a distance, and used heat treated flint acquired from sites up to two-hundred fifty miles away \SMJt

• The tiny space of time when human culture was shaped, was the time of rapid growth and variety in inventions \NEUt

torch *The letter D of the Snake Ring Template.* A metaphor for the light of the sun. *Ref* CANDLE, FIRE, LIGHT.

torque *The letter S of the Snake Ring Template. A metal collar or neck chain. Ref* JEWELRY, RING MOTIF, SOCIETAL ASPECT.

tortoise *The letter A of the Snake Ring Template. Ref* TURTLE.

totemism *The letter E of the Snake Ring Template.* The ritualized identification of an individual or a group with specific metaphors from the primordial religion. *Ref* SOCIETY AS AT THE AXIS MUNDI, SOCIETAL ASPECT, TOTEM POLE.

totem pole *The letter E of the Snake Ring Template. Ref* COLUMN, SOCIETY AS AT THE AXIS MUNDI, TREE, VERTICAL STICK.

tower *The letter E of the Snake Ring Template. Ref* SPIRE, SOCIETY AS AT THE AXIS MUNDI, VERTICAL LINE/ SHAPE.

toys *The letter R of the Snake Ring Template.* Often, objects associated with the metaphors of the young sun's passage through the snake ring which allay the innate fears of the infant mentality through play. *Ref* ART, GAME BOARD/ CHILD/ SPORT, PSYCHOLOGY CHILD, TOOL-MAKING, WAR.

trade *The letter I of the Snake Ring Template. Ref* COMMERCE.

trance *The letter R of the Snake Ring Template. Ref* HYPNOSIS, PSYCHOLOGY CHILD/ DREAMS.

transcultural similarity *The letter R of the Snake Ring Template.* The metaphors and rituals created in terminal Ice Age cave art, to inspire seasonal fertility during the extreme famine and chaos of that time. As in tool-making, they were retained and continuously reused, either consciously or unconsciously, by their descendants as they dispersed to other parts of the world. *Ref* ART, CAVE, CHAOS IN NATURE, FLOOD, FLORA, HOUSE, LORE, PSYCHOLOGY CHILD, RITUAL, SEASON, SOCIETAL ASPECT, SOCIETY AS AT THE AXIS MUNDI, SOCIOBIOLOGY, TOOL-MAKING.

• The Andeans associate Christ with the sun and the Virgin Mary with the earth mother *See* DEMYTHOLIZATION +19a PERU, ANDEAN \AVDt \LEIt

treasure *The letter I of the Snake Ring Template.* A metaphor for the fertility and prosperity brought on by the young sun. *Ref* COMMERCE, GOLD, MATERIALISM, RAINBOW.

tree *The letter E of the Snake Ring Template.* A metaphor for the vertical segment of the serpent path of the old sun from the sky to the underworld joining with the mother goddess. *Ref* CROSS WEST, DEMYTHOLIZATION, MARRIAGE, SNAKE, SOCIETY AS AT THE AXIS MUNDI, VERTICAL LINE/ SHAPE, WEST ORIENTATION.

• At the Ceremony of the Cross, a Maypole formed of a living tree is worshipped while a maiden is serenaded *See* CROSS WEST & RIBBON & SPIRAL & VERTICAL LINE/ SHAPE +19a SPAIN, CHRISTIAN \FONt

trefoil motif *The letter L of the Snake Ring Template. Ref* ARCHITECTURE, SOCIETAL ASPECT, TRINITY.

trepanning *The letter D of the Snake Ring Template.* A ritual practice to release the soul from the head as a metaphor for the passage of the solar soul from the head of the dead old sun to the successor sun of the new season. *Ref* DEATH, HEALING, SEASON, SOCIETAL ASPECT, SOUL, TRINITY.

• In traditional ceremonies, after the individual is cremated, the skull is split to remove the spirit so the soul may join the eternals *See* DEATH & ETERNITY & FIRE & HEAD & SOUL & TRANSCULTURAL SIMILARITY & TREPANNING -19b INDIA, HINDU \NATt

tree worship *The letter E of the Snake Ring Template.* Focus on the tree as a metaphor for the vertical segment of the sun's serpent path into the western horizon. *Ref* TREE, VERTICAL STICK.

triangle motif upright *The letter G of the Snake Ring Template.* A symbol for the mountain-house of the mother goddess as well as the waters of the western horizon. *Ref* MOTHER GODDESS, MOUNTAIN, STAR SIX POINTED.

• An engraved bone from the upper Magdalenian period displays the image of a fish with a series of triangle motifs -350b GERMANY \MAQp

• In the art of the of some of African secret societies, triangles represent lakes +19a ZAIRE LUBA \AFAt

triangle motif inverted *The letter D of the Snake Ring Template.* A symbol for the descent of the old sun within the snake ring path into the western horizon. *Ref* BULL, CROSS,

DEMYTHOLIZATION, DESCENDING MOTIF, STAR SIX POINTED, TRIANGLE MOTIF UPRIGHT.

• Frieze are composed of triangular bulls skulls and flowers *See* BULL & DEATH & FLORA & HOUSE & LETTERS & REGENERATION & TRANSCULTURAL SIMILARITY -20b GREEK, SAMOTHRACE \DANp

• A male deity is depicted riding a horned animal with a large triangle obscuring the front of his face +19a NIGERIA \PAQt

trident *The letter L of the Snake Ring Template.* A metaphor for the path of transference of the old sun's solar soul to the successor sun of the new season. The trinitarian aspect of this division into solar father, son and husk, occurring in the mountain house of the western waters, are symbolized by the division of the shaft into three prongs. *Ref* HOUSE, HUSK, MOUNTAIN, SEASON, SOUL, TRINITY, WATER, WEST ORIENTATION.

triform *The letter I of the Snake Ring Template. Ref* TRINITY.

trinity *The letter L of the Snake Ring Template. See* SECTION TWO.

T-upright *The letter O of the Snake Ring Template.* A symbol for the vertical segment of the serpent path below the eastern horizon. *Ref* CROSS EAST, EAST ORIENTATION, SERPENT ENTWINED, VERTICAL LINE/ SHAPE.

T-inverted *The letter D of the Snake Ring Template.* A symbol for the descent of the old sun within the vertical segment of the snake ring path into the western horizon. *Ref* CROSS WEST, DESCENDING MOTIF, HOUSE, T-UPRIGHT, VERTICAL LINE/ SHAPE.

turkey *The letter B of the Snake Ring Template.* A bird-metaphor for the old sun, reinforced by its beard-like appendage. *Ref* BIRD, CHICKEN, SACRIFICE ANIMAL, TRANSCULTURAL SIMILARITY, WEST ORIENTATION.

turtle *The letter A of the Snake Ring Template.* A reptilian metaphor for the continuation of the snake path into the western horizon underworld. *Ref* CIRCLE MOTIF, HORIZON, SERPENT ENTWINED, WATER.

• India is said to lie between heaven and earth, resting in the back of a tortoise *See* SOCIETY AS AT THE AXIS MUNDI -19b INDIA, HINDU \CAIt \LARt

• To ancient Taoists, the tortoise was a symbol of the forces of earth -1b CHINA \RAWt

• A pillar with an entwined serpent at the top resting on a stylized tortoise, represents the link between heaven and earth *See* PATH & PILLAR & SNAKE & SOCIETY AS AT THE AXIS MUNDI +18a CHINA \CHRt

• The serpents and tortoises depicted in shrines are the symbols of male and female deities respectively *See* HOUSE & PATH & UNDERWORLD +19a NIGERIA \MUNt

• Southwest Indians believe that each day the sun god touches a turtle shell hanging from the ladder at the entrance to their kiva, and moves underneath the kiva to rise again in the east *See* HOUSE & LADDER INFERNAL & SOCIETY AS AT THE AXIS MUNDI +19 USA \SINt

twelve *The letters P & K of the Snake Ring Template.* A numerical metaphor for the sum of the cosmic levels. *Ref* LEVELS CELESTIAL/ UNDERWORLD, PROCESSION, TIME (DAY).

twenty *The letter A of the Snake Ring Template.* A numerical metaphor for the apparent daily journey of the sun around the earth, taking into consideration the zero concept. *Ref* LEVELS CELESTIAL/UNDERWORLD, MATHEMATICS, UROBORUS, ZERO.

• Twenty was one of the most important multipliers in the calendar system, and in other calculations important to the function of the society +7b MEXICO, MAYAN \HAOt

twenty-four *The letter A of the Snake Ring Template.* A numerical metaphor for the apparent daily journey of the sun up and down through the twelve cosmic levels. *Ref* LEVELS CELESTIAL, TIME (DAY), UNDERWORLD, UROBORUS.

twins *The letter N of the Snake Ring Template.* A metaphor to increase the fortune of the young sun, one twin to fight and the other to escape, in the struggle against the old suns of the seasons past who remain in the underworld. *Ref* GAMBLING, HUSK, SEASON, SOCIETAL ASPECT, TRINITY, WAR.

twisted shapes *The letter A of the Snake Ring Template.* A metaphor for the entwined serpent path of the sun. *Ref* PATH, ENTWINED MOTIF.

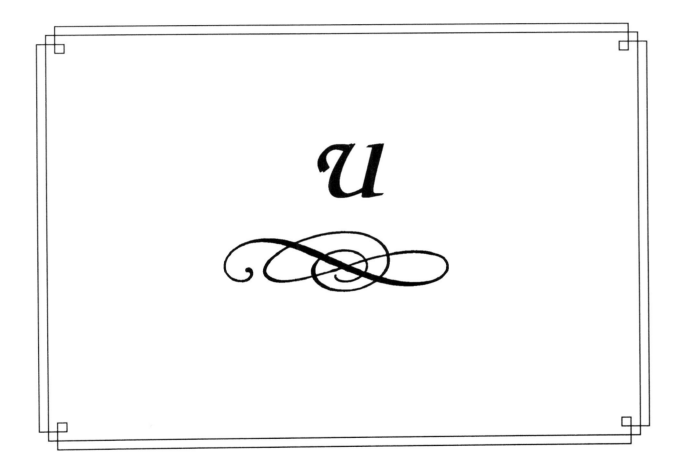

umbrella *The letter A of the Snake Ring Template.* A composite metaphor consisting of its top representing the dome of the snake path in the sky, and its handle representing the vertical path at the horizon *Ref* EAST/ WEST ORIENTATION, RAINBOW, VERTICAL LINE/ SHAPE.

• The top of the king's umbrella has an orb and a bird, both made of gold *See* BIRD & GOLD & ROUND MOTIF & RULER +19a MALI, DOGON \GARt

• Royal umbrellas were adorned with images of the lotus, bird, or elephant *See* BIRD & ELEPHANT & LOTUS & RULER +18a INDIA, IMPERIAL \WESp

• The umbrella is an important part of the Geisha wardrobe. A top-of-the-line "janome" is painted with a wisteria pattern or a white band referred to as the "snake eye" *See* EYE & MARRIAGE & MOTHER GODDESS & PATH & PROSTITUTE & SNAKE & RING MOTIF & TREE +19 JAPAN \NYTp

• Murals covering the interior walls of a Mayan temple include scenes of victims of war with bloodied hands, a royal baby carried away by a warrior, and attendants holding large umbrellas. **[Note:** Possibly depicting the mythic heroes of the underworld battle, wounded so the newborn sun can escape to the serpent path dome of the sky**]** *See* BABY BOY & HAND RAISED WITH MISSING DIGIT & WAR

underworld *The letter K of the Snake Ring Template.* See SECTION TWO.

unicorn *The letter L of the Snake Ring Template.* A metaphor for the virile old sun as a bull, after its horizon death [symbolized by the loss of its horn]. *Ref* BULL, DEATH, MARRIAGE, RHINOCEROS, SEASON, TRINITY.

• The original variants of the mythic unicorn are in many parts of the world. According to legend, if a virgin is placed in a field, the unicorn will lie down in her lap *See* CORNUCOPIA & MARRIAGE & VIRGIN +19a CARL JUNG \CIRt

urn *The letter K of the Snake Ring Template. Ref* VESSEL.

uroborus *The letter A of the Snake Ring Template. A snake apparently biting its tail. This does not occur in nature.* A metaphor for a single coil of the entwined serpent path, as depicted in *the Snake Ring Frontispiece* on the day of the vernal equinox, when the solar soul passes from the old sun of winter to the new sun of the successor season, typical of the sun's regenerations of itself into a newborn form in order to bring on changes in nature. *Ref* CIRCLE MOTIF, LEVELS, PATH, SEASON, SERPENT ENTWINED, SUN OLD/ YOUNG, TRINITY.

• The significance of the uroborus is fundamental to the psychology of the unconscious CARL JUNG \NEUt

• The wholeness in child psychology is determined by the uroborus. Its image has been found in Egypt, New Zealand, India, Greece and Africa *See* PSYCHOLOGY CHILD & TRANSCULTURAL SIMILARITY \NEUt

• The self-generative nature of the uroborus was symbolized by the self-rolling wheel *See* CIRCLE MOTIF & PATH & REGENERATION & WHEEL +19a \NEUt

• The uroborus is used in ornamentation and jewelry in many parts of the world *See* JEWELRY & SOCIETAL ASPECT & TRANSCULTURAL SIMILARITY +19a CERVANTES \MUNt \WEJt

• A Yang-shao pot depicts one of the earliest known images of the uroborus, with its top half colored light and its bottom half dark *See* BLADE & VESSEL(UNDERWORLD) -45a CHINA, NEOLITHIC \MUNp

• The uroborus was depicted even in pre-dynastic time. Its significance is unknown -30b EGYPT \MUNt

• The uroborus was a common decoration at Susa the capital city *See* SOCIETY AS AT THE AXIS MUNDI -29b IRAN, ELLAMITE \MUNt

• The uroborus was "the heavenly serpent" known as Tiammat. It represented "continuity of life" *See* DEATH & REGENERATION & SOUL -20b IRAQ, ACCADIAN \NEUt \MUNt

• The Greeks believed that the celestial serpent biting its own tail could also take the form of a spiral. It was the primal "I am the alpha and the omega" and was also the symbol for alchemy *See* ALCHEMY & LETTERS & SNAKE & SPIRAL -20b GREEK \LEIt \NEUt \JUPt

• The mandala is the continuum of the dragon known by the names Vrtra and Asat. It is the uroboric circle that contains the mysterious powers of the sun gods and demons *See* DEATH & HUSK & MARRIAGE & REGENERATION & TRINITY -19b INDIA, HINDU \MCCt \NEUt

• The Kundelini, a snake coiled into a ring, passes from the base of the spine to the dome of the head, integrating the individual with the absolute *See* HEALING & PATH & PSYCHOLOGY CHILD & SOCIETAL ASPECT +5b INDIA, YOGA \CUPt

• In very old Chinese belief, the uroborus is a dragon connecting the sky to the earth *See* CALABASH & HORIZON & PATH -15b CHINA \MUNt \CIRt

• An undeciphered shrine from king Tutankhamun's tomb depicts a uroborus encircling the king as a mummy *See* RULER & PATH & REGENERATION & DEATH -13a EGYPT *Figure 347*

Figure 347

• Dedicated to the young sun god **Aeo** was the first and last letters, alpha and omega, inscribed on the uroborus. [**Note:** the first and last letters, alpha and omega, are images of a bull and ring motif respectively, the beginning and end result of regeneration of a new sun god in the *Snake Ring*] -5b ITALY, MITHRAIC \LEIt

• According to Plato, the world was formed within the uroborus *See* CHAOS IN NATURE & REGENERATION -4a GREEK \NEUt

• An illustration from a "magic" papyrus depicts a uroborus surrounding the sacred scarab *See* BEETLE(LEAP-UP) & DEATH & MAGIC & REGENERATION +1a GREEK \LEIt

• The circle of the firmament is a uroborus revolving on a spindle held by the goddess. The uroborus is half light and half dark *See* BLACK(UNDERWORLD) & GODDESS & PATH & SPINDLE(AXIS MUNDI) & THREAD +1a GREEK, ORPHIC \SANt \CIRt

• A ritual bowl of the Mesopotamian Gnostic sect has a uroborus at its center *See* VESSEL(UNDERWORLD) +5a IRAQ, MANDAEAN \NEUp

• Bronze warrior figures often have medallions on their headdress of a small bird within an encircling uroborus. The meaning if this medallion is unknown *See* BIRD(SUN YOUNG) & WAR & WARRIOR(HERO) +13a NIGERIA, TSOEDE \EYOp

• The famed "Calendar Stone", with its border of a doubled-headed serpent with an old and young god in its mouths, once stood at the top of the main pyramid-temple Coatepec (snake mountain), named after the mythic western mountain house where the sun god was born. *See* MOUNTAIN & REGENERATION & PATH & PYRAMID & SOCIETY AS AT THE AXIS MUNDI & BIRTH & SUN OLD/ YOUNG & WEST ORIENTATION +13b MEXICO, AZTEC *Figure 348*

• A frequent image on early Tarot playing cards is that of the sun associated with a uroborus *See* GAME BOARD & OCCULT & PATH & SOCIETAL ASPECT & SUN YOUNG +14a ITALY, TAROT \KAPt

• Southwest Indians painted a snake around wagon wheels *See* CARRIER & PATH & WAR & WHEEL +17b USA, HOPI \BOWt

Figure 348

• The door of the king's palace is carved with weapons under a relief of the uroborus *See* PATH(UNDERWORLD) & RULER & WAR +18a BENIN, FON \PAQp

• A brass warrior's shield depicts a uroborus surrounded by felines *See* FELINE & PATH & WAR +18a NIGERIA, BENIN *Figure 349*

Figure 349

• Bracelets, in the form of a feathered uroborus with crossbands on its body interspersed with ring motifs, represent the mythic rainbow snake which encircles the

world. **[Note:** An identical motif, not found in nature, is depicted on the bodies of the serpents forming the head and skirt of the mother goddess statue from the main Aztec temple] *See* JEWELRY & MOTHER GODDESS & PATH & RAINBOW & RING MOTIF IN SEQUENCE & SERPENT FEATHERED & TRANSCULTURAL SIMILARITY & X-CROSSING +18a NIGERIA, BENIN *Figure 350*

Refer also to *Figure 56* SECTION TWO.

• Dancers at the winter rites, parade into an opening of a screen painted with the double headed serpent, "the soul catcher", in the form of a uroborus *See* DANCE & PATH & PROCESSION & REGENERATION & SEASON & SOUL +18a CANADA, KWAKIUTL \NABp

Figure 350

• The lodge-maker of the Sun Dance ceremony wept over the Wheel, a carved image of a water snake curved into a ring and hung with eagle feathers. It stood on a staff above the buffalo skull which was the main ceremonial object on the altar. At the conclusion of the Sun Dance, the Wheel was raised upwards in a circular motion to hasten the appearance of the sun *See* DEATH & SERPENT FEATHERED & PATH & HOUSE & ALTAR & RAPTOR & SUN OLD/ YOUNG & REGENERATION & RITUAL +19a USA, ARAPAHO

Refer to *Figure 43* SECTION TWO.

• Greater Southwest Indians depict the uroborus in their sand paintings +19a USA, NAVAHO \NEUt

• The gypsies of the world use the uroborus as an amulet +19a ROMANIA, GYPSY \NEUt

• An emblem of Free Masonry is a snake biting its tail. The Rosy Cross version of this symbol includes, at its center, a rose superimposed on a cross with an upright triangle at its top. A youth with a star over his head is at the bottom of the uroborus carrying the pack and staff of a traveler. **[Note:** The Masonic Order claims descent from the mamons who built Solomon's Temple. Present scholarship places its roots, instead, in 18th century European mysticism. Probably unconsciously, the Rosy Cross motif depicts the cross at the mountain symbol where the new sun, whose father, the old sun died to give him birth, (the password of the Order is, "I am the son of the widow") leaves on this path through the underworld to bring fertility symbolized by the flower] +19a MASONIC \GOLp \SANt

• The occultist "Mark of the Beast" is a cross within a uroborus *See* CROSS WEST & OCCULT & SOCIETAL ASPECT +19a ALEISTER CROWLEY \OCTp

• One of the earliest books written in the form of a novel, the vastly popular *Don Quixote*, has the hero doing battle with windmills which he saw in the form of rotating dragons *See* PATH & PSYCHOLOGY CHILD & WAR +15a DON CERVANTES \WEJt

• Chemist Friedrich Kekule envisioned the previously unknown structure of the benzene molecule while he was dozing by the fire and had a vision of a snake eating its own tail +19a \OCTt

• Physicist S.L. Glashow used a sketch of the uroborus to envision a new theory relating natural forces to distance +19a \NYTp

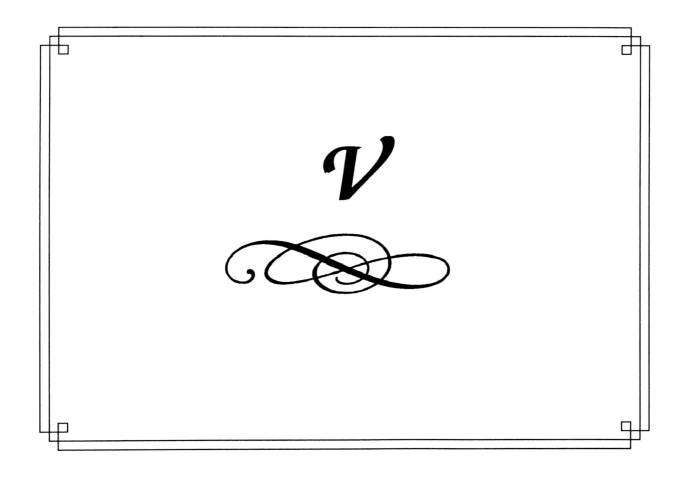

vagina or ***vulva*** *The letter H of the Snake Ring Template.* A metaphor for the mother goddess in the mountain-house of the western horizon. *Ref* BIRTH, CAVE, HOUSE, MARRIAGE, MOUNTAIN.

• From the Rig Veda, the sacred book of the Hindus, "Earth Mother open thyself, let him in lightly. Arch thy broad back on the next lap of his journey" *See* MARRIAGE & PATH & MOTHER GODDESS & SERPENT ENTWINED -19b INDIA, HINDU \NEUt

• Images of women with parted legs are at the entrances to many deep Ice Age art caves *See* BIRTH & CAVE & HOUSE & MARRIAGE & MOTHER GODDESS & REGENERATION -350b FRANCE, LA MADELEINE \RAUt

• An engraved stone from an Ice Age cave depicts vulva signs. One sign has a series of cupules leading away from and returning to it or vice versa *See* PATH & ROUND MOTIFS IN SEQUENCE & STONE(MOUNTAIN) - 990b FRANCE LA FERRASSIE *Figure 351*

Figure 352

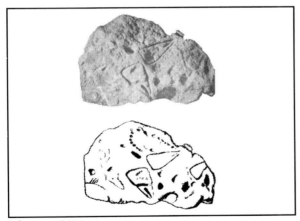

Figure 351

Figure 353

• The woman's mask worn in secret society dances has a bird within the vulva at its top *See* BIRD & DANCE & PATH & MARRIAGE & MOTHER GODDESS +19a SIERRA LEONE, MENDE *Figure 352*

• Many of the old boulders with engraved vagina-signs, at a salt sanctuary sacred to the Indians of the area, "could have been found at the [Ice Age site] La Ferrassie" *See* SALT & STONE & TRANSCULTURAL SIMILARITIES +19a BOLIVIA, CHIMANE \GIEt *Figure 353*

• There are many illustrations in ancient Hindu, Egyptian, Greek and Canaanite art of a goddess showing her genitals. A Hindu wood carving depicts a cobra in a goddess' vagina *See* BIRTH & GODDESSES & MARRIAGE & PATH & SNAKE +16a INDIA, HINDU \NEUt *Figure 354*

• A temple hymn is dedicated to the mother goddess of childbirth and her "womb-serpent" - 35b IRAQ, SUMERIAN \MUNt

Figure 354

• A terra cotta headless figurine from **Ishtar's** temple depicts the goddess offering her breasts. Serpents on her thighs lead to the pubic triangle *See* HOUSE & MOTHER GODDESS & PATH & REGENERATION -19b IRAQ, ASSUR
Figure 355

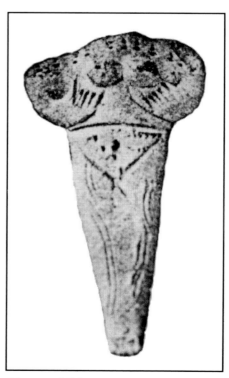

Figure 355

• Goddesses opening their genitals were a common theme in Egyptian art. The images were displayed at ceremonies in honor of the goddess **Hathor**, the mother goddess often shown with cow's horns at her head and/or with the infant sun god **Horus** on her lap *See* ART & BABY BOY & BULL & COW & MARRIAGE & MOTHER GODDESS & SUN YOUNG -30b EGYPT \RAUt

• Explorers to the New World named an island off the east coast "Isla de las Mujeres" because its temple had stone columns depicting half-naked women at each side of the entrance with their skirts raised to their navels *See* GODDESSES & MARRIAGE & TEMPLE & WATER -15a MEXICO \RAUt

• Neolithic art from Utah depicts a complex group of images in association with a rainbow. These include a female with her vagina open, a figure with his hands raised and a vertical row of ring motifs (not shown here) *See* HAND RAISED & MOTHER GODDESS & RAINBOW & REGENERATION & RING MOTIF IN SEQUENCE & STONE -60b USA, NEOLITHIC *Figure* 356

Figure 356

• Statues of women exposing their genitals were in ceremonial houses of the Northwest Coast Indians *See* HOUSE & MARRIAGE & REGENERATION +18a CANADA, KWAKIUTL \NAUt

• Large wood female figures, their hands holding their legs open to expose their privates, are frequently placed on the gables of the men's houses *See* TRANSCULTURAL SIMILARITIES +19a CAROLINE ISLANDS, PALAU ARCHIPELAGO *Figure 357*

Figure 357

• Carved reliefs of grotesque women with their legs spread apart and holding their vulvas open with their hands, called Sheelagh-na-gigs, remain over the doorways of many early Christian churches *See* ART & DEMYTHOLIZATION & GODDESSES & MARRIAGE +4a ENGLAND/ IRELAND
Refer to *Figure 83* SECTION TWO.

valley *The letter G of the Snake Ring Template.* A metaphor for the entranceway into the underworld at the western horizon. *Ref* ABYSS, UNDERWORLD, WEST ORIENTATION.

vase *The letter K of the Snake Ring Template. Ref* VESSEL.

vegetation *The letter I of the Snake Ring Template. Ref* FLORA.

vehicle *The letter M of the Snake Ring Template.* **1.** A metaphor for the hero-carrier of the new sun through the underworld. **2.** *The letter T of the Snake Ring Template.* A metaphor for the speed required for the sun to traverse the sky and underworld in one day. **[Note:** Mankind's fascination with powerful automobiles, particularly those with feline or equine names**].** *Ref* CARRIER, FELINE, HORSE, PATH, SOCIETAL ASPECT.

veil *The letter K of the Snake Ring Template.* A metaphor denoting the wearer as faceless and unseen below the horizons. *Ref* MARRIAGE, MOTHER GODDESS, SOCIETAL ASPECT, UNDERWORLD.

• The sun god **Osiris** who died in the sea, was resurrected by the veiled goddess **Isis** in her palace. The drought ended, and crops were restored *See* FERTILITY & RESURRECTION (REGENERATION) & SEASON & SUN OLD/ YOUNG & UNDERWORLD -30b EGYPT \ELHt

• Aborigines say that the evening sun hides its face with a veil of hair-string, and vanishes from sight +19a AUSTRALIA, ARANDA \CAAt

verb *The letter R of the Snake Ring Template. Gram. A word expressing an action performed by or suffered by a subject.* Symbols, objects, human figures and animals were used in terminal Ice Age art to inspire corresponding actions by the suns and mother goddesses, directed to the attention of either the male or female deities, an association that remains in the masculine or feminine definite article applied to even inanimate objects in the Romance languages. *Ref* ANIMISM, METAPHOR, POLYTHEISM, SOCIETAL ASPECT, SPEECH, WRITING.

verticality *The letter E of the Snake Ring Template.* A metaphor designating the image or article as within the vertical segment of the sun's serpent path at the western horizon. *Ref* ARCHITECTURE, GODS, GODDESSES, HERM, VERTICAL LINE/ SHAPE.

vertical line/ shape **1.** *The letter E of the Snake Ring Template.* **2.** *The letter O of the Snake Ring Template.* See SECTION TWO.

vertical stick *The letter E of the Snake Ring Template.* See SECTION TWO.

vessel *The letter K of the Snake Ring Template.* A metaphor for the infinite paths of the entwined serpent through the underworld. Their aggregate forms an inverted dome which contains the world oceans, with the square earth floating in their center. *Ref* CALABASH, UNDERWORLD.

• The world's top and bottom halves are as bowls -19b INDIA, HINDU \MCCt

• A sacred vessel holds the "yaje" hallucinogen (made from the "yaje" vine that wraps around trees in the jungle) for rituals whose ultimate purpose is to inspire the joining of the **Sun Father** with his daughter, the **Yaje Woman**. This vessel is the "place of death" as well as the "place of origin and rebirth" *See* HALLUCINOGEN & INCEST & MARRIAGE & RITUAL & SUN OLD & VINE +19a COLOMBIA, TUKANO \REJt

victory *The letter N of the Snake Ring Template.* A metaphor for the conquest by the young sun over the husks of old suns in the underworld. *Ref* GAME SPORT/ BOARD, WAR.

vine *The letter A of the Snake Ring Template.* *Ref* PATH, ROPE, SNAKE, TREE.

virgin *The letter H of the Snake Ring Template.* **a**. A female metaphor for the regenerated mother goddess, the daughter of the mother goddess of the previous season, who will join with the old sun in the western horizon. *Ref* GODDESSES, MARRIAGE, MOTHER GODDESS, SEASON, SUN OLD, WEST ORIENTATION. **b**. A male metaphor for the sun whose life ends at the end of the season when he copulates with the mother goddess. *Ref* CIRCUMCISION, MARRIAGE, SEASON, SOCIETAL ASPECT, SUN OLD.

virgin birth *The letter I of the Snake Ring Template.* *Ref* BABY BOY/ GIRL, GODDESSES, TRINITY, VIRGIN.

Virgo *The letter H of the Snake Ring Template. Astron. A woman holding a spike of grain.* A metaphor for the mother goddess who gives birth to the new sun, the bringer of fertility. *Ref* FLORA, MOTHER GODDESS, SPRINGTIME, SUN YOUNG, VIRGIN (FEMALE), ZODIAC.

• Sometimes depicted with the six-pointed star, Virgo was always associated with the birth of a god *See* BABY BOY & VIRGIN & STAR \CIRt

virtual reality *or* ***artificial reality*** *or* ***cyberspace*** *The letter R of the Snake Ring Template. An illusionary environment created through the use of interactive computer graphics,* with the ability to artificially place one within the metaphors at the axis mundi. A possible means to replace the metaphors fading from contemporary life. *Ref* RELIGIONS CONTEMPORARY, DEMYTHOLIZATION, SOCIETAL ASPECT, PSYCHOLOGY CONTMEPORARY PROBLEMS, PSYCHOLOGY QUANTITY, SOCIETY AS AT THE AXIS MUNDI. *Figure 358*

Figure 358

void *The letter G of the Snake Ring Template.* *Ref* ABYSS, HOLE.

volcano *The letter G of the Snake Ring Template.* A metaphor for the fiery mountain at the abyss in the waters of the western horizon where the old sun dies and joins with the mother goddess. *Ref* FIRE, HOLE, MOTHER GODDESS, MOUNTAIN, SOCIETY AS AT THE AXIS MUNDI, WATER.

vulture *The letter Q of the Snake Ring Template. Ref* RAPTOR.

walled enclosure *The letter R of the Snake Ring Template.* *Ref* PRECINCT, SOCIETY AS AT THE AXIS MUNDI.

wand *The letter E of the Snake Ring Template.* A metaphor for the vertical segment of the entwined serpent path at the western horizon. *Ref* SCEPTER, SHAMAN, VERTICAL STICK.

war *The letter N of the Snake Ring Template.* See SECTION TWO.

warrior *The letter N of the Snake Ring Template.* *Ref* HERO, WAR.

water *The letter F of the Snake Ring Template.* A metaphor for the waters surrounding the earth, primarily the waters of the western horizon. *Ref* BIRTH, HORIZON, HOUSE, MARRIAGE, MOTHER GODDESS, MOUNTAIN.

• Euripus, meaning "navel of the sea", was also the name of the center of the Roman circus which took place around their pyramid, claimed to belong to the sun -350 ITALY \SANt

• The primeval waters were referred to as "the mother" -35b IRAQ, SUMERIAN \COTt

• The thirteenth letter of the Hebrew alphabet is "mem", which means "water". It is the source of the English thirteenth letter "M" See LETTER & LEVELS CELESTIAL & MATHEMATICS & WRITING -10b ISRAEL, JEWISH \ENDt

• Traditionally, holy areas of the Hindu and Buddhist faith have sanctuaries surrounded by moats they call "the cosmic ocean" See SOCIETY AS AT THE AXIS MUNDI +19 INDONESIA \EXQt

• Roman Catholics make the sign of the cross with Holy Water when they enter a church See CROSS WEST & HOUSE & SOCIETAL ASPECT +19a ITALY, CHRISTIAN \TULt

waterfall *The letter F of the Snake Ring Template.* A metaphor for the descending waters of the western horizon. *Ref* ABYSS, WEST ORIENTATION, WHIRLPOOL.

wave *The letter F of the Snake Ring Template.* *Ref* WATER.

weapon *The letter N of the Snake Ring Template.* A metaphor for: **a.** The underworld conflict between the old and new suns. *Ref* WAR. **b.** *~ in burial* The regeneration of the new sun, who must fight his way through the perilous underworld. *Ref* BURIAL, DEATH, REGENERATION, SOCIETAL ASPECT, SOUL, SUN OLD/ NEW.

• Some Neanderthal graves contained food, flowers and flint weapons. In one of these, a youth about sixteen years old, was surrounded by charred cattle bones and had an axe near his hand *See* BULL & FERTILITY & FIRE & REGENERATION & WAR -400b FRANCE, LE MOUSTIER \BULt \CAAt

weaving *The letter A of the Snake Ring Template.* A metaphor for the entwined serpent path of the sun around the universe. *Ref* PATH, SOCIETAL ASPECT, X-CROSSING.

• At springtime The goddess **Persephone** was in a cave guarded by two serpents. She was weaving a garment which was to be a beautiful picture of the universe. Her father the sun god **Zeus** approached her in the form of a serpent, and together they conceived the young sun god **Dionysus** *See* BIRTH & CAVE & INCEST & MARRIAGE & MOTHER GODDESS & PATH & SPRINGTIME & SUN OLD/ YOUNG -20b GREEK \CAAt

• Young girls were chosen at the age of ten for their physical perfection. One part of this group spent the rest of their lives in temple shrines as virginal priestesses, the "wives of the sun" weaving textiles. The other group of these young girls became second wives to the Emperor and his nobles *See* HOUSE & MARRIAGE & RULER & SUN OLD +9b PERU, INCA \MASt

• The horizontal bar of the loom is a feminine element, symbolizing the flat roof over the grave of their serpent-god **Lebe** in the primal field. The vertical stake of the loom is the masculine element *See* CROSS WEST & DEATH & HORIZON & MARRIAGE & PATH & SOCIETAL ASPECT & SUN OLD & WEAVING +19a MALI, DOGON \GRKt

• Weavers sing prayers as they work. Their words follow the woof, a zig-zag thread representing the serpent deity **Lebe**. The weavers stop working when the sun touches the horizon *See* MUSIC & PATH & SNAKE & SOCIETAL ASPECT & THREAD & WEAVING +19a MALI, DOGON \GRKt

• The warp in the woven garments of Eastern Woodlands Indians represents the "light of day", and the woof, "the dark of night". The fringes of the garments represent falling rain, and the borders the "standing rainbow" *See* GARMENT & NIGHT & RAINBOW & SEASON(RAIN) & SOCIETAL +19a USA, IROQUIS \WESt

• Peasant women take weaving lessons to be better sexual partners to their husbands *See* MARRIAGE & PATH +19a MEXICO \AVDt

week *The letter P of the Snake Ring Template. AS. A period of seven days.* A metaphor for the sun's passage through the seven celestial layers within the serpent path. At the seventh level, the zenith of its path, the sun appears to rest. *Ref* CALENDAR, DAY OF REST, LEVELS CELESTIAL, SOCIETAL ASPECT.

well *The letter G of the Snake Ring Template. A natural or manmade source of water.* A metaphor for the abyss into the waters of the western horizon. *Ref* CENOTE, HOLE, SOCIETY AS AT THE AXIS MUNDI, WATER.

werejaguar *The letter M of the Snake Ring Template. The composite figure of a jaguar and a human infant.* A metaphor for the feline carrier of the new sun (within the feline's body) through the underworld. *Ref* BABY BOY, FELINE, HERO, SPHINX, SUN YOUNG, UNDERWORLD, WATER.

west orientation *The letter D of the Snake Ring Template.* A metaphor for the sunset location of the mountain-house within the entwined serpent path, where the old sun of the past season dies and the new sun of the successor season is born. *Ref* DEATH, HOUSE, MARRIAGE, MOUNTAIN, RED, SACRIFICE ANIMAL/ HUMAN, SERPENT ENTWINED, TRINITY, VERTICAL LINE/ SHAPE, WATER.

• The decorated temple caves of Cro-magnon Man are clustered near the west coast of Europe -350b \CAIp

• The Indian petroglyphs of Black Canyon are concentrated on the western wall -90b USA \SAMt

• Figures of bulls' skulls in the shrine rooms of the oldest true city in the world are located only on the walls facing the mountains to the west *See* BULL & DEATH & HOUSE & SOCIETY AS AT THE AXIS MUNDI -70b TURKEY, CATAL HUYUK \REAt

• On the west end in the pediment of a temple at the Acropolis is the image of the old sun god **Zeus.** On the east end pediment is the image of the young sun god **Apollo** *See* EAST/ WEST ORIENTATION & HOUSE & PATH & PEDIMENT & SUN OLD/ YOUNG -20b GREEK \BOAp

• One hundred fifty of the colossal statues, some of them still attached to their platforms, and a few still with red stone "top hats" on their heads until recently, are all located on the west side of the island facing west *See* HAT(TOP) & PATH & RED & SUN OLD/ YOUNG & WATER +19a EASTER ISLAND \HEWt

• The westernmost tips of land are called the "souls jumping off place". The dead are believed to sink with the sun into the west *See* DEAD & REGENERATION & SOCIETAL ASPECT & SOUL & SUN OLD & WATER +19 POLYNESIA \ELIt

whale *The letter J of the Snake Ring Template.* See SECTION TWO.

wheel *The letter A of the Snake Ring Template.* A metaphor for the daily path of the sun within a coil of the entwined serpent. *Ref* CIRCLE MOTIF, SERPENT ENTWINED, TIME, UROBORUS.

wheel of fortune *The letters A & I of the Snake Ring Template.* A metaphor for the fertility and prosperity brought on by the young sun within the snake ring path. *Ref* BABY BOY, FLORA, GOLD, SPRINGTIME, TREASURE, WHEEL.

whirlpool *The letter F of the Snake Ring Template.* A metaphor for penetration by the vertical segment of the serpent path into the waters of the western horizon, forming the entrance way into the underworld. *Ref* HOLE, SOCIETY AS AT THE AXIS MUNDI, WATER, WATERFALL.

whistling *The letter P of the Snake Ring Template.* Like music and clacking the tongue, an archaic way of calling the attention of the old sun. *Ref* MUSIC, SOCIETAL ASPECT.

wild man *The letter L of the Snake Ring Template. Ref* BULL, HUSK, TRINITY.

window *The letter H of the Snake Ring Template.* A secondary metaphor for the entrance into the mountain-house of the western horizon. *Ref* DOOR, HOUSE.

wine *The letter I of the Snake Ring Template.* **a.** A metaphor for the blood of the old sun, imbibed as the transference of the solar soul. **b.** A metaphor, particularly its grapes, for fertility. *Ref* BLOOD, FLORA, SOCIETAL ASPECT, SOUL, TRINITY.

• In the Eucharist ceremony, the basis for communion, the bread symbolizes the body of Christ and the wine His blood Ob ITALY, CHRISTIAN \NYTt

• A 2,000 year-old vineyard, one of the oldest vineyards in the world, produces a red wine known as "Bull's Blood" *See* BULL Ob HUNGARY \WESp

• In the Rig Veda, a holy book of the Hindu faith, wine is referred to as "the sun" -19a INDIA, HINDU \OCTt

• When launching a new vessel, it is traditional for a woman to break a bottle of wine on its prow. **[Note:** The vessel as an allegory for the boat of the dead that lands on the western horizon] *See* BOAT & GODDESS & OBJECT RITUALLY BROKEN & UNDERWORLD & WATER \WESt

winged *The letter P of the Snake Ring Template. Ref* FEATHERED.

winter solstice *The Solar Orbit Frontispiece drawing. Ref* BABY BOY, CHRISTMASTIDE, DEMYTHOLIZATION, NEW YEAR, SEASON, SOUTHWEST ORIENTATION.

witchcraft *The letter R of the Snake Ring Template. Ref* OCCULT.

wolf 1. *The letter M of the Snake Ring Template. Ref* FELINE, NIGHT. 2. *The letter L of the Snake Ring Template. Ref* BULL, FAIRY TALE, NIGHT.

woman *The letter H of the Snake Ring Template.* A societal metaphor for the mother goddess in the mountain-house of the western horizon. *Ref* GODDESSES, HOUSE, MOTHER GODDESS, PSYCHOLOGY CHILD/ CONTEMPORARY, SOCIETAL ASPECT.

wood *The letter E of the Snake Ring Template. Ref* TREE.

world axis *The letter E of the Snake Ring Template.* A metaphor for the vertical segment of the entwined serpent path at the western horizon, the societal "center of the world". *Ref* NAVEL OF THE WORLD, AXIS MUNDI, VERTICAL STICK.

worm *The letter A of the Snake Ring Template.* A metaphor for the cosmic serpent; esp. after demytholization. *Ref* DEMYTHOLIZATION, SERPENT ENTWINED, SNAKE.

worship *The letter R of the Snake Ring Template. Ref* BABY BOY/ GIRL, FERTILITY, MOTHER GODDESS, SOCIETAL ASPECT.

woven fabric *The letter A of the Snake Ring Template.* When worn, a metaphor which designates the wearer as the sun or mother goddess within the entwined serpent path. *Ref* GARMENT, SOCIETAL ASPECT, WEAVING, X-CROSSING.

wreath *The letter I of the Snake Ring Template.* A symbol of homage to the seasonal new sun and the fertility it provides. *Ref* FLORA, RING MOTIF.

writing *The letter* ℛ *of the Snake Ring Template.* Evolved applications of the series of graphic metaphors originally created to inspire the regeneration of a new sun along the western segment of the Snake Ring path *Ref* ART, CAVE, LETTERS, PATH, SOCIETAL ASPECT, SPEECH.

• Serious writing deals with the relationship of Man to God +19a \TIMt

• Linguistic universals are an innate mental endowment. How does the human mind have this innate property? +19a NOAM CHOMPSKY \WETt

• The remarkable success of Homo sapiens is due to his ability to file and retrieve [by means of writing] past experiences +19a ALVIN TOFFLER \TOFt

• A child comes to learning with an existing cognitive structure +19a JEAN PIAGET \NYTt

• There is a circle from death to language and from language to life +19a OCTAVIO PAZ \NYTt

• What is the meaning of the megalithic carvings of spirals, serpents, cups, and rings on the megalithic tombs and menhirs of Europe? +19a ALASTAIR SERVICE \SEQt

• Certain images "going together" may have introduced an initial order into the universe +19a CLAUDE LEVI-STRAUSS \PHYt

• Writing was a stupendous invention. Its twenty-four little signs speak to those not yet born +16a GALILEO \SANt

• The objects in the offering pits located in the pyramid platform at the front and rear of the Aztec Templo Mayor in present-day Mexico City were uniformly oriented toward the sunset; leading to the proposition that "the offerings and their placement were a language that needs deciphering" +19a EDUARDO MATOS MOCTEZUMA \MAXt

• The raised hand is the most common symbol in Ice Age cave art -350b FRANCE \MAZt

• Rock art was probably primitive writing, representing a spirit reality *See* STONE(MOUNTAIN) -350b FRANCE \NWSt \HEDt

• The symbols in pre-historic caves of the Americas are the same as those found worldwide: sun, vagina motifs, and raised hand signs *See* CAVE & MARRIAGE & BIRTH -80a BRAZIL, WASUSU \NATt

• The worldwide complex of spirals, meanders, chevrons, and dotted bands represented a sacred script earlier than that of Mesopotamia -50b RUSSIA/ ITALY \RAUt \ARCt

• Inscribed stones at the end of a megalithic passageway bear images of the raised hand, ring motif, spirals, and round motifs in sequence. They are illuminated by the sun one-by-one at the equinoxes, as though the sun is reading the symbols. What is it reading? *See* HAND RAISED & RING MOTIF & ROUND MOTIF IN SEQUENCE & SPIRAL -45b IRELAND, MEATH \MIEp

• Paintings of images on tomb walls were done rapidly at the time of burials as a kind of ritual writing to the gods. The Egyptians believed their writing could influence the gods -30b EGYPT \WESt \EDWt

• The undeciphered Phaistos disk, the earliest known formalized European writing, bears images arranged in a spiral array which include an eagle with a serpent-tail, the head of a youth with thirteen rays, a goddess with pendulous breasts, upside down bulls, hand symbols, some with shortened fingers, ring motifs, cross motif, and snakes -19a CRETE MINOAN \HAWt
Refer to *Figure 237*

• The images of an eagle, snake, and feline found on early Jewish synagogues probably represented a sub-verbal language -10b ISRAEL, JEWISH \ENDt

• The Hebrew consonants [in archaic times there were no Hebrew vowels] which comprise the name Abraham, the Biblical father of the Jews, are derived from pictographs of a bull, house, head, and water respectively. The consonants of his son Isaac's name are derived from pictographs of a hand and arm, an inverted snake, and a raised hand respectively. The consonants of a Hebrew word for priest are derived from pictographs of a snake and cross respectively *See* BULL & CROSS & HAND RAISED & HEAD & HOUSE & DEMYTHOLIZATION & LETTERS & PATH & PRIEST & SUN OLD/ YOUNG & UNDERWORLD & WATER -10b ISRAEL, JEWISH \WESt \ENDp

• The Hebrew consonants for a creature of Jewish mysticism possessing a body without a soul, the Golem, are pictographs representing the number three [initially the images of the Hebrew alphabet represented numbers as well], a spiral, and water respectively *See* GHOST & SOUL & SPIRAL & TRINITY & WATER -10b ISRAEL, JEWISH \ENDt

• The meaning of feline, warrior, and snake designs on the thousands of woven textiles laid in graves is veiled in mystery *See* DEATH & REGENERATION & UNDERWORLD & WAR & WEAVING -2a PERU, PARACAS \STHt

• The Hebrew letters have power for good and for evil. The universe is encompassed by the twenty-two Hebrew letters and the ten Hebrew numbers. When one studies the words of the Torah, one is in danger from the primeval serpent -1b ISRAEL, KABALA \NACt \OCTt

• To indicate the force of the Hebrew letters, if an error is made in writing God's name it cannot be erased. Instead, the whole column must be re-written *See* CHAOS IN NATURE & GOD -10b ISRAEL, JEWISH \CAAt

• The Tun glyph represents the old god at the end of the year, but it also represents the interior of the earth *See* TRINITY & UNDERWORLD -6b MEXICO, MAYAN \THNp

• The painted clay figures found in caches were placed in groups, not alone. These offerings and their positioning was a language that needs deciphering *See* UNDERWORLD & WEST ORIENTATION -6b BELIZE, MAYAN \ARCt \MAXt

• Written prayers are inserted into and spun in prayer wheels as a means of communicating with the deity *See* PATH -5b TIBET, TANTRIC

Figure 359

• Chinese characters were originally pictographs that priests used to communicate with the spirit world -1a CHINA \CRAt \COTt

Figure 359

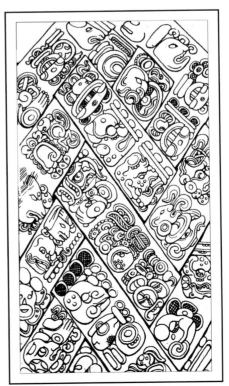

Figure 360

Figure 361

• Much of the Maya codices deal with the passage of time, but their translation is still largely a mystery. The heiroglyphs are sometimes found written in the pattern of a plaited mat, corresponding to a preconquest drawing of the plaited mat of the cosmic serpent with a ring motif among its strands *See* RING MOTIF & SERPENT ENTWINED & X-CROSSING +3b HONDURAS, COPAN \MUTt \NATt \SMIt *Figure 360 Figure 361*

• In an abbey on the island of St. Honorat off the coast of France, one of the first Christian churches was established to convert the pagans from their worship of the sun. [**Note:** St. Patrick studied here the technique of using the Pagan's own images to convert them to Christianity before his mission to Ireland]. A sacred inscription was written along a ribbon snake which hangs vertically from a cross *See* CROSS WEST & LETTERS & PATH & RIBBON +4a FRANCE, CHRISTIAN *Figure 362*

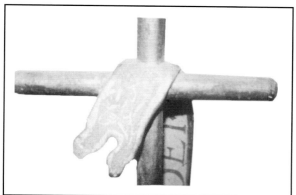

Figure 362

• The sky god **Woden's** power came from the runes which he discovered hanging from a magic tree *See* PATH & TREE +7b GERMAN, TEUTONIC VIKING \ELIt \EXQt

• A rock engraving of the 10th century shows runes along the body of a serpent. Most known runic inscriptions were carved inside medieval stave churches [**Note:** Churches with dragons carved at their gables]. None have been deciphered *See* DRAGON & HOUSE & PATH +9a SWEDEN, TEUTONIC \CAMp \EXQt

• Images on the offerings recovered from the Chichen Itza cenote, a natural sink hole filled with water, relate to the art in the Temple of the Jaguars at the ball-court *See* FELINE & GAME SPORT & UNDERWORLD & WAR +7a MEXICO, MAYAN \COIt

• Explorers to Easter Island were shown Orongo tablets with serpentine writing [**Note:** actually boustrophedon, since returning lines were upside-down] consisting of figures of snakes, trees, falling bird-men, and of rising bird-men with a ring motif on their heads. No one has been able to translate the few remaining Orongo tablets *See* BIRD & CARRIER & DESCENDING MOTIF & LEAF-UP & PATH & REGENERATION & RING MOTIF & SNAKE & TREE +8a EASTER ISLAND *Figure 363*

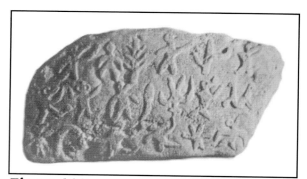

Figure 363

• Thousands of rocks at Turo Muerto are carved with images. No one has been able to determine the text for these images, which include a radiant ring motif as the sun, a lean and fat llama representing the seasons, a series of ring motifs along a snake's body *See* FAUNA & FERTILITY & MOUNTAIN & PATH & SNAKE & STONE & RING MOTIFS IN SEQUENCE +8a PERU, HAURI \STHt

Refer to *Figure 151* SECTION TWO.

• The only extant ideographic script from the Far East is the "road-teach" of the last century which was to instruct the dead the proper road to travel +18a CHINA, NAKHIS \HASp

• Children learn languages best by drawing and writing before learning to read; children naturally write first and read second +19a \WESt \NYTt

• Art was the only "writing" in tropical Africa +19a AFRICA \PAQt

• Images painted in the sanctuaries at the changes of seasons were a type of writing; their purpose was to stimulate, not to symbolize +19a MALI, DOGON \GRKt \LAUt

• In olden times the carving of images was done mostly on the chief's doorway *See* RULER & PALACE +19a NIGERIA, YORUBA \RAUt

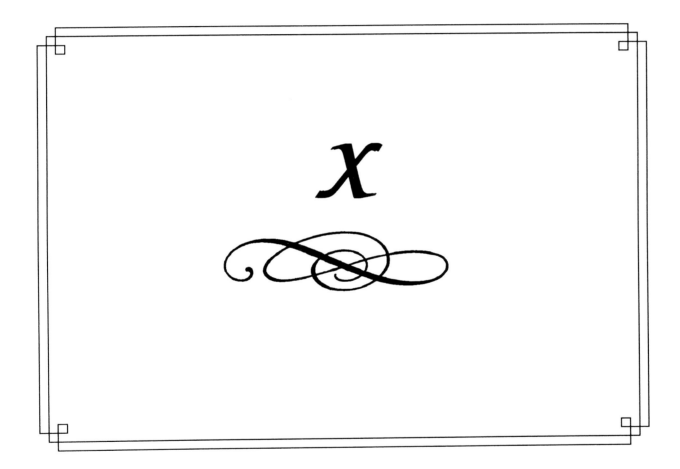

X-crossing *The letter A of the Snake Ring Template.* A metaphor for the apparent spirals of the entwined serpent path of the sun, as they go back and forth between the solstices, each crossing the other at the horizons; the entwined serpent path encompassing the earth and its surrounding waters. *Ref* DRAGON, ELEPHANT, HORIZON, SERPENT ENTWINED, WEAVING.

• X's in their sand painting represent the frame around "space"   +19a COLOMBIA, TUKANO \REJp

• An Ice Age artifact was found in the form of a mammoth with crossmarks carved into its body *See* ELEPHANT(CELESTIAL) & PATH -350b GERMANY \HAWp

• The frame of the sky, or "the skambha", is represented by the letter Khi, which is written as "X" -20b GREEK \SANt

• As illustrated in the Dresden Codex, the feathered rain-serpent in the sky is usually depicted with X-bands in its eyes and/or a large X-band on its body -6b MEXICO, MAYAN
Refer to *Figure 7* SECTION TWO.

• To the Mayan people, woven geometric patterns represent the movement of the sun through the layers of the sky and underworld *See* GARMENT & WEAVING +19a MEXICO, MAYAN \ARCp

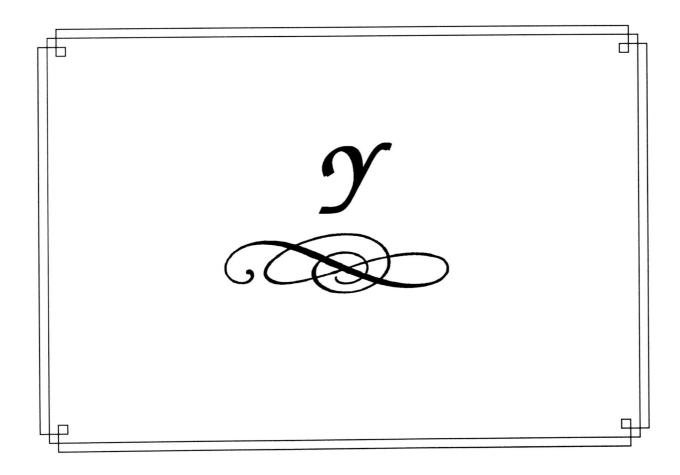

yang-yin *The letter H of the Snake Ring Template. Chin. The active masculine yang principle (as of light, heat) in nature that combines with the passive female yin principle (as of depth, darkness, wetness) in nature to produce all that comes to be.* A metaphor for the joining of the old sun with the mother goddess to produce a new sun at springtime and, by extension, all flora and fauna in the world and mankind as well : HAND RAISED. *Ref* LIGHT, MARRIAGE, MOTHER GODDESS, SOCIETAL ASPECT, SUN OLD/ YOUNG, WATER.

year *The letter A of the Snake Ring Template. Ref* CALENDAR, NEW YEAR, SERPENT ENTWINED, TIME.

yellow *The letter S of the Snake Ring Template.* The color as a metaphor for the sun. *Ref* ART, GOLD, SUN.

yoke motif *The letter K of the Snake Ring Template.* A metaphor for the underworld portion of the sun's path within the entwined serpent. *Ref* CALABASH, LEVELS UNDERWORLD, SERPENT ENTWINED.

• In their art, the "yoke" symbol represents a vagina. It is a doorway of rebirth between one existence and another   +19a COLOMBIA, TUKANO \REJp

youth and old man *The letter S of the Snake Ring Template.* A societal metaphor for the sun at the changes in the seasons. *Ref* SEASON, SUN OLD/ YOUNG.

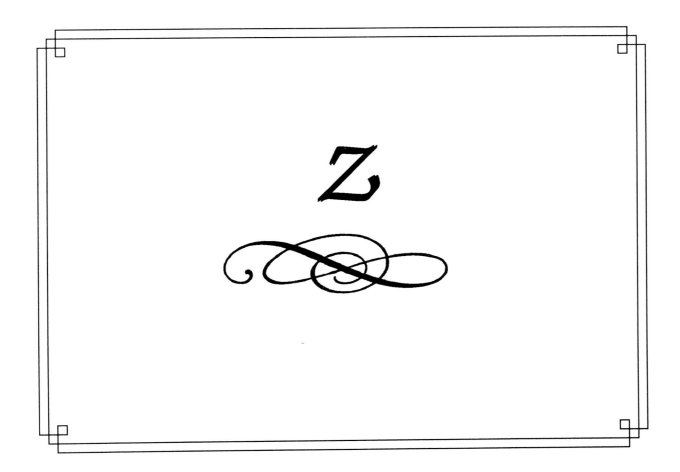

zenith *The letter P of the Snake Ring Template.* A metaphor for the sun in the highest part of the entwined serpent path in the sky. *Ref* DAY OF REST, LEVELS CELESTIAL, SEVEN.

zero *The number 1 of the Snake Ring Template. Arith. Naught; the point of departure in reckoning.* A numerical metaphor for the border between the cosmic layers from which the sun departs up the celestial layers and down the underworld layers. *Ref* LEVELS, MATHEMATICS.

Figure 364

zig-zag motif 1.*~ horizontal The letter F of the Snake Ring Template.* Ref WATER. **2.** *~ vertical The letter A of the Snake Ring Template.* Ref DESCENDING MOTIF & SNAKE.

zodiac *The letter O of the Snake Ring Template.* A group of metaphors associated with the seasonal regeneration of a new sun within the entwined serpent path around the cosmos. Humans are assigned the role and characteristics of the specific metaphor related to the sun's path at the time and date of their birth. *Ref* ASTROLOGY, BIRTH, BULL, CRUSTACEAN, FELINE, FISH, HAND RAISED, HANDS UP AND DOWN, MOTHER GODDESS, RAM, SEASON, SERPENT ENTWINED, SOCIETAL ASPECT, TWINS, WATER.

• In a relief of the young sun god **Phanes**, he is depicted with a lion, ram, and deer's heads on his body, surrounded by the signs of the zodiac. A snake wraps around his body, connecting the upper half of an egg above his head with the lower half of the egg below his cloven hoofs. The snake, together with the signs of the zodiac, represents the sun's path *See* DEER & EGG & FELINE & PATH & RAM & SUN YOUNG +1a ITALY, ORPHIC \LEIp *Figure 364*

• A statue of the sun god **Mithras** depicts a youth with a lion's head for his own and a large snake wound around his body which bears the signs of the zodiac. Other images of this Mythraic cult, popular among the Persian and Roman military, depicts the young sun god Mithras killing a bull along the serpent path *See* BULL & CARRIER & FELINE & PATH & SUN YOUNG & WAR -5b ITALY, MITHRAIC *Figure 365*

Figure 365

• A central axis controls the zodiac *See* AXIS MUNDI & REGENERATION & SEASON +7b SWEDEN NORDIC \ELHt

SELECTED BIBLIOGRAPHY

SOURCES

ABE - Abell, George O. *Exploration of the Universe*, 3rd ed.(Holt, Rinehart & Winston: San Francisco)1964.

AFA - African Arts Magazine April 77, July 1977.

ALB - "Maya Treasures of an Ancient Civilization", Albequerque Museum: , New York, 1985.

AMA - Museo Amano: Artifact from The Collection of

AME - American Antiquity Magazine Volume 54, No.1, 1989.

AMN - American Museum of Natural History: *Gold of El Dorado*, New York, 1979.

AMW - American West Magazine September/ October 1982.

ANA - Volk, J. Geary. Habib Anavian Collection: *Ancient Near Eastern Cylinder and Stamp Seals from the 6th Millennia B.C. to 651 A.D.*, New York, 1979.

ANB - Volk, J. Geary. Habib Anavian Collection: *Iranian Art from the 5th Millennia B.C. to the 7th century A.D.*, New York, 1977.

APP - Appignanesi, Richard. *Freud For Beginners*(Pantheon Books: New York) 1979.

ARC - Archaeology Magazine July 1977/ June 1989.

ATK - Atkinson, R. J. C. *Stonehenge and Neighbouring Monuments*(English Heritage: London)1987.

ATL - Atlantic Magazine March 1983.

AVD - Aveni, Anthony. *Ethnoastronomy and Archaeoastronomy in the American Tropics*, ed. with G. Urton(New York Academy of Sciences: New York) 1982.

AVE - Aveni, Anthony. *Archaeoastronomy in Pre-Colombian America*(University of Texas Press: Austin)1975.

BAE - Smithsonian Institution, Bureau of American Anthropology, bulletin 157, Anthropological Papers 43-48, Washington D.C. 1955.

BAJ - Baines, John and Jaromir Malek. *Atlas of Ancient Egypt*(Facts on File Publications: New York)1980.

BAL - Author's Notes: Information on File.

BAN - Matos, M., Portilla, M. Leon, Portillo, J. Lopez. *El Templo Mayor*(Bancomer, S.A: Mexico City)1981.

BAP - *Pre-Colombian Art*. A Catalog of the Collection, Vol. II (Barakat Gallery: Beverly Hills) 1988.

BEO - Benedict, R. *Patterns of Culture*(Houghton Mifflin Company: Boston)1934.

BEP - Bernal, Ignacio., Andy Seuffert. *The Ball Players of Dainzu:* Artes Americanae 2, trans. Carolyn B. Czitrom(Akademische Druck- u. Verlagsanstalt: Graz, Austria)1979.

BEQ - Bernal, Ignacio. *100 Great Masterpieces of the National Museum of Anthropology*, New York, 1969.

BER - Bernal, Ignacio. *The Olmec World*(Berkeley: Los Angeles) 1969.

BEU - Bettelheim, B. *The Uses of Enchantment*(Vintage Books: New York)1976.

BIB - <u>The Biblical Archaeological Review Magazine</u> September 1978 -August 1987.

BLB - Blacker, I. *Cortes and the Aztec Conquest*(American Heritage Heritage Co. Inc.: New York)1966.

BOA - Boardman, John. *Greek Sculpture, The Archaic Period*(Thames & Hudson Ltd: London)1978.

BOM - Author's Notes; *Information on File*, 1975 -1990.

BOP - Boorstin, Daniel J. *The Discoverers*(Random House: New York) 1983.

BOQ - Borhegyi, Stephan F. *The Pre-Colombian Ball-games a Pan-Mesoamerican Tradition*, Milwaukee Public Museum, 1980.

BOW - Bourke, J. *The Snake Dance of the Moquis of Arizona*(Charles Scribner's Sons: New York)1884.

BRA - Brandon, S.G.F. *Man and God in Art and Ritual*(Charles Scribner's Sons: New York)1975.

BRB - Brain, Robert. *The Decorated Body*(Harper & Row: New York)1979.

BRE - Brecher, K. *Astronomy of the Ancients*(The MIT Press: Cambridge)1979

BRF - Breuil, A.H, "400 Centuries of Cave Art", Paris, 1952.

BRH - The British Museum: *Frozen Tombs, The Culture and Art of the Ancient Tribes of Siberia* London, 1978.

BRP - Brown, D. *Bury My Heart at Wounded Knee*(Pocket Books: New York)1981.

BRU - Bruce, R.D. *Lacandon Dream Symbolism*(Ediciones Euroamericanas: Mexico) City, 1975.

BUL - Bull, C. (consultant) Time-Life series: *Planet Earth, Ice Ages*, Windsor Chorlton (author), Amsterdam, 1984.

BUM - Bullon, J.A. *La Cueva de La Pileta*, Berlin/ New York, 1977.

BUQ - Burland, C. *North American Indian Mythology* (New York, 1975).

CAA - Campbell, Joseph *Primitive Mythology*(Penguin Books: New York)1987.

CAD - Campbell, Joseph *Creative Mythology*(Penguin Books: New York)1987.

CAI - Campbell, Joseph *The Way of the Animal Powers*(Harper & Row: New York 1983.

CAJ - Carnegie Institute of Washington *Ancient Maya Paintings of Bonampak, Mexico*, Boston/ Richmond, 1955.

CAM - Campbell, Joseph *The Mythic Image*(Princeton University Press: Princeton, N.J.)1975.

CAQ - Carpiceci, A.C. *Pompeii 2000 Years Ago*, (review) (Bonechi: Florence)1967.

CAS - Casson, L. Time/ Life series *Great Ages of Man; Ancient Egypt*, New York, 1972.

CAT - Catlin, George. *O-Kee-Pa*(Yale University Press: New Haven/ London, 1967.

CEN - The Center for Inter-American Research *Aztec Stone*, New York, 1977.

CHC - Kwang-Chi, Chang. *The Archaeology of Ancient China*(New Haven/ London, 1977.

CHO - Chou, Hung-hsiang, "Chinese Oracle Bones" <u>Scientific American</u>, April 1979.

CHR - Christie, A. *Chinese Mythology*(Hamlyn Publishing Group, Ltd.: New York, 1975.

CIR - Cirlot, J.E. *A Dictionary of Symbols*(Philosophical Library: New York)1962.

COE - Coe, Michael D. *America's First Civilization*(American Heritage Publishing, Inc.: New York)1968.

COI - Coggins, C.C. *Cenote of Sacrifice*(University of Texas Press: Austin)1984.

CON - Margaret W. Conkey, "A Century of Paleolithic Cave Art," <u>Archaeology</u>, Vol. 34, #4, 1981, pp.20-28.

COS - Cornell, J. *The First Stargazers*(Charles Scribner's Sons: New York) 1981.

COU - Cotlow, Lewis. *The Twilight of the Primitive*(MacMillan Company: New York)1971.

CRU - Crummere, Maria Elise. *Sun-Sign Revelations*(New York)1974.

CUP - <u>Current Anthropology Magazine</u> March 1978/ June 1981.

DAN - Daniel, Glyn. *The Origins and Growth of Archaeology*(Thomas R. Crowell: New York)1971.

DAT - Davis, Wade. *The Serpent and the Rainbow*(Simon & Schuster: New York) 1985.

DAV - Davila, Francisco Gonzalez. *Ancient Cultures of Mexico*(Museo Nacional de Antropologia: Calzada de la Milla-Chapultepec, Mexico)1977.

DED - Sprague de Camp, L. *The Ancient Engineers*(Ballantine Books: New York) 1977.

DIL - <u>Dial, The Magazine</u>, January 1983.

DIS - <u>Discover Magazine</u>, June 1981 -June 1988.

DOC - Dockstader, Frederick J. *Indian Art in America*(Promontory Press: New York).

DOP - Dorsey, George A. *The Arapaho Sun Dance; The Ceremony of the Offerings Lodge*, Field Colombian Museum Publication 75, Anthropological Series vol IV, Chicago, 1903.

DOQ - Dorn, Frank. *The Forbidden City*(New York)1972.

DOR - Wesler, Allan. *Dordogne Field Notes*, 1983.

DUS - Duruy, Victor. *The World of the Greeks*(Editions Minerva,S.A., Geneve)1971.

EDE - "The Working Brain". Interview with Dr. Edelman <u>The New Yorker</u>, January 10, 1983, p. 25.

EDU - Edwards, I.E.S. *Treasures of Tutankhamun*(Ballantine Books: New York) 1976.

EDV - Edwards, I.E.S. *Tutankhamun: His Tomb and it's Treasures*(Metropolitan Museum ofArt: New York)1978.

EDW - Edwards, I.E.S. *The Pyramids of Egypt*(Penguin Books: Middlesex)1985.

ELH - Eliot, Alexander. *Myths*(McGraw-Hill Book Company: Maidenhead)1976.

ELI - Eliade, Mircea. *Patterns in Comparative Religion*(New American Library: New York)1974.

EMN - Emmerich, Andre. *Sweat of the sun and Tears of the Moon*(Simon & Schuster: New York)1965.

END - Encyclopedia Judaica, Jerusalem, 1972.

EXP - Expedition Magazine Museum Bulletin, Univ. of Pennsylvania, Fall 1961.

EXQ - The Explorers Journal Magazine April 1984 -December 1988.

EYO - Eyo, Ekpo. *Treasures of Ancient Nigeria*(Alfred A. Knopf: New York)1980.

FAG - "Civilization", intro. Brian M. Fagan. Readings from Scientific American (W. H. Freeman & Company: California) June, 1978.

FAH - Fagaly, William A. Museum of Art *Shapes of Power, Belief and Celebration*, New Orleans, 1989.

FEJ - Feldon, Victoria. *Lithuanian Folk Art* (Ethnic Art Galleries - UCLA: Los Angeles) 1967.

FIE - Field, Henry. *Arabian Desert Tales*(Synergetic Press: Santa Fe)1976.

FON - Fondo Editorial de la Plastica Mexico 2 Volumes *The Ephemeral and the Eternal of Mexican Folk Art*, Mexico, 1971.

FOU - Foundation For Latin American Art, Culver City, 1984.

FRB - Fraser, Sir James. *The Golden Bough*(The MacMillan Company: New York) 1958.

FRN - Freud, Sigmund. *The Interpretation of Dreams*(Avon Books: New York)1965.

FUR - Furst, Jill and Peter. *Pre-Colombian Art of Mexico*(New York) 1980.

GAR - Garlake, Peter. *The Kingdoms of Africa*(Phaidon Press: Oxford)1978.

GAT - Gates, William. *An Outline Dictionary of Mayan Glyphs*(Dover Publications, Inc.: New York)1978.

GAU - Gaunt, William. *Marine Painting: An Historical Survey*(The Viking Press: New York) 1975.

GAW - Gayley, Charles M. *The Classic Myths*(New York).

GAX - Gay, Carlo. *Chalcacingo*(International Scholarly Books Services Inc., Portland,Oregon)1972.

GEF - Geertz, Clifford. *The Religion of Java*(University of Chicago Press:Chicago)1976.

GIE - Giedion, S. *The Eternal Present*(Pantheon Books: New York)1962.

GIR - Girshman, Roman. *Persia The Immortal Kingdom*(Orient Commerce Establishment: New York)1971.

GRA - Gray, John. *Near Eastern Mythology*(The Hamlyn Publishing Group: London) 1975.

GRB - Grant, Michael. *Eros in Pompeii*(William Morrow & Co., Inc: New York) 1975.

GRE - *Ancient Maya Relief Sculpture*, intro. J. Eric Thompson(Museum of Primitive Art: New York) 1967.

GRH -   Graham-Campbel, James. *The Vikings*(British Museum Publications Ltd: London, England)1980.

GRJ -   Grigson, Geoffery. *Painted Caves*(London) 1957.

GRK -   Griaule, Marcel. *Conversations With Ogotemmeli*(New York)1970.

HAI -   Hagen, Victor W. *The Aztec: Man and Tribe*(New American Library: New York)1961.

HAK -   Hall, James. *Dictionary of Subjects and Symbols in Art*(Harper & Row: New York)1974.

HAO -   Harleston, Hugh. *The Keystone: A Search for Understanding Lubaantun*(The British Museum: London)1972

HAW -   Hawkes, Jaquetta *The Atlas of Early Man*(St. Martin's Press: New York) 1976.

HEA -   Henderson, Robert W. *Ball, Bat, and Bishop; The Origin of Ball Games*(New York)1947.

HED -   Hedges, Ken. *Phosphenes in the Context of Native American Rock Art*, paper, San Diego Museum of Man, 1981.

HEE -   Hedges, Ken *Archaeoastronomical Sites in California*, Ramona, paper, San Diego Museum of Man, 1981.

HEH -   Heiniger, Ernst A. and Jean, *The Great Book of Jewels*(Edita S.A., Lausanne) 1974.

HEK -   Helfritz, Hans. *Mexican Cities of the Gods*(Frederick A. Praeger: New York) 1970.

HEO -   Henry, Francoise. *Irish Art: Romanesque*(Cornell University Press: Ithaca, New York)1970.

HEP -   Henry, Francoise *Viking Art*(Cornell University Press: Ithaca, New York)1970.

HEU -   Heyerdahl, Thor. *Easter Island: The Mystery Solved*(Random House: New York) 1989.

HEV -   Heyerdahl, Thor *The Maldive Mystery*(George Allen & Unwin: London) 1986.

HEW -   Heyerdahl, Thor *Aku-Aku*(Rand McNally & Co.: London)1958.

HEZ -   Author's Notes; *Information on File*, 1975 -   1990.

HIT -   Author's Notes; *Information on File*, 1975 -   1990.

HOY -   Hoyle, Larco R. *Checan*, Geneva, 1965.

HUG -   Hugh-Jones, Stephan. *Hidden Peoples of the Amazon*(The British Museum: London)1985.

HUS -   Husserl, Edmund. *The Origin of Geometry*, trans. John P. Levy(Nicolas Hay, Ltd.: Stony Brook New York) 1978.

ISB -   Isbell, William H. *The Pre-historic Ground Drawings of Peru*, Scientific American, October, 1978.

ISR -   Israel Museum Catalog of the Collection; *Treasures of the Holy Land.*

JAA -   <u>Journal of Psychological Anthropology.</u>

JUN -   Jung, Carl G. *Man And His Symbols*(Doubleday & Company, Inc: New York)1984.

JUP -   Jung, Carl G. *Transformation Symbolism in the Mass* (Paper from the Eranos Yearbooks), Princeton, 1978.

KAP -   Kaplan, Stuart R. *The Encyclopedia of Tarot*(U.S. Games Systems, Inc.: New York)1979.

KER -   Kerenyi, C. *The Mysteries of the Kabeiori* (Paper from the Eranos Yearbooks), Princeton, 1978.

KIR -   Kirk, Geoffrey *Periclean Athens and the Decline of Taste*, Tulane University, 1979.

KRB -   Kraus, Theodor. *Pompeii and Herculaneum: The Living Cities of the Dead* New York)1979.

KRO -   Kroeber, Theodora. *Ishi in Two Worlds*(University of California Press: Berkeley, Los Angeles)1961.

KUN -   Kunstraum Munchen *Peruvian Ground Drawings*, Catalog of Exhibit, 1974.

LAR -   Librarie Larousse *The New Larousse Encyclopedia of Mythology*, Paris, 1978.

LAU -   Laude, Jean. *African Art of the Dogon of Mali*(Brooklyn Museum: New York) 1973.

LEE -   Lee, Sherman E. *A History of Far Eastern Art* (New York)

LEI -   Leisegang, Hans. *The Mystery of the Serpent*, (Paper from the Eranos Yearbooks), Princeton, 1978.

LER -   Leroi-Gourhan, Andre. *Treasures of Pre-historic Art*, New York.

LET -   Levi-Strauss, Claude. *Tristes Tropiques*((Antheneum Publishers: New York)1977.

LEU -   Levi, Peter. *Atlas of the Greek World*(Facts On File, Inc: New York) 1980.

LEV -   Levi-Strauss, Claude. *The Raw and the Cooked*(Harper & Row: New York)1975.

LEW -   Lewin Roger. *The Thread of Life*(Smithsonian Books: Washington D.C.)1982.

LEX -   Taped interview with Claude Levi-Strauss by Richard Wormser, January 26, 1983.

LEY -   Lewis, Brenda R. *Great Civilizations: The Aztecs*, Loughborough.

LIF -   Life Magazine December 1988.

LIT -   J.J. Little and Ives Co. *The Holy Scriptures*, the Jewish Publication Society, 1945.

MAD -   Macfarlan, Alan and Paula. *Handbook of American Indian Games*(Dover Publications, Inc: Mineola, New York)1958.

MAQ -   Marshack, Alexander. *The Roots of Civilization*(McGraw-Hill Book Company: New York)1972.

MAS -   Mason, J. Alden. *The Ancient Civilizations of Peru*(Penguin Books: Baltimore/ New York)1975. 1968.

MAW -   Maternus, Firmicus. *Ancient Astrology: Theory and Practice*(Noyes Press: Park Ridge, N. J.)1975.

MAX - Matos, Eduardo M. *Official Guide to the Great Temple: El Templo Mayor*, Mexico City, 1984.

MAZ - Mazonowicz, Douglas. *Voices From the Stone Age*(Thomas Y. Crowell Co.: New York) 1974.

MCC - McClain, Ernest G. *The Myth of Invariance*(Nicolas Hays Ltd.: New York) 1976.

MER - A Meridian Book: *The Holy Bible*(Tyndale House Publishers, Inc: Wheaton, Illinois)1985.

MET - Metropolitan Museum of Art, *African and Oceanic art.*

MEU - Metropolitan Museum of Art *China: The Bronze Age*, New York, 1980.

MEV - Metropolitan Museum of Art: *Mexico Splendors of Thirty Centuries.*

MIA - The Miami Herald Newspaper, June 1980 -April 1989.

MIB - Michaud, Stephen G., Aynesworth, Hugh. *The Only Living Witness*(Linden Press: New York)1983.

MIE - Michell, John. *Megalithomania*(Cornell Univ. Press, Ithaca: New York)1982.

MOM - Author's Notes; *Information on File*, 1975 -1990.

MOR - Morley, Silvanus Griswold. *The Ancient Maya*(Stanford University Press:California)1956.

MUN - Mundkur, Balaji. *The Cult of the Serpent*(State Univeristy of New York Press: Albany)1983.

MUR - Museum of Fine Arts Boston. *Pompeii A.D. 79*, Boston, 1978/ 1979.

MUT - Muser, Curt. *Fact and Artifacts of Ancient Middle America*(E. P. Dutton: New York)1978.

MYL - Mylonas, George. *Eleusis and the Eleusinian Mysteries*(Princeton University Press: Princeton, N.J.)1974.

NAB - Nabokov, Peter., Easton, Robert. *Native American Architecture*(Oxford University Press: New York)1989.

NAC - Nathan, Rabbi of Breslov. *Advice: Likutey Etzot*(New York)

NAS - National Anthropological Museum, Mexico, Catalog of Exhibit, 1978.

NAT - National Geographic Magazine December 1975 -December 1989.

NAU - Natural History Magazine December 1976 -April 1987.

NEL - The Nelson Gallery *Sacred Circles; Two Thousand Years of North American Indian Art*, Catalog of Exhibit, Kansas City, 1977.

NES - *The Pacific Islands, Africa and the Americas.* Intros. Douglas Newton, et al(The Metropolitan Museum of Art: New York) 1987.

NEU - Neumann, Erich. *The Origins and History of Human Consciousness*(Princeton University Press)1973.

NEV - *New Orleans Museum of Art*, Photographs of Exhibit.

NEW - National Museum of Anthroplogy, Mexico City. *Great Museums of the World*(Newsweek, Inc.: New York) 1970.

NUM - "Estudios Atacamenos", #9, Instituto de Investigaciones Arqueologicas, Universidad del Norte, San Pedro de Atazama: Chile, 1988.

NUN - Nuno, Ruben B. *The Art in the Great Temple*(National Institute of Anthrolology and History, Mexico City)1981.

NWS - <u>Newsweek Magazine</u> December 1970 -August 1989.

NYA - <u>New York Academy of Science</u>, vol. 386; "The Research Potential of Anthropological Museum Collections", New York, 1981.

NYL - <u>New York Public Library</u>, Main Branch, Publications Department/ Photo Collection Department, Information on File, 1975 -1990.

NYM - <u>American Museum of Natural History Magazine</u>

NYT - <u>New York Times</u>, Newspaper, October 1979 -September 1985.

OAT - Oates, David. *The Rise of Civilization*(Phaidon Press Ltd.: New York)1976.

OCT - *The Occult and The Supernatural*(Octopus, London 1975).

OMN - <u>Omni Magazine</u> May 1984 -April 1989.

PAH - Page, R. I. *Reading The Past: Runes*(British Museum Publications Ltd.:London)1987.

PAQ - Parrinder, Geoffrey. *African Mythology*(Paul Hamlyn: London) 1975.

PAT - Patton, Peter C., Holoien, Renee A. *Computing in the Humanities*(Lexington/ Toronto)1981.

PHY - <u>Physics Today Magazine</u> June, 1984.

PIA - Piaget, Jean. *Play, Dreams and Imitation In Childhood*, trans. G. Gattegno and F. M. Hodgson(W. W. Norton & Co. Inc.: New York) 1962.

PIB - Piaget, Jean. *Structuralism*(Harper & Row: New York)1968.

PID - Piankoff, Alexander. *Mythological Papyri*, Bollingen Series XL3.

PIN - Pinsent, John. *Greek Mythology: Library of the World's Myths and Legends*(Peter Bedrick Books: New York) 1984.

POM - Pomerance, Leon. *The Phaistos Disc*, Goteborg, 1976.

PRI - Pritchard, James B. *The Ancient Near East in Pictures*(Princeton University Press) 1969.

PSY - Theodore Melnechuk, "The Dream Machine", <u>Psychology Today</u>, November 1983, pp. 22-34.
David Heller, "The Children's God", <u>Psychology Today</u>, December 1985, pp.22-27.

QUE - Quennel, Peter R. *The Colosseum*, New York.

RAU - Rawson, Phillip. *Primitive Erotic Art*(G. P. Putnam's Sons: New York)1973.

RAW - Rawson, Phillip. *Tao: Eastern Philosophy of Time and Space*(Bounty Books: New York)1978.

REA - *The World's Last Mysteries*(Readers Digest: Pleasantville/ Montreal) 1978.

REC - Recinos, Adrian. *Popol Vuh* (Translation), Univ. of Oklahoma, 1975.

RED - <u>Readers Digest Magazine</u>, "The Living Magic of Indian Art", Dec. 1977.

REJ - Reichal-Dolmotoff, G. *Beyond the Milky Way*, UCLA 1978.

REV - <u>Review Magazine</u> May 1979/ November 1982/ February 1984/ December 1985.

RID - Richter, Gisela. *Greek, Etruscan, and Roman Bronzes*, New York, 1915.

ROB - Robicsek, Francis. *A Study in Maya Art and History: The Mat Symbol*(Museum of the American Indian, New York)1975.

ROD - Robicsek, Francis. *The Maya Book of the Dead: The Ceramic Codex*(University of Virginia Art Museum) 1981.

ROM - Roman, Francisco Tornay. *Ronda; Situation, History, and Monuments* (Barcelona) 1978.

SAG - Saggs, H. Layard; Henry Austen. *Nineveh and Its Remains*(Frederick A. Praeger: New York)1970.

SAM - San Bernadino Museum Quarterly Magazine, San Bernadino, 1978/ 1980.

SAN - Di Santillana, Giorgio and Von Dechand, Hertha. *Hamlet's Mill*(David Godine: Boston)1977.

SCD - Scholes,France V., Roys, Ralph L., et al. *The Maya Chontal Indians of Acalan-Tixchel* 2nd ed. (University of Oklahoma Press) 1968.

SCG - Schafer, Edward H. *Ancient China*(Time-Life Books: New York)1967.

SCH - Author's Notes; *Information on File*, 1975 -1990.

SCI - Scientific American Magazine, Feb. 1980 -Jan. 1983.

SCK - Science Magazine Nov. 1982 -Oct. 1984.

SCM - Science News Magazine Vol. 131.

SCO - Science Illustrated Magazine June/ July 1988.

SEQ - Service, Alastair/ Bradbery, Jean. *A Guide to the Megaliths of Europe*, London, 1979.

SIF - Sielmann, Heinz. *Wilderness Expeditions*(Franklin Watts, Inc.: New York)1980.

SIN - Simmons, Leo W. *Sun Chief*(Yale University Press: New Haven)1970.

SMJ - Smithsonian Magazine April 1977 -February 1990.

SMK - "Helios In Palestine", unpublished paper by Prof. Morton Smith, Department of History, Columbia University, October 22, 1979.

SML - Smith, Stevenson W. *The Art and Architecture of Ancient Egypt*, Penguin Books.

SOP - Sophocles. *Oedipus the King*, Lincoln, 1965.

SOU - *Important Pre-Colombian Art* (Sotheby Park Bernet, Inc.: New York) 1981.

STE - Stern, Theodore. *The Rubber Ball Games of the Americas*(University of Washing Press: Seattle)1966.

STH - Stierlin, Henri. *Art of the Incas*(Rizzoli International Publications, Inc.: New York)1983.

SWB - Swaddling, Judith. *Ancient Olympic Games*(British Museum: London)1980.

TAT - Tattootime Magazine Volume 2, No.1, 1983.

TEL - Tel Aviv Museum Catalog of Exhibit; *Treasures of the Bible Lands*, Tel Aviv, 1987.

TEM - Templo Mayor; Field Notes, Allan Wesler, 1978/ 80/ 85.

TEO - Teotihuacan; Field Notes, Allan Wesler, 1984/ 85.

THL -	Thompsom, J. Eric S. *A Catalog of Maya Heiroglyphs*, Univ. of Oklahoma, 1970.
THN -	Thompson, J. Eric S. *A Catalog of Maya Hieroglyphics*(University of Oklahoma Press: Norman) 1962.
THO -	Thompsom, J. Eric S. *A Commentary on the Dresden Codex*, Philadelphia, 1972.
THP -	Thompsom, J. Eric S. *The Rise and Fall of the Maya Civilization*, Univ of Oklahoma, 1975.
TIL -	*The First Cities* (Time-Life: New York) 1973.
TIM -	Time Magazine March 1977 -April 1989.
TL4 -	*Time Frame 3000-1500 B.C.* (Time-Life: Alexandria) 1987.
TL5 -	*Time Frame 3000-1500 B.C.* (Time-Life: Alexandria) 1987.
TL7 -	*Time Frame 3000-1500 B.C.* (Time-Life: Alexandria) 1987.
TL9 -	*Time Frame 3000-1500 B.C.* (Time-Life: Alexandria) 1988.
TOF -	Tofler, Alvin. *Future Shock*(Bamtam Books: New York)1974.
TOM -	Tomkins, Peter. *Indian Sign Language*(Dover Publications, Inc.:New York) 1969.
TUL -	The Tulanian Magazine, Tulane University, New Orleans, Summer 1984/ Winter 1985.
TUQ -	Turner, Geoffrey. *Indians of North America*(Blandford Press: Poole, Dorset)1982.
TUR -	Turner, Wilson G., Smith, Gerald A. *Indian Rock Art of Southern California* (San Bernadino County Museum, Red Land, California)1975.
VOG -	Vogt, Evon Z. *The Zinacantecos of Mexico; A Modern Maya Way of Life*(Holt, Rinehaeart and Winston: New York)1970.
VOO -	Voor Volkenkunde Museum Catalog of Exhibit; *Expressions of Belief*, New York, 1988.
WEB -	Webster's International Dictionary (G & C Merriam Company, Springfield, Massachusetts)1971.
WES -	Wesler, Allan. *Information on File*, 1975 -1990.
WET -	West, John Anthony. *Serpent in the Sky*(The Julian Press, Inc.: New York) 1987.
WHJ -	White, Randall. *Dark Caves, Bright Visions: Life In Ice Age Europe*(The American Museum of Natural History(W. W. Norton & Co., : New York/ London)1986.
WII -	Wili, Walter. *The Orphic Mysteries: Orphism and the Greek Spirit*, (Papers from the Eranos Yearbooks), Princeton, 1978.
WIK -	Willard, T.A. *The City of the Sacred Well*(New York/ London).
WOO -	Wood, Michael. *In Search of the Trojan War*(Facts On File Publications: New York)1986.
YAL -	Yalouris, Nicholas. *The Search For Alexander*(Little, Brown & Co., New York)1980.
YOO -	Yoshnobu, Tokugawa. *No Robes and Masks*, Japan Society.

SOCIETY FOR THE STUDY OF SYMBOLS AND IMAGES

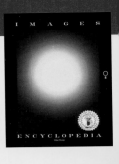

Society Membership

It is in the nature of an encyclopedia to be interdisciplinary. It is also desirable for an innovative approach (such as that exhibited in the Images Encyclopedia) to be interactive. The **Society for the Study of Symbols and Images (SSSI)** will make all efforts to respond to members' communications, and to circulate bulletins of pertinent and new information to its members.

Members will be invited to send comments, criticism, requests for specific information from the Images DataBank, or contributions of

information and/or illustrations they wish to included in the Images DataBank, to:

SSSI, P.O. Box 546665
Surfside, FL 33154-6665
or Send by FAX to: SSSI
(305) 899-1142

SSSI must limit this networking invitation below to readers who have sent in the official information card on this page.

Immediately mail in the information card and Proof of Purchase and you will be registered as a member of **SSSI** for one year, qualified for networking.

To receive your FREE membership and to help the Society serve its members better, now and in the future, please fill out this official questionnaire card to qualify. Sorry, no photocopies or other duplications will be accepted.

Yes, I would like to receive a complimentary one year membership in the Society for the **Study of Symbols and Images** by completing the questionnaire and signing below.

_____
Signature   Date

_____
Name

_____
Address

_____
Phone   FAX

1. Your field(s) of interest/work

_____

_____
Degree(s)

_____
Society Membership(s)

2. Do you have access to a video cassette recorder (VCR)? ☐

3. Do you have access to a computer? ☐
Type of computer(s) and software system you use

_____

4. How did you first learn about the IMAGES ENCYCLOPEDIA or **SSSI**?

_____
_____
_____
_____

5. Please write below anyone who you would like to receive a brochure about the IMAGES ENCYCLOPEDIA.

_____
_____
_____
_____
_____
_____
_____
_____

We are interested in your opinions about the IMAGES ENCYCLOPEDIA. Please write your comments on this card or send us a letter by fax or mail.
Address: **SSSI**, P.O. Box 546665 Surfside, FL 33154-6665.
FAX:305-899-1142

#021395

A-Dragon

B-Bird

C-Bull

D-Fire

E-Cross West, Vertical

F-Crustacean, Water

G-Mountain, Pyramid

H-Cave, House, Marriage

I-Flora, Young Sun

J-Whale

K-Levels Underworld

L-Trinity

M-Feline

N-War

O-Raised Hand, Leaping Animal

P-Levels, Celestial

Q-Raptor

R-Society as at the Axis Mundi

S-Ring Motif

T-Horse

ENTERPRISES
PUBLISHERS

Return Address

_____
_____
_____

Society for the Study of Symbols and Images
P.O. Box 546665
Surfside, FL 33154-6665